Insurance
Rehabilitation

Insurance Rehabilitation

Service Applications in Disability Compensation Systems

Ralph E. Matkin

With Contributions by Jack M. Sink and William C. Wallace

5341 Industrial Oaks Blvd.
Austin, Texas 78735

Printed in the United States of America

Library of Congress Cataloging in Publication Data

Matkin, Ralph E., 1946 —
  Insurance rehabilitation.

  Bibliography: p.
  Includes indexes.
  1. Insurance, Disability. 2. Rehabilitation. 3. Vocational rehabilitation.
I. Sink, Jack M. II. Wallace, William C. III. Title.
     HD7105.2.M38   1985   368.3'86   85-593
               ISBN 0-936104-55-4

5341 Industrial Oaks Blvd.
Austin, Texas 78735

10 9 8 7 6 5 4 3 2 1   85 86 87 88 89

Contents

iii

Figures and Tables

v

Preface

Insurance Rehabilitation: Service Applications in Disability Compensation Systems represents a departure from the traditional content and application of rehabilitation practices found in introductory textbooks on the subject. Its intention is to supplement, rather than supersede, existing philosophies and practices focused on rehabilitating disabled populations within the United States. Accordingly, the goal of this text is to provide information and background about disability insurance compensation systems in order for rehabilitation professionals to become better prepared to provide their services effectively and efficiently within that context.

Although insurance rehabilitation is receiving much attention, and therefore thought by many to be a new area for service application, the fact is that rehabilitation services began comingling with the insurance arena 12 years before the formation of the public vocational rehabilitation program. Thus, the intention of the book is to convey four messages: (1) identify insurance systems and their regulatory frameworks; (2) focus on rehabilitation services practiced within insurance systems; (3) promote increased understanding of vocational rehabilitation and insurance issues among both public and private sector practitioners; and (4) invite the rehabilitation community to become active participants in compensatory systems affecting disabled citizens.

This book was written also to serve as a resource for preservice, inservice, and continuing education programs conducted in applied work settings and academic environments. In addition to these uses, I have made every attempt to include information that will assist rehabilitation professionals who plan to or who are currently providing services to disabled insurance recipients to pass the Certified Insurance Rehabilitation Specialist examination administered by the Board for Rehabilitation Certification. To accomplish these ambitious and challenging goals, the book contains a mixture of history, theory, philosophy, and practical applications of rehabilitation services offered within the insurance rehabilitation arena. This information is contained within the 10 chapters, three glossaries, and 10 appendices that constitute this book.

Each of the 10 chapters begins with an overview of its content and objectives, and concludes with a summary linking the preceding information with the subsequent chapter. Beginning with Chapter 1, the importance of work and the development of disability compensation insurance systems are summarized. This chapter is intended to provide a backdrop, rather than an extensive history lesson, for events leading to present-day disability compensation systems. Chapter 2 proceeds with a presentation of the salient features of various employee compensation programs enacted by both state and federal legislatures. Among the systems discussed in this chapter are state and federal workers' compensation, employers' liability laws, railroad employee insurance programs, Social Security, and occupational safety and health statutes. Chapter 3, coauthored with William C. Wallace, provides information and insight into insurance processes, types of insurance coverages for disabling conditions (other than those identified in Chapter 2), and basic concepts of insurance with which rehabilitation professionals typically are unfamiliar. Chapter 4 provides perspective to the development of the private rehabilitation sector in relation to its public and nonprofit sector counterparts. Chapter 5, once again coauthored with Mr. Wallace, discusses essential elements of disability case management that enhance the effectiveness and efficiency of insurance rehabilitation service planning and implementation.

The next three chapters elaborate several traditional rehabilitation service areas that are crucial when working with disabled insurance recipients. *Assessing Vocational Potential* (Chapter 6) integrates job analysis, job modification, and vocational evaluation as methods through which information is gathered about occupational requirements in relation to disabled clients' functional abilities. *Vocational Counseling* (Chapter 7) stresses the importance of establishing an atmosphere conducive for gathering, identifying, and selecting appropriate vocational goals and objectives. Furthermore, this chapter integrates two important ingredients of vocational counseling; establishing the client-professional relationship, and the vocational substance for which "counseling" is offered. Chapter 8 (*Job Placement*) addresses the ideal goal toward which every disabled insurance recipient and rehabilitation professional seeks to attain. This chapter emphasizes the importance of beginning job placement efforts early in the rehabilitation process as an integral component of vocational assessment and counseling services.

Chapter 9, coauthored with Jack M. Sink, provides information about court systems and legal issues involved in expert witness procedures. Most importantly, this chapter identifies step-by-step methods used for preparation and delivery of vocational testimony in the courtroom. Finally, Chapter 10 identifies and discusses the continuous obligation professionals have to acquire and maintain their levels of expertise in the rehabilitation service delivery process. Similarly, this chapter addresses the need for program (service) evaluation to test the efficacy of the services themselves that are offered.

In addition to the chapter contents, a series of glossaries and appendices are included. The purpose of these additions to the book is to provide an easy-to-access reference to materials that otherwise have been neither compiled, nor collected under one cover.

Before concluding, I must express my sincerest appreciation to those who assisted in the development and completion of this book. Some offered materials, others provided suggestions, and all contributed their time and encouragement. I am particularly grateful to Drs. Brian McMahon, T.F. Riggar, and John Grenfell for their critical review of and valuable suggestions for the material contained. To Malisa Janes, Laura Sanders, and Carol Grant, special thank yous are extended for their assistance in gathering information contained in portions of the book. Furthermore, I want to convey my sincerest appreciation to the family of the late Dr. Jerome Lorenz, and to Dr. Brockman Schumacher for extending to me the space and equipment within the Rehabilitation Institute of Southern Illinois University at Carbondale required to compile this manuscript. Finally, for their valuable and insightful chapter contributions, I want to thank especially Dr. Jack Sink and Mr. William Wallace.

Ralph E. Matkin

1 Insurance Rehabilitation An Introduction

W ork represents a universal activity people have engaged in since before recorded history. Not only does work provide an important method for individual survival and expression, it is a crucial element in social organization. Many turning points in history have occurred as a result of changing relationships between people and work. Indeed, the evolution of workers' compensation insurance, designed as a protection for employees injured on the job, is one example of social change emanating from the people-work relationship. Throughout this book various insurance systems and laws are identified and discussed that pertain to people whose work abilities have become impaired during the course of employment. Combined with this information are aspects of the vocational rehabilitation process that are beneficial for effective service delivery within the context of insurance systems.

The purpose of this chapter is to introduce the reader to insurance rehabilitation. In order to accomplish this goal, two sections are delineated: (1) the importance of work; and (2) industrialization and its effects. The objective of this chapter is to present an overview of events and philosophies that helped shape disability compensation benefit programs, within which increasing numbers of public and privately employed rehabilitation professionals are working.

Importance of Work

According to Black (1968), work consumes approximately one-third of the daily activity of the average wage earner, and as such, represents one of the most important aspects of human existence. However, if one considers the time associated with job skill and knowledge acquisition, periodic refresher training and updating, not to mention travel to and from the work site, it becomes evident that work is perhaps the single most important aspect of life. On the other hand, for those who have had their work life interrupted

1

because of injury or disease, its re-establishment becomes of prime importance in their medical and vocational recovery.

Work is seldom, however, only a means by which people sustain life. It
has many other functions of equal or sometimes greater importance to both
the individual and society. For example, work is one of the functions through
which individuals find an outlet for self-expression and creativity, as well as
relating to society. It provides people, and often their families, with status,
recognition, affiliation, and similar psychological and sociological characteristics essential for participation in a complex society (Menninger, 1964).

Work generally is a purposeful activity that involves both physical and
mental processes, and deliberately extends beyond the present by creating
products or values to be consumed in the future (Quey, 1968). In this way,
the work of individuals contributes to one's own well-being, as well as to the
sustention and maintenance of the immediate family and group, society, and
culture of which they are a part. It is desirable, nevertheless, for work to be
meaningful to the individual. If it is not, then the product of one's labors
contributes less to the benefit of the individual and society alike. Indeed, in
the absence of meaningfulness, or in the presence of unsatisfactory conditions, workers sometimes have resorted to revolt in and destruction of their
work environment (Williams, 1984). On the other hand, the importance of
work has not always included an analysis of its meaning.

In primitive societies the meaning of work was seldom studied. Rather,
work was associated typically with "fatigue" growing out of "drudgery" (Petersen, 1961). Later, as cultures began to emerge and spread their influence
throughout the modern day Middle Eastern regions, the meaning of work
was tied inextricably with prevailing social orders and religious beliefs. More
often than not in those societies, the work performed by any individual
depended upon the class to which he or she was a member. "Work roles"
of this nature, such as they were, continued to exist from pre-Christian times
into the Middle Ages. It was during the latter part of the Middle Ages, especially as the Renaissance and Protestant Reformation periods began to emerge,
that serious attempts were made to separate church from state affairs.

As the Renaissance and Reformation periods developed, the importance
of work assumed new meaning. According to Lucas (1972), work became a
duty for all to perform as the only way, or at least a major way, to serve God.
The "Protestant Work Ethic" began to emerge from the pronouncements of
church reformers such as Calvin and Luther that advocated the virtuousness
of work and the sinfulness of inactivity. It was this philosophy that carried
itself to America in the 17th and 18th centuries as hundreds of thousands
of persons fled political struggles and religious persecutions that enveloped
Europe.

In addition to American immigrants bringing with them many of the social
and religious values of western Europe, so too came traditional work concepts

and methods of labor. For example, the "master-servant" relationship, which emerged during the Middle Ages as a form of protection offered to workers by local rulers in exchange for labor, continued to flourish in early America since many immigrants had their ship passage paid by wealthy land owners (e.g., terms of indenturement). Similarly, as the industrial revolution developed in Europe, bringing with it an age of mechanization, new work methods increased productivity and subsequently changed the relationships between servants and masters on both continents. Along with the development and increase of factories as the predominant mode of productivity (replacing agriculture emphasis), the employer-employee relationship began to emerge, leading eventually to the development of modern day employee compensation systems.

Industrialization and Its Effects

The industrial revolution that was sweeping across Europe in the mid-1700s produced a wave of inventions that not only increased productivity levels, but contributed to the emergence of a new class of workers. As more and more people began migrating to cities and large industrial towns to seek employment in factories, social problems began to arise. Among the most significant problems were the over-crowded living and working conditions endured by factory workers that frequently compromised their safety and well-being. This section reviews the "factory system" and its abuses, the growing unrest among workers and subsequent labor revolts, and the beginnings of work reforms.

The Factory System

The industrialization of western Europe and America brought with it a rapid growth in population, increased agricultural activity, and expanded technological innovations. Generations after 1830 witnessed an apparent uninterrupted advance in virtually all sciences, accompanied by a growth in inventions applied to nearly all activities of daily living. According to Lucas (1972), it was a time when people welcomed and expected material improvements, not just for a privileged few, but for everyone.

In line with these advances (which included more productivity and less average time on the job), there developed a strong sense of individualism in the 1800s that extolled the virtues of pursuing one's own interests with minimum government interference. For example, private interests were thought to promote public welfare such that the accumulative efforts of each individual would be conducive of greater social harmony (Lucas, 1972). It was not long afterwards, however, that the newly formed "class" of entrepreneurs began to combine together to form monopolies in restraint of trade. Similarly, the factory system that developed in the unrestricted business atmosphere of the early industrial revolution fostered the development of rigid class differences among the working populace.

Industrialization raised to pre-eminence a new, prosperous, and influential middle class that derived its wealth from investments in labor and surplus earnings acquired through trade. This newly strengthened economic group also began to exert pressure on government to take a strong position in preserving their economic affluence. According to Lucas (1972), the mounting conservative doctrine of the capitalist middle class (e.g., industrialists) advocated that government not only forbid restraining monopolies by law, but take positive steps to enforce competition. Beneath the middle class affluence, on the other hand, were the masses of workers upon whose labors and suffering business prosperity had been built (see Table 1–1). Indeed, for the underprivileged, life was decidedly miserable.

Although the industrial revolution unquestionably brought prosperity to some, it brought in its aftermath terrible urban slums, child labor, and systematic exploitation. Families were crowded together in poorly built factory tenements, condemned to live out their lives in dark, foul-smelling rooms that periodically were swept with epidemics of typhoid, tuberculosis, and cholera. Those who serviced the growing needs of industry soon became aware that they had exchanged the bondage of servitude for the bondage of the

Table 1–1. Average Hours of Work per Week from 1850 to 1980 in the United States (U.S. Bureau of the Census, 1981)

Year	Average Hours of Work per Week
1850	69.8
1860	68.0
1870	65.4
1880	64.0
1890	61.9
1900	60.2
1910	55.1
1920	49.7
1930	45.9
1940	44.0
1950	40.0
1960	37.5
1970	36.3
1980	32.1

factory. From these conditions arose labor unrest that led to worker revolts of one form or another.

Labor Revolt and Its Aftermath

At first, the new class of factory workers suffered many hardships such as low pay, long working hours, and terrible working conditions by modern standards. In response to these factors, workers began to form organizations, at first known as "combinations," in order to protect themselves from excessive demands of factory owners. Because of pressure exerted by wealthy factory owners, however, almost every government outlawed combinations on the grounds of their potential for conspiring against employers (Tyler, 1944). In many instances, especially in Europe, open revolt and rioting among factory workers broke out against the factory system in general and their owners in particular. Frequently, these "insurrections" were forcibly subdued by local and national militia, or by bands of loyal workers, which often resulted in destruction of private property, death and crippling injuries among the combatants, and a deepening ill-will between employers and employees.

Generally, instances of worker violence (e.g., "Luddism," a term that has come to mean irrational, futile machine wrecking) served only to alienate employers and social reform-minded people against the plight of the working class. More often than not, the results of worker uprisings led to harsh legislation to punish those who wished to change the system through armed rebellion. Although some employers negotiated with their employees (more often from fear of personal and property loss than because of concern for their workers), most attempted to further consolidate their power through laws that would prohibit future organizational attempts by labor groups.

Notwithstanding the developments of organized labor and its impact on improving the conditions of American workers, employers began feeling pressures from society to assume greater responsibility for the well-being of their employees. Indeed, employee well-being was acknowledged as a source of increased productivity. Moreover, soon after the American Civil War, improved production methods and innovative manufacturing techniques led to a dramatic increase in the number of industrially caused or related injuries and deaths among workers, especially those employed by railroads. As a result, early attempts to provide compensation to injured workers and their families began to emerge in Europe for the protection of workers.

Beginning in Germany, followed by Austria, Finland, England, France, Holland, Sweden, Denmark, Belgium, and Hungary, legislation embodying the concept of workers' compensation began to emerge (Eastman, 1969). Although these various foreign systems differed greatly in detail, they generally constitute two categories; those in which employers are required merely to compensate injured workers on a uniform plan, and those in which employers are required also to insure against occupational risk. In the first category, typified by the English laws, workers are assured compensation for accidents by the employer, whereas in the second category, typified by German laws, compensation is doubly assured because employers are compelled to insure employees against injury in addition to providing compensation if injury occurs (Eastman, 1969). Thus, while both systems might be called "workers' accident insurance" programs, it is better to call the English system one of compensation, and the German method one of insurance. Nevertheless, both systems were important because of their contributions to the development of modern-day workers' compensation statutes in the United States.

Work Reform Leading to Workers' Compensation in America

Early attempts to fashion a compensation program for American workers typically studied the German and English systems. In Germany, for example, industrial accident insurance was one of three pioneering social insurance programs adopted in the 1880s. Beginning in 1883, the German Parliament enacted the Sickness Insurance Law, followed in 1884 by the Accident Insurance Law, and finally the Act for Insurance Against Old Age and Invalidity in 1889. According to Rhodes (1917), the consummation of the German system represented the collective ideas of the socialists that advocated protection of individuals and their families against the consequences of misfortunes regardless of fault.

In contrast to the German laws, the English system of compensation emerged from the long periods of worker revolts mentioned previously. Beginning in 1880, the English Parliament passed the Employers' Liability Act which modified the old common law defenses between masters and servants (see Chapter 2 for more discussion about "common law defenses"). Although previous legislation existed that pertained to regulation of working hours and conditions, the distinguishing feature of the 1880 law was that it changed the master-servant rule. In its place, legislative recognition was established that made employers liable to employees for injuries sustained by reason of the negligence of an employee who served the employer in a representative capacity (Rhodes, 1917). On the other hand, because all parties were dissatisfied with "assumption of risk" clauses and limited liability issues contained in the 1880 act, the British Workmen's Compensation Act of 1897 was passed. Like the 1884 German law, the more recent English act declared employers to be liable for industrial injuries to their employees, but unlike the German statute, it did not require employers to carry insurance, although most large firms did take out insurance policies (Gordon, 1963).

Based upon the early German and English systems, the United States began efforts to develop similar legislation in the early 20th century. Generally, state governments formed committees to prepare reports and make recommendations to their legislatures and governors about the most equitable system for workers' compensation programs. Despite the fact that many of the early attempts to establish legislation later were declared to be unconstitutional, they helped pave the way for subsequent laws that were more enduring by 1911 (Obermann, 1965). In that year, 10 states enacted workers' compensation laws that survived constitutional challenges (i.e., California, Illinois, Kansas, Massachusetts, Nevada, New Hampshire, New Jersey, Ohio, Washington, and Wisconsin, respectively). The following year, Arizona, Maryland, Michigan, and Rhode Island were added to the list of compensation states; and in 1913, Connecticut, Iowa, Minnesota, Nebraska, New York, Oregon, Texas, and West Virginia made a total of 22 states. By 1920, all but six states had viable workers' compensation statutes, and in 1948 Mississippi became the final state to adopt such legislation (Alaska and Hawaii had passed their statutes prior to admission to statehood).

Perhaps the major contributor to the eventual successful development of state workers' compensation laws occurred in 1908 with the passage of the Federal Employers' Liability Act. Although this piece of legislation is discussed in greater detail in Chapter 2, the importance of its passage was that it demonstrated to the states the federal commitment to the compensation principle. Thus, subsequent legislation emerging from both state and federal levels were soon seen in rapid succession leading to the modern-day statutes that cover all occupations with few exceptions.

Summary

The importance of work is an underlying consideration for all human activity. Indeed, this proposition is demonstrated throughout history in terms of the relationships work has with individual survival, self-expression, and job satisfaction on one level, and social organization, values, and attitudes on another. In its social context, work activities have been used to differentiate social classes, as well as the treatment of groups by others. During eras of industrial revolution, for example, treatment of workers by employers sometimes resulted in revolt, the formation of labor organizations, and general legislative actions to ease or suppress worker unrest. Industrial revolutions in both Europe and the United States also focused attention on the many abuses suffered by laborers, including increased instances of occupational disabilities and death. It was from concerns about the well-being of workers, especially those in hazardous occupations, that legislative attempts in the late 1800s began to formulate methods by which employee compensation for job-related injuries could be provided. Out of these early laws, fashioned especially by German and English Parliaments, workers' compensation programs began to appear in the United States by 1911. With this introduction in mind, Chapter 2 discusses modern-day disability compensation programs enacted by federal and state legislatures in the United States.

2 Injury Compensation in the Course of Employment

S tatistics reveal that occupational injuries produce significantly more disabled Americans than the commonly regarded human destruction caused by war. For example, the President's Committee on the Health Needs of the Nation (1952) reported that during World War II there were 20,500 major amputations among servicemen in the Armed Forces, whereas there were over 65,000 amputations among civilian industrial workers during the same period. Although these figures represent totals, rather than rates of exposure to hazards (in which war far exceeds occupational injury), the comparative losses sustained to the nation through job-related accidents are significant. More importantly, such losses and their concommitant effects on individual lives are insufficiently considered even today.

The purpose of this chapter is to familiarize the reader with insurance compensation benefits developed for those who have sustained injuries in the course of employment. To accomplish this goal, the chapter is divided into three major sections: (1) the compensation principle; (2) workers' compensation; and (3) related compensation programs. The objective of the chapter is to present an overview of current compensation systems found in legislative enactments.

The Compensation Principle

The compensation principle arose from employer-employee (and earlier "master-servant") relationships that eventually shaped modern worker benefit programs. In order to develop a sense of the reasons underlying modern workers' compensation remedies, it is important to be aware of their historical antecedents in common law rules and employers' liability statutes. Within these early forms of indemnity for industrial injury are concepts that contributed to the rise of workers' compensation as a more equitable benefit program.

9

Common Law Rules

Out of the early master-servant relationship, consisting of personal assurance offered by an employer to an employee (which varied from one work situation to another both in terms of protection offered and willingness of employers to honor their agreements), emerged common law rules. The purpose of these laws was twofold; they provided a standardized method by which injured employees could recover damages through personal injury suits against employers, and yet, they provided three basic defenses designed to protect employers from such suits brought against them either by injured employees or by others whose losses were inflicted by employees in the course of employment (Cheit, 1961; Larson, 1974; Somers & Somers, 1954).

Implicit in the common law rules was the assumption that occupational injuries were always the result of someone's fault. The responsibility of the courts was to ascertain who was at fault and to direct that person(s) to bear the costs associated with the sustained losses. Under the common law rules, however, employers could escape liability by pleading any of the following defenses:

Fellow-Servant Doctrine   Employers were absolved from all responsibility for injuries that were due to the actions or inactions of fellow servants.

Assumption of Risk   An injured employee could not recover damages and lost wages if an injury was due to the inherent hazards associated with a job of which the employee had, or should have had, advanced knowledge.

Contributory Negligence Doctrine   An injured employee had to prove that no oversight or carelessness on his or her part had contributed in any way to the occurrence of the accident regardless of the employer's negligence.

Needless to say, the burden of proof that the employer had not provided the employee due care rested with the worker. Moreover, such a burden was often difficult, if not impossible, to demonstrate. As a result, injured workers frequently failed to bring their cases to court, and when they did, the odds were heavily against their success.

Employers' Liability Statutes

The helplessness of the worker to secure relief for injuries from an employer who used the three common law defenses became so flagrant an example of injustice that change in the system was necessary. Statutory efforts, known as *employers' liability laws,* were made to diminish or remove some of the employers' common law defenses so that the injured worker not only stood a better chance of securing financial compensation for his or her injuries, but would be treated as equal to the employer in the court room (Somers &

Somers, 1954). The resulting early employers' liability laws generally have been classified into three categories: (1) statutes denying the right of employers and workers to sign contracts relieving the employer of liability for accidents as a condition of employment; (2) statutes extending the right of suit in death cases; and (3) statutes abrogating or modifying the common law defenses (Somers & Somers, 1954).

Although employers' liability laws continue to exist today for some occupational groups (and are discussed later in the chapter), major shortcomings of the statutory refinements in these early laws promoted the rise of workers' compensation systems. Among the limitations identified by Dodd (1936) and Somers and Somers (1954) concerning both common law rules and employers' liability laws were their: (1) anachronistic assumptions; (2) inadequate and uncertain recoveries for injuries; (3) wastefulness and high costs of the legal system; (4) delayed settlements; (5) inconsistency of awards; (6) deterioration of labor relations; (7) lack of preventive efforts; and (8) the public burden to support injured workers and their dependents who were unable to resume employment but were unable to win a court settlement in an employer suit.

The Rise of Workers' Compensation

Workers' compensation represents a dramatic departure from the negligence-based methods of handling disability that were prevalent in the common law rules and employers' liability laws. Under the workers' compensation system, employees are assured that they will be compensated for their occupational injuries, but no longer have the right to sue their employers (United States Chamber of Commerce, 1984). Thus, in exchange for the right to bring an action for full indemnification (that is, for lost wages as well as for other elements of damage), the employee is assured recovery of part of the wage loss, and medical and restorative services.

In essence, workers' compensation laws involved an entirely new economic and legal principle — *liability without fault.* According to Cheit (1961) and others, this concept abandoned the moral and legal concept of individual fault as a basis for public policy (that is, behind every disability there is a negligent party), and in its place, substituted the idea that the hazards of work and the employment relationship themselves are reason enough for compensating job-related injuries. Therefore, the resulting economic losses are considered costs of production, and are chargeable, to the extent possible, as a price factor (United States Chamber of Commerce, 1984). Finally, the laws serve to relieve employers of liability from common law suits involving negligence and have six basic objectives to achieve that goal: (1) predetermined, adequate, and prompt benefits; (2) elimination of wasteful litigation and legal fees; (3) certainty of payment; (4) promotion of safety and health activities;

(5) lower overhead ratios; and (6) assurance of medical and rehabilitation services (Somers & Somers, 1954; United States Chamber of Commerce, 1984).

The basic principle of liability without fault also was supported in a series of economic and legal theories, largely developed post hoc and entirely pragmatically. The earliest and most prominent was the theory of "occupational risk" which asserted that each industry should bear the costs of its own occupational risks, and that these costs should be included in the product price (Downey, 1924). A later and far more persuasive formulation, known as the principle of "least social costs," maintained that justification for workers' compensation was that it reduced the economic loss resulting from industrial accidents to a minimum (Witte, 1930). Legal theories, on the other hand, generally were derived from court decisions during subsequent rulings regarding workers' compensation suits.

Two of the best known decisions advocated the "social compromise" and "status" theories. The former held that workers' compensation represents a balanced set of sacrifices by and gains for the worker and the employer which could be legally enforced in the public interest (*Stertz v. Industrial Insurance Commission*, Washington Supreme Court, 1916). The "status" theory, on the other hand, proved to be more enduring legally, as well as more influential for subsequent interpretations of workers' compensation statutes. In the decision rendered by the United States Supreme Court in *Cudahy Packing Co. v. Parramore* (1924), workers' compensation legislation was interpreted as resting on the idea that the worker's contribution of work entitled him or her to equal status with the employer who contributed his or her capital (i.e., worker contribution for the sake of wages and employer contribution for the sake of profit).

Workers' Compensation Remedies

The path between statements of principle and their translation into acceptable legislation often reveals many stumbling blocks and moments of uncertainty. The work of various state and federal commissions, investigating the inequities of employers' liability laws, resulted in near unanimous condemnation of the existing systems. In their place, legislation was enacted that has led to present-day workers' compensation remedies, highlights of which are found in appendices A through C. It is important, however, that the reader remain aware that workers' compensation statutes differ from state to state, as well as between state and federal regulations. This section summarizes the salient features contained in state and federal workers' compensation statutes.

State Workers' Compensation

A basic and often repeated objective of workers' compensation on which there is broad agreement is that coverage under the acts should be universal. That is to say, that workers' compensation should be provided for *all* work-related injuries and diseases, as well as consisting of a uniform statutory definition and tests regardless of jurisdiction. Yet, for various historical, political, economic, or administrative reasons, no state law covers all forms of employment, although a fairly uniform statutory definition does exist which extends benefits to "personal injury caused by accidents arising out of and in the course of employment" (United States Chamber of Commerce, 1984, p. 1). On the other hand, while the tests used to determine whether an injured worker meets the statutory definition are also fairly uniform among the states, their interpretation has not resulted in completely uniform coverage of injuries and diseases according to the United States Chamber of Commerce (1984).

Coverage Boundaries   Although more than nine out of every 10 American workers potentially eligible for work-injury compensation come under the jurisdiction of state laws, the remaining 12% have employers' liability legislation or the tort law as their basic remedies. In addition to certain occupations not covered by workers' compensation statutes (see Appendix A), such laws may be either compulsory or elective. Today there are only three states, however, where employers can choose whether or not to provide workers' compensation benefits for their employees (i.e., New Jersey, South Carolina, Texas). Although an employer may accept or reject the state workers' compensation act, in so doing, an employer also forfeits the ability to use the three common law defenses mentioned earlier (i.e., fellow-servant doctrine, assumption of risk, contributory negligence). A compulsory law, on the other hand, requires each employer to comply with an act's provisions for the compensation of work-related injuries or illnesses.

As mentioned earlier, the principle of liability without fault is the theoretical basis for every American workers' compensation law. With minor exceptions, the remedy offered is an exclusive one, whereby three basic elements or tests are involved. According to Cheit (1961), these tests of eligibility include:

1. An injured worker must be an employee working in a covered employment as defined by compensation laws.
2. The disability must be compensable in nature.
3. There must be a causal relationship between employment and the disability.

Insurance Requirements   Workers' compensation benefits generally are financed exclusively by the employer as a recognized element in the cost of production. Similarly, most states require employers to obtain insurance or prove financial ability to carry their own risk in the form of self-insurance. Basically, the types of insurance available to employers are controlled by the states, and as such, tend to cluster into three distinct groups; private insurance, state insurance funds, and self-insurance. More information about the types and nature of insurance companies is contained in Chapter 3.

Private and Public Employment Virtually all industrial employment is covered by workers' compensation; however, there are specific exclusions among the various state jurisdictions (see Appendix A). Moreover, among the prominent exclusions are those who are employed as merchant marines and interstate railroad workers. Persons employed in these categories, while not covered by workers' compensation statutes, may seek damages under the Federal Employers' Liability Act or the Longshore and Harbor Workers' Compensation Act. Generally, most jurisdictions permit employees in an exempted class to be brought in voluntarily by the employer or by an administrative agency order which is frequently the case (United States Chamber of Commerce, 1984). Finally, Appendix A identifies those states which extend coverage to private employment, the extent of coverage for those working in public employment, the types of occupations excluded from coverage, and those that exclude coverage based on the number of employees.

Occupational Diseases Coverage Although workers' compensation laws initially had no specific provisions for occupational diseases, now all states recognize responsibility for them. On the other hand, two important problems in determining eligibility exist in this area. First, most states do not provide compensation for a disease that is an "ordinary disease of life" or which is not "peculiar to or characteristic of" an employee's occupation (United States Chamber of Commerce, 1984, p. 2). Second, although most occupational diseases become evident during employment or shortly after exposure, others (such as radiation disabilities) may take longer to reveal their symptoms, and thus create difficulty in establishing a causal relationship between employment and the disability.

Disability Classifications Because workers' compensation imposes an absolute, but limited, liability upon an employer for employee disability caused by the employment, the benefits payable to an injured worker attempt to cover most of the worker's economic losses. Losses include both earnings and the extra expenses associated with an injury or disease. When considering the amount of benefits to be awarded for loss of income or earning capacity due to an occupational injury, disease, or death, five classifications of disability are used. These are defined in the following manner:

Temporary-total disability   One in which the injured employee is totally incapacitated for work beyond the day on which the accident occurs, but is subsequently able to return to work without permanent impairment. About 95% of all injuries sustained in the course of employment are in this category (United States Chamber of Commerce, 1984).

Permanent-total disability   One from which an injury permanently and totally incapacitates the injured worker from carrying on a gainful occupation; for example, blindness in both eyes, double amputations, spinal cord injury.

Temporary-partial disability   One in which the injured worker is partially incapacitated during the course of the work day on which the injury occurs, but is able to continue working on the day of the incident, and is subsequently able to work without permanent impairment. Examples of such time-limited injuries include cuts, lacerations, and minor burns that may require immediate attention, but are not expected to result in an employee leaving the job for the remainder of the day or longer.

Permanent-partial disability   One that involves permanent loss of a member of the body, such as an eye, a foot, or a finger.

Fatality   An injury or illness that results in the death of the employee.

According to the United States Chamber of Commerce (1984), most awards and the preponderance of money paid as income benefits are either for temporary-total or permanent-partial disabilities because these, more than any other categories, involve current earnings or wage earning ability. Finally, the basic formula used to determine income benefits in all types of injury claims uses the following seven factors according to Somers and Somers (1954, pp. 60-61):

1. A specified maximum percentage of the worker's normal and average wages.
2. A weekly dollar maximum and minimum.
3. A maximum total or aggregate dollar amount.
4. A maximum duration or amount of time for which benefits must be paid.
5. Variations according to the number of dependents claimed by the employee.
6. The waiting period specified by statutes before payments begin.
7. The formula by which average wages are computed to derive allowable benefit amounts.

Rehabilitation Benefits   These include both medical and vocational services for those cases involving severe disabilities, and generally are considered to be an integral part of the complete medical treatment and care program for injured workers (Cheit, 1961). Moreover, the mutual interests of disabled employees and employer alike tend to favor starting rehabilitation services as soon as possible after the accident incident. While the specific rehabilitation provisions now in workers' compensation laws are outlined in Appendix B, rehabilitation is provided in all states even if unspecified in the law (United States Chamber of Commerce, 1984). More information about the role of rehabilitation, as well as the services offered to industrially injured workers, will be described later in this chapter and Chapter 4. Suffice it to say at this point, however, the contributions of the state, federal, and private vocational rehabilitation programs have and continue to demonstrate the economic benefits to employers and disabled employees of holding down the cost of industrial accidents and diseases.

Second Injury Funds   Second-injury funds were developed to address problems arising when pre-existing injuries, combined with a second injury, produce a disability greater than that caused by the latter alone. The purpose of these funds is twofold in nature: (1) it encourages hiring of disabled workers and avoids discrimination against handicapped individuals; and (2) offers a more equitable allocation of costs for providing benefits to such employees (Somers & Somers, 1954; United States Chamber of Commerce, 1984).

Second-injury funds are designed to provide compensation to an injured worker for the *total* disability resulting from the combined injuries, but the last employer meets only the costs of the last injury; the remainder of the award is paid from the state's special fund. Where no special second-injury fund is provided by the state statutes, however, an employer in whose employ a second injury occurs usually is liable for compensation due for the *total* disability. On the other hand, most compensation laws now limit employer liability in second-injury cases to the payment for the disability resulting from the second injury considered by itself (United States Chamber of Commerce, 1984). Appendix C indicates the nature of the injuries covered, the portion of payment by the employer and by the fund, and the sources of the fund.

Administration of Workers' Compensation   Because workers' compensation grew out of a public dissatisfaction with the manner in which job-related disabilities were being handled, the system was designed with the intention that prompt and effective disposition of disability cases would result. Thus, without an effective delivery system, many of the problems associated with the common law rules and employers' liability laws would still remain. Generally, the states have moved either to administer their laws through the court system, a special commission or board, or combination of both. Regardless of which system is preferred among the states, the principal areas of administration include: (a) supervision of compliance with statutory regulations for employers, employees, insurance carriers, and medical and legal personnel; (b) investigation and decision on disputed claims and the supervision of medical and vocational rehabilitation services; (c) management of second-injury funds and special assessment requirements; and (d) collection of data and evaluation of program performance (see Appendix D).

Federal Workers' Compensation

Nearly 75% of the federal employees come under a workers' compensation law; of these, two-thirds are under the Federal Employees' Compensation Act, the others under the Longshore and Harbor Workers' Compensation Act. The remaining employees under federal jurisdiction, who are not covered by either of these provisions, are covered by separate federal acts identified later. Although federal employees were the first to gain compensation protection under American law, the original 1908 act limited payments to artisans and laborers in hazardous work. Since that time, the changes in both of these federal acts have increased substantially the benefits provided, as well as occupations covered.

Federal Employees' Compensation Act The Federal Employees' Compensation Act (FECA) was first passed by Congress in 1908 and was designed to cover civil employees of the federal government, as well as public employees of the District of Columbia (Somers & Somers, 1954). In 1916, however, FECA was amended to establish a uniform program for all civil employees of the United States regardless of hazard. According to Cheit (1961), five groups of employees were covered: (1) employees of all three branches of the federal government; (2) employees of the government of the District of Columbia; (3) all reserve corps personnel while in training or on active duty in peace time; (4) commissioned personnel of the Public Health Service; and (5) workers employed under various emergency relief acts. Later, in 1949, the FECA was again amended (P.L. 81-357) so as to apply also to workers of wholly owned federal projects such as the Tennessee Valley Authority, Panama Canal, and Alaska railroads. Today, however, government employees of the District of Columbia are no longer covered by FECA, but rather by the District of Columbia Workers' Compensation Act which became effective July 26, 1982 (United States Chamber of Commerce, 1984).

Since its extensive revision in 1949, the FECA remains one of the most liberal compensation laws in the country. Administered by the Division of Federal Employees' Compensation of the Office of Workers' Compensation located in the U.S. Department of Labor, FECA covers injuries which occur in the performance of duty, as well as all diseases which are work related. Unlike most of the state laws, virtually no distinction is made between temporary-total and permanent-total benefits, that is, there are only two classes of disability; *total* and *partial*. Disabled workers receive a minimum of two-thirds of their weekly wage up to $910.31 per week, or up to 75% of their weekly wage where there are dependents (United States Chamber of Commerce, 1984). No duration or total dollar limits are set on indemnity payments to totally disabled workers, whereas benefits to partially disabled employees are paid according to a specific schedule of injuries or to compensate for wage loss.

Medical benefits under the FECA are unlimited for the effects of an injury, and include hospitalization and any necessary appliances without charge to the disabled employee. On the other hand, the employer governs the selection of physicians and hospitals, but allows for the employee to choose from an approved listing of persons and places. The FECA also authorizes any permanently disabled worker to undergo vocational rehabilitation services, as well as providing an additional maximum benefit of $200 per month for maintenance. If a person fails to undergo vocational rehabilitation services, which could increase the injured employee's earnings, the federal administrator has the ability to reduce the benefits received by the claimant.

Longshore and Harbor Workers' Compensation Act   The Longshore and Harbor Workers' Compensation Act provides job disability benefits for all U.S. maritime employment and certain others. According to the United States Chamber of Commerce (1984), however, the courts have held that the Longshore Act does not apply to maritime employment in Puerto Rico. Additionally, privately employed workers in the District of Columbia are no longer covered by the act since enactment of that district's workers' compensation law in 1982. According to the federal act, six groups of private employees are subject to federal workers' compensation jurisdiction: (1) longshoremen engaged in offshore stevedoring; (2) ship repairpersons; (3) certain other employees in maritime occupations; (4) defense base workers; (5) employees engaged in operations conducted on the Outer Continental Shelf working on natural resources of submerged lands; and (6) certain civilian employees under the jurisdiction of the Armed Forces not otherwise covered because they are not paid from appropriated funds (Somers & Somers, 1954).

Originally passed by Congress in 1927, 10 years after longshoremen had been barred from state coverage by a U.S. Supreme Court decision (*Southern Pacific Co. v. Jensen*, 1917), the Longshore Act grew out of the difficult problems posed by the longshoremen's status under maritime laws. According to Cheit (1961), longshoremen generally lived at home and worked for private employers who frequently came under the jurisdiction of the newly created state compensation law. However, because these same workers were employed in settings that were water-based, they were subject to maritime laws and thus were not eligible for state compensation benefits. Therefore, after several unsuccessful attempts to bring these workers under a compensation system, Congress finally passed a bill specifically for them which was found to be acceptable to the Supreme Court.

Today, the Longshore Act is administered by the Division of Longshore and Harbor Workers' Compensation within the Office of Workers' Compensation of the U.S. Department of Labor. The law covers injuries and all diseases arising out of employment, and while its benefit schedule is not as liberal as that of the FECA, it compares favorably with those of many other states' compensation laws. Both the partial and total disability schedules are similar to those of the FECA and no total dollar limit is imposed for the latter cases. On the other hand, death benefits range from 50% to 66.7% of the weekly wage according to the number of dependents, but the maximum weekly benefits payable to dependents is unlimited following a 1979 ruling by the United States Supreme Court (*Director of the Office of Workers' Compensation Program v. Rasmussen*, 44 U.S. 29). Vocational rehabilitation benefits are paid from second-injury funds and only allow a maximum of $25 per week maintenance. Additionally, despite the fact that all administrative costs are financed by Congressional appropriation, liability is privately insured through either commercial or self-insured insurance (Cheit, 1961).

Related Compensation Insurance Programs

It was noted earlier that approximately 75% of all federal employees are covered by either FECA or the Longshore and Harbor Workers' Compensation Act. Similarly, it was reported that among the states' workers' compensation laws, certain classes of employees are not covered, but that these vary from state to state, for example, domestic servants, farm laborers, railroad workers (see Appendix A). In many instances, disabled employees may be compensated for their work-related or nonwork-related injuries or diseases by any of the following pieces of state and federal legislations: Federal Employers' Liability Act, State Employers' Liability Acts, Jones Act, Railroad Retirement and Unemployment Insurance Acts, Social Security Act, Veterans' Readjustment Act, and assorted health and safety acts.

Federal Employers' Liability Act

Since railroading was considered to be a highly hazardous type of employment, railroad workers were among the most conspicuous victims of the inequities of the 19th century common law rules as they applied to occupational injuries. Indeed, at the turn of the century, the railroad accident record was at its worst, insofar as in 1901 it was estimated that one out of every 399 railroad employees was killed at work; for those operating employees, the ratio was one in every 137, and the injury rate was one in 26 (Allen, 1952). Thus, in response to the demands for protection and for reform of the old common law rules of employers' liability, Congress enacted the first Federal Employers' Liability Act (FELA) in 1906.

Although the law as applied and interpreted by the courts has become extremely technical, the basic design of the FELA is quite simple. The employer is responsible for damages to employees for work-related injuries, but only for those injuries that occur as a result of the employer's negligence. Thus, the notion of comparative negligence is still a relative issue in that damage awards are reduced in proportion to the amount of the employee's contributing negligence that is found. For these and other reasons, the use of negligence as a basis for occupational disability compensation on the railroads in particular has been criticized from the beginning. Yet, despite repeated efforts to amend the FELA and introduce workers' compensation on the railroads, these proposals have been consistently rejected. According to Cheit (1961), leading the opposition are the railroad workers themselves, who contend that a switch to workers' compensation would actually reduce their economic security.

State Employers' Liability Acts and Tort Law

If state workers' compensation acts included everyone under state jurisdiction who was potentially eligible, almost all workers would be covered, leaving only about 2.3% under federal, employers' liability, and admiralty systems (Cheit, 1961). Actually, however, workers' compensation is far from complete, as is made evident by its various exclusions, exemptions, and eligibility requirements reported in the appendices. Yet, while approximately 88% of the American work force are covered by either state or federal forms of workers' compensation, over 10% are not. For these employees, redress in cases of work injury must be found within the residual remedies of state employers' liability and tort laws.

In theory, if injured at work, these employees can file against their employers, and the common law generally will not be available for use against them (Riesenfeld & Maxwell, 1950). Both tort law and employers' liability legislation assure that employees have the right to sue for damages on the grounds of employer negligence, as well as serving as aids for barring employers the use of the common law defenses. Furthermore, the money stakes in such suits tend to be high, because tort theory entitles an injured worker to damages sufficient to relieve him or her from all detrimental effects of the injury (Cheit, 1961). Moreover, damages are in theory bounded by no special dimensions, but rather are payable for all losses where there is liability (Malone & Plant, 1963). On the other hand, even though the employers' liability system, under its case-by-case approach, occasionally produces very high damage awards, more frequently than not the right to sue is either not exercised because a settlement is bargained before a suit is begun/completed, or because of ignorance or fear of the injured worker and/or the witnesses. Historically, it was this uncertainty of recovery that led to the enactment of workers' compensation legislation.

Apart from theory, however, the reality of the matter is that actual figures of injuries, deaths, and payments under the employers' liability system are sketchy at best. This is a result of a number of factors among which are the limited number of cases brought before the courts under this system, those cases that are not identified as such (because they are reflected in claims under public liability insurance, manufacturers' liability, and farmers' liability policies), and payments received from uninsured employers (Cheit, 1961). Among the excluded worker and employer categories in many states are employers of small business establishments who employ less than the minimum number of workers required by state law as necessary for workers' compensation coverage, agricultural occupations generally, domestic servants, independent contractors, and casual laborers (see Appendix A). Moreover, the difficulties, delays, costs, and outcome uncertainties employees face when undertaking such a lawsuit further reduce the likelihood that this procedure will realize an increase in cases.

The Jones Act and Admiralty Law

Although seamen represent the smallest occupational group with separate legal status for occupational disability compensation, their situation is more complex than any other since they are covered by two separate legal systems; admiralty and tort laws (Somers & Somers, 1954). Remedies for injuries are provided under both systems and benefits are provided under other statutes. Since the passage of the Merchant Marine Act of 1920 (Jones Act), seamen have enjoyed the same rights and recoveries as are accorded to railway workers under the FELA. Owing to the difference between conditions at sea and on land, and to the historical distinctions between admiralty or maritime law and the common law, the liability of the shipowner today is considerably greater than that of the railroad employer. Today, an injured seaman has available three different, but not mutually exclusive, remedies: (1) maintenance and cure during any disability while he or she is on the payroll; (2) the seaman may sue for tort damages, if negligence can be shown; and (3) the seaman may sue for tort damages, without proof of negligence, where there is an unseaworthy vessel or an unseaworthy appliance (Somers & Somers, 1954). Thus, like the injured railroad worker, the injured seaman has a form of temporary disability insurance in which it is not necessary to establish work connection, plus the right to sue for substantial tort damages in serious cases.

After the passage of the Jones Act, however, shipowner interest in compensation coverage for injured seamen increased. Their later efforts to have the provisions of the Longshore and Harbor Workers' Compensation

Act extended to seamen provided the impetus for the first major analysis of seamen's compensation under the Jones Act. In 1941 a Congressional Inter-departmental Committee issued its report recommending a workers' compensation system for seamen despite the fact that the majority of seamen would appear to lose more than they would gain by transferring to a workers' compensation scheme with the typical standards provided at the time. The proposed workers' compensation system recommended by the committee, therefore, provided standards that were far more liberal than any compensation law then in effect, i.e., (a) no waiting period for benefits; (b) benefits at least equal to those provided under the Longshore Act, but without limits on total benefits payable for death or disability; (c) benefits during periods of out-patient treatment and convalescence not less than the maintenance to which the injured seaman was entitled during a period of temporary disability; and (d) benefits computed on a full-time wage base, together with the value of subsistence and lodging, as well as payment for overtime and bonuses (Interdepartmental Committee to Study Workmen's Compensation for Seamen, 1941). However, the report to Congress did not result in any legislative action.

Later in 1946, the U.S. Bureau of Labor Statistics published its study which further analyzed the data collected by the Interdepartmental Committee five years earlier. The purpose of this second study was to assess the status of seamen's benefits in relation to the Longshore Act, as well as propose a hypothetical compensation act. This group found that, although the total settlements under the hypothetical scheme would exceed total actual net settlements under the then present system, about half of the individual cases would be worse off, only 46% would gain, and less than 5% would neither gain nor lose (Zisman, 1946). On the other hand, those who would gain most from workers' compensation were the fatal and permanent-totally disabled cases, while the temporary cases would lose the most. In view of the results of these two studies, it was little wonder that seamen, through their unions, have continued to resist proposals to bring them under a workers' compensation system. As a result, indemnity payments for work injuries at sea remain a private affair between seamen and their employing companies.

According to Cheit (1961), disability and benefit records, like the disposition of claims of aggrieved shippers or passengers, are maintained only in each shipping line's private business files. If there is no resulting lawsuit, no public record of claims disposition is made. Even when the issue goes to court, the final disposition often is not noted and nowhere are the claims systematically recorded (Cheit, 1961). Based on this account of the "procedures," it is not surprising that very little is known about the effectiveness of the present system of compensating seamen for occupational death or disability. Compounding the problem is the fact that shipping is a relatively small industry where the work relationships have their own peculiar traditions.

Railroad Retirement and Unemployment Insurance Acts

In 1934, Congress decided that there should be a railroad retirement annuity system for the purpose of promoting efficiency and safety in interstate transportation (Rayback, 1966). A year later the Railroad Retirement Act passed Congress, followed in 1938 by the enactment of the Railroad Unemployment Insurance Act. Both laws, which subsequently have been amended to broaden the benefit coverages, expand and further define the regulatory powers of the Railroad Retirement Board, and strengthen the linkages between the railway acts and the Social Security Act.

The railroad retirement disability program dates back to 1935 when the original program provided disability annuities to employees under age 65 who had 30 or more years of service. Today, however, employees with 10 years of railroad service are entitled to disability benefits if their condition is determined to be total and permanent in nature (Boehne, 1982). According to the Tenth Institute on Rehabilitation Issues (1983), disability under this Act has a twofold meaning, insofar as a "permanent disability" is one that prevents an individual from engaging in any regular employment. "Occupational disability," on the other hand, may consist of a permanent condition that prevents an individual from engaging in his or her regular employment, but not necessarily exclude all other employment. Thus, for those railroad employees who are determined to be totally and permanently disabled, benefits are available to present and former employees regardless when their disabilities occurred as long as the 10-year minimum employment requirement is met. For those who do not meet the 10-year requirement, however, application for benefits must be made to the Social Security Disability Insurance program (Boehne, 1982). On the other hand, those railroad employees who do not qualify for total disability benefits (i.e., are occupationally disabled), can receive annuities if they: (a) are at least age 60 or have 20 years of railroad service; *and* (b) have a current connection with the railroad industry (Boehne, 1982).

In 1954, the Railroad Retirement Amendments (P.L. 83-572) added survivor benefits for dependent, disabled children age 18 and older whose disabilities began before the age of 18. Moreover, the 1968 amendments (P.L. 90-257) introduced benefits for totally and permanently disabled widows, commencing as early as age 50. In order to be eligible, a widow's disability had to begin no later than seven years after the employee's death or seven years after she ceased to be entitled to widowed mother's benefits because she no longer had an eligible surviving child in her care. Furthermore, these rules also apply to widowers. Overseeing the program administration for all entitlements under these railroad acts is the Railroad Retirement Board.

It is important to mention that the Railroad Retirement Act should not be confused with benefits provided under the Federal Employers' Liability Act mentioned previously that also covers railroad workers. In order for disabled employees to collect benefits under FELA, it must be proved that the injury was the result of some negligent act of the employer (Tenth Institute on Rehabilitation Issues, 1983). Although the Railroad Retirement Act does not require proof of negligence per se, it does require that a sustained injury resulted from and occurred during the performance of an employee's railroad duties.

Benefits provided by the Railroad Retirement Act and the Railroad Unemployment Insurance Act are financed by taxes paid by employees into the Railroad Retirement Trust Fund. Moreover, the trust fund receives reimbursement from the Social Security Disability Insurance Trust Fund for employees determined to be totally and permanently disabled. This financial arrangement was enhanced considerably by the Act's 1974 amendments (P.L. 93-445) which further coordinated railroad retirement and social security.

Social Security Act and Its Amendments

In 1935, Congress enacted the Federal Social Security Act (P.L. 74-271), followed in subsequent years by several amendments that basically increased coverage to more types of American citizens. The Act represented "a series of related measures designed as a unified, well-rounded program of attack upon the principal causes of insecurity in our economic life" (Social Security Handbook, 1982, p. 2).

Today, the Social Security Administration, housed within the United States Department of Health and Human Services, consists of eight insurance and/or benefit programs: (1) retirement insurance; (2) survivors insurance; (3) disability insurance; (4) hospital and medical insurance for elderly and disabled persons; (5) black lung benefits; (6) supplemental security income; (7) unemployment insurance; and (8) public assistance and welfare services (Social Security Handbook, 1982, p. 2). Among these programs, the federal government operates the retirement, survivors, disability, hospital and medical, black lung, and supplemental security benefits; the remaining are operated by the states with federal cooperation. While each of these programs provides varying degrees of assistance to disabled persons, an overview of the disability insurance and supplemental security income programs are presented. Later, toward the end of this section, a review of the black lung and several other benefit programs will be covered.

Social Security Disability Insurance (SSDI)   This program is a trust fund for workers in the United States which is contributed to by most citizens for use in the event of disability and loss of earnings (Bitter, 1979; Rubin & Roessler, 1983). SSDI benefits are designed to replace some of the lost earnings, with the amount of benefits dependent on the amount of contributions made by the individual worker. This federal program pays benefits to disabled workers under the age of 65 whose disability is expected to last 12 months or more or result in death. Seven types of disability protection are included in the disability provisions of the act: (1) monthly cash benefits for a disabled worker and family; (2) monthly cash benefits for needy individuals under the supplemental security income program; (3) the establishment of a "period of disability" for a disabled person, which protects against the loss of or the reduction in the amount of disability or retirement benefits; (4) monthly cash benefits for a disabled widow(er), or a disabled surviving divorced spouse; (5) monthly cash benefits for a disabled son or daughter of a worker entitled to worker's or retirement benefits or of an insured worker who died; (6) vocational rehabilitation services to a disability beneficiary who is capable of being restored to productive activity by the state vocational rehabilitation agency; and (7) hospital and supplementary medical insurance protection (Social Security Handbook, 1982).

A disabled worker becomes entitled to SSDI monthly cash benefits beginning with the first month in which the disabled worker meets five criteria: (1) has a defined disability; (2) has filed an application for worker's benefits; (3) has achieved a minimum period of employment covered by social security; (4) has completed a 5-month waiting period; and (5) has not attained age 65 (Social Security Handbook, 1982, p. 77). Cash payments are payable monthly based on wages earned during the covered period of employment, plus allowances for spouse and children. Cost-of-living increases are payable also and are effective each June. Finally, combined SSDI and workers' compensation benefits cannot exceed 80% of the average current earnings of the disabled person prior to the occupational injury. Furthermore, the 1981 Omnibus Budget Reconciliation Act requires that SSDI benefits supplement workers' compensation payments unless state law provides for a reverse offset on or before February 18, 1981 (Social Security Handbook, 1982; United States Chamber of Commerce, 1984; United States Department of Health and Human Services, 1982).

Supplemental Security Income (SSI)   The SSI program provides a minimum income for persons who are either disabled or elderly and whose income is within certain limits prescribed by the Social Security Administration. The SSI program was the first federally administered cash assistance program in this country available to the general public. According to the Social Security Administration, SSI establishes that payment may be received as a right by those citizens or legally admitted aliens residing in this country who qualify as elderly, blind, or disabled and who meet the income and resource criteria. The program, which is administered by the Social Security Administration and is funded from general tax revenues, was designed with two objectives in mind. First, the program was designed to transfer to federal rolls those persons who had been recipients of federal-state assistance payments as blind, elderly, or disabled. Second, SSI was established to form uniform national programs of payment for these three disability types.

In order to be determined eligible for SSI payments, which may begin no earlier than the month in which the application is filed, the following criteria must be met: (a) age 65 or older; or (b) is blind; or (c) is disabled; and (d) is a resident of one of the 50 states, the District of Columbia, or the Northern Mariana Islands; and (e) is a citizen of the United States, or a legally admitted alien for permanent residence; and (f) does not have a countable income for a month or more; and (g) does not have countable resources in excess of $1,500 for an individual, or $2,250 for a couple; and (h) is not accepted because of residing in a public institution and not receiving Medicaid, failure to accept treatment for drug addiction or alcoholism, absence from the United States, refusal to accept vocational rehabilitation services, or failure to apply for other benefits, pensions, or the like to which potentially eligible (Social Security Handbook, 1982, p. 327).

Finally, the SSI program offers two vocational-types of services to eligible recipients; a trial work period and vocational rehabilitation. A trial work period is provided in order to create an opportunity to measure disabled persons' ability to work and hold a job. While this service is not considered as a determiner of whether the disability has ceased, income received during the trial work period may be high enough to prevent payment of SSI benefits for some months. Vocational rehabilitation services, on the other hand, are available for blind or disabled persons under the age of 65, as long as they are determined appropriate for such services by a state vocational rehabilitation agency. Moreover, persons who are receiving SSI and who refuse such services without good cause are not eligible to continue to receive SSI payments (Social Security Handbook, 1982).

Veterans' Readjustment Acts

Approximately 10 years after the creation of the Veterans' Administration, which organized all of the veteran-related functions of five separate offices, the Disabled Veterans Rehabilitation Act of 1943 (P.L. 78-16) was enacted. Under this act, the Veterans' Administration was authorized to carry out all necessary services to assist disabled servicemen to adjust to the world of work following their honorable discharge from the Armed Forces (Obermann, 1965). Less than a year later, in 1944, Congress passed the Servicemen's Readjustment Act (P.L. 78-346), commonly known as the "GI Bill," which provided training and education assistance for men and women whose education or career had been interrupted by military service. In addition to these benefits, as well as hospitalization, disability compensation, and preferential employment and referral services, the Veterans' Administration formed a Vocational

Rehabilitation and Education Service organized in cooperation with universities to offer graduate training in psychology and counseling (Obermann, 1965).

After the Korean conflict, the Veterans' Readjustment Assistance Act of 1952 (P.L. 82-550) extended similar benefits under the GI Bill to returning veterans who had served in that conflict. Similarly, in 1962, rehabilitation and other benefits were authorized for honorably discharged veterans who served between 1945 and the Korean conflict, as well as afterward (P.L. 87-815). Finally, shortly after the end of the Vietnam struggle, Congress modified the Veterans' Acts in 1976 by providing a two-to-one matching fund for individuals who wanted to contribute to their own educational and training programs. Additionally, the Act eliminated the termination dates for eligibility for services among service-related, severely disabled veterans (P.L. 94-502).

Occupational Health and Safety Legislation

While it is beyond the scope of this section to provide an indepth review of the historical development of health and safety movements within American industry, it is important to identify significant developments which led to the more important pieces of legislation in this area. For interested readers who desire more detailed information, Somers and Somers (1954) provide an excellent historical accounting of the health and safety movements in their book *Workmen's Compensation*. Additionally, current legislative enactments in this area are more than adequately reviewed annually by the United States Chamber of Commerce and the United States Department of Labor, Employment Standards Administration.

Federal Coal Mine Health and Safety Act of 1969 (P.L. 91-173)   The legislation grew out of the Federal Coal-Mine Safety Act of 1952 which gave the Federal Bureau of Mines authority to close mines under five specified conditions that might lead to a "major" disaster (Somers & Somers, 1954). The 1969 statute, which was subsequently amended in 1972, 1978, and 1981, provides benefits for total disability or death caused by respiratory illness attributable to coal mining. The Act is administered by the Division of Coal Mine Workers in the United States Department of Labor's Office of Workers' Compensation Programs and by the Social Security Administration. Title IV of the Act is the Black Lung Benefits Reform Act of 1977 which was enacted on March 1, 1978. Black lung benefits are payable at the minimum for total disability provided by the FECA, plus an allowance for dependents equal to 50%, 75%, or 100% of the basic benefits for one, two, or three or more dependents respectively (Social Security Handbook, 1982).

The Black Lung Disability Trust Fund, financed by an excise tax on coal production, was established by the 1978 amendments to pay claims where the last employment was prior to 1970 or where no responsible coal mine operator could be identified (Social Security Handbook, 1982). According to the United States Chamber of Commerce (1984), a total of $10 billion in black lung payments have been made to approximately 500,000 claimants between 1969 and 1981. In addition to the benefits provided by the Act, beneficiaries also receive an annual cost-of-living increase.

Federal Occupational Safety and Health Act of 1970 (P.L. 91-596)   The purpose of the Occupational Safety and Health Act (OSHA) is to assure that every worker in America is employed in safe and healthful environments in order to preserve the nation's human resources (Sartain & Baker, 1978). The Act represents the first all-embracing federal health and safety legislation that is labor-oriented. In fact, it has been hailed as one that grants to workers the most extensive "Bill of Rights" in the history of labor legislation (Sartain & Baker, 1978, p. 315). Administration of the Act rests within the Occupational Safety and Health Administration of the United States Department of Labor. Under the provisions of the Act, employees have a right to participate in the development of OSHA standards, to request a public hearing on any standards that are under consideration, and to obtain copies of current OSHA standards from their employer or from the OSHA office nearest them. Moreover, if employees are discharged for their attempts to exercise their rights, management may be required not only to rehire and reinstate them to their former positions, but with retroactive pay. Finally, the Act limits enforcement of health and safety practices to the work environment as it affects employees, *only* but it does not cover similar practices within the community, the latter being within the province of the Environmental Protection Agency.

Summary

Modern-day workers' compensation and other forms of injury compensation arising out of work-related accidents and health hazards are a far cry from early methods designed to ensure employee protection. The development of the compensation principle, evolving from the common law rules and employers' liability laws, is characterized by the concept of liability without fault. This basic concept is found regardless of whether workers' compensation laws are state or federally enacted. On the other hand, because of constitutional challenges to many of the early laws, each state has somewhat different provisions which include covered occupations, exempted classes of workers, benefit entitlements, waiting periods, and overall administration of the program, to name a few. Indeed, it is because of the many dissimilarities among state statutes, not to mention their differences in relation to federal workers' compensation provisions, that additional laws have been enacted by the federal government designed to provide protection to assorted other occupational groups not covered elsewhere. Among these other occupations which have their own compensation statutes are railroad employees and merchant marines. In addition to legislation designed to compensate for disability and death as a result of employment hazards, efforts in state and federal legislatures have prompted enactment of statutes to increase the safety and health standards within work environments. Thus, the compensation principle and accident prevention form an intertwined relationship whereby one enhances the other. Compensation for injuries and occupational diseases sustained in the course of employment notwithstanding, the following chapter provides additional insurance information about coverages and protection in cases where disabilities result from activities outside of and unrelated to employment.

3 Insurance Principles and Concepts

William C. Wallace and Ralph E. Matkin

E very field of knowledge has its own specialized terminology, and terms that have very simple meanings in everyday usage often take on different and complicated connotations when applied in a specialized field. As with rehabilitation, the field of insurance is based upon fundamental concepts that influence the planning and delivery of services to the populations it serves. Understanding the basic concepts of any specialization is a necessary prerequisite for persons responsible for either direct or indirect service delivery in a chosen occupation. For those rehabilitation professionals engaged or anticipating involvement in services provided to insured disabled persons, there is a need to be aware of insurance and legal "rules of the game."

The purpose of this chapter is to provide readers with basic principles and concepts of insurance in order to develop a greater understanding of the framework in which rehabilitation services may be practiced. To accomplish this goal, the chapter is divided into four sections: (1) ethical foundations of insurance; (2) concepts of insurance; (3) life, health, and property and liability insurance; and (4) insurance-rehabilitation interface. Within these sections, new and perhaps unfamiliar terms will be encountered. Although many will be defined within the context in which they appear, readers may wish to refer periodically to glossaries of insurance and legal terms.

Ethical Foundations of Insurance

The sustained and healthy execution of the insuring process depends on more than simply the mechanics of insurance; it rests on an ethical foundation. The "ethical pillars" of insurance concern those generally accepted behavioral standards that are conducive to the long-range availability and use of insurance. According to Long (1971), the insurance institution rests on nine such pillars: (1) achievement; (2) acquisitiveness; (3) preservation; (4) apprehension; (5) honesty; (6) obedience; (7) tradition; (8) personal responsibility;

31

and (9) charity. Thus, before turning attention to the basic concepts of insurance, it is necessary to briefly discuss the underpinnings of the insurance method by examining its ethical foundations.

Achievement   Achievement is one of the ethical pillars upon which sustained use of insurance depends. For insurance to function, achievement must generally be valued by the insured society. In other words, individuals using insurance must believe that achievement is both desirable and possible, and must possess strong incentives that will promote individual motivation. According to Long (1971), the achievement concept of insurance is closely akin to the Protestant work ethic, which is fundamental to much of the historical culture of the United States (see Chapter 1). The general idea of the Protestant ethic is that hard work, self-denial, and self-discipline along with steadfast and vigorous pursuit of one's calling provide serenity, if not happiness, in this life and ensure moral and spiritual progress toward the life that is to come (Weber, 1930). As it pertains to the ethical foundation of insurance, achievement is a similar concept, but not necessarily as strong. For one thing, it need not have the ascetic flavor of the Protestant ethic, nor does it necessarily connote the idea that hard work and self-discipline are important preparations for life after death. For the purposes of insurance, it is enough that achievement be pursued for the joys it can bring in this life both as a means and an end. In short, insurance needs an achievement orientation both on the part of those making the insurance available and those using it. It requires the elements of incentive, work, pride, growth, and optimism that come from a belief in achievement and from a society in which freedom to achieve is both permitted and encouraged (Long, 1971).

Acquisitiveness   Although this term may have a negative connotation of greed or extreme and determined selfishness for some, as it is used here, acquisitiveness refers to a desire to acquire rather than avarice. Acquisitiveness is a form of achievement that must be sanctioned by law to be considered right and just in order for insurance to prosper. Moreover, in an insurance environment there must be some resources susceptible to redistribution; the more the amount of resources, the greater the usefulness of insurance. Without an acquisitiveness common to virtually all members of a given society, the society is not likely to have the income, real property, and other possessions that are the usual objects of insurance. Without this acquisitiveness on the part of virtually all members of the society, no form of economic and social organization is likely to be productive. On the other hand, when acquisitiveness is accepted and approved, any form of economic and social organization is likely to be productive and insurable objects are likely to accumulate.

The sustained use of insurance demands that those using it view ownership not only as a legal right, but as a positive good. According to Long (1971), insurance users must feel that an individual should be able to own at least a large portion of his or her labor and that ownership should transcend the grave through the right of an individual to bequeath a large fraction of his or her estate. Without such an attitude of ownership, for example, life insurance would atrophy, and other insurances might normally be terminated at the death of an insured party. Thus, insurance depends on an ethic that supports ownership and honors the institution of private property (Long, 1971). Finally, the history of insurance is linked closely with the history of private enterprise; where enterprise has flourished, insurance has also. At least part of the relationship has to be attributed to the acquisitiveness that characterizes enterprise.

Preservation A third ethical foundation of insurance is the desire to preserve. The word "preserve" means to keep safe from injury, harm, or destruction, to keep alive, keep intact, maintain, or protect from decay. This word is quite important to the successful operation of a system of insurance because insurance requires that people generally have a distaste for loss of value and waste. Moreover, it is not enough that the general public merely be indifferent to destruction or other decrease in value, the decrease must be a source of displeasure. The basic concept of distaste is sometimes referred to as an "aversion to loss" (Sauvain, 1967, p. 119). In short, the ethics essential to insurance require that the overwhelming majority of the people, whether or not they are insured, cherish and want to preserve value.

Apprehension A person who experiences no excitement or fear about the future, but rather faces it in utter complacency probably has no interest in insurance. Neither does one who views the future with abject futility and despair. Only those individuals who have a somewhat apprehensive, yet positive, concern about the future will be motivated to use insurance in an effort to preserve their options to the maximum. The ethics of insurance require that a mild or moderate degree of apprehension be regarded as a commendable trait among all members of society and as particularly befitting those to whom others look for financial support (Long, 1971).

Honesty Honesty is the fifth ethical issue of insurance, and rests upon the assumption that for insurance to be able to function, most people in a society are honest in most little matters and "compulsively" honest in large matters. Furthermore, in the eyes of the law, insurance long has been a matter of good faith and in some respects, as in marine insurance, a matter of utmost good faith (Riegel, Miller, & Williams, 1976). Good faith is a necessary accompaniment of an insurance transaction because of the looseness and the ambiguity of so many promises, restrictions, and other provisions in the contracts. Indeed, these provisions invite abuse. For example, who is to say whether an insured person who has become disabled for at least 60 months under a long-term disability is in fact unable to engage in any gainful employment for which he or she is reasonably suited in terms of training, education, experience, or prior average earnings?

High standards of honesty are not confined to those who are parties to the insurance contract. Medical advisors, attorneys, jurists, hospital administrators, claims adjustors, rehabilitation professionals, and others who are related to the contract have responsibilities to conduct themselves in an honest fashion. Furthermore, insurance also requires honesty as the customary and dependable action of other persons in society who are not in any way involved in insurance transactions. To illustrate this point, numerous types of insurance contracts promise payment or replacement in kind in the event of certain types of loss by theft. If theft becomes so rampant that losses become excessively common, redistribution of the burden of theft losses will become impractical, and the burdens will have to remain where they fall; with the lost-property owner. Thus, insurance is sustained by honesty such that, major breaches of it at any level of society weaken the viability of the insuring process.

Obedience The principal means of guaranteeing order in human behavior is through the creation and enforcement of law, wherein the willingness to obey the law by members of society constitutes the sixth ethical foundation of insurance. The ethical foundation of insurance demands the establishment of laws that minimize long-term loss. In this sense, then, the law is an institution for regulating human behavior through the maintenance of the status quo or through the encouragement of nonwasteful change. When law serves such a function, violations normally can be thought of as destructions of value or as socially repugnant appropriations of value by one person or organization from another; either of which can produce an insured loss and evoke redistribution of resources. Therefore, if the insuring process is not to be overwhelmed, the violations must be relatively few, there must be general enthusiasm or at least tolerance of the law, and generally the law must be followed and obeyed so that behavior will be predictable and losses will fall within tolerable limits (Mehr & Cammack, 1976).

Tradition Law, however, is not in itself sufficient to introduce and maintain the full degree of order necessary for insurance to function. One reason is that law is not static, but is subject to change, albeit in cautious, deliberate, and predictable ways. Occasionally, however, the implications for insurance of a judicial decision or a new statute can be profound and immediate (e.g., amended statutory mandates of providing vocational rehabilitation services to qualified injured workers covered by workers' compensation provisions). A second reason that law per se is insufficient is that many customs, practices, and other expressions of behavior are outside the law, not because they are violations, but rather because they are not covered by law. Examples may include the manner in which people get to and from work, forms of recreation, generally accepted ways of dancing, and even eating habits. For insurance to be made available and used over a long period of time, the legal and extra-legal aspects of life must be orderly enough to permit predictions. Members of society, therefore, must have at least a moderate respect for tradition in this sense. Tradition, on the other hand, does not have to be sacrosanct. The requirement is only that loss-causing legal or extra-legal behavior change slowly enough to be predictable in time for incorporation into insurance prices. Tradition must be honored at least to the extent that this much stability in human conduct be maintained.

Personal Responsibility Sustained use of insurance requires widespread conviction that each individual is personally responsible and accountable for him or herself and property. Without personal responsibility, an individual might not feel sufficiently motivated to defer current consumption in order to pay insurance premiums. In many ways the ethical concept of personal responsibility is similar to professional responsibility discussed in Chapter 10. In both instances there is a duty on the part of the responsible party to provide services or necessities to others. Moreover, personal responsibility is a presumption of accountability for one's actions or inactions. Unless a majority of people in a society manifests these two ingredients of personal responsibility most of the time, insured losses can become too frequent and too large to sustain the concept of insurance.

Charity The final ethical fundamental of insurance, according to Long (1971), is society's willingness to exhibit a general disposition of goodwill, kindliness, and sympathy (i.e., charity). As has been mentioned previously, insurance involves redistribution, whereby some who pay insurance premiums will, during a given policy period, collect nothing except perhaps a relatively small refund from the insurer and possibly not even that. On the other hand, a few individuals will receive compensatory payments, some of which may be inordinately large compared to amounts that have been paid to the insurer by the beneficiaries. Thus, insurance involves averaging of losses because if insurance were priced so that each insured paid exactly for his or her own loss (plus the share of the cost of the insuring process), the purpose of insurance would be defeated. In other words, each insured party has to be willing for his or her premiums to be used to pay both the losses of others and the expenses of the insuring process, in exchange for personal protection in the event of misfortune. The ethical principle of charity in insurance serves as a formalized loss-sharing process that takes a little from many and gives much to a few.

Concepts of Insurance

Although ethical foundations of insurance provide some measure of definition to the field, they do so only indirectly. For that reason, as well as to provide more substance to the topic, it is necessary that readers become familiar with concepts of insurance. Among the issues presented in this section, readers will be able to: (a) identify early forms of insurance; (b) understand the fundamental principles of risk and risk management; (c) identify basic insurance mechanisms and their uses; (d) grasp legal aspects of insurance; (e) differentiate types of insurance and the structure of the industry; and (f) understand the rationale for reinsurance.

Early Forms of Insurance

The insurance industry in the United States is a tremendous industry measured by any standards. Today there are nearly 5000 companies conducting operations in this country alone that employ over 1.4 million people, and have responsibility for assets of more than $300 billion (United States Chamber of Commerce, 1984). On the other hand, it is obvious that this industry did not develop in a short period of time, nor were current forms of insurance always in existence. In order to avoid confusing terminology between early and present forms of insurance, brief descriptions will use current terms.

Marine and Fire Insurance   Perhaps the oldest of modern branches of insurance is marine insurance issued to shipowners or merchants for their cargo and possessions. Those individuals (rather than companies) who agreed to accept a portion of the risk (i.e., to insure cargos and possessions) wrote their names under the description of the risk and the terms of the agreement. From this practice of "writing under" the agreement arose the term "underwriting" and "underwriter," referring to the one who selects or rejects risks (Pfeffer, 1966).

In the United States, fire insurance generally was the next type of insurance provided. Among the first companies to offer this form of protection was the Insurance Company of North America whose charter gave it broad underwriting powers to engage in all lines of insurance. This "multiple-line" underwriting practice will be explained later.

Casualty Insurance   The first form of casualty insurance written in the United States by the Travelers Insurance Company provided accident protection against injuries resulting from railroad accidents. Later, companies began providing policies to insure against other forms of liability such as public hazards, automobiles, elevators, and physical damage to property. Personal liability coverages also began to emerge to protect employees as a result of the passage of assorted Employers' Liability laws. Finally, with the passage of New York's workers' compensation law in 1910, casualty insurance began to encompass workers' compensation insurance.

Life Insurance The first life insurance company in America was founded in 1759. Known as "The Corporation for Relief of Poor and Distressed Presbyterian Ministers and the Poor and Distressed Widows and Children of Presbyterian Ministers," it continues to be in operation today as the world's oldest life insurance company (Elliott and Vaughn, 1972). Based upon the "principles of probability" and "predicted mortality" tables, life insurance attempts to standardize rates for all insured persons according to their ages in relation to their term of life expectancy.

Monoline Insurance Organizations Although not a type of insurance per se, "monoline" organization was an early attempt by states to limit and regulate the underwriting powers of insurance companies. In other words, in a monoline insurance organization, companies were restricted by law to the writing of only one line of insurance (e.g., fire, casualty, life). According to Elliott and Vaughn (1972), there were three basic reasons for this forced compartmentalization: (1) it would permit insurers to specialize and become proficient in one type of risk coverage; (2) it was believed that through segregation of insurance lines, more accurate appraisal of financial requirements for each line would develop; and (3) insurance regulators believed that there was a danger in either overestimating or underestimating the costs of insured risks when different lines of insurance were combined.

Multiple-Line Transition Because of discontent being expressed about the monoline concept, states began moving more toward "multiple-line" powers for insurance companies. The basic idea of this alternative method was the concept of product diversification common in the manufacturing industry. Thus, through insurance diversification the averaging of fire losses with liability losses, for example, over a period of time should result in greater stability of operation and fiscal management. In other words, the spread of loss principle that is basic to all insurance operations is inherent in the notion of the multiple-line concept.

Principles of Risk and Risk Management

Throughout the preceding portions of this chapter, the term "risk" has appeared in reference to what one insures against. It would seem that the term is a simple enough notion, connoting that in a given situation there is uncertainty about outcome wherein the possibility exists that the outcome could be unfavorable. This loose intuitive definition of risk, which implies a lack of knowledge about the future, is satisfactory for conversational usage, but is less than desirable from an insurance perspective. On the other hand, surveying insurance literature for a definition of risk reveals only general uniformity, insofar as risk represents a chance of loss, is the possibility of loss, means uncertainty, is the dispersion of actual from expected results, or is the probability of any outcome different from the one expected. Putting these definitions together, Elliott and Vaughn (1972, p. 11) define risk as "the possibility of an adverse deviation from a desired outcome that is expected or hoped for."

Compounding the problem of defining risk is the equally perplexing problem of agreeing on what is meant by "degree of risk." Moreover, it is not uncommon for the terms "peril" and "hazard" to be used interchangeably with each other and with "risk." Although degree of risk is more difficult to define, relying on probability averaging for the most part, the latter two terms are easier to differentiate. A *peril* is a cause of loss, such as the peril of fire or theft, while *hazard* refers to a condition that may create or increase the chance of a loss arising from a given peril. Furthermore, hazards are normally classified into three categories: (1) *physical hazards* that increase the chance of loss, such as the type of construction, location of property, and the occupancy of a building; (2) *moral hazards* refer to the behavioral tendencies on the part of the insured party to be dishonest in an attempt to defraud the insurance company; and (3) *morale hazards* refer to a careless attitude on the part of insured parties toward the occurrence of losses (Elliot & Vaughn, 1972). Finally, risk itself can be classified in many ways depending on the situations involved and types of losses incurred.

Financial and Nonfinancial Risks   Although there is some element of risk in every aspect of human endeavor, many of these do not have financial consequences. For the most part the risks discussed in this book, however, focus on those with financial consequences to all parties involved in the rehabilitation process within insurance systems.

Static and Dynamic Risks   Dynamic risks are those that result from changes in the economy, such as price changes, consumer tastes, income and output, and so forth (Willett, 1951). These risks normally are perceived to benefit society over the long run, since they are often the result of adjustments made to misallocation of resources. Static risks, on the other hand, involve the losses that would occur even if there were no changes in the economy. For example, losses resulting from the perils of nature or the dishonesty of others are part of this class of risks. Therefore, static risks, unlike dynamic risks, are not a source of gain to society, but rather involve either the destruction of an asset or a change in its possession as a result of dishonesty or human failure (Willett, 1951).

Fundamental and Particular Risks   The distinction between fundamental and particular risks is based on the differences in origin and consequences of the losses. Fundamental risks are those that involve losses that are impersonal in origin and consequence, such as those caused for the most part by economic, social, and political phenomena (Kulp & Hall, 1968). Particular risk, on the other hand, involves losses that arise out of individual events and are experienced by individuals rather than by the entire group to which they belong (Kulp & Hall, 1968). For example, unemployment, war, inflation, earthquakes, and floods are all fundamental risks, whereas the burning of a house or the robbery of a bank are particular risks.

Pure and Speculative Risks   According to Riegel and his associates (1976), speculative risk involves a situation where there is a possibility of either loss or gain, such as in the case of gambling. Pure risk, however, is used to designate those situations that involve only the chance of loss or no loss. These distinctions are important in an insurance context because normally only pure risks are insurable since speculative risk is voluntarily accepted based on its two-way nature (Bickelhaupt & Magee, 1970). Furthermore, pure risk generally is classified by three types: (1) *personal risks* involve the possibility of loss of income or assets as a result of the loss of income earning ability; (2) *property risks* involve the loss of property; and (3) *liability risks* involve the possibility of loss of present assets or future income as a result of damages assessed or legal liability arising from either intentional or unintentional torts or invasion of the rights of others (Elliott & Vaughn, 1972). Moreover, pure risks constitute areas that considerable attention is given by insurance companies in order to control their financial losses in the form of paid claims. The scientific approach to solving the problem of dealing with pure risks faced by individuals and businesses has come to be known as "risk management."

Many business firms have highly trained personnel who specialize in dealing with pure risk; in some cases, in fact, this is a full-time job for one person, or even for an entire department within a company. Risk management, however, is something more than insurance management, in that it deals with both insurable and uninsurable risks, as well as the choice of appropriate techniques for dealing with these risks. On the other hand, risk management is something less than all management, since it does not deal with business risk per se. The risk management responsibility is for the conservation of assets and income from those losses involved in pure risk situations. Thus, while the objective of management in general is the conservation of the assets of the firm and maximizing of profit, the objective of risk management is the *protection* of the organization's assets and income from serious financial impairment as a result of static losses. In other words, the role of the risk manager is to minimize the adverse effects of losses and the uncertainty in connection with pure risk, while preserving the firm as an operational entity in the business economy. Therefore, the process by which the risk manager achieves the risk management goal includes five steps: (1) identification of the risks; (2) evaluation of the risks; (3) consideration of alternatives and selection of the risk treatment device; (4) implementing the decision; and (5) evaluation and review of the results.

Finally, with the development of risk management as a special functional area of business, increased attention has been devoted to formalizing its principles and techniques, in order to provide guidance to the risk management decision-making process. One of the best contributions was the development of the "rules of risk management" consisting of three simple common-sense precepts applied to pure risk situations. Mehr and Hedges (1963) propose the following rules: (1) don't risk more than you can afford to lose; (2) don't risk a lot for a little; and (3) consider the odds.

Basic Insurance Mechanisms and Their Uses

From a functional perspective, insurance is a social device whereby the uncertain risks of individuals may be combined in a group and thus made more certain, with small periodic contributions by the individuals providing a fund out of which those who suffer losses may be reimbursed. In its legal sense, insurance is a contract whereby the insurer agrees to make good any financial loss the insured may suffer within the scope of the contract, and the insured party agreeing to pay a consideration (premium) for that degree of protection. Thus, the varying forms of organizations that assume risk may be conveniently referred to as the insurer, and the individual who is relieved of the risk called the insured. In order that an insurance contract may operate equitably, produce the desired benefits, and be practical from a business point of view, certain conditions are desirable. Riegel and his associates (1976) identify six characteristics of insurable risks that insurers attempt to satisfy when writing coverage policies: (1) the insured should be subject to a real loss; (2) the loss to be insured against should be important enough to warrant the existence of an insurance contract; (3) losses should be fairly definite in terms of cause, time, place, and amount, in order to minimize adjusting problems; (4) the cost of insurance must not be prohibitive; (5) a large number of insured parties is necessary to spread the cost of risk; and (6) losses that will be incurred should be capable of approximate mathematical calculation. Of these six characteristic conditions, two principles emerge that require brief elaboration; the principles of probability and the law of large numbers.

Principles of Probability   The calculations of premiums for insurance of nearly every kind are based upon the application of the principles of probability to past experience. For example, in life insurance the principles of probability are applied to past experience as represented by a mortality table (e.g., average life expectancy); in fire insurance, the principles may be applied to past experience in fire losses; in workers' compensation insurance to past experience showing compensation benefits paid; and so forth. Premiums in insurance usually are expressed in the form of rates, that is, by the amount of premium per unit of protection or exposure. Thus, in life insurance, a rate is quoted per $1,000 of protection, in fire insurance per $100 of insurance, in workers' compensation insurance per $100 of payroll, and in marine insurance usually per $100 of insurance (Riegel et al., 1976). The most important of the principles of probability is that chance may be represented by a fraction, wherein the numerator expresses the number of times an event happens and the denominator represents the number of times an event may possibly happen. Therefore, when applying the principles of probability to the experience of the past, one arrives at the probability that an event will occur in the future. Furthermore, to justify such a conclusion (by minimizing the likelihood of error), it is necessary that a sufficiently large number of instances be considered to provide a dependable average, and that the conditions of the future coincide with those of the past as nearly as possible (Riegel et al., 1976).

The Law of Large Numbers   Before discussing this issue, a distinction must be made between the chance or probability of an event's happening and the degree of risk connected with the event. From the viewpoint of society, the function of insurance is primarily the reduction of the uncertainty resulting from risk, and only incidently the reduction of probability. For example, there may be a very small probability and yet a great deal of risk when a house is struck by lightning. If, however, a probability is obtained from or applied to a small number of cases (limited exposure), it involves a considerable degree of risk and is not entitled to great confidence. Therefore, according to the Law of Large Numbers, the chance that the relative frequency of an event will differ from the underlying probability by any stated amount approaches zero as the number of trials increases. Based on this mathematical hypothesis, the function of insurance is to combine a large number of risks and thereby reduce the degree of risk and hence uncertainty.

Although the function of insurance is primarily to decrease the uncertainty of events, any inducement that insurance offers toward preventing or reducing the losses involved tends to lessen the probability of the event occurring. For example, life insurance companies may offer lower rates to nonsmokers; fire insurance companies give reduction in rates for property using protective devices; marine rates are lower where aids to navigation exist; and workers' compensation companies give reductions in rates for improvements in loss experience arising out of implementation of employee safety and prevention measures.

Legal Aspects of Insurance Contracts

Transferring risk from the individual to the insurance company is accomplished through a contractual arrangement under which the insurance company, in consideration of the premium paid by the insured and promise to abide by the provisions of the contract, promises to indemnify the insured or pay an agreed upon amount in the event of the specified loss. The instrument through which this transfer is accomplished is the insurance contract, which as a contract is enforceable by law. A great deal of the law that has shaped the formal structure of insurance and that has influenced its content has been derived from the general law of contracts (Mehr & Cammack, 1976). In providing an overview of the legal framework in which insurance operates, it is necessary indeed to include the general requirements of contracts in relation to insurance. Moreover, the interested reader is encouraged to refer periodically to the glossaries of insurance and legal terminology to better understand some of the concepts addressed.

Legal Definition of Insurance   Earlier, insurance was defined as a social device whereby the uncertain risks of individuals may be combined in a group and thus made more certain. Many courts and some state legislatures have defined insurance in various ways other than that stated above. Because of that diversity, no single legal definition of insurance would be appropriate in this context. However, particular attention is given to insurance by the courts and government bodies in terms of the general requirements of enforceable contracts. Insurance policies, as is the case with all contracts, must contain certain elements in order to be legally binding. These elements include: (a) *offer and acceptance* wherein there must be a definite and unqualified offer by one party and the acceptance of the exact terms of the offer by the other party, either written or oral; (b) *consideration* insofar that the insurance transaction requires both parties to exchange something of value (e.g., the insurer's promise to pay if a loss occurs, and the insured's promise to pay the premium); (c) *legal object* whereby the object of the contract has a legal purpose, rather than being unenforceable as contrary to public policy (e.g., criminal acts); (d) *competent parties* with respect to their capability to enter into a contract in the eyes of the law (i.e., of legal age of consent and able to understand the obligations imposed by the contents of the contract); and (e) *legal form* insofar as the contract conforms to state requirements of form (i.e., written or oral), filing procedures, and standard provisions.

Classification of Insurance Contracts   Insurance contracts can usually be classified as personal, unilateral, conditional, aleatory, contracts of adhesion, *uberrimae fidei*, contracts of indemnity, and life and health insurance contracts. Other, more general ways of classifying contracts in the insurance industry are as follows: (a) *personal contracts* that are used to describe a variety of coverages designed to indemnify risks common to private individuals such as life, health, property, and liability; or (b) *commercial contracts* that are used to describe a variety of risks common to businesses, such as property, liability, and certain business undertakings. Still another method of classifying insurance contracts is in terms of the type of coverage provided: (a) *property* insurance (often referred to as fire insurance); (b) *liability or casualty* insurance; (c) *health* insurance; and (d) *life* insurance. As the reader will note, there is sufficient overlap between the content of these classification schemes. For this reason, a brief discussion follows using the initial listing of legal classifications.

Personal Contracts. An insurance contract is usually a personal contract whereby a property and liability insurer usually agrees to insure a specific person or persons against loss (Riegel et al., 1976). Under this form of contract, the person is insured, not the property or source of liability covered under the terms of the contract. In determining whether or not to issue a personal contract, the insurer considers the personal characteristics of the applicant, as well as other factors depending on the nature of the coverage desired. For example, life and health insurers might investigate the applicant's history of illness, require a complete physical examination, and other related factors before issuing such contracts. Finally, the insured party's right to transfer insurance assignments (coverage), with or without the insurer's consent, varies with the type of policy written.

Unilateral Contracts. According to Riegel and his associates (1976), if an insured party pays a premium or premium installment before or at the time the insurance contract becomes effective, the insured has done all that can be required to be done. On the other hand, the insurer has promised and can be forced to perform in the future in case there is a loss. In this situation, the contract is one-sided, or unilateral, because the insurer has yet to perform its obligation. Moreover, if the terms of the contract become effective before the premium is paid, both the insurer and the insured have made unfulfilled promises, in which case the contract is considered to be bilateral (Riegel et al., 1976).

Conditional Contracts. Unless the insured party satisfies certain conditions specified in the contract, such as submitting claims or other documents within a stipulated time, the insurer cannot be forced to perform its obligations of the contract.

Aleatory Contracts. Insurance contracts rest on the concept of risk, which like chance is susceptible to the laws of probability. As such, insurance contracts are aleatory in nature whereby the amount the insurer pays will depend upon whether the insured suffers a loss and the extent of the loss.

Contracts of Adhesion. Unless the insured party participates in the drafting of the insurance contract, a practice usually limited to risk managers for large companies, the insured must adhere to a contract drafted by the insurer. Consequently, if a legal dispute arises over some ambiguity in the contract, courts are likely to rule in favor of the insured (Riegel et al., 1976).

Contract Uberrimae Fidei. Partly due to the fact that an insurance contract is aleatory, the insurer and the insured enter into a contract where mutual faith is of paramount importance. The legal principle of *uberrimae fidei* (utmost good faith) has deep historical roots in its application to insurance (Elliott & Vaughn, 1972). The practical effect of the principle of utmost good faith lies in the requirement that the applicant for insurance must make full and fair disclosure of the risk to the insurance representative and the insuring company. Thus, the risk that the insurer thinks it is assuming must be the same risk that the insured transfers. In disputed issues, however, it is usually the insured party's failure to disclose all the facts that are at issue, thereby allowing the insurer to introduce one of three common law doctrines to be freed of the risk obligation (i.e., doctrines of concealment, misrepresentation, and breach of warranty) (Riegel et al., 1976). On the other hand, to counter the insurer's assertion of these doctrines, the insured may introduce the doctrine of waiver or estoppel (Riegel et al., 1976). However, legal decisions on the effectiveness of waiver and estoppel claims are both complex and varied in their findings.

Contracts of Indemnity. In many forms of insurance, particularly in property (fire, ocean marine, inland marine, theft, surety bonds, title, crops, and foreign credit) and liability (business, personal, professional, workers' compensation), the contract is one of "indemnity." This means that the insured is entitled to payment from the insurance company only if a loss has been suffered and only to the extent of the financial loss sustained (Elliott & Vaughn, 1972; Riegel et al., 1976). Put in its simplest terms, the principle of indemnity maintains that an individual should not be permitted to profit from the existence of an insurance contract, but rather should be placed in the same financial condition that existed prior to the occurrence of the loss. Generally, this is the same concept advanced in many workers' compensation laws requiring that disabled claimants return to work receiving not less than two-thirds of their pre-injury wage.

Life and Health Insurance Contracts. According to Bickelhaupt and Magee (1970), life insurance protects against the financial loss of income earning abilitaused by death or investment for similar loss in old age. Life insurance contracts, however, contain none of the indemnity provisions characteristic of property and liability insurance contracts (i.e., measure of loss, insurable interest, other insurance, and subrogation). On the other hand, health insurance, applicable to protection against the financial impact of illness or injury, does sometimes contain provisions preventing duplicate recoveries because of other insurance, even though health insurance is not a contract of indemnity (Riegel et al., 1976).

Regulation of the Insurance Industry The insurance industry is regulated in every state through a department or commission that is charged with the responsibility of monitoring and governing the activities of insurers who do business in the respective jurisdictions. According to Bickelhaupt and Magee (1970, p. 171), the "general purpose of insurance regulation is to protect the public against insolvency or unfair treatment by insurers." Most states now require standard policy forms that must include certain provisions such as standardized language in an effort to minimize consumer confusion (Mehr & Cammack, 1976). Furthermore, insurance rating is subject to close regulation, especially for property and liability insurance, although less restrictions apply to life and health insurance rates. There are two reasons for this difference in treatment: (1) property and liability insurance rates are often made by insurers pricing (legally) in concert; and (2) property and liability insurance rates are more difficult to understand and to establish (Riegel et al., 1976). Moreover, property and liability rates are regulated in many states in accordance with model rating laws that are designed to consider rate-making practices of an insurer's past and prospective loss and expense experience, catastrophic hazards, reasonable margins for profits and dividends, and savings allowed or returned by insurers; information that must be reported and filed for approval with the state's Insurance Commissioner.

Types of Insurance and the Insurance Industry Structure

The purpose of this section is to provide an overview of the variety of classification systems of insurance companies and the types of insurance lines offered. For a more detailed description of the specific structural functions of these assorted topics, the interested reader is recommended to consult both the Riegel et al. and Elliott and Vaughn texts found in the references.

Classification of Insurers by Domicile Insurance companies are classified as either domestic, foreign, or alien depending upon the location of their charters. *Domestic* companies are those that have obtained their charters from the state in which they were founded; *foreign* companies include those that operate in any given state, but whose charters were organized in a state other than the location of their principal office; and *alien* companies are those that have been organized in a foreign nation (Riegel et al., 1976).

   Classification of Insurers According to Underwriting Authority   The division of the insurance business according to underwriting authority has been discussed to some extent under the concepts of "monoline" organizations and "multiple-line" transactions. In addition to these forms of underwriting authority, insurance companies may be classified as "multiple-multiple" or "financial-services combinations." *Multiple-multiple insurance* refers to the fact that life insurance companies are buying property and liability insurance companies, and the latter are purchasing life insurance companies. According to Riegel and his associates (1976), some persons foresee the future comprised of two policies; one covering life and health insurance and the other covering all property and liability losses. On the other hand, *financial-services combinations* represent a more recent development whereby insurers combine with other companies marketing noninsurance products, such as personal finance companies, savings and loan associations, and income tax services, to name a few. According to Elliott and Vaughn (1972), insurers have sought this product diversification for reasons such as capturing a larger market for equities, providing "one-stop" financial services, and improving and stabilizing their profits.

   Classification of Insurers According to Legal Forms of Organization   In all forms of insurance, the insured is offered the choice of various legal forms of organization for the purposes of insuring risks. These organizations may be broadly classified into six groups: (1) capital stock insurance companies; (2) mutual insurance companies; (3) reciprocals or interinsurance companies; (4) Lloyd's associations; (5) government insurers; and (6) self-insurers.

   Capital Stock Insurance Companies.   The distinguishing characteristics of these types of insurance companies are: (a) the premium charged by the company includes no form of contingent liability for the policyholder; (b) the Board of Directors is elected by the stockholders; and (c) earnings are distributed to shareholders as dividends on their stocks (Elliott & Vaughn, 1972). Thus, stock companies are organized as profit-making ventures, with the stockholders assuming the risk that is transferred by the individual insured parties. Capital stock companies more or less dominate the field of property and liability insurance, accounting for approximately two-thirds of the premium value (Elliott & Vaughn, 1972).

   Mutual Insurance Companies.   In contrast to a stock company, a mutual insurance company is owned by the policyholders, and is organized for the purpose of providing insurance for its members. The essential characteristics of this type of company are: (a) its lack of capital stock; (b) the distribution of earnings; and (c) any money left after all operating costs are paid reverts to the policyholders in the form of dividends (Elliott and Vaughn, 1972).

Reciprocals. The reciprocal or interinsurance exchange is a relative newcomer to the insurance industry, often confused with mutual insurers, comprised of an unincorporated aggregation of individuals who exchange insurance risks (Riegel et al., 1976). Like mutuals, however, reciprocals are fundamentally cooperative organizations wherein each member (or subscriber) is both an insured and an insurer. Moreover, as a member of the group the individual is insured by each of the other members, and in turn insures each of them. According to Elliott and Vaughn (1972), one of the main characteristics that distinguishes the reciprocal is the chief administrator of the program, who is called the "attorney-in-fact." This position carries with it broad powers granted by the members, which can be a source of abuse in unscrupulous cases. Finally, reciprocals confine their operations to the property and casualty fields, and with the exception of compensation paid for the attorney-in-fact and operating expenses, the only expense involved for a subscriber is the amount of losses that occur.

Lloyd's Associations. Within this classification of insurers are Lloyd's of London and American Lloyd's. *Lloyd's of London* is the oldest and perhaps most famous of all insurance organizations in the world, and represents a corporation for marketing the services of a group of individuals. On the other hand, Lloyd's itself does not issue insurance policies or provide insurance protection, relying instead on the actual insurance being underwritten by its more than 6000 underwriting members of the association (Elliott & Vaughn, 1972). Thus, each member of the association technically is a separate "insurance company," issuing policies and underwriting risks separately or collectively with other members. *American Lloyd's*, on the other hand, is an attempt to emulate the success (and perhaps capitalize on the fame) of Lloyd's of London. An American Lloyd's is simply a group of individuals who operate an insurance mechanism using the same principles of individual liability of insurers that the London-based association uses (Elliott & Vaughn, 1976).

Government Insurers. In addition to a vast array of social insurance programs, both the federal and state governments have become increasingly important in the area of private insurance. In many cases they operate monopolistic insurance programs, and in some cases compete with private insurers (United States Chamber of Commerce, 1984). In most cases, however, the government has entered the insurance arena when private insurers were either unable or unwilling to provide desired coverages. Finally, the private insurance coverages provided by the government normally involve a contractual relationship, whereas the social insurance programs also offered may or may not involve a contract.

Self-Insurance. Under some circumstances, it is possible for a business firm to engage in the same activities as a commercial insurance company in dealing with its own risks. However, according to Elliott and Vaughn (1972), what many people refer to as self-insurance is not really insurance at all, but rather assumption of risk. Thus, these authors suggest that in order for self-insureds to be classified as a bona fide insurance plan, three elements must be present: (1) the firm should be large enough to permit the combination of a sufficiently large number of exposure units so as to make losses predictable; (2) the plan must be financially dependable; and (3) the units of loss potential must be distributed in such a manner geographically so as to prevent fiscal catastrophe (p. 77).

Table 3–1. Types of Insurance

Personal Insurance
    Health insurance
    Life insurance and annuities
    Unemployment insurance
Property and Liability Insurance
    Allied fire
    Automobile liability
    Automobile physical damage
    Boiler and machinery
    Commercial multiperil
    Credit
    Fidelity
    Fire
    Glass
    Homeowners' multiperil
    Inland marine
    Miscellaneous liability
    Ocean marine
    Surety
    Theft
    Workers' compensation

Types of Insurance   Although the variety of insurance coverages available are seemingly endless, Table 3-1 reveals two general categories of insurance (personal, and property and liability), as well as the many forms of insurance found within each. At this point, however, discussion of the major components of health, life, property, and liability insurance types will be deferred to the next major section of the chapter.

Reinsurance

"Reinsurance is an agreement between the insurance company that originally issues a policy and another organization (the reinsurer), the latter agreeing to accept a certain share of the former's potential liability on the policy" (Riegel et al., 1976, p. 120). The reason for this type of insurance, which is basically insurance for insurers, is to protect insurers against the catastrophe of a comparatively large single loss or a large number of small losses as a result of a single occurrence (e.g., natural disasters, acute and severe injury claims, and so forth). In a reinsurance transaction the insurer seeking reinsurance is known as the "direct writer" or the "ceding company," while the reinsurer is referred to as simply the "reinsurer" (Elliott & Vaughn, 1972, p. 104). Thus, reinsurance serves two important purposes: (1) it helps in spreading risk for the insurance company itself (much in the same manner as risk is spread among policyholders for coverages previously mentioned), and (2) it serves a financial function by freeing the ceding company's obligation to maintain unearned premium reserves or policy reserves. These two types of reserves represent surpluses that are drawn upon by insurance companies to compensate losses sustained by policyholders. In the absence of reinsurance, however, the surplus of these reserves may decline to a point that requires an insurance company to stop or dramatically curtail its activities until premiums become earned; thus freeing surplus (Baker, 1980).

Origins of Reinsurance   According to Kramer (1980), the idea of reinsurance and its practice are probably as old as the commercial practice of insurance itself. As early as the 16th century, reinsurance was described as a class of contract separate and distinct from the insurance giving rise to it. On the other hand, the conceptual meaning of reinsurance has not always meant the same thing in all places. For example, at one time the word described the practice of re-selling more than the original risk assumed by the direct writer for less than the original premium, thus guaranteeing a profit for the direct writer whether a loss occurred or not (Kramer 1980).

Reinsurance almost certainly arose from the practice of offering risk to more than one insurer when the first insurer could not accept it all. This practice of "syndicating" insurance or issuing a number of policies, each from a separate insurer covering the same risk survives today (for example, policies issued by Lloyd's underwriters). Finally, that portion of a risk that the writer retains is called the "net line" or the "net retention"; the act of transferring a part of the risk to the reinsurance company is called "ceding"; and that portion of the risk that is passed to the reinsurer is called the "cession" (Elliott & Vaughn, 1976, p. 104).

Types of Reinsurance   There are two types of reinsurance policies, known as treaties: facultative and automatic. Under a facultative treaty, the risks are considered individually by both parties, such that each risk is submitted by the direct writer to the reinsurer for acceptance or rejection (Elliott & Vaughn, 1976). Under this type of treaty, the terms under which the reinsurance will take place is specified, and once the risk has been submitted (which the direct writer is not required necessarily to submit) and accepted, the advance arrangements apply. Until that time, however, the direct writer carries the entire risk (Ferguson, 1980). Under the terms of an automatic treaty, on the other hand, the reinsurer agrees in advance to accept a portion of the gross line of the direct writing company or a portion of certain risks that meet the reinsurance underwriting rules of the reinsurer (Baker, 1980). Under this method, the direct writer is obligated to cede a portion of the risk to which the automatic treaty applies.

Benefits to the Policyholder   From the standpoint of the insured (direct writer), the practice of reinsurance is beneficial for several reasons. First, it gives insurance companies that practice it greater financial stability and thus makes the insured's individual policy more reliable. Second, if a large amount of insurance is needed, the insured may obtain it without negotiating with numerous companies (Riegel et al., 1976). Third, it enables the insured to obtain protection promptly. Fourth, all the insurance can be written under identical contract provisions. Finally, through reinsurance, small companies are encouraged by their ability to divide large exposures for safety by being able to spread their fixed costs over a greater volume of business (Ferguson, 1980).

Limitations of Reinsurance   Although reinsurance has many useful functions and purposes, it also has its limitations. The chief of these is that in itself reinsurance cannot change the inherent nature of the business being reinsured (Baker, 1980). In other words, the mere operation of the reinsurance mechanism does not render an inherently uninsurable risk insurable, nor can the mechanism convert an underrated risk into an adequately rated risk. A second limitation is that it is capable of being misused or overused if the ceding company and the reinsurer are not sufficiently knowledgeable about their business. Finally, reinsurance is vulnerable to being used for improper or even fraudulent purposes. According to Baker (1980), through reinsurance, liquid funds can be siphoned by unscrupulous operators from one insurer they control to another, for illegal purposes. Furthermore, reinsurance can be used also as a device to bilk reinsurers and others of funds.

Life, Health, and Property and Liability Insurances

Although Table 3–1 reveals that insurance lines can be separated into two broad categories (personal, and property and liability), Table 3–2 illustrates the unique features of life, health, and property and liability coverages in terms of functions, types, and classifications. By referring to Table 3–2, and the following overviews of each insurance type, an understanding can be achieved regarding their respective effects on rehabilitation service delivery for policyholders.

Life Insurance

Life insurance serves as a means of creating an estate for an insured person's dependents, rather than as an attempt to return an individual to the same financial position after a loss as was acquired before the loss. On the other hand, the contingency insured against has certain characteristics that make it unique from other forms of insurance. Because no person lives forever, the event insured against is an eventual certainty. The requirements of an insurable risk are not violated, however, because *it is not the possibility of death per se being insured against, but rather the untimeliness of its occurrence.* Therefore, the uncertainty surrounding the risk in life insurance is not whether one is going to die, but when one will die.

Strictly speaking, there are only three types of life insurance, as noted in Table 3–2. *Term insurance* provides protection against financial loss resulting from death during a specified period of time. That is, it pays only if an insured person dies within a given period, such as one year, five years, and so forth. In other words, at the end of the policy period, the protection ceases. *Whole Life insurance* (also known as "straight life" or "ordinary life") is the basic type of lifetime policy that provides protection at a level premium for the entire lifetime of the insured person. In other words, as long as an individual continues to pay premiums, protection equal to the face amount of the policy will be provided. *Endowment Life insurance* represents a contract that promises to pay the face amount of the policy if the insured dies within the policy period, or to pay the face amount if the insured lives to the end of the specified period. According to Elliott and Vaughn (1972), this is the famous "you win if you live and you win if you die" contract. That is to say, the endowment portion pays the face amount if the individual survives, while the term portion pays if death occurs during the specified period.

Table 3-2 reveals four basic classes of life insurance based upon how they are marketed. *Ordinary* life insurance premiums are marketed generally with a face amount of over $1,000, and are paid to the insurance company annually, semiannually, quarterly, or monthly. *Industrial* life insurance is a form

Table 3-2. Characteristics of Life, Health, and Property and Liability Insurances

	LIFE	HEALTH	PROPERTY & LIABILITY
FUNCTIONS	Means of creating an estate for dependents. Represents "risk-pooling." Risk of loss increases with time. Insures against untimeliness of occurrence.	Varies with the type of insurance.	When combined, protects against both legal liability for damages from bodily injuries or property damage caused by others, and damage to or loss of the insured's own property.
TYPES	Term insurance. Whole Life insurance. Endowment Life insurance.	Disability Income (loss of income) insurance. Medical Expense insurance.	Varies with the nature of the perils and property (see Table 3-1).
CLASSIFICATIONS	Ordinary. Industrial. Group. Franchise.	Hospitalization. Surgical Expenses. Regular Medical. Major Medical. Comprehensive Major Medical.	Property: Varies. Liability: General. Employer's. Workers' Compensation. Automobile (tort & no-fault).

in which the face value of the policy is less than $1,000 and the premiums are payable as frequently as weekly. *Group* life insurance represents a plan whereby coverage can be provided for a number of persons under one contract; yet, the insurance on each life is independent of that on the other lives (Riegel et al., 1976). Unlike industrial insurance, however, group life premiums are comparatively low and may be contributory in nature, whereby the insured person pays a flat rate and the sponsoring organization or employer (with which the contract is written) pays the balance (Mehr & Cammack, 1976). Finally, *Franchise* life insurance is a mass marketing plan similar to group life insurance, but generally written on groups whose numbers are insufficient to meet the requirements for a group policy.

Health Insurance

There are few areas of insurance that are as confusing as the field of health insurance. One reason for this confusion is the bewildering number of health insurance contracts available. According to Dorken (1980, p. 16), "what is commonly called health insurance is really prepayment of expenditures." Moreover, until recently, there was little general agreement in the terminology used when referring to health insurance (e.g., "accident and health," "accident and sickness," "disability," etc.).

Table 3–2 reveals two types of health insurance. *Disability (loss of income) insurance* attempts to replace the income lost when a person becomes disabled. In this way, it serves as a protection against loss of income by providing periodic payments when the insured is unable to work as a result of sickness or injury. Although the purpose of disability income insurance at first appears to be redundant to workers' compensation, there are are two major differences. First, unlike workers' compensation, disability health insurance can be purchased by individuals and groups, whereas workers' compensation can be purchased only in group form. Second, some disability income policies exclude payment if the illness or accident arises out of the insured person's occupation and if entitlement is provided under a workers' compensation statute. Such contracts are termed "nonoccupational."

Before turning attention to medical expense insurance, it is important to define "disability" and "injury" because of their impact in the coverages of disability income policies. Although different insurance companies define disability in various ways, most definitions conform to one of three categories: (1) an inability of the insured to engage in his or her occupation; (2) an inability of the insured to engage in any reasonable occupation for which he or she is or might become qualified; or (3) an inability of the insured to engage in any occupation (Riegel et al., 1976). Similarly, there is often a considerable difference in the manner in which policies define "injury"; yet virtually all take one of the following forms: (a) accidental bodily injury; (b) bodily injury by accidental means; or (c) bodily injury by violent, external, and accidental means (Riegel et al., 1976).

The second type of health insurance is *Medical Expense insurance*. As the name suggests, payments are made to cover the costs of medical care that result from sickness or injury, such as physician bills, hospital costs, nursing and related health services, and medications and supplies. Benefits may be paid in the form of reimbursement of actual expenses paid by the insured person up to a specified dollar limit, cash payments with specified sums, or the direct provision of care. Similarly, expenses may be paid directly to the service provider(s) or to the insured person.

Among the medical expense coverage classifications, several deserve brief mention. *Hospitalization insurance* is sold under two types of contracts: (1) an indemnity contract that pays all or a portion of the hospital costs of room and board, as well as some of the incidental fees of equipment; and (2) service contracts that pay for actual services of the hospital to the insured person for a specified number of days rather than a cash benefit. *Surgical expense insurance* also is sold under indemnity and service contracts wherein the former lists the amounts the policy will pay for a variety of operations, and the latter provides benefits to pay physicians' expenses. *Regular medical expense insurance*, although normally not written alone, pays for visits to a doctor's office or for visits by a doctor to the insured's home or hospital. *Major medical policy* is the medical contract that is most appropriate for the large expenses that would be financially disastrous for the individual to pay. Characteristic of these policies are provision of benefits for blood transfusions, drugs and prescriptions, prosthetic devices, and mobility aids. Finally, *comprehensive major medical* policies combine the best features of a base plan and the major medical contract into a single policy. The distinction between the comprehensive major medical and the major medical policy is the size of the deductible. Under a comprehensive plan, the deductible may be as low as $25, whereas it is typically much higher (e.g., $100 to $1000) under the major medical policy (Elliott & Vaughn, 1972).

Property and Liability Insurance

Insurance policies designed to protect the individual in connection with loss of or damage to personal or commercial possessions are known as property insurance. Property may be damaged or lost as a result of a wide variety of perils, most of which are considered insurable by the insurance industry. General liability insurance, on the other hand, primarily covers the insured's legal liability for personal injuries or property damage to others, such as workers' compensation and professional liability (negligence and malpractice) policies. Furthermore, combined property and liability insurance serves to protect the insured against both the legal liability for damages for bodily injuries or property damage caused to others, and damage to or loss of one's own property.

An area of risk that confronts almost every person of business is that of behavior that could result in an injury to another person or damage to property of others. The basis of the risk is the liability imposed by law upon the party responsible for injury or damage to others, the result of which could attain catastrophic proportions both for the injured party as well as for the wrongdoer. For more information about negligence and liability, the reader's attention is directed to the Glossary of Legal Terms and portions of Chapter 10.

Liability insurance rarely is concerned with the legal penalties resulting from criminal behavior or intentional torts because it would be contrary to public policy to protect an individual from the consequences of the intentional injury or damage inflicted. Thus, liability insurance is concerned primarily with unintentional torts or losses arising from negligence. Most important, liability insurance serves as a protection against unintentional failures of a person to exercise the proper degree of care required under circumstances that could or do lead to an injury to another, or to damage of another's property. In other words, negligence involves the failure to provide proper care, but in itself might not result necessarily in damage or injury to another or another's property.

All forms of liability insurance are essentially the same in purpose and protection, insofar as being contracts designed to prevent the insured party from undergoing any (or limited) financial loss in accordance with the conditions and stipulations contained in them. In providing protection against the consequences of any negligent act, liability insurance contracts are divided into three classifications: (1) general liability contracts that include a variety of business, personal, and professional liability policies (the latter discussed in Chapter 10); (2) employer's liability and workers' compensation (see Chapter 2); and (3) automobile liability under tort and no-fault systems. It is the "no-fault" automobile insurance system that deserves brief elaboration.

There are presently 24 states and the District of Columbia that have no-fault automobile insurance systems operating, in which first-party coverage is designated as *Personal Injury Protection* (PIP) and generally is outlined as "Coverage P" in the policy contract. "PIP benefits ordinarily cover medical expenses, lost income, survivors' loss, expense for replacement services (expenses incurred for household help, child care, necessary yard work, etc., which the injured person is unable to perform because of the injury), and funeral expense" (Insurance Institute of America, 1982, p. 25).

Issues relating to the application of Coverage P in specific situations generally involve two elements known as "caused by the accident" and "reasonable and necessary medical expenses." In the first, PIP coverage does not pay for expenses caused by illness, disease, or death from natural causes *except* when caused or aggravated by an accidental event arising from the

Personal injury protection

maintenance, use or operation of the insured vehicle. In the second element, PIP coverage provides for payment or reimbursement for *reasonable and necessary* medical, replacement, and funeral expenses. Finally, within those jurisdictions where no-fault automobile insurance exists, the system conforms to one of three broad plans: (1) a *modified plan* designed to limit the right to bring suit, but which stops short of actually eliminating the right; (2) an *add on plan* that does not limit the right to bring suit, but simply expands the typical first-party Medical Payments Coverage of automobile insurance to include benefits for lost income; and (3)a *voluntary plan* that allows an insured person the option to purchase PIP coverage.

Insurance-Rehabilitation Interface

According to Kulp and Hall (1968), an insurance underwriter is responsible for selecting those insured parties whose hazards seem to be least, followed by initiating controls designed to minimize the rising cost problems for the insured and insurer alike by maintaining rate levels. In the event that an insured party suffers a covered loss, the insurance claims representative begins a claim handling process that may require the services of professionals outside of the insurance company to meet the needs of the insured party under the terms of the insurance contract.

In those cases requiring rehabilitation services, the rehabilitation professional typically is one of the "external" consultants used by insurance claims representatives. Although Chapters 4 and 5 identify services generally offered by such professionals and the case selection process used by the insurer, respectively, it is important that insurance rehabilitation specialists understand the rudiments of claim handling and the contractual obligations for their services from the insurance perspective. Moreover, as a contracting party with an insurance company, with the obligation to provide rehabilitation services to eligible insured claimants, the rehabilitation professional enters into an agreement that legally means he or she acts as a representative of the insurer. Furthermore, as a legal representative, the rehabilitation professional must conduct him or herself according to the guidelines set forth in the Fair Claims Practices Act of 1939 and its subsequent amendments. Briefly stated, this Act prohibits rehabilitation representatives of insurance companies from advising claimants of their legal rights, conducting business directly with claimants who are represented by an attorney without the latter's prior consent, and advising claimants against seeking legal advice from an attorney. Thus, acquiring a basic understanding of these issues will facilitate the interaction between contracting parties in the rehabilitation process, and ideally contribute to the smooth delivery of restorative services to insured disabled clients.

The Claim Handling Process

When referring cases involving disabling traumatic injury or disease protection to rehabilitation service providers, most insurance carriers take the position that a contracted rehabilitation professional becomes a *limited* agent of the insurance company. In such a capacity, the professional has authority to bind the insurer in contract. Therefore, it is important that the rehabilitation professional be familiar with contractual issues involved in the application of these legal obligations as they apply to both the insured disabled party and the insurance company.

Role of the Insurance Claims Representative The primary role of all insurance claims representatives is to manage the claim payment function or indemnification of losses covered by the insurer's policies. The claim handling process involves the "adjusting" of payment demands to the contract terms, and indemnifying or paying those that apply to the case at hand. Hence, the term "insurance adjustor" is used frequently to describe those persons responsible for this function of insurance. More recently, however, the term "insurance claims representative" is being used in place of the "adjustor" term (Health Insurance Association of America, 1982). Beyond the occupational designation, however, a claims representative must keep abreast of policy changes and judicial decisions that affect contractual interpretations. These functions are crucial in order to efficiently and fairly adjust a claim in relation to the parameters of various coverages to specific situations.

Upon notification of a loss, the claims representative typically contacts the appropriate records source within the insurance company in order to verify that the contract was in force at the time of the loss. Assuming this was the case, the next step is to verify the loss through an investigation, either by telephone or in person, with the insured party in order to secure an estimate of the nature and degree of injury and/or damage sustained. According to the Insurance Institute of America (1982, p. 31), "investigation is the process of assembling information and evidence from which the insurer can determine the position it should take in respect to its legal obligation." Therefore, the initial investigation and communication by the claims representative with the insured lays the foundation for setting a reserve and the proper management of the case file once it is opened.

Most insurance companies use a system whereby the district or company's average paid loss for the specific coverage is reserved when the coverage is opened. *Reserving* is a process involving the transfer of funds from a company's surplus account to an indemnity account; thereby making them more accessible for benefit payments on behalf of the insured and/or claimant(s). Generally, the claims representative will have authority to expend the claim fund reserve without prior supervisory review and approval, since the majority of claims will "settle" or involve that amount (i.e., the average paid loss) based on the company's experience in the market.

In those situations, however, involving multiple or serious and catastrophic injuries and losses, the claims representative usually will submit the investigation to a supervisory committee that examines the loss closely and "sets" an appropriate reserve. According to Mehr and Cammack (1976), the *loss reserve* includes the amount of liability for the claim, consisting of that which is: (a) reported and adjusted, but not yet paid; (b) filed, but not yet adjusted (i.e., verified); and (c) incurred, but not yet reported. The process of reserving a loss or estimating the value of a claim is extremely important because it involves analysis of the insurance company's financial liabilities and ultimately its ability to compete in the marketplace.

After the reserve is set and proper authority has been obtained by the claims representative, the claim handling process formally begins. Although a variety of methods are used to organize the work involved in claim handling, the most popular approach is the *calendar system.* Under this method the insurance representative reviews the complete inventory of files, pays incurred losses, and investigates and verifies the status of each claim within a specified period of time; generally 30 days. In first party losses, this process continues until the claim is closed either by exhausting the benefits or when the insured recovers from the disabling effects of the injury or disease. In third party liability claims, on the other hand, the process continues until the claims representative effectively can settle the loss with the claimant and secure an appropriate release; that is, whereby the insured gives up the right, claim, or privilege demanded of the insurer (Donaldson, 1976). Finally, upon closure the funds remaining in the indemnity account are returned to the company's surplus in a practice commonly called "releasing a reserve."

Special Claim Handling Techniques Occasionally insurance claims representatives use specialized techniques to assist in the effective and efficient management of claims. Among the more commonly known methods are the nonwaiver agreement, expense advance, and the single payment annuity.

Nonwaiver Agreement. In those instances when a claim does not fall neatly within the provisions of a policy, a coverage question may exist for the insurance representative, whereby a nonwaiver agreement may be executed. Such an agreement "is one by which the insured and the insurance company agree in writing that neither party will waive any of its rights under the policy as a result of the investigation or defense of an action brought against the insured" (Magarick, 1962, p. 198). Sometimes referred to as a "reservation-of-rights agreement," the nonwaiver allows the claims representative to investigate the elements of the claim without formally and possibly prematurely denying coverage.

Expense Advance. Another tool used frequently in the handling and management of personal liability claims is the expense advance. This special technique is a relatively straightforward agreement by the insurance carrier to provide payment to a claimant for expenses incurred or projected as a result of damages caused by the negligence of the insured party. In other words, advance payments generally are offered in those cases where the elements of liability clearly are against the carrier's insured. Advance payments may be made for property damage, medical bills, and loss of income sustained by the claimant, typically with the understanding that these funds will be credited to the insured or insurer in the event a settlement or judgment is reached. The advantages of using the expense advance include its assistance in removing the adversarial relationship, enhancing the claims representative's control of the claim, and simultaneously meeting the needs of the claimant.

Single Payment Annuity (structured settlement) Approach. Instead of the insurance carrier offering a single "lump sum" in settlement of a claim, a method growing in popularity involves the carrier purchasing an annuity that will pay the claimant specified amounts in years ahead. Generally, such an individually designed settlement consists of four parts: (1) payment of special damages such as past wage loss, medical bills, and liens; (2) payment of plaintiff attorney's contingent fees either immediately or on a deferred basis (when an attorney is involved); (3) up-front cash to the plaintiff for the purchase of more accessible living quarters, specially equipped transportation devices, or other personal aids; and (4) guaranteed income for the maintenance of the plaintiff, his or her family, or survivors. The advantages of using this technique of claim handling are many, but most important is the fact that all benefits derived from the settlement are *tax-free* to the claimant, providing that the claimant does not take constructive receipt of the settlement.

The Claim Handling Functions of Rehabilitation Services

Although the majority of health and property and liability claims is relatively uncomplicated, requiring little more than telephone management and mail contacts between the insurance representative and the insured party, there are those that require more personal attention. For example, claims representatives may be overwhelmed with the problems encountered in cases involving complicated serious or catastrophic injuries, illnesses, or diseases. Because the information contained in these cases may be difficult to obtain, beyond the expertise of the insurance specialist, and difficult to interpret, assistance frequently is required from trained professionals in the field of rehabilitation. Notwithstanding the special skills and knowledge brought to the claim handling process and the insured individual by these professionals, it is crucial to the claims handler that the information provided be both thorough in its coverage and timely in its delivery. To a large degree, through the contract obligations between the insurer and the rehabilitation professional, the latter becomes the "eyes and ears" of the claims representative who is responsible for reserving and managing the financial aspects of the loss. Clarification by rehabilitation consultants of factors such as medical prognosis, ability of the insured's family to cope with the financially altered status of their income, estimates of income loss resulting from the nature and degree of the disabling condition, and long-range goals are critical elements the claims representative must consider in planning and managing the financial aspects of cases; particularly those under Long-Term Disability or Catastrophic Health Care plans (Meyer, 1971).

Finally, intervention by rehabilitation professionals may be helpful to insurance claims representatives in the ongoing management and ultimate resolution of serious and catastrophic injury or disease claims, as well as less serious cases when medical and vocational complications occur, in three areas. First, using rehabilitation professionals offers a viable method for controlling the amount of claim dollars spent to achieve timely resolution of claims. Second, information provided by rehabilitation professionals can be useful in establishing accurate reserves, thus allowing the carrier to determine an effective rating posture and maintain a competitive position in the insurance marketplace. Third, using the disability management services of rehabilitation providers can increase and improve the insurance carrier's rapport with not only the insured claimant, but also with the legal, medical, business, and industrial communities.

Summary

The purpose of this chapter was to acquaint the reader with basic concepts of insurance that underlie many of the disability compensation systems. This information, although presented as an overview, reveals two significant aspects of insurance for those practicing rehabilitation. First, insurance systems are exceedingly complex and, like most areas of business, are based on contractual agreements that identify and stipulate services and obligations among consenting parties. Second, the systems of insurance in which rehabilitation professionals practice require knowledge and skills of policies that are quite different from those found in the public rehabilitation sector.

Keeping in mind the various insurance and disability compensation systems contained in this and previous chapters, Chapter 4 identifies and discusses the roles and functions of rehabilitation professionals working in an insurance context. Furthermore, the following chapter identifies the assortment of rehabilitation services offered in this growing area of work with disabled clients, as well as some of the similarities and differences between public and private sector rehabilitation orientations.

4 Rehabilitation in an Entrepreneurial Atmosphere

The information presented thus far has been intended to familiarize the reader with the reasons for and nature of responsibilities employers assume for their employees. Together with that, the essential characteristics of insurance have been enumerated relative to their importance in formulating appropriate and necessary services for disabled workers. With this background in mind, the purpose of this chapter is to acquaint the reader with the rehabilitation process in the private business sector. In order to accomplish this, the chapter is organized into four sections: (1) public sector legacy, (2) growth and development of private rehabilitation, (3) services and settings, and (4) practitioner roles and functions. The culmination of this chapter, in conjunction with those preceding it, provides the reader with an optimal framework with which to best understand subsequent chapters addressing specific professional issues and services that characterize vocational rehabilitation in an entrepreneurial atmosphere.

Public Sector Legacy

As indicated in Chapter 2, concern for the establishment of compensation programs for industrially injured workers generally coincided with the development of the state-federal vocational rehabilitation system. In fact, Obermann (1965) is careful to point out that the early discussions of vocational rehabilitation, with respect to industrially injured workers, emphasized the intent of the public program by opening the Vocational Rehabilitation Act of 1920 (P.L. 66-236) with the following: "That in order to provide for the promotion of vocational rehabilitation of persons disabled in industry or in any legitimate occupation . . ." Over the years federal legislation directed toward the public vocational rehabilitation program has expanded both the scope of services offered and the disabled populations to be served. For example, program expansion and modification were evident first in substantial measure in the Barden-LaFollette Act of 1943 (P.L. 78-113) which increased the physical restoration services available, as well as extending vocational rehabilitation benefits for the first time to mentally retarded and mentally ill clients (Bitter, 1979; Rubin & Roessler, 1983).

More recently, the Rehabilitation Act of 1973 (P.L. 93-112) and its 1978 and 1984 amendments (P.L. 95-602 and P.L. 98-221, respectively) were significant for several reasons. First, the term "vocational" was removed from the title of the Act. Second, service priority emphasis was given to the most severely disabled clients. Third, disabled persons' rights were proclaimed for the first time under Title V. Fourth, program and practitioner accountability were enhanced by provisions such as program evaluation, Individualized Written Rehabilitation Programs for disabled clients, and the recognition that rehabilitation personnel be "qualified" to provide services. The importance of these legislative mandates must be underscored because of their concomitant effects on the purpose and programs of public sector vocational rehabilitation when compared to those of the private sector.

The Purpose and Philosophy of Rehabilitation

The National Council on Rehabilitation in 1942 issued a definition of rehabilitation which is still widely quoted and used: "Restoration of the handicapped to the fullest physical, mental, social, vocational and economic usefulness of which they are capable" (National Council on Rehabilitation, 1944, p. 6). Shortly thereafter the American Medical Association (AMA) began viewing medical care as a three-phased process; prevention, cure, and vocational rehabilitation (Allan, 1958). In large part, the addition of the rehabilitation component resulted from medical advances achieved in the treatment of wounded soldiers in World War II which not only prolonged life, but often times required long-term medical management. This period saw the development of physical medicine as a specialty area such that the AMA established the Council on Physical Medicine in 1944 and created a specialty Board of Physical Medicine in 1947, whose name was changed in 1949 to the Board of Physical Medicine and Rehabilitation (Allan, 1958).

During the 1940s, the practice of vocational rehabilitation was confined almost exclusively to the public sector (although Travelers Insurance Company employed nurses to care for the vocational needs of injured workers of its policyholders since as early as 1908). The legacy of the public sector purpose and philosophy of vocational rehabilitation found its way into the area of private sector rehabilitation through workers' compensation systems, although an important modifying distinction was made later. Since its beginning, workers' compensation systems have been based on the premise of providing adequate medical care and adjustment to claims. In fact, as noted in Chapter 2, the first workers' compensation legislation included a promise that attention would be given not only to the prompt payment of cash benefits, but also to the rehabilitation and reemployment of injured workers. It is not surprising then to see the striking similarity in definitions of rehabilitation between the National Council on Rehabilitation and that of the International Association of Industrial Accident Boards and Commissions (IAIABC): "The restoration of an occupationally disabled employee to that person's optimum physical, mental, vocational, and economic usefulness" (IAIABC, 1977, p. 3). Furthermore, Larson (1974) and others have indicated that vocational rehabilitation occupies the same place of importance in the workers' compensation system as it does in the AMA medical care process in order to restore the worker to the maximum usefulness attainable in employment considering the nature of the disabling condition (e.g., Berkowitz, 1960; Cheit, 1961; Cheit & Gordon, 1963; Jaffe, 1961).

On the other hand, in spite of the high degree of similarity of rehabilitation definition and role in the care and treatment of disabled persons between the public sector program and the workers' compensation system, differences do exist in terms of interpretation that eventually affect the nature and type of services rendered. It was noted earlier that recent legislation affecting vocational rehabilitation in the public sector omitted the word "vocational" and placed service delivery priority to those with severe disabilities. These modifications are significant because they alter the basic definition of rehabilitation from a "restoring" process to one of an "educational" process. In other words, federal legislation currently requires those employed in the public vocational rehabilitation program to provide both rehabilitative and habilitative services to disabled persons who may or may not have vocational potential. Within this context, the terms "rehabilitation," "habilitation," and "potential" require additional clarification.

According to Whitehouse (1953) and Jaques (1970), rehabilitation is concerned with reeducation or readaptation for persons following a disabling injury, disease, or disorder. Not only do rehabilitation clients require services that will *restore* them to self-sufficient or nearly self-sufficient living, they need services that will capitalize on their past training and skill assets. Habilitation, on the other hand, refers to an initial educational learning process for persons who have *never* learned to live independent lives. These disabled persons generally were born with a disability or became afflicted by one very early in life and therefore, require services to develop fundamental capabilities, knowledge, experiences, attitudes and skills (Jaques, 1970; Whitehouse, 1953). Thus, for the habilitation client, reemployment is not so much the primary goal, but instead, development of the person's potential to live as independently as possible which may or may not include first-time employment as an outcome.

Rehabilitation practitioners in both public and private settings stress the identification of assets that can be used in mobilizing resources that might assist a person to overcome a handicap. To that end, the definitions of rehabilitation offered by the National Council on Rehabilitation (1944) and the IAIABC (1977) each contain reference to restoring disabled persons to their "fullest" or "optimum" capabilities or usefulness. Another way of phrasing this goal might be to call it "maximization of vocational potential." Herein lies the fundamental philosophical difference, according to some authors, between public and private vocational rehabilitation sectors. In the words of Diamond and Petkas: "The traditional State/Federal Rehabilitation Agency approach is to maximize the client's potential. The Workers' Compensation approach is to rehabilitate the injured worker to the level of functioning prior to injury" (1979, p. 30). While on the surface a difference appears to exist, it may be one of interpretation rather than of philosophy.

What constitutes vocational potential? In writing about this subject, Super defined the term "potential" as "the aptitudes, the abilities, the interests, the personality traits, the motivations, and the concepts of self that have been isolated in clinical and psychological studies and that have been observed to have direct or indirect bearing on vocational behavior" (1969, p. 76). More importantly, everyone, no matter what his or her endowment, has some potential. Yet, potential exists only in possibility, but not in actuality. As a result, "no one — such is human imperfection — can be viewed as having become all that he is capable of becoming" (Super, 1969, p. 75). Basically then, what Diamond and Petkas have identified is that in the workers' compensation system rehabilitation practitioners attempt to maximize the client's potential to return to employment at a level of functioning (and wage-earning) which closely approximates the pre-injury level. On the other hand, while they are less specific about what constitutes attainment of a client's potential in the public rehabilitation sector, it can be assumed that rehabilitation or habilitation goals are identified that are achievable, although they may be considerably less than the client's maximum potential.

The Rehabilitation Process

"The rehabilitation process is a goal-oriented and individualized sequence of services designed to assist handicapped people achieve vocational adjustment" (Bitter, 1979, p. 4). In the public rehabilitation sector, this process begins with case finding or referral and it culminates, if successful, in employment or other means by which a disabled person can live as independently as possible. If it results in employment, the disabled person becomes a productive wage-earning and tax-paying member of society; or if the process results in an increased ability of living independently, even though employment may not be feasible, the disabled person becomes less of a tax burden to society.

Thus, the rehabilitation process in the public sector consists of three distinct and interrelated activities; goal orientation, individualization, and sequential service delivery (Bitter, 1979).

Goal orientation includes the identification of an appropriate vocational or independent living activity that the disabled client will attempt to achieve. The appropriateness of the identified goal is a function of such variables as the nature of and the limitations imposed by the disabling condition, the client's background training and skills, his or her aptitudes, interests, and abilities, as well as the current labor market and availability of jobs in a given occupation. Moreover, selection of an appropriate vocational or independent living goal is contingent on the wage to be paid if the goal is vocational in nature, or the cost of the independent living services to be purchased, transportation to and from the work site or activity center, and so forth.

Individualization in the rehabilitation process refers to the cooperative planning between the rehabilitation practitioner and the disabled client. In other words, the rehabilitation professional focuses on the individual needs of each client in his or her case load and develops goals, as well as implementing strategies for goal-attainment, *with* the client. This form of personal attention to the needs of each disabled client is recorded in a document referred to as the Individualized Written Rehabilitation Program (IWRP) of services. In the public vocational rehabilitation sector, each client is provided an IWRP that specifies the vocational goal, the objectives required to facilitate goal-attainment, and the specific services to be offered.

Sequential service delivery emphasizes the delivery of services at the proper time and in the most appropriate sequence for each person (Bitter, 1979). Generally speaking, the sequential nature and timing aspects of this part of the rehabilitation process is known as "case management" which typically includes the following service components; intake interviewing, medical evaluation, psychological evaluation, vocational evaluation, work adjustment evaluation, treatment, training, job development and placement, and follow-up service monitoring (Roessler & Rubin, 1982).

The rehabilitation process outlined above for the public system typically generalizes to the private vocational rehabilitation sector. This is especially true for those cases involving workers' compensation, although the process of goal orientation, individualization, and sequential service delivery is useful for any client populations and services provided in the rehabilitation field. The efficacy of the three-phase process for public and private vocational rehabilitation service providers alike is demonstrated by its attention to accountability and client involvement in the rehabilitation program.

Economic Benefits of Rehabilitation

Among the rationales for the conduct of a public vocational rehabilitation program has been the economic benefits derived from such services for society in general and the disabled individual in particular. In a study conducted by Conley (1965), it was indicated that for every dollar spent for services by state and federal vocational rehabilitation agencies, between one and a half and five times the cost of services was realized in tax returns. Later, Conley (1969) elaborated on his earlier work by computing a benefit-cost ratio that indicated between five and eight dollars in increased lifetime earnings for disabled clients were realized for every dollar spent for vocational rehabilitation services. Other studies have demonstrated more dramatic economic impact from rehabilitation programming. For example, Bitter (1979) reports a 1966 study conducted by the Department of Health, Education, and Welfare that revealed a benefit-cost ratio estimated at $30 for each $1 spent. Similarly, Reagles and Wright (1971) calculated ratios of 25 and 27 to one for the rehabilitation of medically disabled persons in Wisconsin. While it must be understood that factors such as the present economic health of a nation, availability of jobs in the labor market, and the ability of disabled to overcome their handicap(s) sufficiently to enter competitive employment affect these benefit-cost ratios, the vocational rehabilitation program is unique among human service programs. Its uniqueness comes from the fact that it is the *only* public-sponsored human service program that actually pays money back into the system at a level equal to or greater than its costs.

The economic benefits of vocational rehabilitation are yet another example of the public sector legacy to private sector rehabilitation. Insurance companies and employers have recognized the economic value of rehabilitation since at least 1929. At that time, Professor David McCahan stated:

> From an economic point of view, the idea of rehabilitation is sound. Like accident prevention, it may be regarded as an outgrowth of compensation. And, like accident prevention, when embodied in a sensible, consistent and well-operated program, it tends to reduce compensation costs and to pay for itself in dollars and cents, besides contributing to the well-being of those whom it has reached. (1929, pp. 73-74)

From this statement, however, it appears that vocational rehabilitation in the private sector is more a matter of cost-savings than a "return on investment" in terms of money coming back to third-party funding sources (e.g., insurance companies, self-insured employers, etc).

Within the workers' compensation system, cost-savings provided by vocational rehabilitation services frequently take the form of returning the industrially injured client to work as quickly as is medically feasible (Deneen & Hessellund, 1981; Silberman, Rothaus, & Scharpnick, 1980). By returning the injured worker to his or her previous job, vocational rehabilitation saves money in several ways. First, the insurance carrier's expenses are reduced insofar as the need for extensive and prolonged training for a new occupation are minimized or eliminated, and the duration of temporary total disability payments is reduced. Second, vocational rehabilitation saves the employer money when the injured worker is returned to the former job in two ways: (1) increasing insurance premiums are minimized for the workers' compensation policyholder (i.e., employer) because the expenses of rehabilitation to the insurance company are less than if the injured worker must be retrained and seek new employment, and (2) the employer's expenses are minimized in terms of hiring and training a new employee to replace the injured worker, as well as return to the former level of production.

Aside from the workers' compensation system, vocational rehabilitation in the private sector promotes and provides cost-savings to employers in the form of Employee Assistance Programs (EAP). Not only is it well documented that EAPs save industry money by reducing absenteeism, on-the-job sluggishness, too frequent use of medical benefits, accidents, tardiness, and related production-reducing behaviors (Brisolara, 1979), such programs have been found to have pronounced effects on improving worker satisfaction (Dickman & Emener, in press). Since their earliest beginnings in 1939, the numbers and scope of EAPs have proliferated; today over half of the 500 largest industries in the United States have them (Land, 1981; McMahon et al., 1983; Roman, 1981).

Keeping in mind the public vocational rehabilitation sector's legacies of purpose and philosophy, rehabilitation process, and economic benefits, it is time to see how these factors operate in the private rehabilitation sector.

Growth and Development of Private Rehabilitation

Private, profit-making firms are rapidly becoming a significant component of the delivery system of vocational rehabilitation services to the nation's disabled population. Total revenues of private, entrepreneurial rehabilitation firms were estimated to be approximately $35 million in 1978, nearly $70 million in 1979, and over $150 million in 1980 according to the U.S. Department of Health, Education, and Welfare (DHEW, 1978, 1979, 1980). Additionally, the private sector is estimated to serve approximately 150,000 to 200,000 disabled clients annually compared to a total active caseload of about 1.8 million in the state-federal vocational rehabilitation program (DHEW, 1978). Looking toward the future, the private sector can be expected to take on an even more critical role in shaping the total delivery system of rehabilitation services.

Since its inception, the state-federal vocational rehabilitation program has been the primary employer of rehabilitation professionals. In fact, in the mid-1970s it was estimated that 50% of the approximately 20,000 rehabilitation counselors nationwide worked in state agencies (Schumacher, 1977). The vast majority of the remaining 10,000 was reported to work in sheltered workshops, vocational rehabilitation centers, school settings such as colleges and universities, medical centers and hospitals, correctional institutions, and mental institutions (Feinberg & McFarlane, 1979). On the other hand, private sector rehabilitation employment accounted for only 10% of the total number of rehabilitation counselors in 1978, but was expected to increase to approximately 23% in 1979 and to 31% by 1983 (Gutowski, 1979). Furthermore, a study of employment trends conducted by the Washington, D.C. -based Urban Institute projected that by 1983 twice as many employment opportunities would exist in the private sector than in the state-federal vocational rehabilitation system (Gutowski, Harder, & Koshel, 1980). On the other hand, employment opportunities in the the state-federal vocational rehabilitation program have revealed a gradual decline in recent years as a result of budgeted resources that have barely kept pace with the rate of inflation (Matkin, 1980b, 1980e; Matkin & Riggar, 1985; Rule & Wright, 1981).

The real and anticipated growth of private sector rehabilitation is not without reason. Among the most crucial and specific factors contributing to its rapid growth in a relatively short time span are changes recommended by a Presidential Committee responsible for studying state workers' compensation laws. After reviewing and deliberating the collective states' statutes, the Commission concluded that a stronger and more active role for physical and vocational rehabilitation services be instituted within the workers' compensation framework (National Commission on Workmen's Compensation Laws, 1972). Moreover, the Commission (1972) emphasized that the employer be responsible for the costs of vocational rehabilitation, by noting that in the past much of the costs were paid from sources outside the workers' compensation program (e.g., federal grants to states' departments of vocational rehabilitation). This recommendation was based on two important considerations: (1) "allocations of vocational rehabilitation costs to the responsible sources, the employer, for all work related injuries should be made, and (2) state departments of vocational rehabilitation have been less than consistent in attending to the occupationally disabled" (National Commission on Workmen's Compensation Laws, 1972, Vol. 1, p. 82).

On the heels of the Commission's report, the Interdepartmental Worker's Compensation Task Force was created in 1974. Although its report, issued in 1977, generally considered that the state-federal vocational rehabilitation system adequately served most industrially injured workers, the public program was found not to be adequately prepared to consider the claims and settlement issues in the workers' compensation system, that is, the long-term costs and benefits of a vocational rehabilitation program were not adequately considered in the settlement decisions (Interdepartmental Workers' Compensation Task Force, 1977). As a result of the recommendations made by both the Presidential Commission and the Task Force, state legislatures moved to amend their workers' compensation statutes to bring them up to the recommended standards. Thus, while the specific changes made varied from state to state, the net result was a virtual explosion of growth in the private vocational rehabilitation sector.

Although the growth of private rehabilitation has not been uniform across all states, because of the differences found in workers' compensation statutes from state to state, approximately 80% of all services are directed toward insurance companies and self-insured employers and deal with workers' compensation referrals (Gutowski, 1979). While workers' compensation programs are by far and away the single largest source of client referrals, Chapter 3 provided information about other potential sources of client referrals. These and other sources include:

1. Workers' Compensation
   a. insurance carriers
   b. self-insured employers
   c. claimant attorneys
   d. state workers' compensation boards and commissions
2. Long-Term Disability Insurance
3. Automobile No-Fault Insurance
4. Federal Workers' Compensation Programs
   a. Federal Employees Compensation Act
   b. longshore and harbor workers
   c. railroad workers
   d. coalminers
5. Third-Party Liability
6. Social Security Administration
7. Contractual Agreements
   a. employee assistance programs
   b. hospitals, corrections, schools, business and industry, employment agencies, etc.

While the sources of client referrals to private vocational rehabilitation firms and providers may vary, it is important to understand that the services offered represent a goal-oriented, individualized treatment, and sequential process of service delivery similar in most respects to that found in the public rehabilitation agency system. Before identifying the types of services offered, the typical employment settings, and the roles and functions of rehabilitation personnel in the private sector, it is necessary to emphasize the concept work has to the private practitioner.

Interdisciplinary Teamwork

Vocational rehabilitation has been defined in both the public and private sector contexts earlier and was found to be virtually identical in both instances. Most definitions, however, include the concept of eliminating or alleviating a disability to the greatest degree possible and the individual achieving his or her maximum level of gainful employment and social living within the limits imposed by a disability. For fear of being misunderstood, the various professions and sub-specialties involved in the rehabilitation of disabled persons have adopted the term "total rehabilitation" to emphasize the all-inclusiveness of their services (Gulledge, 1963). Therefore, as the concept is broadened, the problems of semantics are multiplied, and it is not safe to assume that "rehabilitation" has the same meaning to everyone concerned in the process. According to Gulledge (1963) and other authors such as Roessler and Rubin (1982), the organization and use of community resources are to a very large degree the function of vocational rehabilitation. In other words, the vocational rehabilitation service provider (in either public or private employment) more often than not is a case manager or coordinator of services. The "team approach" brings together members of many different occupations who are concerned with the overall rehabilitation of the client. Generally speaking, however, the variety of services offered and the professionals concerned with their delivery can be categorized as either medical rehabilitation or vocational rehabilitation.

Although medical and vocational rehabilitation services may be provided concurrently or consecutively, they tend to be separated by the professional disciplines involved and the institutions used. There are also differences in the extent to which the disabled person is able to make his or her own decisions and participate in the planning of medical and vocational rehabilitation services. In most states, the separation of vocational rehabilitation from medical rehabilitation (comprehensive medical care) is made by the provisions of workers' compensation law. Medical rehabilitation frequently requires the skills and services of many specialized paramedical personnel such as physical therapists, occupational therapists, nurses, social workers, speech and hearing therapists, prosthetists and orthotists, psychologists, and others. By the very nature of the problem, the physician typically controls and directs all of these services.

Since the medical profession is oriented toward improving the physical condition of the patient, by widening the range of vocational opportunities, it fits in well with the goal of vocational rehabilitation. Vocational rehabilitation includes all services necessary to return an injured worker to suitable gainful employment which must include the provision of medical services. Yet, the vocational rehabilitation professional may authorize medical treatment only upon the recommendation of a medical specialist, with all phases of medical treatment remaining under the supervision and direction of the physician. In the private sector, however, it must be understood that vocational rehabilitation practitioners seldom, if ever, have the authority to authorize medical treatment. Rather, *recommendations* are made generally to the referral source who typically has the *authority* to seek and fund such services.

Once a disabled worker's need for vocational rehabilitation has been established, the client and counselor begin to *jointly* explore the problems associated with his or her returning to work. This *individualized treatment* approach continues throughout the service delivery process so that an identifiable vocational goal is established and agreed upon by all concerned parties in the rehabilitation operation, as well as clearly defining the objectives necessary to accomplish the vocational goal. Within the private rehabilitation sector, especially with regard to workers' compensation coverage, goals and objectives stress reemployment. Moreover, insurance carriers and rehabilitation practitioners alike are concerned with returning the injured worker to employment as quickly as the medical condition will allow. As was mentioned earlier, a prompt return to work provides cost savings to the insurance carrier and employer alike, minimizes the disruption of family income for the disabled worker, and enhances the chances of successful vocational rehabilitation (Cheit, 1961).

Return-To-Work Goals

When providing rehabilitation services within the private sector, key ingredients for successful job placement include being responsive to the needs of both the referral source and the disabled worker. According to Cheit (1961), the most effective method to ensure successful vocational rehabilitation is to return the injured worker to the former job if at all possible. Indeed, 93% of those cases which involved a return to the job held at the time of injury proved to be long-term successes (Cheit, 1961). As a result of this finding, the "return-to-work" philosophy of the private rehabilitation sector permeates its goals according to the hierarchy identified by Matkin (1981a, 1982b) and Welch (1979):

1. Return the client to work performing the same job with the same employer.
2. Return the client to work performing the same (but modified) job with the same employer.
3. Return the client to work performing a different job, that capitalizes on transferable skills, with the same employer.
4. Return the client to work performing the same or modified job with a different employer.

5. Return the client to work performing a different job, that capitalizes on transferable skills, with a different employer.
6. Return the client to work performing a different job, that requires extensive and prolonged training, with the same or different employer.
7. As a last resort, return the client to work in a self-employed capacity.

Finally, the "return-to-work" philosophy of private sector vocational rehabilitation has a direct bearing on the nature and duration of services offered by the majority of practitioners. This will be evident in the next section dealing with the types of services offered in the private sector and various employment settings represented.

Services and Settings

It was mentioned that the vast majority of services offered by private vocational rehabilitation professionals is directed toward serving workers' compensation claimants (Gutowski, 1979). As such, the Office of Workers' Compensation Programs has stated that it considers "private rehabilitation agencies a useful alternative to the public rehabilitation agencies in providing the best and all necessary services to expeditiously return the injured worker to employment" (U.S. Department of Labor, 1980, p. 1). In order to meet the challenge of returning disabled clients to employment, a sequential set of services are set in motion with the goal of returning people to work. Within the public sector, it has been noted that this sequence generally consists of evaluation, treatment, training, job placement, and follow-up services. Services offered in the private vocational rehabilitation sector basically are a reflection of these, although the emphasis may be different, as well as some services offered exclusively among private providers of vocational rehabilitation (Organist, 1979; Shrey, 1979). The differences between public and private sector service emphasis are accurately reflected in the following statement by Diamond and Petkas (1979, p. 31):

> The private-for-profit vendors generally do not provide a unique range of services. The key differences are in timeliness of services and more personalized case management. The emphasis is on short-term vocational evaluations looking for transferable skills, court testimony (where required in litigated cases) and job placement. The State VR Agency emphasizes diagnostic workups, physical restoration, long-term vocational assessments and training.

In addition to court testimony, several other vocationally oriented services appear to receive more attention, and as a result, are identified as specific services by the private sector rather than as such within the public rehabilitation system. Examples of these service areas are job analysis, labor market surveying, job restructuring consultation, and medical case management (McMahon, 1979; Sales, 1979). Moreover, research conducted by Matkin (1982d) revealed 29 service areas offered among members of the National Association of Rehabilitation Professionals in the Private Sector (NARPPS). These are found in Table 4–1 along with the percentage of members offering the various types of services.

It is apparent from the percentages reported in Table 4–1 that a dramatic division in services occurs between "Job Restructuring Consultation" (#10) and "Psychological Evaluation" (#11) (i.e., 70.1% and 40.8%, respectively). Keeping in mind the private sector's goal of returning the injured worker to employment and the hierarchy of objectives listed earlier, the data reported by Matkin (1982d) tend to confirm claims that private sector service emphasis is directed toward job placement, vocational in nature, and short-term in duration. Furthermore, from a workers' compensation perspective, it is understandable that longer-term services, such as independent living skills training, work adjustment, psychological counseling, and job seeking skills training, are less frequently offered than is the case in public vocational rehabilitation.

Up to this point the term "private sector rehabilitation" has been used to differentiate services and people working in profit-making enterprises as compared to those working in public vocational rehabilitation agencies or not-for-profit rehabilitation facilities such as sheltered workshops. Among the assorted businesses subsumed by this broad category are corporations in any industry, rehabilitation companies, insurance companies, large law firms, private hospitals, nursing homes, and private practitioners (Hasbrook, 1981). On the other hand, investigations of the NARPPS membership in 1981 revealed that the majority of private vocational rehabilitation professionals is employed by for-profit rehabilitation firms.

In a study conducted by Lynch and Martin (1982), approximately 42% of the 147 respondents were employed by for-profit rehabilitation firms, 19% indicated they were private consultants, and 16% were employed as rehabilitation specialists by insurance companies. These findings were supported in large measure by a second study, which revealed that 40.2% of the 174 respondents were self-employed owners or co-owners of rehabilitation companies that employed a staff of rehabilitation specialists, 20.7% were employees of private rehabilitation companies, 17.8% worked within insurance companies, and 14.9% consisted of persons in private practice without additional rehabilitation personnel (Matkin, 1982d).

Table 4–1. Services Offered among Members of the National
Association of Rehabilitation Professionals in the Private Sector
(*N*=174)

Services	%
1. Vocational Counseling	94.8
2. Job Analysis	92.0
3. Job Placement	90.8
4. Job Development	88.5
5. Case Monitoring and Follow-up	86.8
6. Labor Market Surveying	84.5
7. Vocational Evaluation	76.4
8. Medical Case Management	76.4
9. Vocational Testimony	71.3
10. Job Restructuring Consultation	70.1
11. Psychological Evaluation	40.8
12. Psychological Counseling	40.2
13. Work Adjustment	35.6
14. Group Counseling	35.1
15. Program Evaluation Consultation	29.3
16. Personnel Selection Consultation	24.1
17. Marriage and Family Counseling	21.3
18. Insurance Claims Adjusting	20.1
19. Independent Living Skills Training	14.4
20. Labor Union Negotiation	9.8
21. Job Seeking Skills Training	5.2
22. Mobility Training for the Blind	4.6
23. Employee Assistance Programs	2.3
24. Architectural Barrier Removal Consultation	1.7
25. Pain and Stress Management	1.1
26. Financial Counseling	0.6
27. Business Consultation	0.6
28. Alcohol Counseling	0.6
29. Independent Medical Examinations	0.6

In view of the types of services offered most frequently in Table 4–1 and
evidence that suggests that the majority of private practitioners are employed
by rehabilitation firms or else are in private practice, it is important to identify
the work characteristics that constitute their jobs. The necessity for work role
and function information about the private rehabilitation sector is essential

for several significant reasons: (1) to determine the most appropriate training and preparational needs required for job entry, (2) to assess the representativeness of curriculum content in rehabilitation training programs in terms of private sector job responsibilities, (3) to remediate areas of curriculum deficiency and increase the body of knowledge within the rehabilitation field, and (4) to continue developing and expanding the occupational professionalism of vocational rehabilitation.

Roles and Functions

Vocational rehabilitation is a relatively young field by comparison to other human service-oriented occupations (e.g., physicians, nurses, psychologists, educators). As indicated in Chapter 2, vocational rehabilitation was created, for all intents and purposes, from federal legislation with an initial purpose of providing services to disabled American war veterans needing vocational assistance and training. As federal legislation continued to expand the scope of vocational rehabilitation programs and the populations to be served, it soon became evident that there existed a shortage of trained personnel to attend to the needs of disabled persons. Similarly, vocational rehabilitation in the private sector generally was provided by rehabilitation nurses who worked for large insurance companies to serve the needs of injured employees of workers' compensation policyholders (Lewin, Ramseur, & Sink, 1979). In order to meet the need for more persons trained in vocational rehabilitation, federal financial support to educational institutions began in 1954 as part of the Vocational Rehabilitation Act Amendments (P.L. 83-565). Thus, to meet the needs of practicing rehabilitation counselors, as well as to develop appropriate training curricula for would-be practitioners, work role and function studies were undertaken to discover the tasks and duties performed by this newly emerged occupational group (i.e., vocational rehabilitation counselors).

As you will recall, current estimates of the numbers of rehabilitation counselors nationwide report nearly 20,000 persons engaged in this occupation, half of which work in settings other than the state-federal agency system (Feinberg & McFarlane, 1979; Schumacher, 1977). Moreover, Gutowski and his associates (1979, 1980) have indicated that while approximately 10% of the total employment of vocational rehabilitation counselors (i.e., 2000) in 1978 were in the private sector, that number was projected to increase to over 30% (i.e., 6000) by 1983. Recently Field (1981) estimated as many as 5000 rehabilitation practitioners were represented by the nearly 300 members of NARPPS. This figure, however, was not limited to rehabilitation counselors per se, but included a more generic vocational rehabilitation *specialist* group (e.g., administrators and supervisors, counselors, job placement specialists, nurses, and vocational evaluators). More recently, Matkin's (1982d) survey of NARPPS members revealed that out of 174 persons who reported being employed in a profit-making rehabilitation business, the number of offices exceeded 1200 and the number of rehabilitation staff employed in them was nearly 5300. Notwithstanding the variety of occupational backgrounds subsumed by this vocational rehabilitation specialist group, their numbers are significant enough to warrant investigation of their work roles and functions as compared to the duties and responsibilities of rehabilitation personnel in the public sector.

Rehabilitation Counselors

Reviewing the curricula content of rehabilitation counselor training programs has resulted in a variety of reactions among authors over the years. Some believed that the psychological content was over-emphasized while areas of industrial sociology, labor market trends and analysis, and workers' compensation were neglected (Matkin, 1980d; Olshansky, 1957; Olshansky & Hart, 1967; Scher, 1979). Others have made cases for rehabilitation personnel serving as counselors rather than coordinators of services (Patterson, 1957, 1966, 1967, 1968, 1970). Still others have suggested that problem solving needs more emphasis (Angell, DeSau, & Havrilla, 1969), as well as basic service management (Rubin & Roessler, 1983).

Because of the suspected differences in work activity emphasis between the public and private rehabilitation sectors, which to some degree is reflected in Table 4–1, two important investigations were undertaken. In the first, Matkin (1982e) surveyed members of NARPPs to determine the roles and functions of private rehabilitation specialists. The second investigation, sponsored by the Commission on Rehabilitation Counselor Certification and conducted by Rubin and Matkin and their associates (1984), surveyed all Certified Rehabilitation Counselors (CRC) to identify their work activities in a variety of employment settings in relation to the content knowledge areas contained in the CRC national examination. Both investigations used self-reporting instruments relying greatly on the contents of both the Muthard and Salomone (1969) and Wright and Fraser (1975) instruments. On the one hand, Matkin's (1982e) "Rehabilitation Specialist Task Inventory" contained 132 work statements, while on the other, Rubin et al.'s (1984) "CRC Job Task Inventory" contained 130 items. In both cases, rehabilitation specialists and counselors indicated the degree to which each work task was part of their job. Likewise, both investigations reduced the total responses into meaningful categories of work functions using similar methods of statistical analyses. Table 4—2 presents the five categories of work functions identified in each of these studies.

While the findings of these two investigations reveal similar categorical titles of job functions, it is necessary to know the specific nature of each, and more crucially, how important these various activities are for rehabilitation counselors in the private sector. Thus, to ascertain this information, Rubin et al. (1984) were able to isolate CRCs according to their respective work settings as well as divide the five work groups found in Table 4—2 into subcategories. Table 4—3 identifies the 11 subcategories and also reveals those areas perceived to be important job activities for CRCs employed by private vocational rehabilitaiton firms or who work in private practice.

Job Placement and Development   It was noted in Table 4—1 that job development and placement are among the most frequently offered services in private rehabilitation work. Among the many work activities that private rehabilitation counselors perform in terms of providing placement services are: (a) using supportive counseling to prepare clients emotionally for the stresses of job hunting, (b) instructing clients in ways to find employment, (c) exploring alternative ways for clients to respond to employers' questions about the presence of a disabling condition, (d) providing information about the availability of job openings that best suit clients' needs and abilities, (e) assessing labor market trends within the community in relation to specific job classifications, (f) visiting training facilities to determine their suitability for clients, (g) surveying the local labor market to determine wage and salary

Table 4–2.   Comparison of the Roles and Functions of Private Rehabilitation Specialists (Matkin, 1982e) and Certified Rehabilitation Counselors (Rubin et. al, 1984)

Private Sector Categories [a]	CRC Categories [b]
1. Planning & Coordinating Client Services	1. Job Placement & Development
2. Business & Office Management	2. Case Management
3. Job Development & Placement	3. Professional/Policy/Test Development
4. Diagnostic Assessment	4. Vocational Counseling & Assessment
5. Other Professional Activities	5. Affective Counseling

[a] Surveyed a random sample of 850 private rehabilitation specialists nationwide with a usable response rate of 254.
[b] Surveyed the total population of CRCs (N=approximately 7000) with a usable response rate of 1135. Work role categories were determined by factor analyzing only responses made by practicing CRCs (N=715).

Table 4–3. Sub-categories of Work Functions for Privately Employed[a] Certified Rehabilitation Counselors (Rubin et al., 1984)

Job Function Sub-Categories

---

    1. Job Placement & Development
        A. Employment Development
†   B. Placement Counseling
*   C. Supportive Placement Service

    2. Case Management
†   A. Service Planning
        B. Vocational Service Coordination
        C. Medical & Psychological Services
**   D. Fiscal Management

    3. Professional/Policy/Test Development
        A. Professional Development & Administrative Planning
        B. Test Administration & Development

    4. Vocational Counseling & Assessment
†   A. Vocational Counseling
†   B. Vocational Assessment

** 5. Affective Counseling

---

† Important job functions for CRCs employed by private firms or in private practice.
* Important job function for CRCs employed by private firms but *not* for CRCs in private practice.
** Important job function for CRCs in private practice but *not* for CRCs employed by private firms.
[a] CRCs employed by private rehabilitation firms ($N=109$) and CRCs working in private practice ($N=42$).

---

ranges for various jobs suited to clients' abilities, (h) assessing the transferability of clients' skills across specific jobs and job families, (i) meeting with representatives of insurance companies, attorneys, physicians, and training personnel to coordinate vocational rehabilitation activities, (j) performing job analyses in order to determine the work requirements of specific jobs in terms of their physical, intellectual, and training requirements, and (k) providing expert testimony about the vocational abilities of disabled clients.

Case Management Case management generally describes activities that are performed to plan and coordinate the rehabilitation services deemed most appropriate to return the disabled client to work in the most effective and expeditious manner. For vocational rehabilitation counselors working in the private sector, important case management activities include: (a) developing a written rehabilitation plan with the client that identifies the vocational goal and the services required to achieve that goal, (b) integrating information from vocational, medical, and other diagnostic reports in order to determine the most appropriate vocational goal feasible, (c) monitoring the client's progress toward attainment of the identified vocational goal, (d) ensuring that clients understand their responsibilities in the rehabilitation process, (e) conducting intake interviews to determine how best the counselor and agency can help the client, (f) discussing the counselor's role and responsibilities in the rehabilitation process with the client, (g) determining the client's expectations of the rehabilitation services to be offered, (h) explaining the nature and limitations of counselor confidentiality to clients before engaging in services, (i) establishing timetables for performing assorted vocational rehabilitation services and making these known to the client and other interested parties in the rehabilitation process, (j) explaining available rehabilitation entitlement benefits to clients, (k) obtaining an understanding with the referral source about the financial responsibilities for a client's rehabilitation, and (l) checking and verifying billing fees for services received and rendered.

Vocational Counseling and Assessment Table 4–1 revealed that vocational counseling is the most frequently offered service area within private vocational rehabilitation. Furthermore, vocational evaluation constitutes a frequently provided service as well as an important method for determining the most appropriate and feasible vocational goal for disabled workers. For those persons engaged in private vocational rehabilitation, regardless of whether they are employed by a firm or work as independent practitioners, the following work activities are among the most important: (a) assessing client's past training, work experience, hobbies, and other significant factors in relation to vocational choice; (b) assessing the vocational significance of the client's disability; (c) exploring with clients their vocational assets and liabilities and their acceptance of them; (d) reviewing materials and reports concerning medical, educational, training, and other important information that will be important for determining a feasible vocational goal; (e) discussing factors related to good work adjustment with clients in order to help improve their employability; (f) assessing the consistency of clients' vocational choices with their personality, medical condition, and other significant vocational factors; (g) using test results as a diagnostic aid in the process of gaining a thorough understanding of the whole client; (h) interpreting test results to clients in a manner that relates them to both broad and specific occupational areas and jobs; and (i) consulting with experts in a particular occupational field to determine the potential for placement prior to recommending a specific vocational goal.

Affective Counseling   Counseling skills generally transcend many areas in the day-to-day activities of the rehabilitation counselor. In this context, however, affective counseling refers to those activities that focus on client motivation and assist rehabilitation counselors to better understand the client and help him or her to overcome the fears and anxieties of returning to work. On the other hand, it is important to mention that affective counseling activities, because of their tendency to become rather involved, time consuming, and prolonged in nature, generally are performed more often by rehabilitation counselors working in private practice than by their counterparts in private rehabilitation firms (Rubin et al., 1984). Activities characteristic of affective counseling include: (a) assisting clients to achieve emotional and intellectual acceptance of the limitations imposed by their disability, (b) interpreting the motivations underlying clients' behavior in order to identify methods to modify inappropriate or less than optimal behaviors in relation to vocational choices, (c) discussing with clients their interpersonal relationships in order to help them more fully understand their nature and quality, (d) providing information about clients' motivation and other significant factors affecting vocational outcome to members of a diagnostic treatment team, and (e) helping reduce clients' anxiety about their medical condition and other aspects affecting vocational outcome that may seem insurmountable to clients.

Rehabilitation Nurses

Rehabilitation nurses reportedly were the first occupational group to perform vocational rehabilitation services in the private sector (i.e., circa 1908). The work of the nurse on the medical rehabilitation team constitutes a vital adjunct to the services of the physician and serves as a linkage to the vocational rehabilitation counselor. Rehabilitation as an integral part of nursing has always manifested itself in the form of concern for the physical and psychological reactions of patients to disease and injury (Allan, 1958). In the typical role as a staff nurse in a general hospital, some of the very early functions of nursing included areas that later became the province of specialists trained in social work, counseling, and psychotherapy. More importantly, it must be recognized that the nurse is often the first contact patients have when entering a hospital, following treatment, and throughout most of the convalescent period. The impact that nurses have on patients/clients, therefore, is tremendous in terms of being associated with understanding, alleviation of posttreatment fears, acting as a liaison between patient and physician, and ministering to the day-to-day needs of clients during the period of hospitalization.

The nurse who works in the specialized environment of medical facilities designed for rehabilitation of either chronic or acute patients learns to apply rehabilitation techniques in a well-defined pattern and as part of a medical team whose goal is comprehensive restoration and adjustment to disability. As Morrissey (1951, p. 62) has indicated so accurately, the principal contributions of the rehabilitation nurse are in the areas of "service management, clinical teaching, and basic bedside nursing." Therefore, in the controlled environment of a hospital rehabilitation service, the nurse recognizes and uses the hygiene, nutrition, exercise, elimination, relaxation, recreation, and occupational preparation which contribute toward the maximum possibility of successful rehabilitation (Allan, 1958). Notwithstanding these responsibilities, the nurse may have other roles in relation to the rehabilitation process. Those who are in nursing education have the task of finding the ways and means to interest more persons to enter nursing schools and subsequently the profession. The field of industrial nursing offers an opportunity for the development of human relations, for the practice of selective job placement, and for the organization of a medical department within an industrial setting which is oriented to rehabilitation ideas and practices. Public health nursing, in particular, demonstrates the need for knowledge and use of community rehabilitation services, as well as the practical counseling, follow-up nursing routines, and social awareness which are the bases for home-care programs (Morrissey, 1951).

Rehabilitation nurses working within the workers' compensation system are employed primarily by large insurance companies (Matkin, 1982d, 1982e). In his investigation of the roles and functions of private rehabilitation specialists, Matkin (1982e) reported that rehabilitation nurses, more than any other occupational group, were responsible for planning and coordinating client services. This broad area was broken down further into six sub-areas consisting of: (1) client orientation and service planning, (2) resource identification and referral, (3) service coordination, (4) gathering and synthesizing information, (5) guidance and counseling, and (6) disseminating information (Matkin, 1982e).

Client Orientation and Service Planning   Among the work activities performed by rehabilitation nurses in this area are: (a) interviewing hospitalized clients in order to orient them to the rehabilitation program and make initial plans for services, (b) ensuring that clients understand the role of the rehabilitation nurse, as well as their own responsibilities in the rehabilitation process,

(c) explaining rehabilitation entitlement benefits to hospitalized clients, (d) explaining the nature and extent of confidentiality between themselves and clients, (e) determining clients' expectations of rehabilitation services, (f) involving clients in the decision-making process, (g) evaluating clients' needs in relation to necessary rehabilitation services, (h) developing intermediate rehabilitation objectives for clients during convalescent periods, (i) establishing timetables for performing various rehabilitation services, (j) monitoring clients' progress toward vocational goal attainment, and (k) evaluating the degree of client participation in the rehabilitation process.

Resource Identification and Referral   Because of the familiarity rehabilitation nurses have with medical care and its adjunctive services, it is not surprising that nurses more than others in private sector rehabilitation perceive the following activities as important aspects of their job: (a) identifying rehabilitation facilities, centers, agencies, or programs within the community that provide services to disabled persons; (b) discussing the purpose and need for referral when referring clients to cooperating agencies; (c) referring clients for medical evaluations; and (d) referring clients to rehabilitation facilities to assess their physical limitations, work tolerances, motivation, and level of vocational functioning.

Service Coordination   Working primarily in an insurance setting, rehabilitation nurses perhaps have the best opportunity to coordinate the variety of services and programs being received by injured workers. This comes from the fact, as noted earlier, that the vast majority of referrals to the private rehabilitation sector comes from the insurance company which handles workers' compensation policies. Therefore, as the leading source of referrals, information about the needs of injured workers naturally returns to the insurance carrier from a variety of sources. For those companies employing rehabilitation nurses, these persons are in a position to keep abreast of the current state of affairs in any client's case. Among the duties of a rehabilitation nurse in this capacity are (a) meeting with representatives of training facilities, attorneys, and attending physicians to coordinate rehabilitation activities; (b) contacting clients' attorneys to arrange an initial interview with the client; (c) scheduling appointments to see clients; (d) working as part of an interdisciplinary team to determine when clients are ready to enter training or employment; and (e) discussing the progress of clients with members of the treatment team, as well as with the client.

Gathering and Synthesizing Information   Activities constituting this area are similar to those of case management for rehabilitation counselors insofar as they deal with developing an understanding of the needs of clients in order to institute a viable rehabilitation plan. Such work responsibilities for the rehabilitation nurse include: (a) compiling client information to initiate a case file; (b) reviewing background materials in terms of past training, work experiences, pre-injury earning level, and related factors to be considered in selecting an appropriate vocational goal; and (c) examining with clients the consequences of their disability and its significance in relation to work, family, and self-sufficiency.

Guidance and Counseling   It was mentioned earlier that the role of the rehabilitation nurse incorporates a concern for the physical and mental well-being of disabled persons under their care. As such, guidance and counseling activities serve as a vehicle for the nurse to communicate with the client in order to reduce fears and anxieties clients have about the ramifications of their condition. Some of the more important responsibilities rehabilitation nurses have to assist in restoration and recovery are (a) facilitating diagnostic procedures by enlisting the cooperation of clients themselves, (b) working with clients to identify mutually acceptable methods to resolve personal conflicts, (c) discussing ways in which clients can communicate to others about their disability, and (d) helping clients to identify alternative methods of coping with their disability.

Disseminating Information   Earlier studies of rehabilitation counselor roles and functions have found that much time is spent preparing and processing reports and other information about clients. Needless to say, the same holds true for the rehabilitation nurse. More specifically, the need to communicate with other members of the rehabilitation team or other members within the rehabilitation process requires skills in letter composition, report writing, and verbal skills. The ability to summarize long reports, as well as making clear and concise, yet comprehensive, recommendations is necessary.

Rehabilitation Administrators

There are an estimated 12,000–13,000 administrators, managers and supervisors employed in the field of rehabilitation in the United States according to Lorenz (1977). These individuals primarily work either in state-federal rehabilitation agencies or in approximately 5,000 private, not-for-profit rehabilitation facilities (Lorenz et al., 1981). While the number of similar positions in the private rehabilitation sector has yet to be determined, a rough estimate among the NARPPS membership revealed over 55% were administrators or supervisors. This figure includes the 40.2% who reported being self-employed owners or co-owners of private rehabilitation firms that had a staff of rehabilitation personnel, plus the 14.9% who indicated being in private practice as sole practitioners (Matkin, 1982d). In view of the fact that role and function information available for CRCs in the private sector indicates that fiscal management is part of the duties being performed, especially for those operating as sole proprietors (see Table 4–3), the need arises to determine what activities these persons perform.

According to Young (1977), the theory and practice of rehabilitation administration may not be unique, but the administrative application requires specialized knowledge and skills to attain rehabilitation-specific goals. This view is contrary to the position advocated by many schools and colleges of administration that promote the concept of generic management in which a broadly trained administrator is prepared to manage *any* organization (Suojanen, 1977). On the other hand, Lorenz (1977) has suggested that generic management training programs have failed to respond to the unique management problems of the applied fields and as a result, more specialized areas of administrative training have evolved. Examples of these specialized fields include hospital administration, social work administration, educational administration, and public administration. While rehabilitation administration has joined this group recently, it was not until 1981 that an effort was made to identify the roles and functions of practicing administrators in the rehabilitation field.

The problem of finding qualified individuals to manage the increasing number of rehabilitation facilities and to provide management training for established administrators was not fully realized in the public and not-for-profit sectors until the mid-1960s. Prior to that time, a lack of formal preparation and training were not considered to be serious problems since many programs were small and accountability was not a major issue. Since that time, the gap between a rehabilitation administrator's body of knowledge and the amount of information needed to fulfill the management role continued to widen. This problem has been exacerbated further by a deficiency of management training available specific to rehabilitation (Sawyer & Schumacher, 1980) and the lack of administrative experience prior to assuming the role (Feindel, 1980a, 1980b; Matkin, 1982a; Riggar & Matkin, 1984; Sullivan, 1982). Therefore, in 1981, research was begun to identify not only the roles and functions of rehabilitation administrators working in state-federal rehabilitation agencies or private not-for-profit facilities, but also their training needs.

In order to determine the work characteristics of practicing rehabilitation administrators, Matkin and his associates (1982) developed and administered the "Rehabilitation Administrator Task Inventory" which consisted of 64 work statements drawn from the rehabilitation literature, descriptions of curricula in graduate rehabilitation administration training programs, descriptions of inservice training courses, and administrator input. Responses were obtained from a random sample of members of the National Rehabilitation Administration Association (N=178) and were later analyzed using factor analysis procedures to reduce the information into meaningful groups of work categories. Table 4–4 reveals the 10 groups of work tasks reported by

Table 4–4. Work Role Categories among Rehabilitation Administrators and Supervisors Employed in either Nonprofit Rehabilitation Facilities or State-Federal Rehabilitation Agencies (Matkin et al., 1982)

Work Role Categories

---

* 1. General Personnel Management
* 2. Professional Management
* 3. Fiscal Management
* 4. Production Management
* 5. Program Planning and Evaluation
* 6. Public Relations
* 7. Marketing Services
* 8. Labor Relations
  9. Purchasing
 10. Research

---

* Important work functions of rehabilitation administrators employed in nonprofit rehabilitation facilities. These job activities were more important for administrators in private settings than for those in public agencies.

the authors, along with asterisks (*) denoting those areas which administrators in private not-for-profit facilities indicated were important functions in their work setting.

Although the information collected by Matkin et al. (1982) specifically dealt with rehabilitation administrators and supervisors working in either public agencies or private *nonprofit* facilities, the latter group's work activities closely parallel those working in the private, for-profit rehabilitation arena. In fact, the term "nonprofit" represents an Internal Revenue Service designation applicable to business entities whose profits are in part or totally tax exempt. This is not to say, as the term "nonprofit" seems to imply, that these businesses are not concerned with generating income revenues. Indeed, administrators of nonprofit rehabilitation facilities must be concerned with developing, maintaining, and even increasing their companies' income in order to stay in business (Lorenz et al., 1981). Therefore, the work activities of administrators employed in either private not-for-profit or for-profit rehabilitation companies are similar in nature. On the other hand, the individual working in the private sector as a sole provider of services (i.e., sole proprietor or private practitioner) must be concerned with two work roles—service provider and administrator. As a result, it is important to understand what duties and responsibilities are required of rehabilitation managers or administrators in the private sector as adopted from Matkin et al.'s (1982) research.

General Personnel Management   These activities represent responsibility for the overall supervisory management of personnel within a rehabilitation firm. Examples of the duties performed under this heading include: recruiting, interviewing and selecting applicants for hiring, conducting periodic personnel evaluations, developing strategies for the retention and promotion of existing personnel, managing employee conflicts, disciplining employees, and monitoring the duties assigned to subordinates.

Professional Management   Related to the general area of personnel management is an area dealing specifically with the supervision of direct client service professional staff members. Tasks related to this area include: developing and maintaining an appropriate system for case finding and referral intake, coordinating active client caseloads, assigning work to counselors and other professional disciplinary members, and assisting professional staff in the preparation of individualized written rehabilitation programs.

Fiscal Management   For the private rehabilitation professional working for a company or in private practice, fiscal management skills are necessary in order to maintain solvency, and therefore, minimize either deficit spending or bankruptcy. Responsibilities associated with overall budget management and financial analysis in rehabilitation business settings include identifying appropriate financial resources, preparing budgets, establishing and managing appropriate bookkeeping and financial and cost accounting systems, controlling business expenses, preparing financial analysis reports, and making and implementing financial decisions.

Program Planning and Evaluation   Among the primary responsibilities of any administrator or manager in a business operation is the development and assessment of goals, policies, and objectives upon which the business is based. For example, if job placement services are offered by a private rehabilitation firm, the administrator needs to identify how well this service is being performed in terms of its goals, and the degree of profitability attained relative to the costs of providing the service. Without this information, the administrator may have difficulty budgeting sufficient resources for this service, or perhaps might be wasting revenues in the event that the service is performed in an inefficient or ineffective manner. In either case, the administrator needs to be aware of the status of services and make decisions to modify them if necessary to become more in line with their goals. Duties generally performed as part of program planning and evaluation include conducting needs assessments within the community to identify those services most in demand, developing written goals, objectives, and policy statements, developing resource materials, conducting program evaluations and preparing evaluation reports, and using program evaluation outcomes to reformulate business policies and procedures.

Public Relations and Marketing Private sector rehabilitation does not survive for long if no one is aware of the services available, or worse yet, if people are either misinformed or have a preconceived idea of what private rehabilitation is all about. Among the key ingredients to the early survival of a private rehabilitation company and especially for a private rehabilitation practitioner is community recognition. This means taking the time and making the effort to inform the public in general and potential referral sources in particular of the services available, their costs, and other factors that will enhance present and future referrals. Among the duties a rehabilitation administrator assumes in this work function are: conducting marketing and sales activities for the rehabilitation firm, soliciting client referrals from third-party funding sources, performing public speaking activities, preparing and sending brochures and other materials that adequately describe the rehabilitation services offered, and establishing affiliation or other contractual agreements when necessary.

Summary

More frequently than not private sector vocational rehabilitation draws upon the heritage and legacy of its public sector program counterpart. The importance of work in the rehabilitation process in the private sector has its foundation in public rehabilitation legislation dating back to 1920, as well as in workers' compensation statutes since the early 1900s. The "return-to-work" philosophy advocated by vocational rehabilitation professionals in the business community differs from the public vocational rehabilitation program only insofar as the latter has more recently been mandated by federal legislation to expand its services to severely disabled persons who, by virtue of their disability, may have little or no vocational potential. As in the public sector, the vocational rehabilitation process in the private sector follows a systematic and sequential series of services designed to identify a goal best suited to meet the medical, psychological, and socioeconomic needs of each disabled client. Moreover, private sector rehabilitation is viewed as a cost-saving program for returning injured workers to gainful employment — an economic benefit legacy long associated with vocational rehabilitation services provided to disabled persons by state-federal agencies.

The "return-to-work" philosophy of private rehabilitation permeates most, if not all, of the services most frequently provided by persons in this sector. By far and away, services such as vocational counseling, job analysis, job development and placement, labor market surveying, vocational evaluation, and job restructuring consultation are short term in nature and duration. Their primary emphasis is to return a disabled client to work as expeditiously as possible by providing all necessary services to effectively achieve that goal. By capitalizing on the acquired and transferable skills of injured and disabled workers, private rehabilitation professionals first attempt to return clients to their former job with their most recent employer. This strategy has been demonstrated to be the most effective for several reasons. First, the client is familiar with the nature of the work performed, the work environment, and has an established rapport with his or her coworkers. Second, the familiarity with the work environment minimizes the client's need to learn new policies and procedures, thereby minimizing the time it would take to return to full productive capacity. Third, by returning to the former job, the disabled client enhances his or her ability to return to the pre-injury wage level, thus creating the least amount of income disruption. Finally, the employer benefits in terms of cost savings by reducing the likelihood of paying higher insurance premiums, minimizing production disruption, and absorbing the costs associated with hiring and training a new employee.

Working in the private vocational rehabilitation sector brings with it many challenges regardless of employment setting or occupational classification. Most privately employed rehabilitation personnel work for rehabilitation business firms or are in practice alone. Whether initial training was in the area of rehabilitation administration, rehabilitation counseling, rehabilitation nursing, or other skills such as job placement or vocational evaluation, each of these persons needs to develop a sense of organizational management. The *business* of rehabilitation requires effective and efficient administration of the services to be offered to disabled persons and third-party funding sources. Without these skills, regardless of how well one can counsel, nurse, find jobs, or give tests, it is only a matter of time before the business itself fails, and with it the opportunity to provide such services in an entrepreneurial atmosphere.

5 Disability Case Management

Ralph E. Matkin and William C. Wallace

As indicated in the preceding chapter, planning and coordinating services for disabled persons are not only the most important job functions reported by private sector rehabilitation professionals, but also the most frequently performed tasks. An effective initial case assessment and appropriate case management are crucial services because they set the stage for future case activities. In addition to their contributions for enhancing successful goal attainment and outcome, effective management of cases provides an efficient means for controlling the costs associated with rehabilitating disabled persons.

The purpose of this chapter is to concentrate on that aspect of rehabilitation service planning and coordinating known in the insurance sector as disability management, medical care coordination, or medical management. The significance of disability case management is twofold; it clarifies and plans subsequent medical and vocational treatment and restorative services to be rendered to a disabled person. In order to familiarize the reader with the substance of effective disability management, the chapter is divided into four major sections: (1) medical care costs and disability; (2) case selection by the insurer; (3) initial evaluation; and (4) planning and developing rehabilitation goals.

Medical Care Costs and Disability

To rehabilitate means to restore. The simplicity of this definition, however, grossly understates not only the multiservice aspects typically involved in physical restorative processes but also the costs associated with such services. In terms of medical care alone, each year Americans spend more money for services, resulting in part from a combination of factors such as inflation, greater demands for health service, the growth and availability of private health insurance, and the introduction of newer and more costly medical techniques and procedures. In fact, the total health care spending in 1980, represented by the National Health Expenditure figure (which includes public and private expenditures for personal health care, medical research and construction of facilities, administrative and health insurance costs, and government-sponsored public health activities) reached $247.2 billion, or 9.4% of the Gross National Product (Health Insurance Association of America, 1982). Moreover, according to projections made by the Health Care Financing Administration, national health expenditures will reach $462 billion in 1985, $821 billion by 1990, and over $2 trillion by the year 2000 (U.S. Department of Health and Human Services, 1981).

Aside from medical expenses, the devastating effect of disability on family earnings, workdays lost, and the cost to the private and public sectors cannot be underestimated. In 1980, according to the U.S. Department of Health and Human Services, approximately 339 million workdays were lost as a result of some acute health condition among employed persons 17 years or older. More specifically, the Bureau of Labor Statistics estimated some 40.9 million workdays were lost because of work-related injuries in 1980, resulting from approximately 5.5 million job-related accidents. This rate translated to one injury or illness for every 12 workers in the private economy (U.S. Department of Labor, 1981). Table 5-1 reveals the number of occupational injuries and illnesses by industry in the United States in 1980. Notwithstanding the time lost on the job, group disability income insurance in 1980 paid nearly $4.3 billion (Sabini, 1983). Yet, even when disability income benefits are received they are rarely sufficient to allow the pre-injury life-style to continue for the disabled person and his or her family.

In view of the spiraling costs of providing rehabilitation services and income replacement benefits, as well as the adverse social effects of disability, insurance carriers seek avenues to effectively control these losses. One such method of documented value, either provided by in-house personnel or through outside referral and consultation, is rehabilitation. Where traditionally rehabilitation may once have been considered only when all else had failed, for a steadily increasing number of insurance carriers and self-insured employers it now represents an immediate course of action (Sabini, 1983). Quite simply, rehabilitation has become a cost-effective means for maximizing medical care and work capacity following the onset of illness, disease, or injury, and represents a practical claim control method available to insurers who recognize its value.

In the context of claim control, it is helpful to view rehabilitation as both a process and a goal in which the insurer has, or else partially has delegated

Table 5-1. Number of Occupational Injuries and Illnesses, and Lost Workdays, Private Sector, by Industry Division, in the United States, 1980 (U.S. Department of Labor, 1981)

Industry	Total Cases* (000)	Total Lost Workdays (000)	Average Lost Workdays
Injuries and Illness			
Private Sector**	5,606	41,817	16
Agriculture, Forestry, Fishing	84	579	14
Mining	115	1,683	25
Construction	588	4,386	18
Manufacturing	2,354	16,746	16
Transportation & Public Utility	453	5,045	19
Wholesale Trade	407	2,893	15
Retail Trade	804	5,039	15
Finance, Insurance, Real Estate	90	559	14
Services	712	4,889	15
Injuries			
Private Sector**	5,476	40,895	16
Agriculture, Forestry, Fishing	79	569	15
Mining	114	1,675	25
Construction	580	4,352	18
Manufacturing	2,278	16,222	16
Transportation & Public Utility	445	4,987	19
Wholesale Trade	402	2,838	15
Retail Trade	797	4,997	15
Finance, Insurance, Real Estate	88	533	14
Services	693	4,722	15
Illnesses			
Private Sector**	130	992	19
Agriculture, Forestry, Fishing	4	10	10
Mining	2	9	9
Construction	8	34	11
Manufacturing	76	524	18
Transportation & Public Utility	8	58	15
Wholesale Trade	5	55	18
Retail Trade	7	42	21
Finance, Insurance, Real Estate	2	25	25
Service	19	167	28

* Includes fatalities.   ** Excludes farms with fewer than 11 employees.

to another party, an active disability management role in appropriate cases. This process involves purposeful assessment and active intervention in an insured person's disability situation with the goal of ameliorating the disabling condition in order to restore the capacity to be a productive member of society. Thus, for an active rehabilitation service management role to be effective, essential elements of disability management include early recognition of the need for medical rehabilitation, proper coordination of medical providers and facilities, and monitoring progress throughout the service delivery process. Therefore, when the process of disability management accomplishes its goal, it becomes an instrument that can reduce expenses and adverse social effects of disability by returning disabled individuals to work as soon as possible.

Use of rehabilitation services meets a variety of needs within an insurance context of fundamental claims handling. Aside from the more global social, economic, and humanitarian benefits, the rewards of rehabilitation to the insurance company, employer, and disabled person require examination.

Insurance Company   According to Sabini (1983), rehabilitation benefits insurance companies in three broad ways: reduction of liability, competitive advantage, and corporate social responsibility. When a disabled individual returns to work on either a part-time or full-time basis, or when effective disability management identifies, treats, and checks the progression of a potentially protracted disease or injury early on, the insurance company's financial liability is usually reduced quite significantly. These types of outcomes not only increase the profit gains by eliminating or reducing the need for actual benefit payments, but also assist in stabilizing reserve funds. Second, a sound rehabilitation program enhances an insurance company's competitive position within the industry. It does this in a number of ways through (a) minimizing disability duration and/or medical costs, which in turn reduce loss ratios and therefore assist in keeping premium rates stable; (b) reflecting a progressive and innovative benefit administration that addresses the larger societal problem of ameliorating the effects of disability; and (c) enhancing marketing competitiveness (Sabini, 1983). Finally, an effective rehabilitation program benefits insurance companies by meeting, in part, their implicit corporate responsibility to contribute to society by assuming an active role in returning disabled individuals to satisfying occupational endeavors.

Employer/Policyholder   Provision of rehabilitation programs benefits employers in four ways according to Sabini (1983): (1) insurance premium rate maintenance or stabilization, (2) enhancement of employers' benefit packages, (3) human resource utilization, and (4) corporate social responsibility. In an era of spiraling inflation, the cost of employee benefit programs is of increasing concern. An effectively managed rehabilitation program reduces disability benefits and/or promotes the most cost-effective disability management. These, in turn, serve as significant contributors toward maintaining or reducing insurance premiums paid by employers for their employees. Second, demographic characteristics and current trends in the work force are forcing employers to provide comprehensive benefit packages that reflect progressive features and innovative benefit administration in order to attract and retain employees (Sabini, 1983). A sound rehabilitation program adds a new and extremely important component to an employer's benefit package. Third, in many instances an effective rehabilitation program allows an employer to continue to utilize an injured employee's previously acquired skills in either the pre-injury occupation or in one that uses transferable expertise. Therefore, by retaining an injured employee, the employer avoids additional costs inherent in hiring, orienting, and training new employees. Fourth, as in the case with insurance companies, employers have a social responsibility to assist disabled persons in employment opportunities in an attempt to counterbalance the adverse social, economic, and human suffering consistent with disability.

Disabled Person   Four areas of benefit to disabled individuals are provided by effective rehabilitation program management: (1) income, (2) societal expectations, (3) social and family relationships, and (4) psychological factors (Sabini, 1983). First, an effectively managed rehabilitation program can facilitate not only the reduction of medical costs involved in treating a disability, but also a return to gainful employment with the potential for earnings approximating or exceeding the predisability income when performed in a timely manner. Second, as witnessed in previous chapters, society places a high value on productive employment as part of an individual's complete life. Effective rehabilitation can counteract feelings of demoralization that often accompany disability by assisting the person to regain a sense of self-worth in terms of his or her capacity to meet societal expectations. Third, the employment environment is an arena in which social relationships are formed, social skills are developed or enhanced, and social status is confirmed. These aspects of work are integral to a normal family life-style especially with respect to the family's "self-concept" and status within the community. The deleterious effects of disability can be lessened or eliminated by restoring an individual's capacity to return to productive employment as soon as is medically feasible. Finally, effective disability management enhances the restoration of the disabled person's dignity and self-worth as an individual through the timely provision of services designed to reduce the disability and increase employability.

Medical and Vocational Rehabilitation

Although medical and vocational rehabilitation services may be provided concurrently or consecutively, they tend to be separated by the professional disciplines involved and the institutions or facilities utilized. There are also differences in the extent to which disabled persons are able to make their own decisions and participate in the planning of their medical and vocational rehabilitation services. For example, in many states the separation of vocational rehabilitation from medical rehabilitation is made complete by the provision of workers' compensation, wherein medical care is the legal responsibility of the employer and vocational rehabilitation is not.

According to Gulledge (1963), medical rehabilitation frequently requires the skills and services of many specialized medical and paramedical personnel such as physicians, physical therapists, occupational therapists, nurses, social workers, prosthetists and orthotists, and clinical psychologists. By the very nature of the medical situation, the physician controls and directs all medical rehabilitation services that are focused on the physical improvement of the patient. Vocational rehabilitation, on the other hand, typically is viewed as job oriented rather than medicine oriented, and as such, frequently is not incorporated into the medical treatment program in a timely manner (Gulledge, 1963). By expanding the focus of vocational rehabilitation to include the medical services aspect, however, the presence of a vocational rehabilitation specialist during the initial medical treatment and planning phase enhances the cost containment of services, as well as providing reassurance to the disabled person that vocational planning is congruent with the medical treatment.

Finally, rehabilitation costs can be controlled to a large degree, and successful outcomes can be enhanced when disability case management attends to the following conditions recommended by Cheit (1961, p. 288):

1. A rehabilitation orientation on the part of physicians who treat disabled persons.
2. Rehabilitation facilities and personnel in the right places at the right times.
3. Maintenance payments for disabled persons, should vocational rehabilitation be indicated.
4. Employment opportunities for disabled persons, and broadened subsequent injury provisions to help make placement possible.
5. The refashioning of compensation laws and administration so they will operate to encourage the disabled person's will to recover rather than providing sources of disincentives to employment.
6. Prompt identification of the cases needing rehabilitation services.

Case Selection by the Insurer

In serious and traumatic injury cases, the process of medical recovery and rehabilitation begins with immediate medical intervention. In cases of disease, the process generally begins when the disabled person is no longer able to adequately perform his or her job duties and/or maintain independent activities of daily living. The process of disability management typically is initiated, and ultimately controlled, by the referral source; that is, the insurance company, the self-insured employer, or any other agency responsible for providing insurance benefits to disabled individuals. The reason for this is that the claims representative generally is the first person who becomes aware of a pending situation wherein a policyholder and/or employee of a policyholder is in need of service. The claimsperson has the additional tasks of referring the disabled claimant for appropriate services, monitoring the activities provided in each case by various professionals who have direct service contact with the insured or claimant, monitoring and projecting service costs in each case, and recommending/authorizing payment for appropriate services best suited to the needs of the disabled client and the insurer. Thus, case selection by the insurance claims representative is the crucial first step in any subsequent disability management activity.

The decision to refer a case for rehabilitation services involves a number of considerations by the claims representative because of the variety of factors that may influence a disabled person's recovery process and return to work. For example, factors such as the extent of the injury or disease and recovery prognosis, the family situation, the individual's occupation, his or her age, the employer, geographic determinants, and the extent and limitations of the insurance policy coverage contribute to formulating the decision of whether or not to refer a case for rehabilitation. Because of the importance these factors have in assisting the insurance claims representative to make a determination to refer a case, a number of key questions are presented in each category. The purpose of these questions is twofold: (1) they are designed to address critical changes in the disabled person's life resulting from the injury or disease that should be investigated and considered by the claimsperson when determining the appropriateness of referral; and (2) they provide the rehabilitation professional who receives the referral an opportunity to gain insight into the decision-making criteria of the claims representative.

Injury/Disease and Recovery Processes   The primary consideration in each case is the impact that the injury or disease has on the disabled person's ability to function. Additionally, questions intended to assist in the selection of appropriate referrals for subsequent rehabilitation services should consider what, if any, resulting limitations caused by the injury or disease disrupt or otherwise restrict the disabled person's vocational, social, recreational, and personal activities. Among the most important questions to be asked by the insurance claimsperson when assessing the individual's injury or disease and the recovery processes are:

1. What is the treating physician's diagnosis and the prognosis for recovery?
2. What is the treatment plan?

3. What is the disabled person's age?
4. What was the physical condition of the disabled person prior to the injury or disease process?
5. How long has the insured person been disabled?
6. Are multiple injuries or medical complications involved?
7. Will there be significant permanent, functional limitations in daily activities resulting from the present condition (e.g., dressing, eating, driving, cooking)?
8. Is there a possibility that a complicated or extended period of treatment or therapy will be necessary?
9. Will the fitting and training in the use of prosthetic equipment be required?
10. What additional treatment or therapy is foreseen in this case?

Family Situation   The primary consideration in the area of the disabled person's family situation is the impact the injury or disease will have on them, as well as the potential psychological and social implications for both the family and the disabled claimant. Among the most important questions that the claims representative must have answered are:

1. Is the insured person married?
2. What is the family's financial situation?
3. Are there additional or alternative sources of income available to the family during the period of treatment and convalescence?
4. How many dependents are being supported by the disabled claimant?
5. What is the disabled person's reaction to the injury; for example, depression, optimism, devastation, no reaction?
6. What is the reaction of the spouse and/or children?
7. Will the home require modification for the disabled person to return safely and comfortably during convalescence?
8. Will structural modifications to the insured person's home be required for other aspects of the disabled person's activities after the convalescent period?

Employer, Education, Geographic Factors   The primary concern in all cases is that the disabled client return to gainful employment as soon as is medically feasible. If the person is threatened with loss of employment due to the nature of the injury or disease and requires job site modification, referral for evaluation and job analysis should be considered by the insurance claimsperson. If modifications must be made at the job site or to the insured's work schedule and/or job duties, the employer should be encouraged by the claims representative to allow and assist in making the necessary accommodations. Among the questions that need to be asked in the area of employer, education, and geographic factors are:

1. Is the disabled person employed? If not, how long has the person been unemployed, and why?
2. How long has the insured person been affiliated with the present employer?
3. Does it appear that there is good rapport between the employer and the disabled person?
4. Is the employer willing to retain the injured worker in the current employment situation, or in another job within the employment environment?
5. Does it appear that the injury will interfere significantly with the disabled person's ability to perform his or her job duties?
6. Are the job duties and responsibilities of the disabled worker easily modified?
7. Are the skills required for the pre-injury job transferable to other jobs within the work setting?
8. What is the disabled individual's educational background?
9. Does the person have experience and training in one or more different occupations? Are these acquired skills potentially transferable to other jobs within the employment setting?
10. Is the disabled person a union member? If so, what benefits have been accrued through the present employment situation (e.g., retirement, sick leave, disability or other insurance, annuities)?
11. What is the present employment position of the employer in terms of market for the company's products (i.e., hiring freeze, anticipated increase, anticipated decline)?
12. Are similar jobs available in the immediate geographic area?

Because vocational rehabilitation is the specific goal of a significant number of insurance rehabilitation programs, an accurate job description, obtained through a detailed job analysis, is extremely important and worthy of special mention. For that reason, Chapter 6 contains a more thorough discussion of the essential characteristics of job analysis than presented at this time. Suffice it to say for the moment, however, a detailed description of the disabled person's regular job, analyzed in the context of his or her employment situation, is one of the most basic instruments in the evaluation of rehabilitation potential. The most obvious reason for reviewing a detailed decription of the duties, tasks, and requirements of the person's regular job is to ascertain his or her potential to return to that job or to a modified version of it if necessary. On the other hand, even when there is no possibility of returning to the regular occupation, the job description provides an important source of information for identifying transferable job skills and knowledge to other work within the disabled person's range of ability.

Insurance Coverage and Liability Issues Different insurers will place varying degrees of emphasis on the criteria that must be present, or absent, to constitute a rehabilitation case with potential for successful completion or outcome. Among those criteria, differential emphasis also may be placed on the insurer's financial liability for a claim as a criterion for referral. Within this area, there are several imperatives in the decision-making process about the appropriateness of rehabilitation referrals. First, the insured must be considered in the context of his or her total life circumstances. Second, it is important not to lose sight of either common sense or flexibility when considering rehabilitation as a possible enhancer to reducing the claim and increasing the claimant's well-being. Among the questions the insurance claims representative should consider with reference to coverage and liability issues are:

1. What is the insurer's potential exposure in the case?
2. In first party cases, would involvement by a rehabilitation professional reduce the exposure?
3. Could the involvement by a rehabilitation professional reduce the value of a personal injury liability claim and decrease the insurance company's exposure and/or possible award in excess of the policy limits?
4. Could information about potential wage loss or future projected medical expenses assist in the development of an individually designed annuity settlement?
5. Is this a second-injury case? If so, what is the extent of liability to the current insurer for the second injury?

Insurance companies place varied emphasis on the analysis of these questions depending on a company's experience with rehabilitation services, claim experience in geographic regions, and experience with specific policyholders. Two elements of the claim's situation are always paramount in the decision of whether or not to refer a case; monetary expense and projected length of disability.

Initial Evaluation

Once these questions have been addressed satisfactorily, the insurance claims representative is in a position to decide whether or not to refer a case for rehabilitation services. Assuming that these services are justified and a referral is made, the next major step in the rehabilitation process is for the rehabilitation professional to conduct an initial evaluation/interview. According to Silberman and his associates (1980), the initial interview sets the pace for the entire rehabilitation process that follows. It is the responsibility of the rehabilitation professional to develop rapport with the disabled client and gain that person's confidence so that both may work together toward identification and fulfillment of mutually agreed upon goals. Toward that end, rehabilitation is a team effort involving the rehabilitation professional, the treating physician, the disabled client, the client's employer, the insurance representative, and all other interested parties in the rehabilitation process.

The purpose of the initial evaluation is to assess all pertinent aspects of the disabled person's life situation in order to begin appropriate vocational planning (Silberman et al., 1980). Among the principal questions that must be answered are:

1. Is the disabled person's medical condition stable? If not, when will maximum medical improvement be achieved, and what is the proposed treatment program to attain such a level?
2. Is the treating physician willing to release the disabled person to return to work, with or without restrictions on the activities to be performed?
3. Will the disability prevent the person from returning to the pre-injury job? If so, could the job be altered to accommodate the restrictions imposed by the disability?
4. Is the employer willing to reinstate the disabled person in the pre-accident job, a modified version of the job, or in a different job? If not, is the situation negotiable?

Ideally, the initial evaluation should result in a target date for the disabled person's return to work, specifying the positive and negative factors that affect this goal (Sabini, 1983). In order to better understand the components of the initial interview, three primary areas are identified: (1) individual status; (2) medical status; and (3) environmental status.

Individual Status

Generally, the disabled client is visited by the vocational rehabilitation professional wherever appropriate for the purpose of evaluating his or her present status; that is, the physical condition, social and psychological reactions to the disability, vocational and educational background information, and financial situation. This information may be gathered in the hospital, at the client's home, or in the office of either the treating physician, client's attorney, insurance carrier, or rehabilitation professional. An inportant "rule of thumb" to follow, however, is to assess the disabled person's strengths and weaknesses *as soon as possible.* In this way, necessary services may be secured in order to develop an appropriate plan to return the disabled person to work as expeditiously as possible.

Physical Condition Through the use of effective interviewing and observational techniques, the vocational rehabilitation professional can evaluate the current status and progress of the disabling condition. This will include the handicapped person's description and understanding of the progress as described by the treating medical staff as made available through verbal and written communications. Attention must be given to the medications and other therapies prescribed, as well as past medical conditions and history, in order to present a clear picture of the individual's current physical condition.

   Social and Psychological Status   The rehabilitation professional should assess the individual's adjustment to the conditions imposed by the disabling condition. This includes an evaluation of the handicapped person's reaction to the disability and whether or not there is demonstrated progress toward acceptance of limitations and/or changes precipitated by the condition. Similarly, it is important for the rehabilitation professional to evaluate the support systems available to the disabled client. These include the family structure and their contributions/impediments to the insured's acceptance of the disabling condition and subsequent rehabilitation efforts.

   Vocational and Educational Backgrounds   The disabled person's vocational skills must be examined to determine the effect, if any, of the medical condition on the performance of the pre-accident job. This involves a thorough and detailed analysis of the work activities of the client's job which will be discussed in the following chapter. Educational background information and other occupational experiences should be explored in order to identify potential transferability of work skills if the need arises to consider alternative forms of gainful employment.

   Financial Status   A sensitive and thorough evaluation of the disabled person's current situation is not complete without obtaining information about the client's financial resources and the impact the medical condition potentially has on them. If any undue hardships become evident that may be delaying or otherwise are impeding progress of the rehabilitation program, the vocational rehabilitation professional should be able to identify these issues, as well as propose methods to reduce or eliminate their influence. In some situations, however, the insured client's income, while under the care and treatment of rehabilitation professionals, may equal or exceed the pre-accident net income. For obvious reasons, this can represent economic disincentives to return to work, and thus threaten successful rehabilitation efforts. (A more detailed description of employment disincentives is presented in Chapter 7.)

Medical Status

   The next phase of the initial evaluation is to discuss the current medical situation of the disabled client with the medical treatment team, as well as ascertain their proposed plans of treatment for ameliorating the existing condition. Ideally, the vocational rehabilitation professional will be part of this team effort so that planning of the total rehabilitation care process will effectively integrate and work toward a viable vocational outcome. Thus, as part of the treatment team, the rehabilitation professional not only is kept fully appraised of the medical situation so that proper and timely vocationally oriented services can begin as soon as are medically feasible, but more importantly, the mere presence of such a professional allows for maximum continuity of services by reducing the perception among medical personnel and the patient alike of being an "outsider." Thus, when assessing the medical status of a disabled person, the rehabilitation professional must attend to three factors: (1) the client's physical condition; (2) the treatment plan; and (3) treating facilities.

Physical Condition   Typically, a meeting between the rehabilitation specialist and the treating physician(s) is held so that an assessment of the medical status of the disabled person can be obtained. Not only does this meeting provide an opportunity for the vocational professional to become familiar with the treated person's medical history, but also the current prescriptions for care and treatment of the present condition. It goes without saying, that familiarity with the disabled individual's medical condition requires the rehabilitation professional to be knowledgeable of medical terminology, medications and their potential side-effects, and the vocational implications of a variety of disabling conditions.

Treatment Plan   An equally important aspect of assessing the medical status of any disabled client is comprehension of the medical treatment plan and its integration into the vocational process. The medical treatment plan (as well as the vocational plan) should include a diagnosis, prognosis, and time parameters in which various stages of recovery (and activities) can be expected to occur. At this point, the vocational rehabilitation professional may provide information about the work characteristics of the pre-accident employment, based on the job analysis, which can be used to assist in the development of a viable plan for returning the disabled person to gainful employment.

Facilities   If the disabled client is currently in a hospital or rehabilitation facility, or is expected to enter a facility for further evaluation, treatment, therapy, and/or training, either as an inpatient or as an outpatient, the vocational rehabilitation professional may be requested/expected to evaluate the appropriateness of the facility in terms of its services. While it is imperative that the facility chosen be the most appropriate and effective for the type of service recommended, the vocational rehabilitation professional must be aware of the sensitivity demanded in this type of assessment. For instance, in those situations wherein the choice of facilities has been established *a priori* by someone other than the vocational professional, such an assessment might be considered not only impractical and unnecessary, but may be considered to be beyond the purview and expertise of the professional, especially when a non- vocational oriented facility is in question. On the other hand, in those circumstances where the vocational rehabilitation professional has the authority to recommend or select appropriate facilities commensurate with the vocational objectives, such a request is not unreasonable and should be the responsibility of the vocational professional.

Environmental Status

This phase of the initial evaluation, despite being listed third, may occur either before or after the medical status phase. In many cases, however, when the rehabilitation professional is not involved as part of the medical treatment team, assessment of the environmental status may be the first (or sometimes the only) service requested by the referral source. Typically, evaluation of the disabled person's environmental status covers two areas; work activities performed prior to the accident, and activities of daily living or nonwork activities such as hobbies and interests.

Work Activities   The evaluation of work activities generally takes place at the site of employment. Ideally, written job descriptions should be available from the employer and can serve as a supplement to a formal job analysis. As mentioned previously, the specific activities of a job analysis and information contained in such reports will be discussed in Chapter 6. Suffice it to say at this point, however, the job analysis and the job description provided by the employer should contain information such as a description of the tasks performed on the job, education and/or training required, physical demands of the work activity, environmental conditions present in the work site, and types of equipment and other tools used to perform the job tasks. It cannot be stressed enough that the more specific and detailed the job analysis is, the more useful it will be in assisting the treating physician to comment on the disabled client's current and potential ability to return to the work described, and/or what modifications might be required to the job in order to accommodate any medical restrictions imposed on the disabled person.

In addition to the job analysis, by visiting the work site of the disabled individual, the vocational rehabilitation professional can develop a "feel" for the employer's willingness to reinstate the client either in the previous job, a modified version of the job, or a different job which would capitalize on acquired and transferable skills requiring little, if any, on-the-job training. Similarly, during the assessment of the work activities of the disabled client, the vocational rehabilitation professional may have the opportunity to obtain information about the person's work habits and peer interactions from among coworkers at the job site.

Activities of Daily Living   It is important to evaluate non-occupational activities to discover potential barriers and/or enhancers that potentially will affect successful rehabilitation outcomes. For example, if the disability affects ambulation, will the physical construction of his or her home require modification? Similarly, what are the avocational and recreational activities of the client, and how will the disability affect continued involvement in them? Furthermore, as mentioned earlier, how will the disability affect the client's family and friends in terms of structural modifications to the living environment, let alone interpersonal relationships?

Initial Evaluation: A Procedural Model

While it is important to understand the content of an effective and thorough initial evaluation, it is equally important to be aware of the sequential steps required to perform the process, communicate the findings, and make recommendations for subsequent action to be taken. What follows is a procedural model to achieve those results, based on recommendations of the California Association of Rehabilitation Professionals' *Guidelines for Standards of Professional Behavior* (1982), Deneen and Hessellund (1981), and Silberman and his associates (1980).

A. Preclient Contact
    1. Review the medical file.
    2. Obtain the attorney's permission to contact the disabled client (if the client is represented by legal counsel).
B. Client Contact
    1. Arrange for an appointment by telephone or letter to interview the disabled client.
    2. Explain vocational rehabilitation to the client.
        a. Clarify the role of the vocational rehabilitation professional to the client.
        b. Clarify the role of the client to the client (e.g., participatory requirements).
        c. Explain the vocational rehabilitation process.
        d. Identify and explain the "return-to-work" sequential hierarchy in the vocational rehabilitation process.
    3. Collect data base.
        a. Social history.
        b. Family/living situation.

    c. Effect(s) of the accident on the client's lifestyle.

    d. Client's perceptions of the limitations imposed by this and/or previous medical problems.

       (1) Significant prior medical factors.

       (2) Present medical status from observation and discussion with the client.

    e. Financial information.

4. Vocational/Educational background information.

    a. Education/Transferable skill resources.

       (1) Formal schooling: Specific classes taken, subjects liked and disliked.

       (2) Occupational/Technical training: Formal and informal.

       (3) Military training and type of discharge.

    b. Employment history.

       (1) Present job as perceived by the client: Duties, physical demands, relationship with the employer and coworkers (job satisfaction), dates of employment, job title, tools and equipment used, salary/wages, benefits.

       (2) Past jobs.

       (3) Job analysis of the present job (for comparison to the client's description and for physician review).

    c. Vocational interests, hobbies, avocational activities.

5. Assessment of present readiness for vocational rehabilitation.

    a. Physical considerations.

    b. Evaluation of motivation.

6. Conclusions.

    a. Evaluation of medical, environmental, and individual status.

    b. Evaluation of the client's present feasibility to enter into vocational rehabilitation.

7. Recommendations.

    a. Statement of short-term plans to be executed next in the rehabilitation process.

    b. Time frames for initiation and completion of subsequent steps.

Planning and Developing Rehabilitation Goals

Upon completion of the initial evaluation, the rehabilitation professional proceeds with development of a rehabilitation plan based on the needs of the disabled person. A variety of formats may be used to present the plan to all interested parties involved in the rehabilitation process, although most frequently such a plan consists of a narrative outline which may be either a section of or an attachment to the initial evaluation report. The plan generally contains specific information about short-term and long-range rehabilitation goals, proposed objectives required for goal attainment, projected time parameters for initiation and completion of each objective, an approximated overall time frame for achieving the identified goals, and estimated costs involved. In addition to these areas, it is extremely helpful for the sake of continuity and clarification to identify the persons assigned to provide the services indicated, as well as their responsibilities in those areas. Moreover, the same care should be taken to identify the responsibilities of the disabled client within each of the objectives. By taking the time to provide such detail in the rehabilitation plan, not only can the plan itself be evaluated (see Chapter 10 on Program Evaluation), but the likelihood for ambiguity to exist in role responsibilities is reduced.

Before proceeding further, it is important to note that the development of a rehabilitation plan at this stage in the process, by necessity, consists primarily of proposed medical care services for ameliorating the disabling condition assuming that the client is still in the process of convalescence. In terms of the vocational aspects of the rehabilitation process, the tentativeness of the identified goals and objectives cannot be overstated at this point since their initiation are contingent on the stability of the medical condition as determined by the treating physician(s). With this perspective in mind, the remainder of the chapter focuses on the role of medical case management within medical care and vocational service activities.

Medical Care Coordination

A significant portion of serious or catastrophic injury and disease cases require planned intervention by the rehabilitation professional to ensure that all aspects of the medical rehabilitation process are organized properly. This segment of the rehabilitation process must be performed by a person with appropriate medical training and experience, such as received in nursing, physical therapy, or occupational therapy. Medical care coordination has three goals in the rehabilitation process: (1) to minimize the recovery period without jeopardizing medical stability; (2) to assure that proper medical treatment and other restorative services are received in a timely and sequential manner; and (3) to assist in the containment of medical costs. In order to accomplish these goals, the medical care coordinator should attend to three objectives; establishment of treatment goals, medical facility discharge planning, and monitoring the recovery process.

Establishing Treatment Goals   The first phase of medical care coordination requires development and clarification of a medical care plan in consultation with the treating physician(s). This step frequently is performed and completed by the rehabilitation professional during the initial evaluation process when the physician's treatment plan is being developed. The medical care plan contains information regarding the disabled client's diagnosis, prognosis, and medical goals. Furthermore, it should specify the restorative methodologies that will be used in treating the disabling condition, as well as their duration and costs. Moreover, *all* medical precautions, complications, and contraindications need to be reported for future reference by involved professionals in the rehabilitation process. Finally, the importance of providing accurate, clear, and thorough information about the nature, extent, and anticipated duration and cost of the disabling condition is twofold. First, it provides information that can be evaluated in terms of appropriateness, and second, it assists the insurance claims representative to more accurately estimate case reserves to be set aside for needed services.

   Discharge Planning   In many cases hospital discharge planning is a critical element in the medical care coordination phase of the rehabilitation process. Its two primary goals are (1) to minimize hospital/facility confinement and (2) to promote a smooth, safe, and well-planned transition from the medical care facility to the community. Thus, effective discharge planning often involves making arrangements with hospital personnel to move the disabled person from an acute care center to a more specialized facility, residential care facility, or in most cases, the client's home. In some instances, the arrangement of special services (e.g., attendent nursing, physical therapy, etc.) in the home will enhance an early discharge from the hospital. More importantly, early discharge contributes to cost savings of insurance claims dollars and enhances the medical recovery process by returning the disabled client to familiar surroundings. It is for these reasons, however, that the rehabilitation professional *must* possess sufficient medical knowledge to effectively gauge the medical progress of the client, the effects of prescribed treatment away from the close scrutiny of the medical facility, and the capability of the "new" environment to attend to the convalescent needs of the disabled person.

   Monitoring the Recovery Process   Ensuring that the medical care plan proceeds expeditiously is perhaps the most important rule for the rehabilitation professional in the medical care coordination process. Not only must the professional actively monitor all of the activities in which the disabled person is engaged away from the medical care facility, but these activities must be evaluated both individually and collectively in terms of their impact on medical recovery, physical (or mental) restoration, and personal and occupational adjustment. Indeed, it goes without saying that reporting the progress of recovery to all concerned parties is an ongoing activity throughout the duration of the rehabilitation process. In this way, the rehabilitation professional provides two services. First, he or she provides the disabled client with reassurance that rehabilitation support systems continue to be present. Second, effective and systematically performed case monitoring provides an opportunity for the rehabilitation professional to assess changes in the disabled client's progress and recommend appropriate measures to enhance continued progress toward recovery.

Vocational Service Coordination

Throughout the rehabilitation process it is important and crucial to involve the disabled client in as many decision-making activities as possible. Nowhere is this more necessary than when planning and developing vocational rehabilitation goals. For example, in subsequent chapters, issues such as client consent, confidentiality, and reporting the progress of client activities will be discussed. Moreover, the need for input from the client provides the rehabilitation professional with information about the accuracy of statements, descriptions, and conclusions made by others about the client, and contributes to the client's motivation to recover as completely as possible through the active participation in the rehabilitation process. Simply stated, the disabled client has the right to choose his or her vocational goal and the rehabilitation professional serves as a person whose expertise in a given field assists the client to realistically appraise the goal and facilitate acquisition of it. Therefore, realistic planning and development of vocational rehabilitation goals begin only after the professional has collected all of the necessary client information acquired through the initial evaluation, medical data, and other sources which may include job analysis, vocational and/or psychological assessments, and labor market surveys. Once the disabled client and the rehabilitation professional have reviewed these sources of information and agreed on a suitable vocational goal and objectives, it will be necessary for review, comments, and agreement of the vocational plan to be obtained from the other concerned parties in the rehabilitation process (e.g., the insurance claims representative, the disabled client's attorney, and the attending physician). Thus, coordination of vocational services involves the selection of services and facilities, monitoring the vocational progress of the disabled client, and follow-up and closure.

Selecting Services and Facilities According to the "return to work" hierarchy indicated in Chapter 4, the vocational rehabilitation professional should first attempt to place the disabled client back in the pre-accident job with the same employer. If this placement proves unfeasible, based on the degree of disability, resistance of the employer, or any number of other factors, the rehabilitation professional must attempt other alternatives. If, on the other hand, a complete and thorough evaluation of the disabled client's abilities is not within the capability of the rehabilitation professional, appropriate selection of services and facilities that will best provide this information is necessary. For example, if the client's vocational potential in other occupations requires assessment, referral to an evaluation center may be appropriate. The responsibility of the rehabilitation specialist, in this situation, would consist of any number of the following activities: (a) learning what assessment instruments and/or techniques are used by the facility and its staff; (b) inquiring about the professional qualifications of the staff who are responsible for performing the evaluations; (c) inquiring about the credibility/accreditation of the facility to provide the services it advertises; (d) asking about the timeliness of the services requested and reporting procedures; (e) investigating the presence of potential architectural and/or transportational barriers to be encountered by the disabled client; (f) observing and inquiring about environmental and/or safety hazards within or outside of the facility's premises; (g) noting the starting date, hours of operation, and length of the services requested; (h) asking if the disabled client needs to supply his or her own tools and equipment; (i) making certain that the facility and its staff are trained and/or equipped to deal with the client's specific type of disability; and (j) ascertaining the costs of the services to be rendered.

Monitoring Vocational Progress   Making certain that the disabled client is progressing toward attainment of the identified vocational goal is paramount in the vocational service coordination process. The vocational rehabilitation professional periodically must monitor the client's activities in order to determine the viability of the vocational goal once the client has returned to work, is involved in a vocational evaluation program, an on-the-job training situation, or is enrolled in a formal training program. The purpose of such monitoring activity resembles what was earlier mentioned under the heading of Monitoring the Recovery Process. Namely, the rehabilitation professional is responsible for determining if the disabled client has the capability of performing the vocational goal specified in the rehabilitation plan in view of the nature of the medical condition, in terms of aptitudes, abilities, and interests, and in relation to social and personal adjustment. In the event that a real or simulated work situation provides information that is contradictory to earlier assessment results, the vocational professional must convey this information to others involved in the client's rehabilitation process so that corrective measures or alternative goals can be developed.

Follow-up and Closure   Assuming all activities discussed thus far have been completed satisfactorily, such that the disabled client has returned to gainful employment, a period of follow-up after job placement is appropriate. Follow-up monitoring is a supportive measure designed to assist the disabled client sustain his or her morale while adjusting to and maintaining employment. Frequency of contact between the disabled client and the vocational rehabilitation professional should be reduced gradually during this period in order to foster more self-reliance by the client on his or her own resources. Generally speaking, a follow-up period of not longer than 60 days is recommended once the disabled person has returned to gainful employment. During that period, but depending on the specific needs of the disabled person, contact will initially be maintained on a one-time-a-week basis for several weeks, gradually being reduced to once a month, until the end of the 60-day period. Thus, when adequate adjustment is made by the client, the case is closed.

Summary

Disability management is a method within the rehabilitation process designed to move a newly disabled client from the hospital bed back to gainful employment. It accomplishes this goal by integrating both the medical and vocational aspects of rehabilitation service delivery systems with the objectives of reducing the length of hospitalization, maximizing client involvement in the rehabilitation process, and thereby minimizing the period of time away from work resulting from an injury or disease. When disability management is performed effectively by qualified rehabilitation professionals, the outcome not only is beneficial to the disabled client, but is cost-saving to the insurance carrier responsible for claim benefits. For these reasons, as well as others, effective disability management involves a team effort consisting of highly trained professionals in the field of insurance claims handling, medicine, and vocational rehabilitation. Most importantly, however, disability management must involve the disabled client, as well as other significant persons concerned with the client's welfare, to effectively plan and implement vocational rehabilitation goals. The next chapter will focus on the process of vocational evaluation and its contribution in the rehabilitation process of returning insured clients to work.

6 Assessing Vocational Potential

The successful culmination of any project must recognize the important contributions made by sound planning and accurate appraisal. In the absence or the unsystematic application of these elements, successful goal attainment may be a result of little more than chance. Within the rehabilitation process, medical diagnosis and treatment represent the initial appraisal and planning phases leading toward restoration of a disabled person's physical, mental, and ultimately vocational capabilities. Indeed, the previous chapter revealed the importance of disability case management for identifying and recommending appropriate services designed to assess vocational potential, thereby enhancing the expeditious return to work of disabled individuals.

The purpose of this chapter is to acquaint the reader with the most frequently offered services in private rehabilitation practice that are designed to assess vocational potential. To accomplish this goal, the chapter is divided into three major sections: (1) job analysis; (2) job modification and restructuring; and (3) vocational evaluation. The objectives of the chapter are to familiarize the reader with the purpose of each technique, identify their characteristic components, and discuss their interrelatedness for providing a firm foundation for subsequent vocational recommendations.

Job Analysis

Textbooks devoted to vocational rehabilitation topics typically include a discussion of job analysis within chapters or sections concerned with job development and placement (e.g., Bitter, 1979; Roessler & Rubin, 1982). This is unfortunate because it may give readers the impression that job analysis, although an important component for successful job placement, neither occurs early in the rehabilitation process, nor is a form of evaluation designed to assess work requirements in relation to a disabled person's residual capacities. On the contrary, job analysis information gathered early provides rehabilitation

113

professionals with a more accurate understanding of work limitations imposed by a disabling condition in relation to effective vocational goal planning, potential job modifications that may be required for the person to return to work, and/or identification of alternative pathways to employment through more extensive evaluations. It is for these reasons that the following discussion of job analysis methodology is more appropriately part of vocational assessment than a function of job placement activities.

Perhaps the most frequently cited information about job analysis is the 1972 *Handbook For Analyzing Jobs* by the Manpower Administration of the United States Department of Labor. Although this publication is no longer available from the Government Printing Office, its content has been reprinted for distribution by the Materials Development Center of the Stout Vocational Rehabilitation Institute in Menomonie, Wisconsin. Furthermore, an equally useful companion available since 1982 from the Materials Development Center is *A Guide To Job Analysis: A "How-To" Publication For Occupational Analysts*. Together these references provide practitioners with the most comprehensive information about preparing for, conducting, and reporting job analysis services. For these reasons, this section relies heavily on those sources because of their relevancy for rehabilitation professionals working in an insurance context.

What Is Job Analysis?

According to the United States Department of Labor (1972, p. 1):

> Job information is the basic data used by industry, government and private agencies, and employee organizations for many manpower programs. The nature of the required job information varies in type and approach according to program needs. Regardless of the ultimate use for which it is intended, however, the data must be accurate; inclusive, omitting nothing pertinent to the program; and presented in a form suitable for study and use. The techniques for obtaining and presenting this information are known as "job analysis."

Because this statement indicates that job information data can be used for a variety of purposes, it is important to briefly identify some of those areas. For example, among the possible uses for job analysis information are personnel selection and training, vocational choice, compensation cases, job design, job enlargement, jurisdictional disputes, job satisfaction or dissatisfaction studies, promotion considerations, job transfers, and many more (McCormick, 1979). Moreover, the results of a survey about jobs conducted by the Bureau of Business Research at California State College in Long Beach revealed that approximately 76% of private firms responding to the questionnaire had some use for job analysis programming (Jones & DeCloths,

1969). These uses are identified in Table 6–1. For the purposes of this section, however, job analysis discussion will be focused on identifying job specifications, matching the abilities of disabled persons with appropriate job requirements, and restructuring existing jobs to accommodate disabled workers' limitations imposed by an injury or disease.

Table 6–1. Frequency with Which Organizations with Job Analysis Programs Report Various Uses of Job Analysis Results (Jones & DeCloths, 1969)

Job Analysis Uses	# Firms
Job Evaluation	193
Setting wage and salary levels	180
Appraising personnel	103
Establishing incentives	25
Determining profit sharing	8
Other	3
Recruiting and Placing	188
Making job specifications	149
Promoting, transferring, and rotating	139
Constructing tests	32
Vocational counseling	51
Matching persons with jobs	126
Placing handicapped persons	42
Structuring jobs	112
Diluting jobs	38
Enriching jobs	51
Other	7
Conducting Labor and Personnel Relations	162
Developing performance standards	90
Establishing responsibility	126
Establishing accountability	110
Handling grievances	61
Conducting labor negotiations	42
Establishing channels of communication	56
Organizing personnel records	71
Other	2
Utilizing Workers	139
Organizing and planning	103
Engineering jobs	33
Controlling costs	51
Controlling quality	30
Predicting changes	24

Table 6–1   *(continued)*

Job Analysis Uses	# Firms
Avoiding excess task duplication	85
Other	2
Training	124
Developing courses	69
Selecting trainees	68
Orienting employees	72
Programming teaching machines	4
Other	2

During the post-World War II period, the Employment and Training Administration of the United States Department of Labor began shaping its occupational descriptions in the following manner with respect to physical demand characteristics: (a) classification of work into one of a number of strength categories ranging from sedentary to very heavy work activities; (b) identification of a significant need for climbing and crawling activities; (c) specifying the need for physical manipulation, such as reaching, handling, fingering, and feeling; (d) reporting the need for talking and hearing on the job; and (e) noting the need for sight in specific work positions (Lytel & Botterbusch, 1981). An important outgrowth of the approach taken by the United States Department of Labor was the development of job definitions in the form of job summaries. This information is updated periodically in the form of the *Dictionary of Occupational Titles* (DOT), with the most recent edition appearing in 1977 and supplemented in 1981 (United States Department of Labor, 1977, 1981). The technique used to assess and define jobs contained in the DOT was developed by Sidney Fine and his associates, and is known as "functional job analysis" (Fine, 1973; Fine, Holt, & Hutchinson, 1974; Fine & Wiley, 1971). Table 6–2 identifies the worker function arrangements, along with their definitions, that appear in the latest edition of the DOT.

The advantages of the DOT for job analysis are (a) it classifies and describes occupations in the United States; (b) it identifies occupational and work characteristics; (c) it specifies general qualifications required or needed for various occupational areas; and (d) it permits a job analysis to be conducted (Issacson, 1977). On the other hand, the data gathered on physical demands is not detailed enough to be useful, in and of itself, when attempting to assess a disabled person's ability to perform a specific job in relation to his or her medical limitations (Lytel & Botterbusch, 1981).

Table 6–2. Worker Functions Defined by the 4th Edition of the *Dictionary of Occupational Titles* (1977)

Data	People	Things
0 Synthesizing	0 Mentoring	0 Setting up
1 Coordinating	1 Negotiating	1 Precision working
2 Analyzing	2 Instructing	2 Operating-controlling
3 Compiling	3 Supervising	3 Driving-operating
4 Computing	4 Diverting	4 Manipulating
5 Copying	5 Persuading	5 Tending
6 Comparing	6 Speaking-signaling	6 Feeding-offbearing
	7 Serving	7 Handling
	8 Receiving instruction	

The Purpose and Definition of Job Analysis

The purpose of job analysis is to determine what jobs are and to define their limits; that is, where job activities begin and end. To accomplish this purpose in the most meaningful and useful manner, jobs should be analyzed as they exist, rather than relying on written descriptions which may be provided by an employer and/or through the DOT alone. For a job analysis to be specific and useful for effective rehabilitation planning, it should report a specific job as it exists at the time of the analysis, not as it should exist, nor how it existed in the past, or how it exists in similar employment situations (United States Department of Labor, 1972). Furthermore, the job analysis should be conducted at the place of employment where a disabled person worked, currently works, or anticipates working. Finally, when a job analysis is conducted on the work activities being performed by a disabled person prior to an accident (in order to assess the client's ability to return to that job), it is recommended that the disabled worker accompany the vocational rehabilitation professional to the work site in order to add specificity to the actual duties performed in the course of his or her employment. If that is not possible, however, the accuracy of the information gathered by the vocational rehabilitation professional should be verified during an interview with the disabled individual.

In addition to defining the limits of activities comprising a specific job (see Glossary C definitions), job analysis involves a systematic study of the worker in terms of: (a) what the worker does in relation to people, data, and things; (b) the methodologies and techniques employed to perform work requirements; (c) the machine, tools, equipment, and work aids used; (d) the materials, products, subject matter, or services which result from the work activities; and (e) the traits required of the worker to perform the job (United States Department of Labor, 1972). The latter include information about the required or necessary training to perform a job, personality variables, educational criteria, aptitudes, and other factors related to the performance of specific work activities.

Finally, when attempting to describe job tasks, the United States Department of Labor (1972) recommends that they be arranged in either a chronological or a functional order/sequence. While a chronological order is preferred, a functional sequencing of activities may be necessary when no regular cycle of operations appears to be present. Additionally, tasks that are *temporarily* assigned in addition to the regular job duties should *not* be considered part of the basic job being described in a job analysis. Therefore, in an attempt to further define the situations which a vocational rehabilitation professional may encounter in job analysis studies, as well as what activities should be considered in the job, the United States Department of Labor (1972, pp. 3–4) reports the following guides:

1. *The worker performs a specific cycle or sequence of operations.* The analyst should begin with the first task the worker is called upon to do and consider the work steps successively.
2. *The worker has no regular cycle of operations.* This situation is usually more difficult to analyze since it frequently involves a considerable variety of tasks. The analyst should organize the information according to function [as well as] study the work activities involved in the performance of these functions.
3. *The worker frequently changes from one set of tasks to another.* The tasks should ordinarily be analyzed collectively and recorded in one job analysis, since the tasks involved, although performed by individual workers, actually constitute only one job, all phases of which are performed by all the workers.
4. *The worker performs a given set of tasks although in emergencies he/she performs other sets of tasks involved in other jobs.* Situations such as these should be considered separate jobs, and separate job analyses should be performed for each.

Job Analysis Process

Preparing for the Analysis   The first step in the job analysis process is for the vocational rehabilitation professional to become familiar with the technologies and terminology associated with a given industry and the occupations to be studied. Information for these purposes may be obtained from such sources as books, periodicals, technical literature from trade associations and/or professional societies, or pamphlets prepared by local, state, or federal governments about jobs. The importance of taking the time to become familiar with such details *before* conducting a job analysis is twofold. First, it allows the vocational rehabilitation professional to speak in a language common to management, supervisors, and workers about particular work activities. Second, by preparing for the job analysis in such a manner, the vocational rehabilitation professional can observe and evaluate work tasks and processes efficiently and effectively.

Arranging for the Analysis Making arrangements to conduct a job analysis is best handled in a three-step process; contacting the employment site to schedule an appointment to meet with key personnel, visiting the employment site to become oriented to the establishment, and revisiting the employment site to conduct the job analysis. If no job studies have been conducted by or within an employment setting in the past, initial contact should be made with the head of the firm or, in large companies, with the person who has jurisdiction over such matters (e.g., personnel director, industrial relations director). The purpose of the first visit is to become acquainted with the personnel and operations of the work site which will be necessary to enhance the data gathering process. Furthermore, the first visit provides the vocational rehabilitation professional the opportunity to obtain assurance that management understands the aims of the study and authorizes it. Moreover, during the first visit the rehabilitation practitioner can request copies of employer job descriptions that will be useful in preparing for the subsequent analysis. The final step is to arrange for a second visit in order to conduct the job analysis itself.

Performing the Job Analysis The optimal method suggested by the United States Department of Labor (1972) to conduct a job analysis is by obtaining information through observation and interview. This method involves analyzing jobs by observing a job being performed and interviewing the workers, supervisors, and others who have pertinent information about the job. The benefits of collecting and recording data in this manner are (a) it involves firsthand observation; (b) it enables the analyst to evaluate the interview data and sift essential from nonessential facts in terms of that observation; and (c) it permits the worker to demonstrate various functions of the job rather than describing it orally or in writing (United States Department of Labor, 1972, p. 12). Use of the observation-interview method can be accomplished in two ways. One method involves observing a worker performing a complete work cycle before asking questions, noting all of the job activities included during the observation phase. The second method involves observation and interviewing simultaneously. Using this method requires a note of caution for several reasons. The vocational rehabilitation practitioner should take care in distracting workers who are performing hazardous activities for obvious safety reasons. Also, if a worker is involved in activities requiring attention to detail, assembly-line operation, and/or is working at a piece-rate wage, any undue interruptions may adversely affect the quality or quantity of production or both.

Finally, some important "do's and don'ts" for conducting job analysis interviews, suggested by the United States Department of Labor (1972, p. 13), bear repeating:

1. Do not take issue with the worker's statements.
2. Do not show any partiality to grievances or conflicts concerning the employer-employee relationship.
3. Do not show any interest in the wage classification of the job.
4. Show politeness and courtesy throughout the interview.
5. Do not "talk down" to the worker.
6. Do not permit yourself to be influenced by your personal likes or dislikes.
7. Be impersonal. Do not be critical or attempt to suggest any changes or improvements in methods of work.
8. Talk to the worker only with permission from the immediate supervisor.
9. Verify job data, especially technical or trade terminology, with the foreman or department head.
10. Verify the completed job analysis with the proper official, as well as with the disabled person whom you are serving.

Reporting the Job Analysis   Once all of the information has been gathered about a specific job, the final step is to prepare the job analysis report. Although many reporting styles and formats exist for job analysis, the information contained should be quite similar in terms of descriptive headings and the objectivity of the report. Based on the recommendations of the California Association of Rehabilitation Professionals (1982) and other organizations, the content of a thorough job analysis should contain the following information:

   I. Job Title (provided by the employer and the DOT)
     A. DOT code number
     B. Employer's name, address, telephone number
     C. Supervisor's name
     D. Date of the analysis
  II. Job Description (provided by the employer, DOT, and observation)
 III. Method Used to Obtain the Job Analysis
     A. Representative (similar job)

       1. Interview
       2. Observation
       3. Discussion with observed worker
  B. On site (same job)
       1. Interview
       2. Observation
       3. Discussion with observed worker
  C. Job eliminated (verbal description only)

IV. Observation of Job Particulars
  A. Union affiliation requirements
  B. Salary range
  C. Tools, equipment, work aids used
  D. Work hours

V. Physical Demands

A. Standing	J. Stooping	S. Talking
B. Walking	K. Bending	T. Hearing
C. Sitting	L. Kneeling	U. Tasting/Smelling
D. Lifting	M. Crouching	V. Seeing
E. Carrying	N. Crawling	1. Near vision
F. Pushing	O. Reaching	2. Midrange vision
G. Pulling	P. Handling	3. Far vision
H. Climbing	Q. Fingering	4. Accommodation
I. Balancing	R. Feeling	5. Color vision
		6. Field of vision

A through G should consider strenuousness of the activity, i.e., sedentary, light, medium, heavy, or very heavy work (see Glossary C).

VI. Environmental Conditions
  A. Location of work (indoors, outdoors, both)
  B. Temperatures (hot, cold, alternating)
  C. Wet and/or humid conditions
  D. Noise
  E. Vibrations
  F. Atmospheric conditions
  G. Inherent hazards

VII. Name, Signature, and Date of the Job Analyst
VIII. Disabled Person's Name, Signature, and Date (when appropriate)
  IX. Disabled Person's Attorney's Name, Signature, and Date (when appropriate)
   X. Attending Physician's Name, Signature, and Date (when appropriate)

Job Modification and Restructuring

Once a job has been analyzed, perhaps the rehabilitation professional becomes aware that the majority of work activities involved in the job described do not present problems for a disabled client in terms of his or her residual capabilities. On the other hand, there are either a few movements (steps) in the process and/or physical activities present in the job which now are difficult or not possible to perform because of the client's impairment(s). What should the rehabilitation professional do next?

Perhaps each of us has been faced with similar circumstances in our own lives and daily activities. For example, when we begin to "test drive" a car we consider purchasing, among the first activities we perform is to rearrange specific items in the car to accommodate our personal habits, preferences, and physical characteristics; adjusting the seat so that we can operate the foot pedals and steering wheel comfortably, adjusting the rear view and side mirrors to have an unobstructed view of objects behind us in traffic, and so forth. Later, perhaps we change or add other features of the car as we learn more about its makeup in relation to our needs and desires; we reset the radio channels, a plastic holder is added to accommodate beverage containers during trips, a cushion is placed on the seat to ease the discomfort of sitting for long periods, or substantial changes are made to the body and major mechanical parts to satisfy aesthetic and/or performance desires. The point is, each of us attempts to shape and mold our environments to satisfy us as much as possible. Job modification and restructuring serve the same purpose.

What are Job Modification and Restructuring?

Job modification and job restructuring are synonymous terms used in the literature to describe a process whereby existing jobs or work tasks can be changed to accommodate the capabilities of workers while maintaining or increasing the expected level of productivity (Brolin & Webster, 1978). Throughout the remainder of the book, however, only the term "job modification" will be used for two reasons; consistency, and because in the author's opinion, job restructuring connotes a more substantial and costly process to employers than does the term "job modification." When defining job modification, it is important to identify its relationship to other aspects of the rehabilitation process, such as job analysis, rehabilitation engineering, vocational evaluation, and job placement.

Job Analysis and Job Modification   According to the United States Department of Labor (1970, p. 1), job modification constitutes a "special application of job analysis that involves viewing jobs within the context of the system of which they are a part, analyzing them, and then rearranging their tasks to achieve a desired end." Mallik (1979, p. 145) elaborates this basic definition by adding that the job modification process allows the rehabilitation professional to "combine, eliminate, redistribute, add, or isolate tasks from one or more jobs within the same job family to form part-time or full-time positions." Since jobs rarely exist in isolation from other jobs in a system, job modification should be thought of as not changing one job, but rather as rearranging the contents of many or all jobs within a system. Therefore, any activity in this area should begin with the identification of the jobs within a system, using job analysis as the basic technique for identifying the separate tasks of each job activity, followed by an evaluation of the characteristics and relationships of the tasks involved.

As a special application of job analysis, job modification provides rehabilitation professionals with insights into how work environments, processes, and machines can be changed to enhance disabled persons' abilities to perform work tasks in a manner which will be productively comparable to nondisabled workers. For example, environmental modifications consider the physical layout and location of work activities in terms of whether they are accessible to disabled persons (Brolin & Webster, 1978; Reich, 1980). Process modification considers the sequence of activities in jobs which may be altered to improve productivity, reduce fatigue, time, and motion, and lead to a simplification of perceptual, physical, and cognitive tasks required (Mallik, 1979; Shinnick, Black, & Decker, 1983). Modification of machines may range from a relatively inexpensive addition of a fixture or guide (jig) to major redesigning of machinery. While the latter is more a function of rehabilitation engineering, which will be discussed next, the Fourth Institute on Rehabilitation Issues (1977) suggests the following constraints be considered by rehabilitation professionals when recommending modifying machines to accommodate disabled persons: (a) simple modifications should be of low cost to the employer; (b) design and fabrication should follow human ergonomics; (c) modification of existing equipment and systems should be such that it will accommodate both disabled and nondisabled persons; (d) redesign should not result in confusing servicepersons responsible for equipment maintenance; and (e) criteria for safety should be observed.

Rehabilitation Engineering and Job Modification A generally accepted definition of rehabilitation engineering reported by the Sixth Institute on Rehabilitation Issues (1979, p. 10) is:

The application of engineering to improve the quality of life of disabled persons through a team approach to rehabilitation combining medicine, engineering, psychology, counseling, and other rehabilitation disciplines.

More specifically, rehabilitation engineering involves the analysis, design, manufacture, and alteration of adaptive or other equipment for use by disabled persons. In order to accomplish the application of science and technology for the improved functioning of disabled persons, a rehabilitation engineer should have a working knowledge of mechanical and electrical engineering, possess skills in solving functional problems economically, and have a comprehension of aesthetics so that the disabled person's self-image is not unduly compromised or undermined (Sixth Institute on Rehabilitation Issues, 1979; Thomas, 1981; United States Department of Education, 1980).

Rehabilitation engineering applies to machines and people alike. In the former instance, equipment redesign can range from the simple (and least costly) to the complex and expensive. However, as costs increase, so does employers' resistance to modification of existing systems and methods of operation. Human engineering also reflects a range of complexity and costs similar to equipment redesign, but may be accomplished with little or no cost for employers. For instance, interfacing people with machines or tools to function more effectively and efficiently may include simply rearranging the work station environment, such as raising, lowering, or tilting equipment, or placing objects within a person's reaching radius to reduce unnecessary motion and/or accommodate physical limitations (Shinnick, Black, & Decker, 1983). Human engineering also applies to the use of technology and/or medicine to substitute a prosthetic instrument in order to at least partially compensate for a person's disability. In vocational terms, this means that the disabled person can be equipped with a device which serves as an extension of the person and assists in accomplishment of work tasks that would not be possible otherwise (e.g., wheelchairs, sensory feedback appliances, artificial limbs).

Vocational Evaluation and Job Modification   While methods of vocational evaluation will be covered in more detail later in the chapter in terms of its uses for assessing vocational potential, its relationship with job modification deserves mention at this point. When identifying the strengths and weaknesses of disabled persons, rehabilitation professionals can apply their knowledge of job modification techniques to increase the list of vocational strengths and decrease the list of limitations. Brolin and Webster (1979) have noted correctly, however, that many of the diagnostic devices available such as tests, work samples, and situational assessments usually do not take into account the performance of an individual after job modification. One notable exception among vocational evaluation instruments is the Methods-Time-Measurement Analysis developed and applied to the rehabilitation process in the Netherlands (Mink, 1975).

The Methods-Time-Measurement Analysis is an industrial engineering technique which may be used to develop work samples based on industrial and commercial norms. According to Vactor and Hubach (1979), the value of the work samples lend themselves to environmental alterations so as to make the participant's behavior observable and measurable. The norms used in this evaluation process are based on scientific calculations of movements, rather than being based primarily on the timed performance of nondisabled or disabled persons (Mink, 1975). Thus, from the measured characteristics, strengths and weaknesses of movements can be determined which not only provide a basic profile of abilities, but isolate strengths and limitations according to specific movements which can be incorporated into job modification or engineering design.

Job Placement and Job Modification   Job placement represents the ultimate goal of the vocational process in insurance rehabilitation as noted in preceding chapters. Among the advantages of job modification reported by Mallik (1979) are its assistance in developing job opportunities for disabled individuals and creating additional part-time or full-time employment for more job seekers. Along these lines, the United States Department of Labor (1970) lists how job modifications benefit industry and workers alike. First, job modification increases employment opportunities at entry level positions for persons who do not possess the necessary skills to compete in the labor market. It does this by freeing experienced personnel from lower level tasks in order to have more time to perform work activities in their areas of expertise. Second, job modification creates meaningful opportunities for inexperienced workers to advance to higher level jobs as they acquire new skills through on-the-job training, formalized classroom instruction, and work experience. Moreover, job modification is one of several avenues that can be used to assist employers to make their employment sites more accessible for qualified disabled workers, and thus, more in keeping with the Federal Architectural Barriers Act of 1968 (Francis, 1983).

Job Modification Process

Preparing for a Job Modification Study   Approaching a job modification study is very similar to the steps recommended when preparing for a job analysis, insofar that the support of the employer is crucial for success. In addition to following guidelines such as becoming familiar with the organization to be studied and enlisting the support of key personnel within the employment setting, the rehabilitation professional must be aware of the abilities and potentials of disabled clients before beginning the analysis or at least *before* the actual modification to the job begins. Furthermore, the rehabilitation professional should be prepared to answer any or all of the following employer questions identified by the United States Department of Labor (1970, p. 3):

1. Will the study interrupt operations?
2. What costs may be incurred by the employer?
3. Will the intent of the study or its outcome affect the morale of present employees?
4. How long will the study take to complete?
5. How much time will be required to implement the modified jobs to achieve full production or render more effective service?
6. Will a restructured job be used by other employees in the absence of the person it was designed for initially?
7. What assistance, if any, could be expected from the federal government in terms of financial assistance or tax credits?
8. What effect would a restructured job have on established wage structures, on-the-job training programs, and promotional opportunities, or established career ladders?

Since job modifications affect more than one job within a system of jobs, adequate preparation requires studying the relationships between the overall organization and the purpose of work being conducted within an establishment, hierarchical relationships and promotional possibilities, and the sequence of operations (work flow) and the plant layout. In order for the rehabilitation professional to gain a more thorough understanding of these relationships, it is recommended that he or she prepare an organizational chart, a materials process flow chart, and a staffing schedule as soon as possible in the preparational phase of the job modification study. Examples of organizational and process flow charts are depicted in Figures 6–1 and 6–2, respectively.

The Organizational Chart, depicted in Figure 6–1, graphically shows the setup of a firm or other organization, including the relationships between its subdivisions, and the composition and distribution of its personnel. The Process Flow Chart seen in Figure 6–2 depicts the workflow of an establishment, as well as the normal sequence of operations within it. Finally, the Staffing Schedule is an inventory of an establishment's work force. It shows current staffing patterns of a firm and indicates the distribution of work skills, as well as the uses being made of those skills. Typically, the information contained in a Staffing Schedule consists of an accurate description of *all* jobs in the establishment in terms of plant titles, DOT titles, and DOT occupational codes (United States Department of Labor, 1970).

Procedures for Job Modification   Because job modification constitutes a special application of job analysis, as noted earlier, objective information

Figure 6–1.
Simplified Organizational Chart.

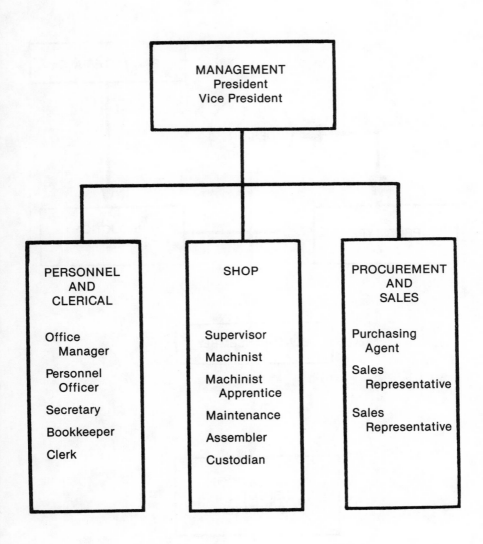

Figure 6–2.
Process Flow Chart.

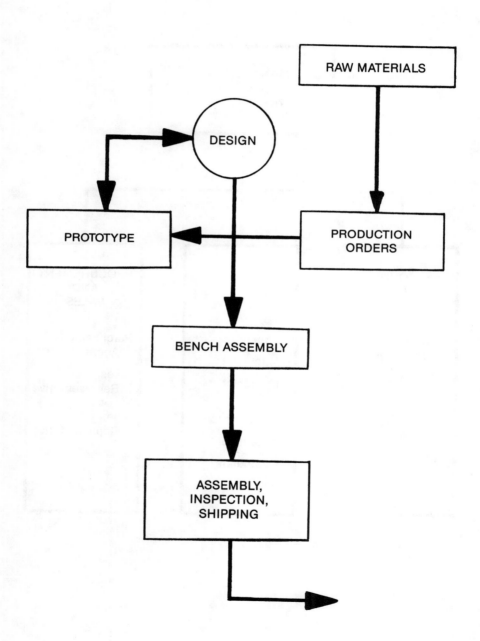

about the jobs to be modified can be obtained in several ways: (a) by observing the work situation; (b) by interviewing workers, supervisors, and personnel specialists; or (c) by referring to prepared company job descriptions or previously prepared job analysis materials. The most complete information can be obtained, however, through a combination of observation and interview methods as described under job analysis. Thus, for each job to be studied for possible modification, the following sequence of events is recommended by the United States Department of Labor (1970, p. 13):

Step 1: Determine the relationship of the job(s) to the system of which they are a part.

Step 2: Describe in detail the tasks that comprise each job (following the job analysis method).

Step 3: Estimate or time the amount of time required to perform each task during the work cycle or the average work day.

Step 4: Rate each task in relation to worker functions, i.e., data, people, things.

Step 5: Rate each task in terms of general educational development.

Step 6: Rate each task in relation to important aptitudes required to perform the activity.

Step 7: Evaluate each task in relation to other important worker traits such as physical demands and environmental conditions.

Step 8: Group tasks according to worker functions, educational development, aptitudes, and other important worker traits.

Step 9: Record task groupings.

Step 10: Evaluate task groups in terms of the kind of work performed or technology involved.

Step 11: Review the process flow, establishment layout, and machinery and equipment to determine if tentative groups are feasible in this respect.

Step 12: Consider career lattice possibilities.

Step 13: Determine if cumulative totals of work time for the tasks in the tentative groups justify full-time jobs.

Step 14: Evaluate and adjust groups until the most feasible and practical arrangements of tasks are developed.

Step 15: Prepare detailed job descriptions (in the same manner as the job analysis method).

Step 16: Prepare career lattices.

Step 17: Follow up after implementation of the job modification has been completed (approximately three months afterward).

Reporting the Job Modification   A detailed description of the steps identified above will closely parallel the reporting categories of a job analysis report (sections I through VII). In addition to that information, it may be extremely helpful to include diagrams of the workflow process of jobs being studied before modification (see Figure 6–3) and the proposed workflow to be implemented (see Figure 6–4). While graphic illustration is not intended to replace a more formal descriptive narrative of work activities, much can be said in support of "a picture being worth a thousand words" in terms of providing conceptual clarity for such an analysis. Finally, when job modification reports are being prepared by rehabilitation professionals, it is wise to ask *and answer* five basic questions according to Warren (1979):

1. *What* is the purpose of the operation or activity being studied? Does it accomplish what it is supposed to?
2. *Why* is the activity being done? Should it be done? Could the same result be accomplished without it?
3. *Where* is the activity taking place? Why is it located where it is rather than somewhere else?
4. *When* is the activity being performed? Is it proceeding in the proper sequence? Is there a better sequence?
5. *Who* is performing the activity? What are the qualifications required? Are the qualifications possessed by the worker being used in the activity?

Vocational Evaluation

In its broadest meaning, vocational evaluation includes all medical, psychological, social, cultural, vocational, and educational information that helps define a disabled person's problems in order to better identify, understand, and work toward achieving realistic rehabilitation goals. As used here, however, it will pertain more narrowly to information and techniques for specifically assessing vocational aptitudes, abilities, and prognosis. Obtaining these types of information is important, especially in an insurance rehabilitation context, because collectively they provide a foundation to support recommended vocational goals and objectives, particularly in those instances when a disability precludes the continuation of the pre-injury occupation. Thus, vocational evaluation provides a method to assist rehabilitation professionals in their determination of a disabled person's employability and ability to benefit from rehabilitation services by systematically assessing residual levels of functioning.

What is Vocational Evaluation

Although vocational evaluation techniques have been used differentially by various cultures throughout recorded history (Alexander & Selesnick, 1966; Neff, 1968; Shaffer & Lazarus, 1952), the full scale development and systematic employment of such techniques is a 20th century phenomenon

Figure 6-3.
Work Flow Diagram.

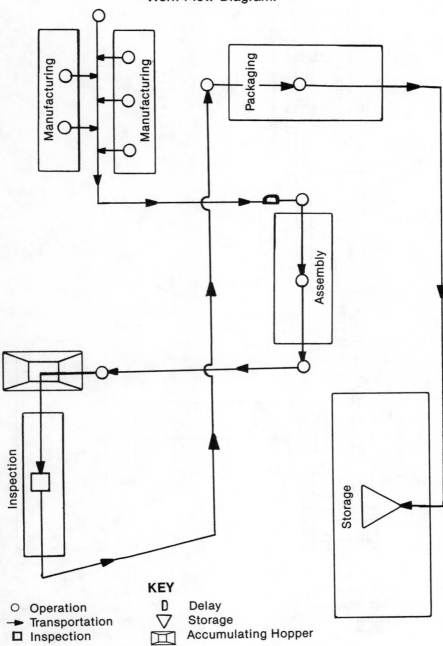

KEY

○ Operation
→ Transportation
□ Inspection

D Delay
▽ Storage
⬡ Accumulating Hopper

Figure 6-4.
Modified Work Flow Diagram.

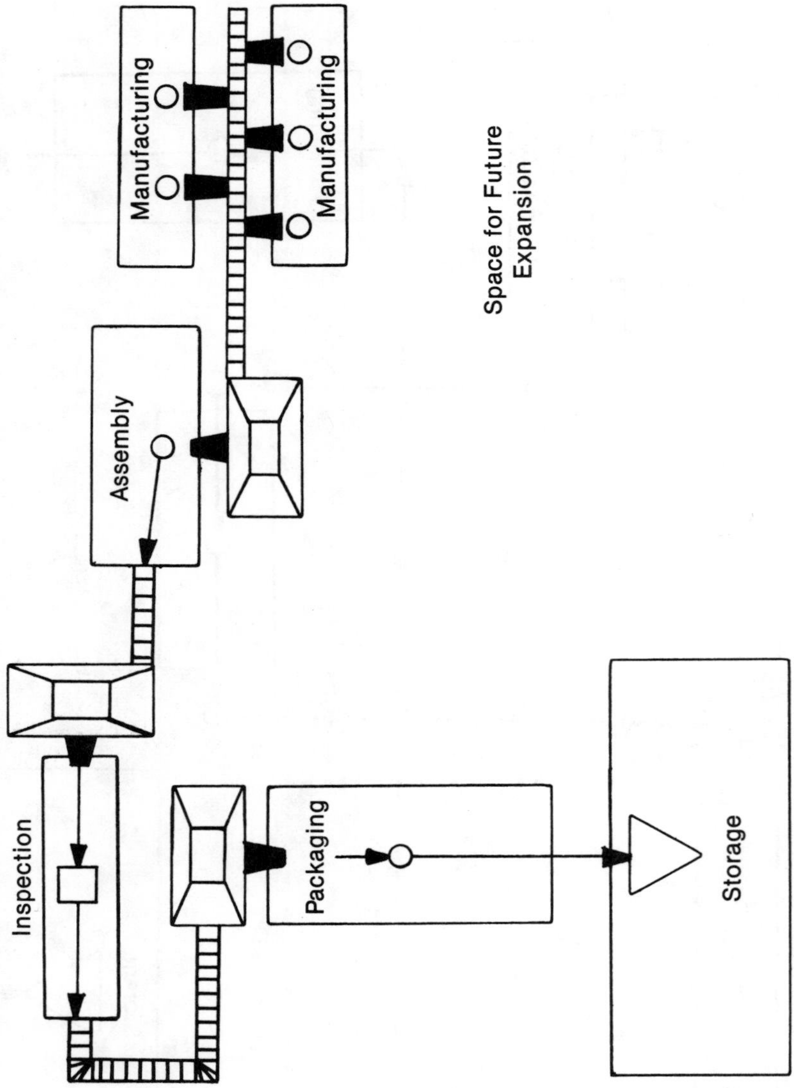

KEY

○	Operation	▽	Storage
→	Transportation	▼	Gravity Feed Shute
□	Inspection	▦	Powered Conveyor Belt
▯	Delay	⬡	Accumulating Hopper

(Nadolsky, 1972). Furthermore, the growth and acceptance of vocational evaluation techniques during the first half of the 20th century was confined primarily to the United States. Even today, concern for vocational assessment in other industrialized nations does not equal that in this country. Neff (1968) attributes this difference, in large part, to the long-standing unique political and social systems maintained by the United States that are based upon equal opportunity through mass education.

According to Nadolsky (1972), most of the current attitudes underlying the concept of vocational evaluation are derived from the American culture and can be traced to the delayed impact of the Industrial Revolution upon this culture. The emergence of mass education within American society was in response partially to the demands of a growing industrial system which required producers and consumers alike to attain a relatively high degree of literacy (Lucas, 1972). Therefore, Nadolsky (1972) contends that interest in assessment was essential to the survival of America's equal opportunity ideal since the creation and maintenance of such a concept in our heterogenous society must based upon a firm understanding of each person's abilities and limitations in relation to educational and industrial criteria. In order to obtain such an understanding, however, it is important and necessary to know the purpose of vocational assessment and types of evaluations used.

Purpose of Vocational Evaluation In 1972, the Tenth Insitute on Rehabilitation Services developed the following definition for vocational evaluation, cited by Bitter (1979, p. 148):

> Vocational (work) evaluation is a comprehensive process that systematically utilizes work, real or simulated, as the focal point for assessment and vocational exploration, the purpose of which is to assist individuals in vocational development. Vocational (work) evaluation incorporates medical, psychological, social, vocational, educational, cultural, and economic data in the attainment of goals of the evaluation process.

From this definition, the reader can see the need for a comprehensive evaluation philosophy incorporating work activities in relation with other factors that have contributory effects on a disabled person's employability. By measuring each variable (e.g., medical, psychological, vocational, economic) in a systematic manner, and combining them to understand their interrelatedness, the vocational rehabilitation professional is better able to determine an individual's strengths, limitations, and work potential (Gellman, 1968; Rubin & Roessler, 1983). Such a level of comprehensiveness is crucial for the development and justification of vocational goals and objectives upon which service recommendations are based.

Because vocational evaluation serves a diagnostic purpose, by gathering data for identifying realistic employment goals and services needed for their achievement, the rehabilitation professional should expect specific information to be provided. For example, Baker (1982, p. 86) mentions eight areas vocational evaluations are expected to address: (1) information about a client's current vocationally relevant levels of social, educational, psychological, and physiological functioning; (2) detailed analysis of client vocational functioning; (3) estimation of the individual's potential for behavior change and/or skill acquisition; (4) determination of a client's most effective learning style; (5) identification of jobs the client can perform without additional vocational services (e.g., transferable skills); (6) identification of educational or occupational training programs that might increase a client's employability; (7) identification of potentially feasible jobs contingent on further vocational services; and (8) identification of community and other support services and programs that might augment job retention.

Types of Evaluation   Before focusing specifically on vocational evaluation techniques, it is important to briefly mention the major categories of assessment incorporated by vocational evaluation according to the Tenth Institute on Rehabilitation Services (1972). These include medical, psychological, sociocultural, vocational, and educational evaluations. Each type will be described in relation to its contributions to a comprehensive vocational assessment.

Medical Evaluation.   Assists in the identification of major and secondary disabilities, functional limitations imposed by the disability, and the general health of the disabled client. The medical evaluation generally consists of a medical examination, as well as any special medical examinations and procedures required. The medical evaluation provides useful information for the vocational evaluation in terms of identifying current and predicted functional limitations, precautions, and contraindications imposed by the disabling condition in relation to activities of daily living. In addition, it may include other relevant data such as type and dosage of prescribed medications being administered, therapies prescribed and their anticipated duration and effects, and a brief descriptive medical history.

Psychological Evaluation.   Aids in the determination of a client's present level of functioning in terms of intellectual capacity, personality, and other traits and abilities relating to an individual's personal characteristics. Psychological evaluations contribute to comprehensive vocational evaluations by providing information about how a client perceives him or herself in relation to the disabling condition, as well as adjustment to it. Furthermore, such evaluation measures assist in understanding more fully a client's needs which are necessary for effective vocational planning. Such information is obtained usually through interviews, observation of behavior, standardized testing measures, and a review of any previous information gathered about the disabled individual. (For a thorough discussion and listing of psychological instruments associated with vocational evaluation, the interested reader is referred to the following books listed in the Reference Section: Anastasi's *Psychological Testing* and Bitter's *Introduction to Rehabilitation*.)

Sociocultural Evaluation. Consists of identification of personal and impersonal factors and events in a client's life. For example, information gathered may consist of social functioning; cultural background; age; special relationships with others such as parents, siblings, spouse, and children; and economic issues which might include level of income, receipt or eligibility for benefit subsidies, and sources of expenses. Information contained in sociocultural evaluations are useful for vocational evaluations in terms of identifying factors that will contribute to selection of a viable goal (e.g., appropriate working wage, location of work environment, need for travel, and the like). Information about the social functioning of clients is gathered through client interviews, client observation, and other sources.

Educational Evaluation. Consists of a determination of a client's educational level, past training completed and skills acquired, learning capacity, attitudes toward learning, and special areas of interest or achievement. Information of these types are useful for vocational evaluations by identifying potential areas to explore in terms of transferable skills (e.g., hobbies, past training, or avocations) and selected characteristics of training programs (e.g., prerequisite knowledge and/or education level). Most information about educational factors can be obtained from school records and client interviews, although sometimes these are supplemented with the administration of achievement and aptitude tests.

Vocational Evaluation. Focuses on a disabled client's work skills and attitudes through information gathered from a vocational history of work activities, administration of standardized tests related to job interest and aptitude, and assessment of vocational potential by using such methods as on-the-job evaluation, sheltered employment, situational assessment, functional assessment, and work samples. When data from these sources are combined with information provided by each of the aforementioned evaluations, vocational evaluation provides a comprehensive basis for subsequent rehabilitation planning.

Vocational Evaluation Methods

Each rehabilitation professional has a responsibility to select (or recommend selection of) the most appropriate techniques and testing instruments to be used to assess each disabled client's vocational feasibility and potential. Currently, there are literally hundreds of standardized testing instruments from which to choose that measure personal traits and abilities, and require varying degrees of training and expertise to administer, score, and interpret accurately. Since a review of these instruments is beyond the scope of this text, and are contained in previously mentioned sources, the remainder of this section identifies and discusses two major methods for assessing vocational potential, along with their advantages and disadvantages. These methods consist of situational assessments and work samples.

Situational Assessments Situational assessment involves observing client behavior using a systematic procedure for observation, recording, and interpreting work activities performed on the job, much in the same manner as described earlier for job analysis (Pruitt, 1977). Situational assessments can be conducted in nearly any work setting, real or simulated, such as within sheltered workshops or on job sites within competitive industry. In either environment, the rehabilitation professional has the opportunity to evaluate a disabled person's performance under working conditions in relation to restrictions imposed by the disabling condition, as well as behavioral dynamics between the client, the supervisor, and coworkers. When conducting this type of assessment, however, it cannot be stressed enough that observational procedures follow the guidelines reported by Dunn (1973): (a) describe behaviors in observable terms; (b) describe the situation in which the behavior occurred; (c) describe what happened rather than what did not happen; (d) describe the frequency, rate, and duration of activities whenever possible; (e) begin each descriptive statement with an action verb; (f) use terse, direct language when describing activities, that is, avoid the use of adjectives to add "color" to the observations; and (g) record observations immediately.

Among the advantages in using a situational assessment approach in vocational evaluation are (1) it offers a real or nearly real work situation and environment for the client; (2) it provides an opportunity to observe how the client interacts with tasks and others within the work situation; and (3) it reduces or eliminates possible test anxiety that is associated with more standardized procedures and instruments that may appear to the client to have little or no relationship to the activities reportedly measured. On the other hand, some of the disadvantages associated with situational assessments include: (1) their dependence on observer reliability, especially when rehabilitation professionals must depend on others to carry out this function; (2) the large amount of time required for a client to become familiar with the work tasks assigned so as to provide as accurate an estimate as possible of performance capability; (3) possible employer unwillingness to provide on-the-job evaluation opportunities; (4) a limited variety of work tasks within sheltered workshops to adequately assess a client's vocational capabilities; and (5) potential violations of provisions of the Federal Fair Labor Standards Act if clients are paid less than minimum wage, yet whose efforts are contributing to an employer's profitability through the production of goods or services.

Work Samples   A task force of the Vocational Evaluation and Work Adjustment Association (1975) defined work samples as any well defined work activity involving tasks, materials, and tools which are either the same as or similar to those used in an actual job or job family. Interestingly, despite the usually high reliance on such instruments in vocational evaluation, work sample systems have begun to proliferate only since the mid-1970s. Prior to that time, only two systems were generally available (i.e., the TOWER system and the Philadelphia Jewish Employment and Vocational Service battery), whereas today at least 14 commercial work sample systems exist (Botterbusch, 1980). Generally, work sample systems combine features of standardized testing procedures, using performance norms established from a variety of sample groups (e.g., mentally retarded, orthopedically disabled, competitively employed workers), and behavioral observation (Matkin & Rice, 1979). Finally, work sample systems range from the very simple to very complex operations in terms of administration, scoring, and interpretation expertise required by the rehabilitation professional. Moreover, they can be designed to measure a single characteristic relevant to one or many jobs, reproduce an entire job operation, or interface with many jobs through the recent use of computer technology.

Among the advantages of work sample systems are (1) their close approximation to real work which tends to hold a client's interest longer than typical "paper and pencil" tests; (2) the concrete nature of most tasks involved in these systems; (3) direct performance feedback to the client; (4) the opportunity to directly observe a client's performance by the rehabilitation professional; (5) the opportunity to explore various job tasks and jobs by both the client and the rehabilitation professional which may not be possible in situational approaches; (6) enhanced predictive validity of vocational potential in a variety of job tasks; and (7) the minimal academic requirements necessary for both administration and scoring by the rehabilitation professional, as well as for participation by the client.

Among the disadvantages of work sample systems, on the other hand, are (1) the need to continuously reconstruct and standardize work samples to keep pace with changing technologies; (2) a need to upgrade the predictive validity of work samples in terms of the norm groups used to establish performance standards in relation to the specific disability of a client being tested; (3) since they are typically a "one-shot" evaluation, it is difficult to determine the effects of sustained performance in an activity that may be required in competitive employment; and (4) the expense of many different work sample systems can restrict many rehabilitation professionals from purchasing them.

Considerations for the Use of Vocational Evaluation and Testing

It is not uncommon for rehabilitation professionals, disabled clients, and third party payors to ask if testing is needed to assist in identifying feasible vocational goals or is merely a means to charge more fees. In spite of the ethical implications of the latter (which will be addressed in the final chapter), rehabilitation professionals should be prepared to substantiate the need for testing *prior* to recommending or implementing such procedures. In order to assist rehabilitation professionals in determining whether or not a need exists for testing, the California Association of Rehabilitation Professionals (1982, pp. 12–13) offers the following guidelines:

1. To provide information about a person's interests, mental and physical abilities, and temperament with respect to work.
2. To support, clarify, and document impressions gained during interviews of a client's interests and abilities.
3. To discover job interests and potential vocational objectives when neither the counselor nor client can verbally state a client's job interests, likes, or dislikes.
4. To more objectively and accurately describe a person's likes, dislikes, needs, and abilities than can be inferred from verbalized interview statements.
5. To individualize a client's reasons for choosing and being motivated towards a particular occupation.
6. To match and compare tested abilities with stated abilities and tested interests with stated interests.
7. To motivate and stimulate vocational decisions into a realistic direction.
8. To support and enhance a person's self-esteem and self-concept as related to job-seeking.
9. To document and validate the reasonableness and feasibility of a rehabilitation plan for regulatory agencies.
10. To compare the tested aptitudes of a person with the necessary level to perform various jobs as specified in the Dictionary of Occupational Titles (DOT) or Occupational Aptitude Profiles of the General Aptitude Test Battery (GATB).
11. To observe and evaluate the physical stamina, endurance, agility, and range of motion that a person possesses in relation to industrial performance requirements.
12. To evaluate the degree that a particular impairment is a physical disability or handicap.

Principle One: Vocational tests and work samples *should be* administered and interpreted to clients when reason for testing is indicated.

Principle Two: If no reason exists or if no questions can be answered by testing, then clients *will not benefit* from the testing.

Principle Three: If a client has a vocational problem that is diagnosed and if the problem matches with the purpose of testing, then tests or work samples are indicated.

When used properly, tests can be valuable tools in the vocational evaluation process for clients and rehabilitation professionals alike. In the hands of persons with inadequate training, however, their use can result in unsound decisions and costly mistakes. It is for these reasons that the American Psychological Association (1982) classifies commercial tests into three levels of complexity in relation to the amount of training required for their proper administration, scoring, and interpretation. These classifications are (1) *Level A* which can be administered, scored, and interpreted by nonpsychologists with little or no training beyond the aid of the test manual; (2) *Level B* which requires some technical knowledge of testing and suitable psychological training; and (3) *Level C* which requires a qualified psychologist with substantial knowledge of tests and measurements, as well as a supervised period of training in the administration, scoring, and interpretation of psychometric instruments.

Finally, when reporting results of vocational evaluations which use testing procedures and instruments, the rehabilitation professional should include a description and purpose of the various tests and/or work samples. The report also should note the client's reaction to the testing process, as well as environmental factors, attitudes, or rapport variables that may have been present during test administration and contributed to their outcomes. Furthermore, an accurate statistical interpretation of the results should be presented along with their validity in measuring the traits in question. The report should conclude with the practical implications of all results tied together in order to support any final recommendations for subsequent services and identified goals.

Summary

Assessing vocational potential requires detailed and systematically derived data focused on the work activities of disabled clients that were performed prior to injury, as well as on those that might be engaged in subsequently. The purpose for gathering such information is to assist the rehabilitation professional and disabled client in formulating and identifying realistic vocational goals, and ways to achieve them, that will result in returning the disabled client to gainful employment as soon as possible. The three methods discussed in this chapter that are generally used to assess vocational potential were job analysis, job modification, and vocational evaluation. Each method attempts to provide information about the characterisitics of work activities in relation to the restrictions imposed by the nature of clients' disabilities. Moreover, each method attempts to provide information that can be used to assist in identifying the next feasible step in the vocational rehabilitation process. For example, job analysis provides information about the characteristics of specific jobs in specific locations. This information can be useful in making determinations about work activities that might require modification or elimination to accommodate a client's disability. Job modification represents a special application of job analysis whereby work activities are studied to determine if alternative methods can be devised to not only accommodate a specific disability, but maintain or increase the production flow of the job. Finally, vocational evaluation provides information about potential activities that disabled clients can perform which are compatible with a person's personal traits such as intelligence, aptitude, education, and abilities. For additional information about specific assessment instruments and assistive devices available, the reader can consult with resources found in the appendices.

7 Vocational Counseling

Throughout the rehabilitation process, trained service providers assist disabled clients to identify and define, as well as achieve, realistic and attainable vocational goals. Although employment goals can change during the rehabilitation process as a result of service and evaluation outcomes, vocational counseling and job placement must receive continuous consideration throughout service delivery. When viewed as an interactive and complementary set of activities, vocational counseling provides direction and meaning to the tangible outcome focus of job placement. The interrelatedness and importance of these activities within an insurance rehabilitation context are evident in the "return-to-work" hierarchy, types of services offered in the private sector, and practitioner roles and functions presented in Chapter 4.

The purpose of this chapter is to provide the reader with information and considerations that are important for effective vocational counseling of disabled insurance recipients. To accomplish this goal, the chapter is divided into two major sections: (1) vocational counseling; and (2) occupational information. The objectives of these sections are to emphasize the importance of an integrated rehabilitation service approach leading to job placement, and to acquaint the reader with issues and alternatives that potentially affect employment outcome.

Vocational Counseling

Before proceeding with this section, it is important that the reader be aware of its intended purpose. This section is designed to identify and provide information about significant elements, beyond the limitations imposed by a disability, that potentially affect vocational planning and rehabilitation outcomes achieved. The importance of rehabilitation professional and client consideration of factors such as the onset of disability, work incentives, and disincentives is stressed as part of the vocational counseling process. Indeed,

141

recognition of these characteristics can facilitate subsequent vocational planning activities designed to enhance achievement of vocational rehabilitation goals.

Vocational counseling also is an extension of case management services discussed in Chapter 5. As in casework, the core of the counseling process is the relationship expressed through the interaction between the rehabilitation professional and the disabled client being served, regardless whether the former party is a contractual agent of an insurance carrier, attorney, or disabled client. Although this section does *not* attempt to define or discuss the variety of counseling theories and techniques used by rehabilitation professionals, it does identify and discuss elements within the counseling process that are useful for achieving maximum client participation in and satisfaction with the vocational rehabilitation process.

Essential Elements of Vocational Counseling

Developing a Counseling Relationship: Rapport Building   The development of rapport between a rehabilitation professional and a disabled client is the first and most crucial step in vocational counseling. Rapport building begins at the time of initial client contact, regardless of the means used (e.g., letter, telephone, face-to-face), and continues throughout the rehabilitation process. Most importantly, rapport involves confidence and understanding between the service provider and the client. Furthermore, it requires an interest in and responsiveness to the disabled person's needs, as well as a permissive atmosphere in which to express one's self (Bitter, 1979). Simply stated, an effective counseling relationship involves treating the client as a responsible person, demonstrating an attitude of caring, being considerate of another's feelings, being patient, and being sensitive to another's needs.

Communication   Effective communication requires interpretation of a message in the same manner in which it was intended. While achieving such a level of accuracy between two or more people is very difficult, it can be enhanced in an atmosphere of mutual trust that allows for clarification through the use of verbal or nonverbal feedback. Additionally, effective communication involves a two-way interchange between parties in order to facilitate accuracy and understanding, not to mention the importance of listening (Benjamin, 1974).

Individualization   Each person, regardless of the presence or absence of a disabling condition, is unique in some manner. Taking into consideration the individual differences disabled clients bring to the rehabilitation process, it is important that services be "tailored" to clients' unique characteristics. Beyond the development of an individualized written rehabilitation plan specifying behavioral objectives and treatment goals, vocational counseling can be individualized in the following manner: (a) scheduling appointments that are mutually convenient to the client and practitioner's daily routines; (b) providing privacy during interviews; (c) taking care to arrive promptly or beginning the interview on time; (d) being prepared for interviews; (e) involving clients in decision-making activities; and (f) being flexible in adjusting vocational goals and service delivery methods based on continuous development and changes occurring in the client's situation (Biestek, 1957).

Client Participation   Active participation by disabled clients in the rehabilitation process, not to mention within vocational counseling, is extremely important to the successful outcome of services rendered. Indeed, the importance of client participation within an insurance rehabilitation context cannot be stressed enough. For example, *lack of active* client involvement in rehabilitation services can be interpreted to mean uncooperativeness or malingering behavior which can be used to justify suspension or termination of insurance benefits (Deneen & Hessellund, 1981). On the other hand, not only do disabled clients have the right to make their own decisions, but the more active they are in the process the greater their investment in achieving identified goals. During vocational counseling, as in other service areas, the rehabilitation professional's role is to guide and promote change in client functioning. Through guidance provided by rehabilitation personnel, clients retain their capacity for self-determination and personal responsibility for vocational goal selection.

Purposefulness   Rapport, communication, individualization, and participation are important elements for two or more persons to carry on a conversation. However, vocational counseling requires more than simply people talking to one another to be effective. It is intended to be a purposeful activity designed to obtain and transmit factual information regarding circumstances affecting clients' vocational choices and alternatives. Thus, establishing a purpose enables both the rehabilitation practitioner and the disabled client to identify and move in a meaningful direction to remediate and/or overcome vocational deficiencies or barriers imposed by handicapping conditions. As in the rehabilitation process, vocational counseling is most effective when it is goal oriented and identifies specific objectives to facilitate goal acquisition.

Recording   Taking notes during vocational counseling activities serves several useful functions for rehabilitation practitioners. These include refreshing one's memory of important facts obtained during the interview, documenting agreed upon or still-to-be resolved issues, synthesizing information to better understand the disabled client's needs, reviewing case progress, identifying services rendered, planning future activities, and providing continuity in the rehabilitation process (Bitter, 1979). On the other hand, note taking during vocational counseling interviews should not interfere with the interaction between rehabilitation professional and disabled client. Keeping that advice in mind, Benjamin (1974) offers a few "don'ts" when recording an interview:

1. Don't take notes if clients object.
2. Don't be secretive about taking notes.
3. Don't use note taking as a form of "cross-examination" by pointing out inconsistencies in an accusatory manner.
4. Don't permit recording to interfere with the flow of the interview.
5. Don't use note taking as an escape from meaningful participation in the interview.

Factors Affecting Client Motivation/Participation

A disabled client's motivation to participate in the rehabilitation process can be affected by many personal and external factors; some of which the client brings to the vocational counseling relationship, and some that the rehabilitation professional contributes. According to Deneen and Hessellund (1981), rehabilitation professionals contribute to enhancing or dampening client motivation through their own attitudes and communications with clients. Typically, attitudes are expressed in the form of "expectations" the practitioner has for/about the client. For example, beliefs about a client's ability to return to work, desire to return to work, or willingness to overcome the disabling condition(s) can be communicated by the rehabilitation professional either verbally or nonverbally. Indeed, the nature of such beliefs, not to mention how they are expressed, potentially has tremendous impact on a client's feelings of self-worth, expectations, and willingness to trust the rehabilitation practitioner (Deneen & Hessellund, 1981). Thus, keeping in mind those elements that the rehabilitation professional brings to the vocational counseling process, it is important to identify and discuss factors surrounding and brought by the disabled client to the relationship. On the other hand, failure to recognize and attend to the following factors can result in significant obstacles that will undermine or defeat vocational rehabilitation goal attainment.

Onset of Disability   Vocational development and choice of occupational goals are affected by the onset of a disabling condition(s). Disabilities occurring early in a client's life may retard vocational development and therefore restrict opportunities clients might otherwise have been able to pursue. In those cases wherein the disabled individual approaches working age unable to cope adequately with social, interpersonal, and job skills characterized by ordinary work situations, the rehabilitation professional must provide services that assist clients to learn the role of the worker (Neff, 1968; Rubin & Roessler, 1983). Work role characteristics must precede and are prerequisite to any serious discussion of vocational alternatives. Without the necessary skills to cope with the range of demands present in the workplace, competitive employment goals are likely to be unrealistic or short-lived following job placement.

Disabilities occurring later in a client's life, notwithstanding, can also impair vocational development. This is particularly the case for disabled clients with progressive disorders or diseases that interfere with activities of daily living (Goldberg et al., 1972; Goldberg & Freed, 1973; Kunce, 1969). Similarly, clients whose disabilities require additional medical attention in order to maximize stability of the condition (e.g., follow-up surgery and treatment), tend to demonstrate more unrealistic vocational planning because of the uncertainties surrounding anticipated medical outcomes (Goldberg et al., 1972). The research findings of Goldberg and his associates suggest that for clients whose medical conditions can be stabilized further, the rehabilitation practitioner would be wise to *delay* advising clients to make a vocational choice until medical stability has been achieved.

Work-Related and Non-Work-Related Injury Compensation   Chapters 2 and 3 identified and discussed assorted insurance laws, policies, and coverages pertaining to industrial and nonindustrial accidents and diseases. Insurance compensation for work-related injuries (e.g., workers' compensation) generally provides coverage for treatment and rehabilitation services, as well as disability payments during recovery, to workers for accidents to their person that were sustained during their normal work activities. Under workers' compensation statutes, for example, the issue of negligence is waived in order to reduce incidents of law suits and increase the likelihood of prompt and certain relief. Despite such a waiver, however, employer and disabled employee attitudes concerning the injury/disease, and wherein blame lies, are often in conflict. On the one hand, employers tend to view an injured worker as incapable of functioning productively not only in the preinjury job capacity, but in any capacity involved in the employment setting (Eaton, 1979). In this circumstance, the disabled worker is considered a liability by the employer who erroneously believes insurance premiums will increase if the worker is retained (Matkin, 1983b; Reagles, 1981). According to Eaton (1979), the employer simply desires to be divested of any association with and responsibility to the injured worker by expecting the insurance company to assume the medical, financial, and vocational obligations of the case. On the other hand, the injured worker frequently believes that the employer is "uncaring" and simply looking for an excuse to terminate the employer/employee relationship. More importantly, in their anger and resentfulness toward the employer, injured workers often misunderstand their benefit entitlements under workers' compensation provisions (Eaton, 1979; Lynch, 1978). Many disabled employees firmly believe that they justly deserve a monetary settlement which they believe will increase the longer they are away from the job and the more they prolong their pain and the handicapping effects of their disabilities (Deneen & Hessellund, 1981; Eaton, 1979). Therefore, during vocational counseling, it is incumbent on the rehabilitation professional to examine whether these attitudes are present, the degree to which they exist, their impact on developing realistic vocational goals, and methods to reduce, eliminate, or circumvent their negative side effects on subsequent vocational planning.

Although approximately 80% of the disabled clients served by rehabilitation practitioners in the private sector are covered by workers' compensation statutes (Gutowski, 1979; Gutowski et al., 1980), the remaining 20% generally receive disability benefits and services under other insurance provisions (e.g., automobile no-fault coverage, personal injury policies, Social Security Disability Insurance). In many cases, these disabled clients may seek vocational rehabilitation services from public or private agencies, companies, and professionals. Although these clients represent nonindustrially injured workers, their disabilities nevertheless can affect their ability to perform their usual and customary occupations. Regardless that an accident or illness was not work related, this group of compensation recipients remain susceptible to many of the same fears, anxieties, and other psychological difficulties experienced by their industrially injured counterparts. It is important to note, however, that nonindustrially injured clients generally are not perceived in as negative a manner by their employers as those injured on the job. This "advantage" serves to ensure a greater willingness among employers to retain the injured employee if at all possible. On the other hand, if the nature and extent of the disability preclude reemployment with the same employer, the nonindustrially injured worker is confronted with employer attitudes about hiring disabled workers in the same manner as other disabled persons seeking employment.

Length of Time From Injury to Referral   Another variable that appears to affect the successful outcome of vocational rehabilitation services is the length of time between onset of a disability and the initiation of rehabilitation services. Research findings suggest that the longer a disabled client waits to seek treatment, the less likely the probability of medical improvement (Beals & Hickman, 1972; Krusen & Ford, 1958). According to Beals and Hickman

(1972), injured workers increasingly elaborate and exaggerate their symptoms with the passage of time, but are less depressed by their current situation than immediately following onset of the disability. More recently, the California Department of Industrial Relations (1979) reported that if disabled clients were referred for rehabilitation services within 180 days (as is the rule) instead of over 280 days postinjury (as is the average), not only would the number of successful cases increase, but the length of time from injury to plan completion would decrease by 28%. Consequently, because evidence suggests that the probability of successful vocational rehabilitation decreases with the passage of time, rehabilitation practitioners in both public and private employment settings must convey this information to the insurance community who control the timeliness of referrals.

Number of Surgical Procedures   Another variable that has been found to affect successful completion of vocational rehabilitation services is the number of surgical procedures. Beals and Hickman (1972) found that no disabled client who had undergone more than three operations returned to work. Similarly, White (1969) reported that of those persons treated in a medically conservative manner, 87% were still maintaining employment two years postinjury. Conversely, among those persons who had had operations subsequent to the initial medical treatment at the time of injury, only 40% still remained employed two years later. Beals and Hickman (1972) also noted that there seemed to be a positive correlation between the degree of psychopathological symptoms and the number of operations; especially among clients with lowback injuries. Interestingly, these researchers found that those "low-back" injured clients who underwent repeated surgeries tended to have the highest "masculinity" scores on personality tests. Furthermore, many of these disabled clients exhibited what Beals and Hickman labeled a "strong man syndrome," that is, they were unable to tolerate chronic disability because it was perceived to interfere with their masculinity.

Within the workers' compensation insurance system, injuries to the back account for the highest number of reported work-related disabilities (Cheit, 1961). In California, for example, back injuries comprised 55% of the disabilities among workers' compensation recipients who received vocational rehabilitation services in 1978; injuries to the hand or knee were the next most frequently reported disability types, i.e., 6% each (California Department of Industrial Relations, 1979). When providing vocational counseling for low-back injured clients, rehabilitation practitioners must be mindful of the inverse relationship between number of operations and successful employment outcome suggested by previous research. However, a note of caution is in order: *Do not overgeneralize, but rather take care to assess the needs of each disabled client and the effects of surgical procedures in his or her particular case.*

Family Support Systems   When a disabled worker or other form of insurance compensation recipient does not have access to the usual sources of self-esteem and self-worth (e.g., employment) by virtue of the disabling condition, efforts to obtain these may be more intensely directed toward others with whom the client is involved emotionally. Family members may come to be valued not only as loved ones, but as sources of reassurance and information linkages between the disabled client and the community. According to Eaton (1979), members of an injured person's family become surrogates in a sense for the former employer and coworkers, and are seen as sources of interpersonal reinforcement that was received from people associated with the workplace. However, burdensome demands may ensue because family roles may be altered by the presence of the client's disabling condition. This must be recognized and attended to by the rehabilitation professional on a periodic basis throughout the counseling process; indeed, throughout the rehabilitation process. For example, in their zeal to help and their devotion to the suffering person's needs, family members may contribute to that person's helplessness and inactivity. In effect the family's sensitivity provides a source of "secondary gain" for the disabled member that may result in that person's reluctance to recover sufficiently to return to work.

Psychologists use the phrase "secondary gain" to refer to gratification received for dependency yearnings or attention seeking (Hinsie & Campbell, 1973). According to Dollard and Miller (1950), secondary gains may help to reinforce disability symptoms and thereby reduce a client's motivation for treatment. Similarly, Weiss and Bergen (1968) report that secondary gains, in the form of "sick role" behaviors, enable impaired persons to receive gratification for their dependency needs without loss of self-esteem. Within insurance compensation systems, the degree of "sick" behavior demonstrated by claimants also can be used to determine the final monetary settlement. Thus the disability may become a source of positive reinforcement for a client, thereby delaying a speedy recovery (Eaton, 1979; Lynch, 1978; Matkin, 1983c). It is necessary for the rehabilitation professional to evaluate the client's feelings about "rewards" received in relation to their impact on selecting and moving toward vocational goal attainment.

Work Disincentives   The disincentive issue in vocational counseling arises because of the existence of various insurance benefit programs that provide cash and income transfers only to those people who withdraw from the labor market either temporarily or permanently. According to Berkowitz (1981, p. 40), the efforts of rehabilitation professionals "to assist people to return to the labor market are hampered by the natural disinclination of clients to lose their assured stream of benefits, which they regard as necessary for the very sustenance of life." Within the United States are a variety of compensation systems of disability transfer payments (see Chapters 2 and 3). For example, in the private sector, people buy policies or work for employers who provide these on a group basis. Social insurance payments, on the other hand, are contingent upon whether a person has contributed to a program over the years. Moreover, indemnity program payments depend on whether one can prove negligence in an individual tort action. Finally, income support programs transfer payments to people who are not only disabled, but also meet economic need criteria defined by various programs. It is only in certain workers' compensation programs and in the indemnity programs, however, that workers continue to receive benefits in spite of earning income simultaneously (Berkowitz, 1981). In all other wage replacement programs, earnings in the competitive labor market constitute prima facie evidence of one's ability to work, thus resulting in payment termination. In general, the more adequate the benefit provisions are in achieving *income replacement* goals, the greater their work disincentive effects (Munts & Garfinkel, 1974).

Table 7–1 shows the growth in disability transfer payments to persons of working age from 1970 through 1977. A quick review of the dollar amounts paid by each program over the years reveals anywhere from a 100% to 300% increase in compensation payments. In addition to these sources of transfer payments, a whole host of direct service program benefits are available to disabled clients who have limited income or assets. Table 7–2 lists 46 federal programs in which vocational rehabilitation clients or their families might participate. Thus, a person receiving disability insurance payments may be eligible for Medicare, food stamps, housing subsidies, possibly Veterans' Administration benefits, and a series of other social services; all or most of which might be lost, in addition to medical and transfer payments, should the disabled client return to work.

Perhaps the most important factor influencing the extent of a worker's unemployment, and subsequently a major contributor to employment disincentive, is the availability of jobs in the competitive marketplace. Similarly, the degree of job seeking activity and a client's concept of an "acceptable" job also affect the extent of that person's unemployment. How hard a person searches for a job and how rigid one's definition is of an acceptable job will depend upon several personal factors; the cost of being unemployed, the amount of personal income and assets in reserve, the income and assets of other family members, the degree of preference and flexibility for one type of job versus another, and one's attitude about work in general (Munts & Garfinkel, 1974; Roche, 1973).

Table 7-1. Disability Transfer Payments

Disability Payments	1970	1975	1976	1977
Insurance Programs				
Whole life	$ 232,900	$ 426,000	$ 458,000	$ 495,000
Health-long-term				
disability	1,817,000	2,618,000	2,795,000	3,109,000
Accidental death and				
dismemberment	150,000	300,000	330,000	360,000
Federal life	29,579	47,772	53,015	61,999
	2,229,479	3,391,772	3,639,015	4,025,999
Retirement Plans				
Federal civil service	525,671	1,255,876	1,548,583	1,900,782
State and local	295,000	490,000	560,000	630,000
Railroads	219,336	389,198	411,758	441,272
Armed forces	488,041	842,444	919,708	967,328
Private pensions	1,126,000	2,234,000	2,314,000	2,369,000
	2,654,048	5,211,518	5,740,049	6,308,388
Social Insurance Programs				
Social Security				
Disability Insurance	2,778,118	8,413,941	9,965,698	11,462,635
Workers' compensation	1,947,461	3,612,384	4,175,560	5,103,146
Black lung	7,000	537,990	561,490	565,828
	4,732,579	12,564,315	14,702,748	17,131,609
Total Indemnity Payments				
Automobile bodily injury	4,125,178	6,160,726	7,139,320	7,859,738
Miscellaneous bodily				
injury	848,602	2,332,702	2,805,498	3,168,823
Veterans' compensation	2,335,311	3,432,786	3,787,519	4,174,041
	7,309,091	11,926,214	13,732,337	15,202,602
Income Support Programs				
Supplemental Security				
Income	1,073,000	2,946,543	3,202,563	3,371,653
Aid to Families with				
Dependent Children	301,000	580,000	643,000	655,000
Veterans' pensions	1,050,405	673,194	752,713	899,008
	2,424,405	4,199,737	4,598,276	4,925,661
Totals	19,300,000	37,300,000	42,400,000	47,600,000

Source: From Berkowitz, M. (1980). *Work disincentives*. Falls Church, VA: Institute for Information Studies. Reprinted by permission.

Table 7–2.   Federal Programs for Income Security by
Eligibility Rules for Current Income

No-Income Rules
Medicare, for aged and disabled persons
Veterans' compensation for service-connected disability
Veterans' compensation for service death
Veterans' housing loans
Veterans' medical care for service-connected disability
Veterans' educational assistance for veterans, dependents, and survivors
Veterans' vocational rehabilitation allowance for 30% disability
Retirement (federal civil service and military)
Social security for persons aged 72 and over
Federal employees' compensation for job-related injuries
Meals for certain persons aged 60 and over

Limit on Wages (for beneficiaries under age 72)
Social Security: Old Age, Survivors, and Disability Insurance

Limit on Wages and Some Public Benefits
Railroad retirement, disability, and survivor benefits
Unemployment insurance (federal, state, railroad, and trade adjustment)
Black lung benefits for miners, dependents, and survivors

Limit on Wages, Some Public Benefits, and Unearned Private Income
Cash Aid
  Aid to Families with Dependent Children
  Supplemental Security Income
  Veterans' pensions for nonservice-connected disability or death
  General assistance to specific groups (Cubans, Indians, disaster pop-
    ulations, and emergency assistance)
Food Benefits
  Food stamps
  School programs (breakfast, lunch, and milk)
  Special supplemental feeding for women, infants, and children
Health Benefits
  Medicaid
  Medical care for veterans with nonservice-connected disability
  Comprehensive health services
  Children's programs (dental, comprehensive health, infant care proj-
    ects, and crippled children's services)
Housing
  Low-rent public housing
  Rent supplements
  Homeownership loans, urban and rural, private and rental
  Rural housing (technical assistance, site loans, repair loans)

Table 7-2 *(continued)*

Indian housing (improvement and technical assistance)
Education
   Basic educational grants
   College work-study
   Student loans (various kinds for special fields)
   Head Start and Follow Through for primary school children
   Upward Bound and Talent Search for high school students
   Work-study vocational education
Jobs and Training
   Job Training Act
   Work incentive projects
   Vocational Rehabilitation (public agencies)
   ACTION-sponsored programs (foster grandparents and senior companions)
   Career opportunities program
Social Services
   Services to needy families on welfare (counseling, day care, homemaker
      service, health care)
   Services to needy, aged, blind, or disabled
   Legal services for the poor

Source: From Walls, R.T., Masson, C., & Werner, T.J. (1977). Negative incentives to vocational rehabilitation. *Rehabilitation Literature, 38*, 143–150. Reprinted by permission.

Although no grand solutions are on the horizon to minimize the fact that for some being unemployed provides more income and service benefits than working provides, rehabilitation practitioners and disabled clients must work toward vocational goals that are realistic. One method by which work disincentives can be reduced is to assist clients to find work that at least approximates the benefits available through programs in which a client is eligible. Although this suggestion is no guarantee that work disincentives will be overcome, or instill a desire to work in those clients who do not possess it, it focuses attention on one of many "secondary gains" that can undermine rehabilitation services if left unattended.

Unions   Another potential obstacle to vocational rehabilitation, that must be identified and addressed in vocational counseling, is whether or not labor union involvement must be considered. In those cases wherein the disabled client is a union member, it will be necessary to determine if the union in question incorporates a seniority system and how that affects members injured on the job. On the other hand, some unions do not have provisions that allow for injured members to return to work in any other capacity than the one held at the time of injury, despite transferable skills. More important, in those cases where union policies exist that jeopardize accrued seniority if a member returns to a different job in the same pre-injury work environment, loss of work incentive may follow. Therefore, prior to helping the client focus too narrowly on one vocational choice, it is wise for the rehabilitation practitioner to investigate and discuss potential problems such as these with appropriate union representatives who are or might be involved.

Hidden Agendas In many ways much of the preceding factors concern what Deneen and Hessellund (1981) appropriately label "hidden agendas" (e.g., attitudes, biases, expectations, and other variables brought to vocational counseling by all interested parties in the rehabilitation process). Before proceeding further, however, it is important to mention that not all conscious or unconscious hidden agendas sabotage the rehabilitation process. Some are positive, such as the need to maintain or further develop self-esteem, and can be used by the rehabilitation professional to enhance and facilitate successful vocational outcomes. Nevertheless, it is important, indeed necessary, for rehabilitation practitioners to be aware of hidden agendas of others that may surface through the disabled client.

In seeking to advocate unconditionally for the disabled client, plaintiff (i.e., injured worker) attorneys attempt to build the best case possible to justify maximum benefits and allowances for those they represent. It should be remembered too that plaintiff attorney fees represent a percentage of the client's final settlement; that is, the larger the award, the more substantial the sum received for legal services. Similarly, defense (i.e., insurance program) attorneys seek the best solutions for their clientele in the form of the least expense possible within the spirit and letter of legal mandates of compensation. On the other hand, defense attorneys frequently are employees of those they represent which reduces the likelihood of their salaries fluctuating on a case by case basis. In both instances, however, attorneys attempt to provide what their respective clients *want*; albeit, in an adversarial relationship the outcomes may be at odds. Within this situation, an effective and skilled rehabilitation practitioner communicates with attorneys by emphasizing the *objective* data upon which rehabilitation plans and services are based to best serve the *needs* of clients (Deneen & Hessellund, 1981). It is incumbent upon the rehabilitation professional to be able to justify recommendations made and actions taken throughout the rehabilitation process based on information gathered, received, processed, and transmitted as objectively as possible. In this manner, realistic plans can be developed and their acceptance by others be enhanced.

Cost containment is a necessary and pivotal concern among insurance representatives responsible for referring disabled clients for rehabilitation services. Although insurance representatives are willing to provide the necessary services to facilitate a client's return to work, their main concern is to remove the injured worker from the "cost" side of the ledger (Deneen & Hessellund, 1981). When dealing with insurance representatives, rehabilitation professionals should be mindful of several other variables besides reducing costs as quickly as possible. For instance, a case may be referred simply because the insurance representative has too many claim files to process effectively, or not enough clerical support to assist in proper screening of referrals. On the other hand, the insurance representative may be responding to company pressure to "move" cases, or taking a more personal initiative to demonstrate to supervisors how cost conscious he or she is. Additionally, rehabilitation professionals may receive cases in order for the insurance representative to determine how the practitioner compares with other service providers in terms of cost, timeliness, recommendations, services delivered, and so forth. Regardless of the purpose(s) underlying client referrals, however, rehabilitation practitioners should approach each case in as an objective manner as possible, taking no particular side, and keeping all interested parties informed throughout the progress of the case.

Finally, rehabilitation professionals have their own hidden agendas also. As Deneen and Hessellund (1981, p. 160) indicate, the rehabilitation professional "believes in work." This belief may conflict with values expressed by others, but should not be used in a judgmental manner if vocational recommendations are not accepted by a client who opts for nonparticipation because work disincentives are not offset sufficiently. Most importantly, rehabilitation service providers must be cognizant that they should attend to the needs of *all* concerned parties within the service delivery process as best as possible. This includes the practitioner's employer unless one is in private practice. This concern deals more with accountability issues and the delicate balance of professional and business ethics that will be discussed in Chapter 10. Suffice it to say at this point, however, private rehabilitation practitioners cannot escape the fact that because their personal income depends on the number of clients served, fees for services must be defensible in terms of the amount charged, the need for the services rendered, and the time taken to provide the services requested by referral sources.

Occupational Information

The reader will recall from Table 4-1 that vocational counseling was reported to be the most frequently offered service within the private sector, as well as being perceived to be the most important rehabilitation service regardless of employment setting. Through vocational counseling, rehabilitation professionals assist disabled clients to better understand the relationship between themselves and their present or anticipated environment. Therefore, while vocational counseling provides the structure within which clients can select vocational goals and work toward possibly changing their behaviors and attitudes to facilitate goal attainment, the substance upon which vocational selection rests is occupational information. Although the basic purpose of vocational counseling remains constant (i.e., clarification of a client's situation leading toward a client's self-determination of vocational choice), the techniques used by the rehabilitation professional obviously will vary according to the individual needs of each client. Thus, the use of career information in vocational counseling similarly is based upon the client's situation and needs.

The rehabilitation professional's decision about whether to use career materials, and if so, when, which ones, and how to present them in the most meaningful manner, cannot be prescribed automatically. Although it is not practical to construct in "cookbook" fashion those ingredients to combine for certain results, it is necessary to consider important areas that require attention when formulating realistic vocational choices. In addition to those factors that clients bring to the rehabilitation process that must be considered when developing vocational plans, the rehabilitation professional is responsible for providing occupational information to enable clients to select suitable careers. In order for this information to be meaningful and useful, it should be as up-to-date and accurate as possible, taking into consideration current labor market trends, government policies concerning wage and hour regulations, affirmative action and accessibility issues and policies, and organized labor issues. Armed with these areas of vocational knowledge, the rehabilitation professional can provide occupational information that will enable disabled clients to select the most appropriate vocational goals to meet their needs.

Acquiring Occupational Information

The United States Department of Labor recently reported that Americans change occupations four times during their work careers; suggesting further a need for job retraining for entry into newly developed technical fields (Alexander, 1983). For disabled and nondisabled people alike, acquisition of occupational information provides knowledge to facilitate career choice, identify training programs to remediate skill deficiencies, and establish realistic job placement goals. According to Andrisani (1978), vocational knowledge incorporates a general description of the world of work, specific descriptions of discrete jobs, job search information, and work adjustment requirements to meet job demand characteristics. Functioning in a vocational counselor capacity, rehabilitation professionals serve as brokers of occupational information, relying on many resource materials to provide accurate and current data about jobs and training programs. Although compiling a comprehensive collection of occupational resource materials is time-consuming and requires periodic updating, it is an essential component for vocational counseling to be effective.

Notwithstanding the importance of possessing comprehensive occupational resource materials, attempting to collect everything that provides information about careers is impractical. Considerations such as space needed for storage, cost, and degree of utilization are sufficient to rule out such an extravagant approach. Careful selection is necessary to assure the acquisition of pertinent and useful materials, as well as developing effective and efficient methods for storage and retrieval. Thus, before undertaking the collection process, attention must be given to several factors identified by Isaacson (1971). These include: (1) determining the group of clients who will make major use of the materials and selecting materials appropriate for them; (2) assessing the nature of the community in terms of resources and information available that will be useful for the specific group of clients to be served; (3) determining the level of personal and/or staff expertise to use acquired materials; (4) planning the manner in which materials will be used, taking into consideration their durability and the number of copies to order; (5) identifying materials one already has or has access to from cooperating sources; (6) identifying auxiliary local resources where similar or additional materials can be found, such as the local library or clubs; and (7) assessing the funds necessary to purchase materials, as well as identifying alternative methods of securing needed information (e.g., grants, donations). Following these steps, the rehabilitation professional will be able to begin collecting career materials.

Initiating Collection   The extent or range of materials that will need to be considered obviously is based upon the range of client disabilities and work types within the group. Ordinarily, the rehabilitation professional should assign highest priority to selecting materials in the following order: (1) first attempt to meet those needs that are most urgent within the group; (2) select materials that are likely to have the broadest appeal and application among clients served; and (3) select specialized materials or those that provide depth in areas of greatest interest. Finally, Isaacson (1971, pp. 409–410) identifies eight steps that should be taken by rehabilitation professionals in order to gain familiarity with what is currently available in the occupational literature:

1. Subscribe to some of the indexes listing occupational materials, e.g., *Career Index, Guidance Exchange, Occupational Index.*
2. Request price lists from those state and federal agencies that publish materials, e.g., the Government Printing Office's *Monthly Catalog.*
3. Obtain some of the more recent bibliographies of occupational materials such as the National Vocational Guidance Association *Bibliography* or other materials contained in the appendices.

4. Check recent professional publications in the rehabilitation and related occupational fields.
5. Obtain price lists from commercial publishers that have materials directly related to occupations.
6. Ascertain from appropriate professional organizations and societies, private industries, industrial associations, and private companies what materials they have available that are appropriate for the disabled clients served.
7. Contact educational institutions for publications.
8. Determine what general items or basic resource volumes are essential for immediate use (e.g., *Dictionary of Occupational Titles, Occupational Outlook Handbook, Occupational Outlook Quarterly*).

Once collection of occupational resource materials has begun, it is necessary to begin evaluating the materials received.

Evaluating Career Information   Evaluation is an integral part of building an adequate or better career library. A rehabilitation professional should always keep in mind the group that will be using the materials, and the needs of that group. Furthermore, it is important to remember the staff that will use the materials and the ways in which the materials will be used. Finally, evaluation of career information materials must consider the costs in relation to use, not to mention in relation to funds available. Additionally, there are several criteria against which each possible acquisition should be measured. These criteria are accuracy, recency, usability, reader appeal, and thoroughness of content (Isaacson, 1971).

Storage and Retrieval   Once the rehabilitation professional has initiated the collection process and later becomes involved in maintaining needed materials, methods of storage and retrieval require attention. Indeed, despite selecting only those materials pertinent to the needs of disabled clients served, it will soon become obvious that the content and volume of information are overwhelming. More importantly, without a system of storage that allows for easy and quick retrieval, the information acquired becomes virtually useless. Perhaps the easiest method of filing is by arranging information alphabetically. This method works best when filing unbound occupational materials that can be contained in folders, each of which is labeled with the occupational title according to content. On the other hand, as occupational files grow larger, simple alphabetizing becomes less efficient. As this occurs, the rehabilitation professional may wish to select methods of coding or cross-referencing materials by job title, year of publication, location of job, and so forth. Moreover, with the advent of home and small office computers, those able and willing to make the financial investment for such equipment will quickly discover the efficiency of these systems in terms of information retrieval.

Before leaving this section, it is important to mention that acquisition of occupational information should not be thought of as confined strictly to job descriptions and similar materials related only to vocational exploration, training, and job availability. Acquiring occupational information refers also to gathering materials and data pertaining to issues that affect vocational selection, job placement, and eventually rehabilitation outcome. For example, current files must be maintained regarding state and federal regulations affecting compensation policies and statutes, guidelines for selecting and hiring employees, rules and regulations pertaining to architectural and transportation barrier removal, and organized labor issues. Although this and other chapters, along with many of the appendices address current compensation policies, it would be remiss not to include these other issues requiring attention during vocational counseling and job placement processes.

Wage and Hour Regulations

In order to facilitate employment or training of disabled clients who are receiving rehabilitation services, federal regulations have been established by Congress and the Secretary of Labor. Provisions contained in the Fair Labor Standards Act of 1938 as amended in 1966, 1971, and 1980, and the Walsh Healy Public Contracts Act allow certificates to be issued that exempt employers from minimum wage requirements in certain instances. Under these regulations, public vocational rehabilitation agencies have the authority to issue 90-day certificates permitting employers to pay disabled clients less than minimum wage rates based on client productivity levels. However, these certificates do not allow less than 50% of the current minimum wage to be paid regardless of whether client productivity is below that level.

On the other hand, if a client is so severely disabled that productivity is below 50% of the average among nondisabled workers, a regional office of the United States Department of Labor's Wage and Hour Division may, upon adequate documentation provided by the employer, issue a certificate below the 50% level but not less than 25% of the prevailing minimum wage. According to Bitter (1979), the wage identified in a *temporary* certificate must reflect the client's productivity and be consistent with wages paid nondisabled workers in the community performing the same quality and quantity of work. Although wage and hour certificates are temporary by nature, in order to minimize abuse, it is possible for employers to apply for a continuing certificate that can be issued for a period not to exceed one year. Typically, such an application would be made during the 90-day temporary certificate period (Bitter, 1979). Moreover, special certificates for payment of subminimum wages can be made to competitive employment firms, sheltered workshops, and sheltered workshop clients, although the latter two groups generally are thought to be the only ones eligible for these considerations.

Within sheltered workshops, three program categories may apply for certificates in which no minimum wage guarantee is required (i.e., evaluation, training, and work activity center programs). In the case of evaluation and training programs, a written curriculum and progress reports for each disabled client must be maintained on a regular basis. However, if goods are produced while in evaluation or training, the client must be paid wages commensurate with the level of productivity (Bitter, 1979). In the case of a work activity center program, statutes require physical separation of the center and its programs from all other activities of the sheltered workshop. Additionally, in order for such a program to be considered to be a work activity center, the nature of the activities must be primarily therapeutic for disabled clients possessing an inconsequential productive capacity.

Nondiscrimination Employment Regulations

The world of the personnel manager has changed dramatically as the Equal Employment Opportunity Commission (EEOC) and the courts have enforced and interpreted Title VII of the Civil Rights Act of 1964 (P.L. 88–352). In addition, there has been a plethora of other laws and government regulations related to equal opportunity in the workplace that rehabilitation professionals must be aware exist as they may pertain to their disabled client populations. Among the groups affected and protected by such laws are minorities, women, handicapped persons, disabled veterans, and Vietnam veterans.

Equal Employment Opportunity   Title VII of the Civil Rights Act became operative in July, 1965, and stipulated that it is an unlawful employment practice for employers to (a) discriminate against hiring an individual or (b) limit, segregate, or classify employees by virtue of race, color, religion, sex, or national origin. Since that time, Title VII has been amended to include other affected groups identified in the Equal Employment Opportunity Act of 1972, the Rehabilitation Act of 1973, and the Civil Service Reform Act of 1978. Before 1965, however, the only major legal constraints on employer selection practices were the state and local Fair Employment Practice statutes dating back to 1945; their effectiveness varying considerably from one jurisdiction to another depending on the political climate and funds available for enforcement (Miner & Miner, 1979).

As with any federal legislation, the final impact of prescribed legal remedies is determined by the United States Supreme Court. Currently, the definition of discrimination in employment opportunity encompasses what is known as unjust treatment, or *denial of equal treatment* (Pati & Adkins, 1981). Under this theory, employers would not be found guilty of employment discrimination if all job applicants or all employees are treated equally in matters of hiring, promotion, discipline, and so forth. In the absence of equal treatment or allegations to that effect, the EEOC has been given direct enforcement powers under the Equal Employment Opportunity Act of 1972 to seek remedies and injunctions against employers if conciliation efforts fail to yield an acceptable disposition of a charge. Moreover, the EEOC is responsible for enforcement of portions of rehabilitation legislation concerning affirmative action.

Affirmative Action and Accommodations   Equal employment opportunity legislation for handicapped citizens rest primarily in Congressional acts and Executive Orders enacted since 1973. For handicapped people these recent laws protect their rights to equal opportunity for education, housing, mobility, and employment; information that should be considered by the rehabilitation professional when presenting occupational information. Among the laws providing a legal framework for the employment of disabled people are the Rehabilitation Act of 1973 and its amendments, the Vietnam Era Veteran's Readjustment Assistance Act of 1972 and its amendment, and Executive Orders 11914 and 12250.

The 1973 Rehabilitation Act (P.L. 93–112), and its amendments in 1974 (P.L. 93–515), in 1978 (P.L. 95–602), and in 1984 (P.L. 98–221) prohibit discrimination against individuals on the basis of a physical or mental handicap if the individual is qualified to perform the specified job and reasonable accommodations are possible by the employer. These provisions are contained in Sections 501 through 505 of Title V of the Act and are discussed briefly below, as well as presented in Table 7–3:

Section 501.   This section mandates federal agencies to develop affirmative action programs to recruit, promote, and fully use handicapped people. It covers nonelected, nonappointed jobs and positions in executive agencies, the legislature, and the judiciary of the federal government and the District of Columbia.

Section 502.   This section establishes the Architectural and Transportation Barriers Compliance Board within the federal government to enforce the Architectural Barriers Act of 1968. This Act requires government funded or assisted public buildings and facilities to be made accessible to handicapped people.

Section 503.   Any organization or business that receives federal contracts or subcontracts of more than $2,500 annually must have an affirmative action program to recruit and more fully use handicapped persons in their employment.

Section 504.   This section prohibits discrimination against present employees, beneficiaries, and applicants for employment or admission to programs by recipients of federal assistance. This provision is applicable to recipients of federal funding grants, including virtually every public and private institution or business.

Section 505. This section provides for remedies and attorneys' fees in an action involving violation of the rights of handicapped people.

Table 7–3. Legal Framework of Nondiscrimination in Employment

Legislation	Base(s) of Nondiscrimination	Employers Covered	Enforcement Agency
Civil Rights Act of 1964, Title VII	Race, color, religion, national origin, sex	All firms with more than 15 employees	EEOC
Executive Order 11246 as amended by Executive Order 11375 (1965 and 1967 respectively)	Race, color, religion, national origin, sex	Firms with federal contracts in excess of $10,000	OFCCP
Equal Employment Opportunity Act, amendments to Title VII	Race, color, religion, national origin, sex	State and local governments and federal contractors	EEOC
Rehabilitation Act of 1973 as amended in 1974 and 1978:	Handicapped		
Section 501		Federal agencies	EEOC
Section 502		Public and private sectors	A&TBCB
Section 503		Federal contractors and subcontractors	OFCCP
Section 504		Federally funded grants and programs	* Dept. of Health and Human Services

Table 7–3   *(continued)*

Legislation	Base(s) of Nondiscrimination	Employers Covered	Enforcement Agency
Vietnam Era Veteran's Readjustment Assistance Act of 1972 as amended in 1974, Section 402	Disabled veterans and Vietnam era veterans	Federal contractors and subcontractors	OFCCP
Executive Order 11914, 1976	Handicapped under Section 504 of the 1973 Rehabilitation Act	Federally assisted programs	Dept. of Health and Human Services
* Executive Order 12250, 1980	Transfer jurisdiction of Executive Order 11914 to the Dept. of Justice		

In 1972 the Vietnam Era Veteran's Readjustment Assistance Act was passed by Congress (and subsequently amended in 1974) to provide affirmative action for that group of disabled veterans. Section 402 of the Act stipulated that employers who receive federal contracts or subcontracts of $10,000 or more annually must take affirmative action to employ, advance, and fully use disabled Vietnam era veterans.

Executive Order 11914, issued by President Ford in 1976, mandated the Department of Health and Human Services (formerly the Department of Health, Education, and Welfare) to issue guidelines to enforce Section 504 of the 1973 Rehabilitation Act. Late in 1980, President Carter issued Executive Order 12250 that transferred lead agency coordination responsibility for Section 504 enforcement to the Department of Justice.

Organized Labor

Traditionally, employment opportunities for disabled clients have been greatest in the public sector; in large part supported by federal mandates such as those above and others found in Chapter 2. As rehabilitation professionals begin the process of assisting disabled clients to identify and explore realistic vocational goals directed toward employment in the competitive labor market, information must be gathered and communicated regarding organized labor union functions. Becoming familiar with the structure and practices of labor unions in terms of their influence on working conditions and entry requirements for applicants in certain trades and professions is essential prior to job placement activities. Therefore, by taking the time to learn about unions during the occupational information stage, rehabilitation professionals and clients will be better prepared to enter job placement knowing how labor unions can enhance employment outcomes, rather than being perceived as a barrier to employment.

Central to the structure of organized labor are the international unions, each of which consists of regional organizations, that in turn are composed of local unions (Bitter, 1979). As indicated, most international unions belong to a federation of independent internationals, called the American Federation of Labor-Congress of Industrial Organizations (AF of L-CIO). The purpose of the federated structure is to influence policy and legislation at national, state, and local levels, provide technical assistance to affiliated local unions, and represent members in contract negotiations with management representatives (Bitter, 1979; Mallik & Moretti, 1982).

At the local level, organized labor unions generally are composed of three levels. At the top is an elected representative of the union membership whose responsibility is to interact with the international union office and serve as spokesperson for the local union membership with management. At the middle level, most unions have a business agent. This person generally is paid by the union to recruit personnel, introduce new employees to the job, be involved in contract enforcement between the union and management, and handle grievances (Bitter, 1979). Finally, at the third level is the shop steward who is either elected or appointed by the member coworkers or higher level union officials. Typically, the shop steward is responsible for interacting with employees on a day-to-day basis in order to provide informal personal counseling and facilitate cooperative activities between coworkers, as well as between management and union members (Bitter, 1979).

Beyond the organizational structure of unions, the rehabilitation professional needs to become familiar with union policies regarding seniority, wage structures, and the ability among members to change jobs within a union shop. These areas are necessary to explore especially when consideration is being given to returning a disabled client to the former job, or one that can be performed with transferable skills, within the pre-injury work site. Activities designed to keep the rehabilitation professional informed of labor union practices and policies include gathering current brochures and pamphlets about local unions, developing and maintaining working relationships with union representatives to obtain information about manpower needs and job openings that can accommodate disabled clients, and assisting local unions to better understand the nature and purpose of vocational rehabilitation services.

Labor Market Surveying

Once the rehabilitation professional and the client have begun exploration of a variety of occupations that possibly are within the client's capability and interests, vocational decision making becomes more focused. Thus, as specific vocational goals become more clear, as well as the necessary activities required to enhance job readiness and placement in a specific occupation, it is incumbent on the rehabilitation professional to determine in advance the extent of job availability in the local community. Needless to say, if a specific occupation is agreed upon by all parties in the vocational rehabilitation process, but either the job per se does not exist or else there are neither openings nor immediate prospect for them, then the time, effort, and monies invested pursuing that occupational goal will be difficult to justify. More important, should these investments prove to be fruitless, confidence in the rehabilitation professional's ability to make sound vocational recommendations will decrease among the client, insurance representative, and all other concerned parties involved in the case. Thus, *before* recommending and implementing strategies to achieve a specific occupational goal, a labor market survey should be conducted.

Labor market information indicates what jobs exist, estimates their frequency in the economy of a given region, and forecasts their growth or decline in the future (Vandergoot, Swirsky, & Rice, 1982). Coupling labor market information with occupational information enables a disabled client and rehabilitation professional to select an occupation that is not only suitable, but also is or will be available when job placement activities begin. It is necessary then for rehabilitation professionals to know where such information can be obtained, what information is needed, and when a labor market survey is most appropriate.

Where to Locate Information   The United States Department of Labor regularly publishes forecasts of the national economy, as well as state and local regions, in terms of affected jobs and manpower needs. Although these sources are useful in providing a general overview of labor markets, and as such should be obtained by rehabilitation service providers, their accuracy can fluctuate when applied locally. For example, within a local economy, a labor strike, a plant closing, or changes in area tax rates can have significant consequences on job availability that are not predictable from national or regional forecasts (Vandergoot et al., 1982). Similarly, another factor that must be considered about national and regional labor market forecasts is their timeliness. Because the length of time required to gather, analyze, and publish data generally takes a year or more, and costs for such studies affect the number of times they are repeated, large scale labor market forecasts may not be as reflective of the present job situation as one would like. Furthermore, specific details about work characteristics of jobs are less than adequately covered by virtue of the volume of data contained. However, using this information as a starting point, along with other sources such as the *Dictionary of Occupational Titles*, the *Occupational Outlook Handbook*, and job analysis data (see Chapter 6), rehabilitation professionals can conduct their own surveys of local labor market trends.

What Information to Gather When plans are being made to conduct a local labor market survey regarding a specific occupation, it is important to be as thorough as possible since the information gathered will be used to substantiate or reject plans to pursue a particular career goal. Therefore, when gathering and reporting labor market information, the following areas require attention according to the California Association of Rehabilitation Professionals (1982, pp. 18–20):

1. Specify the resources used to obtain the labor market information.
   A. Statistical information found in federal, state, and regional publications, as well as newspaper want ads.
   B. Employer contacts that document the name and job title of the person providing the information.
   C. Training program contacts that specify the skills taught for specific jobs, names and locations of employers who have hired graduates, average length of time needed to acquire competitive employment skills, and program costs and salary ranges of employed graduates.
2. Indicate the scope of the survey to obtain the labor market information.
   A. Report the number of employers contacted and their geographic distribution in the community (the California Association of Rehabilitation Professionals recommends that seven to 10 employer contacts per occupation serve as an acceptable minimum).
   B. Estimate job availability in terms of short- and long-range projections, potential growth of the market and upward mobility, and the frequency of job turnover and hiring recency.
   C. Report the level of earnings at entry levels, as well as ceilings.
   D. Specify the qualifications required with regard to physical capacities, education, training, and experience, and job temperament factors (following the guidelines indicated in Chapter 6 for job analyses).

When to Perform a Labor Market Survey Not every disabled client's vocational goals will require that a labor market survey be conducted (e.g., those who return to work with the same pre-injury employer). On the other hand, when a vocational goal is being considered that requires retraining directed toward a new occupation, or self-employment, a labor market survey is recommended (California Association of Rehabilitation Professionals, 1982).

Thus, information gathered about current and potential labor market trends can assist in shaping the most appropriate career goals and methods by which they can best be achieved. Indeed, this knowledge can enhance and facilitate subsequent job placement efforts.

Summary

Vocational counseling represents a means through which to transmit and receive information about the world of work. When providing such a service to disabled clients, it is important for rehabilitation professionals to create an atmosphere that is as least threatening as possible in order to enhance the free and unrestrained exchange of information. Although the methods by which rehabilitation professionals attain and foster two-way communications depend on factors such as personal style and the type(s) of counseling theories used, another necessary component is the information itself to be communicated and received. In this case, the rehabilitation professional attempts to provide comprehensive and useable information about occupations. In order for it to be useful, occupational information must take into account the characteristics of the client's disability, current labor market trends for specific occupations, income requirements of the disabled client, governmental regulations affecting hiring practices, the presence or absence of union membership requirements, and many other real-life work considerations. Thus, it is through the use of effective communication of relevant and comprehensive vocational information that the rehabilitation professional and disabled client can move closer to attaining job placement.

8 Job Placement

E mployment development for and job placement of disabled clients are perhaps the most unique characteristics that set apart the vocational rehabilitation field from other human service professions. Indeed, locating job openings may be the most important phase within the rehabilitation process after a client's abilities have been identified. The effectiveness of job placement services, however, evolves from an ongoing interrelationship between onset of the disability and timeliness of referral, nature of the disabling condition and residual capacities, job analysis data, vocational evaluation results, vocational counseling, and occupational information, not to mention the background and psychological features brought to the process by the client, and the legal system in which services are provided.

Although it can be argued that considering job placement details at the outset of rehabilitation may be premature, it is important that job development activities be considered early in the process in order to facilitate and enhance subsequent job placement planning. Rather than repeat much of the rehabilitation literature concerning job placement techniques, the purpose of this chapter is to provide readers with information that can be useful for avoiding job placement "pitfalls." In order to accomplish this goal, the chapter is divided into four sections: (1) the importance of job placement; (2) the role of the rehabilitation professional as a placement specialist; (3) job placement alternative approaches; and (4) the business of marketing job placement.

Importance of Job Placement

Regardless of employment setting or whether a practitioner is operating within a public or private insurance rehabilitation system, vocational rehabilitation represents a goal-oriented program culminating in gainful activity. As part of the total rehabilitation process, job placement represents more than simply "icing on the cake." Rather, it is an "ingredient" that must receive continuous consideration initiated as close to the beginning of the rehabilitation process as possible. By keeping job placement in mind in the early stages of the rehabilitation process, rehabilitation professionals will be able to begin gathering information and resources that will be needed when job placement activities are ready to be implemented. In other words, the effectiveness of job placement, as well as all other services, is enhanced tremendously by anticipating, preparing for, coordinating, and timing properly the implementation of its activities. Moreover, the importance of job placement of disabled persons is reflected in various statutes and rehabilitation research investigations. However, before implementing job placement strategies, the issues of job readiness must be understood.

Work Readiness Versus Job Readiness

According to Bitter (1968), work readiness refers to a general concept that compares an individual's personal attributes to the world of work. In this sense, people are work ready when they express a desire to work and are able to perform basic skills necessary for getting and holding any job. Examples of work readiness characteristics might include proper grooming and appearance for work in general, punctuality, politeness and responsiveness in dealing with supervisors and coworkers, and safe working habits. Job readiness, on the other hand, constitutes a specific aspect of work readiness. Bitter (1968) suggests that job readiness is the extent to which an individual's qualifications fit the skill requirements of a particular job. In each instance, readiness is defined in terms of how attributes of an individual correspond to the characteristics of jobs, both generally and specifically. Obviously, an individual needs both general and specific skills to be a successful worker, and the precise balance between the two varies from job to job.

Closely related to work/job readiness are the concepts of employability and placeability. According to Sinick (1969), employability refers to requisite skills and work personality factors necessary for specific jobs; whereas placeability refers to the perceived attractiveness of an applicant to an employer. Thus, labor market conditions and an employer's willingness to hire a disabled person affect a client's placeability independent of employability variables. Further clarification of the distinction between employability and placeability is offered by Dunn (1974), who defines the former term as "the capacity of the individual to function in a particular work situation or occupation"; whereas, "placeability . . . refers to the probability that the individual will obtain work in a particular occupation" (p. 39). This distinction is clearer than Sinick's because the difference between functioning on a job and obtaining a job suggests that different skills are involved. For example, Dunn (1974) includes factors such as social development, work personality, work methods, work habits, physical tolerance, basic academic skills, job site accessibility, and a client's ability to get to and from a job as part of employability. Placeability variables are refined further to include three components; job search activities, employer selection procedures, and job interviewing (Dunn, 1974). The job search includes knowing how to find job leads; employer selection procedures include providing credible information to employers seeking applicants; and job interview skills consist of an ability to make a good impression (Vandergoot, 1982).

Finally, the rehabilitation professional must be prepared to assess the readiness of a disabled client to return to employment. By taking into account the interaction between personal attributes of disabled clients and work environment factors, Rosove (1982) suggests the following *readiness criteria* be met by clients:

1. An individual must be able to pick an occupation that is likely to be satisfying.
2. The individual must possess all of the skills and qualifications required of workers in his or her chosen occupation.
3. The individual must be able to perform an effective job search.
4. The individual must be able to demonstrate attitudes and behaviors congruent with the expectations of employers.
5. The individual must be able to cope with personal issues such as transportation, care of dependents, physical disabilities, and others in order to be ready and able to succeed on the job. (p. 115)

Importance of Job Placement in Rehabilitation Research

An annotated bibliography of job development and placement studies conducted between 1950 and 1982, available from the National Rehabilitation Information Center, reveals over 250 citations. Obviously, it is beyond the scope of this book to adequately cover such a vast array of job development and placement techniques, methods, and outcomes. On the other hand, several studies do require brief mention as they relate to the perceived importance of job development and placement activities among rehabilitation professionals.

Within the private rehabilitation sector, job development and placement services were reported to be offered by 88.5% and 90.8% (respectively) of the members of the National Association of Rehabilitation Professionals in the Private Sector (see Table 4-1). Notwithstanding the prevalence of these services within the private sector, Lynch and Martin (1982) indicate that private rehabilitation professionals report job development and placement to be among the most important areas in which training is needed. Although the importance of these two rehabilitation service areas seems apparent, especially for those employed by private rehabilitation companies that primarily serve workers' compensation caseloads, job development has received the least attention from rehabilitation personnel in terms of technological advances and practice according to Ugland (1977). Furthermore, this lack of performance of employment development activities is apparent particularly when examining role and function studies of rehabilitation counselors regardless of work setting (Emener & Rubin, 1980; Matkin, 1982e; Muthard & Salomone, 1969; Rubin et al., 1984).

According to Minton (1977, p. 144), a reluctance among rehabilitation counselors to engage in job development tasks may arise from "feeling(s) that talking to employers about hiring disabled people is comparable to a door-to-door salesman and as such is somewhat 'unprofessional'." For whatever reasons offered by practicing rehabilitation counselors to minimize their involvement in the job development process, the question of whose responsibility these duties are remains unclear. For example, Matkin's (1982e) research of the roles and functions of private rehabilitation professionals (i.e., counselors, nurses, and other practitioners) offered little clarification, although nurses reported significantly less involvement in this area than either of the other two groups. In spite of such inconclusive findings, and regardless of who performs job development activities, two facts are clear. First, research indicates that rehabilitation administrators, supervisors, and especially educators perceive job development to be more a part of a counselor's work than do counselors themselves (Emener & Rubin, 1980; Muthard & Salomone, 1969; Rubin et al., 1984). Such an inconsistency between perceptions can be a potential source of "professional burnout" or role strain for rehabilitation counselors. Second, in order for job placement activities to be performed efficiently, rehabilitation professionals must devote time to pursue employment development strategies.

Role of the Rehabilitation Professional in Job Placement

Kelso identifies a continuum of five rehabilitation role orientations to job placement: Arranger, Agent, Instructor, Guide, and Therapist (Bitter, 1979). Although each of these "roles" are used with specific reference to the job placement process, the alert reader will see how they are a microcosm of the entire rehabilitation process. For example, an *arranger* considers the placement function to be an opportunity to refer disabled clients to others who are best able to develop suitable employment contacts. This activity consists of coordinating, conferring, and cooperating with other agencies or persons that have knowledge of employment opportunities (Bitter, 1979). The *agent* role is one in which a rehabilitation professional considers placement to be a job of convincing employers of the abilities of disabled clients. In the agent role, job development activities are performed that may include job analysis, labor market surveying, public relations and educational seminars to inform potential employers of the capabilities of disabled persons, and solicitation of job openings.

The *instructor* attempts to teach disabled clients those behaviors that will assist in obtaining employment (i.e., work readiness training). According to Bitter (1979), this process begins with an analysis of a client's present level of job-seeking skills, followed by job-seeking rehearsal exercises such as completing job applications, presenting a favorable impression during job interviews, and learning how to respond to questions about work history, job skills, and disabling condition(s). A job placement *guide* functions as an information provider or resource to a disabled client. In this approach, the client is given occupational information and advice, as well as ultimate responsibility for decision-making about seeking and obtaining suitable employment. Finally, the *therapist* role seeks to assist disabled clients to better understand themselves in order to be better able to match their capabilities and limitations to the opportunities in the available employment market (Bitter, 1979). Before leaving this section of job placement, it is important to mention that the roles Kelso identifies are intended to maximize a disabled client's skills to function as independently, responsibly, and as confidently as possible when making vocational choices and seeking employment opportunities.

Job Placement Alternative Approaches

The reader will recall from Chapter 4 that approaches to job placement in the private rehabilitation sector typically follow a seven-point hierarchical strategy (e.g., first attempt to return a disabled client to the same job with the same employer, followed by returning to a modified job with the same employer). Although the merits of this method have been discussed previously, they bear repeating. According to Cheit (1961), when the individual work histories of insurance compensation cases are examined, it becomes clear that of all the paths to economic recovery, as well as for effectiveness and long-term success, none compare with a return to the job held at the time of injury. Moreover, a 1956 report of the International Association of Industrial Accident Boards and Commissions found this type of placement outnumbered "a thousandfold" all other forms of vocational rehabilitation (Cheit, 1961, p. 301). The report also found that for many workers, particularly those with limited educational background or heavy family responsibilities, vocational training, particularly prolonged academic programs, was not feasible. Finally, a return to former surroundings enables injured workers to take advantage of their background skills, contacts, and perhaps even accrued health and welfare benefits.

What happens, however, when a disabled client is unable to return to his or her former job, modified or not, and does not possess sufficient transferable skills to immediately assume a different type of work? In those cases where training might be indicated, one state found the following methods to contribute to successful rehabilitation outcome for its workers' compensation clients: 25% received formal training and were placed on a job at completion; 11% received formal training followed by on-the-job training; 9% were placed only in on-the-job training that led to subsequent employment; and 7% of the successful case closures represented self-employment (California Department of Industrial Relations, 1979). Although there are many specific methods to accomplish job placement, only four will be discussed because they perhaps have the greatest potential for returning disabled clients in a timely manner when training is required. These include on-the-job training, projects with industry, apprenticeships, and using employment agencies.

On-The-Job Training

Some employment situations require neither specialized educational preparation nor specific vocational experience as a prerequisite. The absence of such requirements means that the worker operations either can be learned readily in a brief demonstration period, or are such that only a minimum general education is sufficient to prepare the worker for the tasks. In addition to these characteristics that are generally subsumed in on-the-job tasks, workers with transferable skills and/or prolonged opportunities to observe other tasks going on around them during the course of their work routine might be able to learn new skills without need for formal training. Most commonly, however, employers offer on-the-job training when basic essentials of production can be learned in a relatively brief period of time, so that the worker is assigned soon to the task for which he or she was employed.

On the other hand, when the basic operation of a job is performed by a team or crew of skilled workers, the new employee may be assigned to a more skilled worker or to a team as a helper. This provides an opportunity to learn a complex task by observing and assisting skilled employees for a specified period. Some employers may rotate the beginner, so that the novice serves a period with several teams involved in different aspects of the work, thus becoming familiar with several phases before assignment to a specific job. Frequently, however, job rotation does not provide a trainee comprehensive preparation in all parts of the work.

When deciding to explore the possibility of placing a disabled client in an on-the-job training situation, rehabilitation professionals must be aware of regulations established by the United States Department of Labor governing such training programs. It is very important that all of the criteria listed below are met by the on-the-job training program, or else the client will be considered to be an employee rather than a trainee. If this occurs, not only might the disabled client risk losing a portion or all disability compensation benefit payments received during the "training," but also may lose the employment position. According to the United States Department of Labor Fair Labor Standards Act (1980), *all* criteria must occur for work to be considered on-the-job training:

1. The training, even though it includes actual operation of the facilities of the employer, must be similar to that which would be given in a vocational school;
2. The training is for the benefit of the trainees;
3. The trainees do not displace regular employees, but work under their close supervision;
4. The employer who provides the training derives no immediate advantages from the activities of the trainees, and on occasion the operations of the employment may actually be impeded;
5. Trainees are not necessarily entitled to a job at the conclusion of the training period; and
6. The employer and the trainee understand that trainees are not entitled to wages for the time spent in training.

Projects with Industry

Despite the emphasis on employment, little had been done to systematically bring private industry into partnership with vocational rehabilitation programs until 1968. In that year, amendments to the Vocational Rehabilitation Act (P.L. 90–391) introduced the Projects With Industry (PWI) authority to link public rehabilitation agencies closer with employer groups. Under the regulations governing PWI, any private employer has the opportunity to hire, train, and provide other necessary services to handicapped persons. Employers are paid for their identified costs under either stipulations contained in a federal contract, or through a jointly financed cooperative agreement with the Rehabilitation Services Administration with the United States Department of Education (Pati & Adkins, 1981; Tenth Institute on Rehabilitation Issues, 1983). PWI represents a recognition that the "customer" of vocational rehabilitation products is industry, insofar that the "product" is a productive, capable, and skilled worker who is qualified to meet the personnel needs of industry. Thus, PWI becomes the marketing arm of the rehabilitation system by identifying the manpower requirements of industry and providing a supply of qualified workers who meet those requirements.

In order for private employers to be involved in PWI projects, the following standards must be met: (a) the employer must agree to offer training for recognizable jobs; (b) there must be a planned and systematic sequence of training that will assure acquisition of the needed occupational skills; and (c) there must be a reasonable assurance of continued employment after on-the-job training has been completed (Tenth Institute on Rehabilitation Issues, 1983). In addition, jobs and their actual requirements must be identified (i.e., job analysis) to ensure that disabled clients will be properly selected in terms of abilities, as well as realistic training offered in relation to the type of job(s) performed. Finally, all support services needed by a disabled trainee must also be available and must be coordinated, either directly or by subcontract (Pati & Adkins, 1981).

Besides employers meeting specified criteria for eligibility in PWI programs, disabled clients must also be evaluated to determine their eligibility for assistance. PWIs are limited to "handicapped individuals" or those who have a physical or mental disability that constitutes or results in a substantial handicap to employment. Most important, however, eligibility is contingent on a reasonable expectation that a disabled client will benefit from the provision of vocational rehabilitation services in terms of employability (Tenth Institute on Rehabilitation Issues, 1983). Finally, because PWIs are founded upon and funded through federal agencies, disabled clients must be referred by public rehabilitation offices. Although this stipulation is consistent with policies of public-sponsored programs, nevertheless, it results in a closed job placement avenue for private rehabilitation companies and practitioners. On the other hand, an alternative route for private rehabilitation professionals might be through work with Private Industry Councils (PICs).

PICs were created in 1978 to determine whether input by business into training programs would improve the chances of reducing unemployment among the so-called "hard-core" unemployed workers. Initially, PICs were established as $400 million-a-year pilot programs to find solutions to the weaknesses found to exist in the Comprehensive Employment and Training Act (CETA). The basic idea was that councils would be formed composed primarily of business representatives rather than government officials or designees. The rationale for the predominating business orientation of PICs was that training programs could be designed that were more applicable to the job market and would lead to permanent job positions, as compared to the questionable applicability of 18-month jobs "created" under CETA (Matkin, 1983b). Today, there are over 460 PICs nationwide with an estimated $3.5 billion federal budget proposed to provide training to disadvantaged workers regardless of the origin of the referral source (Alexander, 1983).

Apprenticeship

In many ways, job placement resulting from on-the-job training, PWIs, and PICs is similar to apprenticeships, although less formal or lengthy than the latter. This form of knowledge and work skill acquisition dates back at least to the Middle Ages when various guilds of skilled craftsmen developed a regular practice of indenturing young workers to master craftsmen. The general use of apprenticeships has continued since those early times, such that in 1937 Congress established the National Apprenticeship Program with the support of both labor and management organizations. Not long afterward, the Fitzgerald Act authorized the Secretary of Labor to establish standards to guide industry in employing and training apprentices; to bring management and labor closer together to develop plans for training; and to promote general acceptance of the standards and procedures agreed upon (United States Department of Labor, 1964). The federal agency that was created to implement this program was subsequently known as the Bureau of Apprenticeship.

A basic policy of the Bureau of Apprenticeship has been that programs for employment and training of workers should be developed jointly by and mutually satisfactory to both employers and employees. Under the provisions of the Bureau, an apprentice is a person at least 16 years of age who works under a written agreement registered with a state apprenticeship council. The registration provides for not less than 4,000 hours of reasonably continuous employment for the person, and for his or her participation in an approved schedule of work experiences supplemented by at least 144 hours per year of related classroom instruction (United States Department of Labor, 1964). Moreover, qualifications for employment such as age, education, aptitude, wages, hours of work, length of apprenticeship, schedule of job processes, and the amount of class time required are usually indicated in detail in local standards. These standards typically include procedures for executing and registering the agreement and methods of supervising apprentices both at work and school.

Local apprenticeship programs specify the criteria used for selecting and employing applicants. Often there are more applicants than openings which means that children of workers in the affected occupation are given first priority if they meet the established standards (United States Department of Labor, 1964). Furthermore, a person who has had previous trade training in school or in military service may also have an increased opportunity of being selected. Moreover, if the previous training was of sufficient quality, the subsequent training period under the apprenticeship may be shortened. Finally, there are approximately 300 apprenticeable occupations listed under nearly 90 trade classifications. These include training periods ranging from two to six years in length, with the most common period being three to four years.

Employment Agencies

It has been estimated that approximately 7,500 private placement firms with nearly 12,000 offices exist in the United States and Canada (Matkin, 1982c). An effective employment agency has both a sizable and varied inventory of job orders (i.e., notice of position vacancies from employers), as well as a steady flow of job seekers representing a wide range of work skills and career experiences. By using a job placement firm, such as the public Job Service or private employment agencies, employers are relieved of the costs of advertising job openings and the time it takes to screen out unqualified applicants. Generally, private employment agencies differ from other similar service agencies by charging a fee for activities that result in an applicant being hired for a job. The placement fee is paid to the employment agency either by the hiring employer or the newly hired job seeker. However, approximately two-thirds of all jobs listed with private placement firms are fee-paid by the hiring employer at a cost ranging from 7% to 15% of the employee's first year income (Matkin, 1982c).

In spite of the fact that employment counselors working in private employment agencies attempt to match persons to available jobs, much in the same manner as rehabilitation professionals perform selective job placement with disabled clients, Johnson and Heal (1976) note that private employment counselors are reluctant to serve disabled clients. Indeed, Zadny and James (1978) found that the use of employment agencies accounts for less than 5% of the jobs obtained by disabled persons. On the other hand, when vocational rehabilitation professionals use the "job order" techniques required by private placement firms, not only are more job placements obtained, but the number of rehabilitated clients increases while the number of cases closed as "not rehabilitated" decreases (Zadny & James, 1979).

Rehabilitation professionals appear to have at least two methods to increase employment development and job placement by using employment agency techniques. According to Matkin (1983b), job orders are perhaps the most effective method for both determining the availability of job openings and securing job placement. A job order generally consists of information provided by an employer about a specific job within his or her work setting. For example, information may include the employer's name and address, the title of the job position and a brief description of the duties and skills required, salary or wage range paid, starting date, and the date that the job order was initiated. Job orders also identify the contact person authorizing the employment request, as well as the person within the employment agency who receives the job information.

A second method that may enhance job placement for disabled clients is for rehabilitation professionals to work with private employment agencies, much in the same way as they should with public Job Service offices. This technique can take the form of providing consultation to employment agencies about vocational rehabilitation issues and the needs of disabled clients, offering time and space within the rehabilitation work setting for a private employment counselor on a part-time basis, or providing a rehabilitation professional to work part-time within a private employment agency to serve the needs of disabled job applicants. Before moving to the next section, it is very important to state briefly two points about adapting the techniques and activities of an employment agency. First, when sending disabled clients to prospective employers for work consideration, clients must be capable of performing the specified job in terms of the prerequisite knowledge and skill requirements. Second, activities of employment agencies typically are regulated by state licensing boards and commissions; that is, in order to practice job placement in the private sector, an employment agency license must first be obtained. For a partial listing of the licensing requirements in each of the states and the District of Columbia, the interested reader is referred to the appendices, as well as Chapter 10 dealing with licensing.

Marketing Job Placement

"He who has a thing to sell and goes and whispers in a well, is not so apt to get the dollars as he who climbs a tree and hollers." This saying was found on a Kraft sugar package by public relations director, Jeanne Palluzzi (1981). A marketing approach to job placement, indeed any rehabilitation service, requires some adjustment in the typical rehabilitation professional's thinking. In order to adapt a marketing approach to the goals of a rehabilitation company or an individual's practice, some parallels must be drawn to its applications by commercial enterprise wherein marketing is a complex discipline. According to the Ninth Institute on Rehabilitation Issues (1982), the marketing philosophy insists that every facet of the marketing effort be built around the customer. Within this framework, the employer or referral source (e.g., insurance company, attorneys) is the customer or "client" and the disabled person being rehabilitated is viewed as the "product." In no way should this approach be presumed to offer less concern for the disabled population(s) being served. That is to say, rehabilitation professionals should tend to the needs of potential and actual purchasers of rehabilitation services as they attend to the details of providing quality services for disabled persons.

What is marketing in a rehabilitation context? Bell (1979) identifies two types which he labels "macromarketing" and "micromarketing." As the two terms denote, macromarketing includes a system of organizations and processes by which a nation's or the world's resources are distributed to people in order to satisfy their wants. Micromarketing, on the other hand, is a much narrower view consisting of a process for managing an individual business firm in such a way so as to satisfy its particular customers. In the latter sense, *every* organization, business, and practitioner engages in activities that are considered marketing whether this is recognized or not. For example, all businesses, whether manufacturing or social in product orientation, are concerned with the quality of their products and how those products are perceived and accepted by would-be consumers. Marketing tools serve as methods to enhance both public awareness and product quality by: (a) using persuasive communications to bring about changes in opinions and behavior; and (b) performing necessary adaptations to existing behavioral patterns by designing products and services that are easy to use, as well as easy to find in the marketplace (Rados, 1981). In many ways the goals of marketing and vocational counseling are similar, insofar as both attempt to change behaviors and opinions by communicating information in an organized and persuasive manner. To achieve these goals, however, the ingredients of marketing must be known, just as those used in counseling.

The Ninth Institute of Rehabilitation Issues (1982) identifies two ingredients that must be present for a rehabilitation marketing program to be successful. First, rehabilitation professionals must be prepared to seize opportunities in the market. This can be greatly enhanced by taking the time and making an effort to identify consumer needs, rather than taking a passive role by waiting for opportunities to present themselves. Second, successful marketing involves development and implementation of operating activities that promote the product and its benefits. These activities include things such as advertising, identifying and developing distribution channels, deciding the target group of consumers, providing follow-up servicing, and personal selling.

At this point, a distinction between marketing and selling should be made. Personal selling, according to the Ninth Institute on Rehabilitation Issues (1982), is concerned with the actual presentation of services and/or disabled clients to would-be consumers (i.e., employers responsible for hiring employees). Selling generally is concerned with achieving an exchange between two or more parties; goods for services, employment for job applicants, and so forth. Marketing, on the other hand, is concerned with *having* what the consumer wants; skilled job applicants to fill available job openings, vocational counseling for persons seeking career exploration. Thus, selling represents the applied practice of distributing those products that have been identified through marketing that consumers want. Therefore, under the marketing concept, a management responsibility is fourfold: (1) to determine the consumer's needs; (2) to identify the market of consumers with those needs; (3) to deliver the services and products requested; and (4) to follow up consumer needs and their satisfaction with the services and products received.

The marketing of rehabilitation services and products must be viewed in the context of a comprehensive marketing approach. For a perspective on the scope of what is involved in formulating a viable marketing program, Bloom and Novelli (1980) suggest looking at the basic decision areas to be addressed in terms of their relevance to vocational rehabilitation. These include market analysis and segmentation, product and communication strategies, and channels strategy.

Market Analysis and Market Segmentation

These two areas form the basis for an effective marketing effort that can be built only through an analysis of consumer wants, needs, perceptions, attitudes, and satisfaction levels. From this kind of research comes the foundation for designing marketing strategies. Market segmentation follows as a fundamental step to divide the market into homogeneous segments (e.g., insurance programs, insurance carriers, attorneys, other service areas) and then tailor marketing programs to address their unique needs.

Product and Communication Strategies

Having analyzed the market and determined its segments, rehabilitation professionals are in a position to address real desires and needs and to apply strategy variations unique to each segment. Within this context, communication strategies set the tone and create familiarity between rehabilitation service products and the targeted markets. This is known as "conditioning the market" and includes promotional methods such as presentations before groups and through the media, as well as developing resource materials for distribution and advertising (Ninth Institute on Rehabilitation Issues, 1982).

Channels Strategy

Any organization or individual that is marketing something must determine very carefully the best ways to distribute its products and services. Channels strategy addresses the selection of appropriate intermediaries through which to distribute products or offerings, as well as developing approaches to optimize support from these intermediaries. Access to the markets may take any or all of the following forms suggested by the Ninth Institute on Rehabilitation Issues (1982); membership in business, labor and service organizations such as PICs, labor councils, professional rehabilitation service associations, and the like; community involvement and board memberships; and direct employer contacts.

In conclusion, the marketing discipline is complex and requires direction and careful application in the same manner the rehabilitation professional provides services to disabled clients. To treat it otherwise will result, at best, in a haphazard approach to unite the intricate processes of vocational rehabilitation services. On the other hand, when planned and implemented in a systematic manner, marketing approaches applied to vocational rehabilitation enhance service goal attainment not only in the areas of vocational counseling and job placement, but in all other related service components as well.

Summary

Vocational counseling and job placement service activities are among the most important in the rehabilitation process. Indeed, the degree to which they are offered as service areas in applied work settings and as part of the roles and functions of rehabilitation professionals underscores their significance. This is especially true for rehabilitation professionals working within an insurance context. Reinforcing their importance is the fact that activities comprising vocational counseling and job placement must be linked together, for it is the identification of a realistic vocational goal that provides focus to subsequent job search activities. Similarly, occupational information represents a substantial portion of the foundation upon which both service areas depend for confirmation of the efficacy of vocational choices, rehabilitation planning, and service implementation. Clearly, armed with these rehabilitation service "tools," service providers will be better prepared to recommend suitable goals for disabled clients. Furthermore, when called upon to justify the selection of one or more vocational goals instead of others, knowledge of labor markets and worker characteristics are essential pieces of information that rehabilitation professionals must possess. The necessity of thorough preparation regarding vocational recommendations is the subject of the next chapter dealing with expert testimony. Although an atypical activity within traditional rehabilitation work settings, the role of vocational expert is commonplace among rehabilitation professionals who provide services in the insurance arena.

9 Vocational Rehabilitation in the Courtroom*

Jack M. Sink and Ralph E. Matkin

Whether employed in public or private settings, rehabilitation specialists are being requested more frequently to make professional judgments about the employability of handicapped persons. Moreover, these judgments may be requested or subpoenaed for court testimony, for preparation of legal briefs, or for a decision about whether it is worth going to court with a case. The importance of vocational factors in legal proceedings is becoming increasingly apparent to attorneys and others involved in court systems because work is a pervasive activity that reflects and influences nearly all aspects of human behavior and well-being. For example, Lynch (1983) reports that most legal definitions of disability reflect the importance of work in relation to normal functioning. This includes factors such as pre-injury and postinjury earning capacities, projected medical cost analysis, and functional disability ratings, to mention only a few.

The purpose of this chapter is to provide the reader with information useful for the preparation of vocational information that may be communicated to others such as arbitrators, attorneys, hearing officers, judges, and juries, in the form of depositions and testimony. To accomplish this goal, the chapter is divided into three major sections: (1) judicial systems; (2) methods of legal inquiry; and (3) expert vocational opinion. The objectives of these sections are to assist the reader to better understand legal systems in which vocational information is communicated, and to become aware of the skills and procedures required to respond effectively in legal situations. Finally, the reader may find it helpful to consult the legal terms found in Glossary B while reading this chapter.

---

* Portions of this chapter were adapted from *The Vocational Expert* by Timothy F. Field and Jack M. Sink and are used with permission.

Judicial Systems

In order to understand legal systems, it is important to realize that the source and nature of laws vary, and for this reason, require brief description of their origins to better appreciate their application in various judicial systems. For example, if a disputed question is reserved to state jurisdiction, then the law of the state prevails. On the other hand, if jurisdiction over the dispute has been delegated to the federal government, then federal law takes precedent. In order to better illustrate these and other differences in the formation of and rulings made about laws, this section is divided into five parts: origins of law; criminal and civil law; due process; court structures; and types of hearings.

Origins of Law

Broadly speaking, there are three equally powerful types of law in the United States. *Constitutional law* derives its authority from the federal and various state constitutions. *Statutory law* derives its authority from and is enacted by legislative bodies of government, such as the United States Congress, state legislatures, and administrative agencies within federal, state, and local governments. Finally, *common law* (also called "case law" or "judge-made law") is evolved by judges in the course of their deliberations and interpretations of the many cases and situations presented to the courts that are not covered specifically by statutes (Cohen, 1979).

According to Sandor (1957), common law has a history dating back to the Norman Conquest in 1066. Originating in the laws of Anglo-Saxon England and old English customs, the common law as it developed "was a flexible system that adapted itself to conditions as they arose" (p. 459). Later, in the 12th century, it became the practice to keep an official record of cases decided by the courts of common law. Known as the "plea rolls," these records eventually led to the development of court decisions beiof its own appellate courts or, on federal questions, by the precedents of the United States Supreme Court (Sandor, 1957).

One of most striking features of the English common law is its adjerence to precedent. According to Sandor (1957), these precedents control the litigated question, and, if the court departs from them, it is likely to have its ruling overturned by the higher courts. When a unique question arises, for which there is no precedent, in a state court in the United States, the court usually will look to the precedents of other states for a decision on a similar matter. Ordinarily, however, a given state is bound only by the precedents of its own appellate courts or, on federal questions, by the precedents of the United States Supreme Court (Sandor, 1957).

In addition to the preceding types of law, two other sources deserve mention. *Regulations* are the products of executive actions at three levels of government; national, state, and local. Regulations are addressed to administrative and line staff in order to specify in greater detail the rules to be followed when implementing legislative acts. These detailed rules of implementation are frequently referred to higher levels of government for approval and are focused on resolving frequently occurring situations (Martin, 1976). Often referred to as "Administrative Law," the methods and processes created by governmental regulatory agencies are distinguished from judicial procedures, the latter applying to courts. Finally, *decisions* are the resolution of direct conflicts between individuals that require the application of general and/or specific rules. Although the term "decision" is a popular term, rather than a technical or legal term, it may be used when referring to ministerial acts as well as to those that are judicial or of judicial character (Black, 1979). Table 9-1 summarizes the source and nature of United States laws.

Table 9–1. Origins of Law and Their Products

	Legislative	Executive	Judicial
Federal	U.S. Congress	Administrative Agency	Federal Courts and U.S. Supreme Court
State	State Legislatures	Administrative Agencies	State Courts and Appellate Courts
Local	City Councils	Board and Commissions	Municipal Courts and Trials
Product	Statutes and Ordinances	Regulations and Rules	Decisions

Criminal and Civil Law

The distinction between criminal and civil law is important for several reasons. First, the type of actions being regulated determine the judicial system responsible for deciding the question before it. Second, the amount of evidence needed to prove guilt or fault varies according to whether criminal or civil laws are in question. For example, criminal law regulates those actions that may be offensive to society in general (e.g., murder, rape, robbery, assault), while civil law regulates those actions that may be offensive to particular individuals under specific conditions (e.g., negligence, disputes about property rights). Although no private individual can bring a criminal action to trial (only a district attorney's office can proceed in such a matter), individuals can initiate a civil action (Cohen, 1979). Finally, the elements of proof needed to prove criminal action are considered to be more exhaustive than required to demonstrate civil violations. That is to say, in criminal proceedings, guilt must be proven "beyond a reasonable doubt," whereas in civil proceedings, a defendant has incurred liability only if the "preponderance of the evidence" indicates it (Cohen, 1979, p. 35).

Due Process

The government always has had the power, under the United States Constitution, to take those actions necesary to maintain the safety of society. These powers are referred to broadly as the "police powers" of government (Gutheil & Appelbaum, 1982, p. 39). The extent to which each state can go to protect the public is limited not only by the state's constitution, but also by the Fourteenth Amendment of the U.S. Constitution that guarantees all citizens *due process* and equal protection of the laws; both substantively and procedurally. To better illustrate these points, Martin (1976) notes that due process of the law means substantive justice and fundamental fairness are applied in each case in accordance with the basic rights guaranteed to each citizen under the provisions of the Constitution. Furthermore, procedural due process of the law has been interpreted to mean that "reasonable notice be given to parties of a pending action in a court," and that recognized and established procedures be followed by the court in its conduct and deliberations of questions before it (Martin, 1976, p. 122).

Court Structures

Although many different types of courts exist in this country (e.g., military courts, tax courts, probate courts), there are two basic court systems; the federal court system and the state court system. The court system is the societal institution through which individuals who violate criminal law are prosecuted and those involved in civil disputes can attempt to resolve their differences. As provided in the Constitution, federal judicial power is vested "in one Supreme Court, and in such inferior Courts as the Congress may from time to time ordain and establish." Most of the cases handled by federal courts concern violations of federal laws. Generally, federal courts handle all questions concerning the U.S. Constitution, all cases of maritime jurisdiction, conflicts between states, conflicts between a state and a nonresident of the state, many of the cases involving suits between citizens of different states, and some bankruptcy proceedings (Cohen, 1979). Furthermore, the Supreme Court has

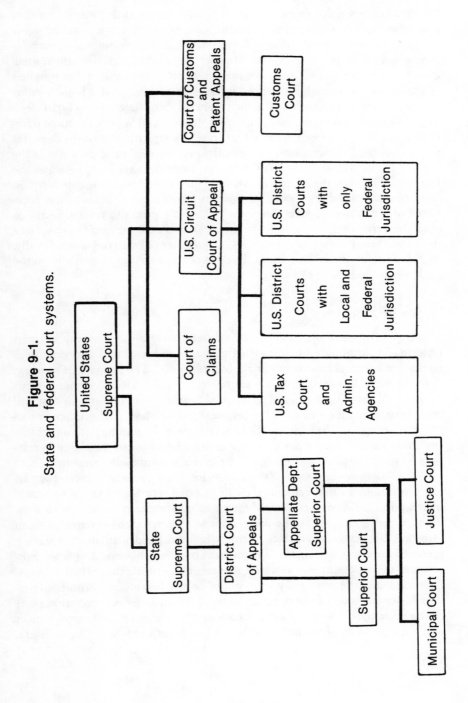

Figure 9-1.
State and federal court systems.

original jurisdiction in cases involving ambassadors, consuls, and comparable foreign dignitaries.

State courts generally handle questions concerning violations of state laws and most questions concerning contracts, wills, personal injuries, and domestic relations (see Chapter 3). Although each state judicial system and nomenclature reflect duties associated with particular functions (e.g., traffic court, small claims court), most state court systems have a three-tier system that parallels the federal system; a trial court, an intermediate court, and a highest court (Cohen, 1979; Schwitzgebel & Schwitzgebel, 1980). Referring to Figure 9–1, examples of trial courts include Municipal, Justice, and Superior Courts; intermediate courts are represented by the Appellate Department of the Superior Court and the District Court of Appeals; and the highest state court is the State Supreme Court. Cohen (1979) notes, however, that in some states the Court of Appeals is the highest court. Appellate courts generally rule on questions of law (e.g., due process), and usually consist of judicial panels composed of three, five, or seven judges who have the power to reverse decisions made by a trial court, affirm the trial court's decision, remand the case back to the trial court for retrial, or modify the judgment of the trial court. Finally, Appellate courts never have juries, but rather come to decisions solely on the basis of the judges' majority ruling.

Types of Hearings

Generally speaking, legal hearings differ from trials and appeals in terms of formality; although sometimes hearings are conducted and their outcomes decided in a formal courtroom (Field & Sink, 1981). The purpose of hearings is to establish facts in disputes and to reconcile any and all disagreements between the involved parties. The types of hearings vary in terms of cost and complexity, but all are intended to resolve issues at a level in the judicial process that can reduce the likelihood of a trial by jury. Beginning with a prehearing conference, several types of administrative hearings are discussed in relation to their purpose and the role of the participants who are involved.

A *prehearing conference* is a relatively informal meeting between the parties involved in a disagreement, their designated representatives, a stenographer, and a hearing officer. Recording the session begins typically with a summary of events that led to the disagreement. Following these statements, an informal discussion takes place during which both sides attempt to reach a mutually satisfying agreement. Whatever the outcome, however, a written transcript of the proceedings is available for later use. During the prehearing conference each of the principal parties in the dispute has an opportunity to present his or her side of the issue at hand. If an attorney is representing one of the principals, his or her job is to attempt to convince the hearing officer and the other side of the merits of his or her client's argument. In so doing, especially in a situation involving vocational issues, a vocational expert may be requested by the representing attorney or the hearing officer to provide an opinion on that specific topic for consideration by all parties involved. Finally, the hearing officer must be an impartial decision maker.

Administrative hearings represent the most prevalent type of hearing situation. These may consist of due process hearings or "evidentiary" hearings to review rules, regulations, and actions taken in matters requiring resolution. According to Martin (1976), the objectives that can be achieved by an administrative hearing include: (a) an appellant's (plaintiff) opportunity to assert his or her right to secure equity in the situation in relation to the law and agency policies; (b) ascertaining factual information upon which the overseeing agency can make a just and fair decision; (c) achieving uniformity in application of agency laws and policies; (d) safeguarding an appellant from mistaken, negligent, unreasonable, arbitrary, or prejudicial action or inaction by an agency or its staff; and (e) calling attention to policies that are inequitable, injurious, or present undue hardship so that needed modification and clarification may be made (pp. 26–27).

Although administrative hearings generally are informal, they are conducted in an orderly and prescribed manner. Hearings such as these typically are held at the convenience of the appellant before the chief administrative officer or designee of an agency for the purpose of allowing the dissatisfied appellant, or designated representative (including legal counsel), to present his or her case in a manner of his or her choosing to show why actions, inactions, or agency policies affecting his or her case should be corrected. Generally, the administrative hearing procedure established by an agency contains timetables setting forth deadlines for accomplishing various steps in the hearing process. For example, a petition for a hearing may be required within a specified time period following occurrence of the disputed action. Furthermore, when petitions are made for a hearing, all parties involved must be afforded an opportunity for hearing after receiving reasonable notice has been given. Such a notice should include a statement of the time, place, and nature of the hearing; a statement of the legal authority and jurisdiction under which the hearing is to be conducted; and a reference to the particular sections of the statutes and rules involved (Martin, 1976). Finally, an opportunity must be given to all parties to respond and present evidence as agreed on all issues involved.

Prior to and during an administrative hearing, the appellant, or his or her designated representative, must have been provided an adequate opportunity to examine all documents and records that are to be introduced at the hearing. Moreover, the opportunity must be provided for the appellant to bring witnesses, to establish all pertinent facts and circumstances about the situation in question, provide arguments without undue interference, and to question or refute any testimony or evidence presented by the defense, including the opportunity to confront and cross-examine witnesses under oath (Martin, 1976). On the other hand, administrative hearings are quasi-judicial in nature, and as such do not follow generally the strict rules of evidence governing a court proceeding. Yet, because such hearings are not open to the public typically (as they are generally in court proceedings), all persons attending the hearing must be present at the invitation of the appellant or the defendant, and as such are given the opportunity to present materials and relevant information pertinent to the issues under consideration.

At the conclusion of an administrative hearing, the hearing officer (usually an Administrative Law Judge in agencies such as the Social Security Administration or Workers' Compensation Offices or Commissions) makes a decision on the basis of the information presented and prepares a record of the hearing. This record serves as an official transcript of the hearing, provides a statement of the points at issue, summarizes the appeal hearing, reports findings of fact and conclusions of law, summarizes the hearing officer's evaluation of the evidence presented, records the nature and type of evidence submitted in the hearing, serves as the official decision of the hearing officer, and serves as the official record of a dismissal or withdrawn appeal (Martin, 1976). In conclusion, the finality of the decision of the hearing officer varies from state to state and from agency to agency. Whereas at one extreme the decision may be the definitive and final administrative action and appeal from such decision is directed to the courts, in other jurisdictions the decision of the hearing officer may be only a "screening" process prior to subsequent review by the administrative head of an agency and its policy board.

Methods of Legal Inquiry

Before approaching the topic of "expert witness," it is important to identify basic methods used to secure information to be used as evidence in quasi-legal and courtroom situations. Among the most commonly used methods of gathering vocational rehabilitation information, for example, is by subpoena, deposition, and testimony. The purpose of each of these methods is to make available information that can be useful for rendering a fair and impartial decision by hearing officers, Administrative Law Judges, or court judges.

Subpoenas

Any of the principal parties (plaintiff/appellant or defendant) in a judicial proceeding can obtain a subpoena to compel the appearance of a witness and/or the production of relevant documents in court for the purpose of examination. Specifically, a subpoena directs an individual to appear as a witness, whereas documents and other materials are obtained by a *subpoena duces tecum.* On the other hand, the mere fact that a subpoena has been issued does not compel the individual to testify, only to appear (Gutheil & Appelbaum, 1982). At that point, however, it is for the judge to decide whether the testimony or records in question are subject to a claim of privilege (a concept that will be discussed later as it differs from confidentiality). Receipt of a subpoena or subpoena duces tecum should be followed by contact with the attorneys or principal party serving the court order who are involved to determine the information being sought. Finally, this may be a good time also for the person receiving the subpoena to contact his or her own attorney to clarify individual rights and responsibilities in the case at hand. Most important, however, *under no circumstances should records be altered or destroyed when a subpoena is received.*

Depositions

According to Brandon (1983, p. 106), a deposition is "a procedure permitted in most states whereby an opposing attorney has the right to question any witness *under oath* before a notary public or other officer of the court for the purpose of giving the opposing side information desired from the witness." This process of information gathering (commonly referred to in the legal profession as "discovery") can be used during the trial or hearing in lieu of the witness' physical presence. On the other hand, it can be used also during the hearing or trial to corroborate a witness' earlier remarks, or to highlight inconsistencies between earlier sworn statements and courtroom testimony. Therefore, if called upon to provide a deposition, a prudent rehabilitation professional should listen carefully to the questions being asked, seek clarification when they are unclear or ambiguous, and carefully consider the substance and interpretability of responses offered. It is also important to consider during a deposition, any communications that the rehabilitation professional may consider to be confidential in nature do not have to be revealed unless directed to the contrary by the court (judge) directly.

Testimony

According to Brandon (1983), the professional rehabilitationists called most frequently to testify as expert witnesses are the counselor and the vocational evaluator, and in some instances the job development or placement specialist. During testimony, questions frequently asked of vocational specialists concern their professional qualifications for testimony, methods by which a vocational opinion was developed in the case at hand, and hypothetical questions based upon admissible evidence submitted in the case (Andersen, 1979). As a result, testimony demands that vocational witnesses be well prepared, accurate in their statements, and objective in their presentation.

Preparation for Testimony   Effective presentation of vocational testimony requires that the rehabilitation specialist not only be knowledgeable about the laws and regulations governing the case, but also be thorough in the collection, organization, and evaluation of information to be included in the testimony. In order to enhance this degree of thoroughness, Lynch (1983) suggests that prior to testifying, the vocational specialist should meet with the attorney requesting the testimony to assist with the organization of the information to be presented. At that time, the attorney should explain the methods involved in presenting evidence before the court or hearing, what questions may or will be asked during direct examination (including those related to professional qualifications of the witness), and what questions could be asked potentially during cross examination. Simultaneously, the vocational specialist should assist the attorney in the examination of information assembled that led to the specialist's conclusions in the case. For example, the attorney should understand fully the purpose and usefulness of each assessment instrument that was used, the contents of records and files about the client's vocational progress, and the methods and resources used by the vocational specialist in developing his or her conclusions and recommendations. Thus, being overprepared for testimony in legal proceedings identifies both the case's strengths and weaknesses; hopefully taking steps to overcome the latter in order to minimize the case's vulnerability during cross examination.

Examinations During Testimony   During the time that a vocational witness is providing testimony, he or she will be asked a sequence of questions by opposing attorneys (as well as possibly the hearing officer or judge). The sequencing of who is asking the questions of a witness determines whether testimony is in response to direct examination, cross examination, redirect examination, or recross examination. Regardless of the type of examination, however, effective testimony is characterized by simplicity; that is, the ability to translate technical information into everyday language that can be understood by the average layperson (Kornblum, 1974). Furthermore, effective testimony is enhanced when the vocational witness demonstrates objectivity, insofar as information is presented about a client, not for or against a client, regardless of the source of one's fees (Lynch, 1983). At this point, it is important to describe briefly each of the types of examination used in judicial proceedings, as well as suggested "rules" for vocational witnesses to follow.

Direct Examination.   This type of questioning involves interrogatives asked of a witness by the attorney who first calls a witness to the witness stand. Typically, a witness will be called first by the attorney who requested the testimony be provided by the witness in the case at hand. During direct examinations, questions typically cover areas such as the witness' current job duties and descriptions, educational background, past work experience, and professional credentials as related to the area of expertise to which testimony is being provided. In addition to these general and specific background questions (used to establish the witness' expertise in the eyes of the court), the attorney will ask the vocational witness to specify the details of services provided to the client in the case, which would include evaluation methods and instruments, the reliability and validity of such methods used, the results obtained, conclusions drawn, and supporting rationale for such conclusions (Lynch, 1983). During direct examination, Brodsky (1981) suggests the following actions to be taken by a vocational witness:

1. Prepare all basic exhibits and outlines of testimony carefully, arranging them in an orderly sequence, before taking the witness stand.
2. Speak loud enough for all to hear and do not talk too fast. Endeavor to obtain and hold the interest of the judge and jury.
3. Avoid unnecessary conversations with the judge or opposing legal counsel. Be courteous, fair, and frank. Keep calm and even tempered, even in trying circumstances.
4. State qualifications fully, but without "puffing" or indulgence in the trivial. Do not be flattered by offers to concede qualifications; for this may be a ploy to prevent the judge or jury from learning important details.
5. After reviewing qualifications, state results and opinions. Follow with a clear and adequate explanation of methods employed in reaching conclusions.
6. Present testimony as you would wish to have it presented if you were the judge. Observe any doubts which may appear to arise in the judge or jury's mind; and try to assist in resolving them. This, after all, is a primary function of an expert witness.
7. Hold to the essentials of the testimony. Develop a sense of proportion. Avoid unimportant detail.
8. Avoid the appearance of being an incorrigible partisan. Face up to the strong points which may be presented by opposing witnesses. Endeavor to demonstrate that, while those points should be given consideration, they must be viewed in the context of the total picture.
9. If not prepared to answer a question, be honest enough to say so. A bluffer is easily detected; and then a cloud is cast over the entire testimony.
10. Be concise. After a point is made, stop talking. (p. 7)

Cross Examination.   After direct examination has been completed, the opposing attorney has the opportunity to question the witness. This sequence of questioning is known as "cross examination." According to Kornblum (1974), there are five objectives in cross examination: (1) to question/challenge the witness' qualifications; (2) to demonstrate the witness' bias, rather than objectivity; (3) to challenge a procedure used in obtaining the vocational information, and thereby question the witness' concluding opinion; (4) to discredit the factual bases of opinions presented; and (5) to establish favorable facts for the opposing side through admissions by the witness. Indeed, cross examination can be intimidating and anxiety provoking, especially if preparation for testimony was absent or haphazard. In order to reduce the intimidating aspects, and to better understand the general rules and format of opposing attorneys, Kornblum (1974) suggests the following:

1. Expect all questions to be brief, to the point, and leading. Questions will be designed to elicit "yes" or "no" responses and not a narrative answer.
2. Expect to be required to give a precise response to the question asked. If an evasive, nonresponsive answer is given, do not expect to be "let off the hook" easily.
3. Once the cross examining attorney's desired point has been established, expect the examination on this topic to cease and turn to another area.
4. As a general rule, the opposing attorney will only ask a question for which he/she knows the answer the expert will give, usually because during deposition the expert committed him/herself to a reply.
5. Do not expect a logical sequence of questioning on cross examination. The opposing attorney recognizes that the chances of getting spontaneous testimony are greater if the expert does not have an opportunity to contemplate a line of questioning and anticipate answers. Expect cross examination to commence and end (as these are the most impressionable moments) on an important area.
6. Expect the opposing attorney to be well prepared. If an expert has been deposed, testimony is known and therefore research and critical questions can be prepared by the cross examining attorney beforehand.
7. Be prepared to hear (and probably be expected to comment about) contrary opinions expressed by expert witnesses called to testify by the opposing attorney.
8. Lastly, remain polite and courteous at all times.

Redirect Examination. When and if points have arisen during cross examination that might seem to be misinterpreted or misunderstood by the court and jury, the witness may be requested by the attorney who asked all direct examination interrogatives to elaborate or clarify such answers. This sequence of questioning is called "redirect examination." Thorough preparation for testimony, however, should include anticipation of a case's weaknesses, and the best methods for recovering from such exposure or exaggeration during cross examination.

Recross Examination. After a vocational witness has been asked to clarify and elaborate any points questioned during the redirect phase, the opposing attorney once again can question the witness. This final sequence of questioning, however, is confined to information brought out only during redirect examination.

Privilege Versus Confidential Communications Before moving to the area of expert witness opinions, it is necessary to distinguish between communications that are privileged and those that are confidential. The distinction between these two concepts is important for vocational witnesses to consider because questions asked during testimony may attempt or be designed to elicit potentially sensitive and personal client information that was given to the witness by the client in confidence. Thus, revealing information such as this, in the presence of others, under oath, and on the record, without a client's prior knowledge or consent, may be anxiety provoking for the rehabilitation professional. Moreover, the importance of the issue is such that further discussion is provided in Chapter 10 within the section dealing with ethics.

Attempting to distinguish "confidentiality" from "privileged communication," Jagim, Wittman, and Noll (1978) point out that, "whereas confidentiality concerns matters of communication outside the courtroom, privilege protects clients from disclosure in judicial proceedings" (p. 459). On the other hand, the mere fact that a communication is made in confidence to a professionally competent person is not enough for the relationship between the client and the professional to be granted a privilege. In other words, unless a privilege is granted under common law or statute in a particular jurisdiction, the courts generally have held that in fact no privilege exists for the particular relationship. Thus, with few exceptions, vocational witnesses are required to reveal confidential information in judicial proceedings when ruled to do so by the court, or risk a contempt citation ruled against them.

Expert Vocational Opinion

The use of vocational experts within a legal context began as early as 1960 when the United States Court of Appeals for the second circuit, in *Kramer v. Flemming* (283 F 2d 916, 1960), required the Social Security Administration Office of Hearings and Appeals to use vocational expert witnesses in disability cases (Grenfell, 1980). Because of the impact these witnesses had on early Social Security Disability Insurance hearings, the concept of vocational witness spread to other legal situations such as industrial hearings (e.g., workers' compensation), personal injury suits, product liability cases, and divorce settlements, to name a few (Andersen, 1979; Capshaw, Grenfell, & Savino, 1982; Grenfell, 1980; May, 1983).

Today, rehabilitation specialists are entering the legal arena in greater numbers, bringing with them a host of disciplinary backgrounds and training (e.g., counselors, job placement specialists, nurses, psychologists, vocational evaluators, and work adjustment specialists). Before a person can testify in court as an expert witness, however, one must first "qualify" as an expert. In other words, an individual posing as an "expert" must demonstrate that, based upon training or experience, he or she has acquired a degree of expertise that will assist the nonexpert members of the court and jury in understanding a subject matter not known by common experience or knowledge (Cross, 1979; Field et al., 1978; Lynch, 1983; Treon, 1979). Therefore, to better understand the role of the vocational expert witness, it is important to know how to qualify as an expert, what the scope of expert testimony involves, the role of experts in an adversarial system, the ethical issues surrounding expert witnesses, and how to prepare for an expert role.

Qualifying as an Expert Witness

Generally speaking, an individual's education, training, or experience offer a basis for establishing the expertise of a witness, as well as preparing the foundation for the admission of testimony. According to Andersen (1979), individuals who have a master's degree in vocational rehabilitation and have significant experience in the field and practice of vocational rehabilitation are found most often to have the qualifications necessary to provide opinions that enable a judge to make decisions about a disabled person's employability. Yet, the degree of vocational expertise remains a matter for the judge to determine. For example, a person who is not otherwise recognized as an expert may be qualified to give expert opinions, because the qualifications to give expert testimony are a relative matter. That is to say, a judge may consider that only vocational evaluators are qualified to interpret work sample systems, or only nurses are qualified to interpret medical case management, and so forth. Thus, the status of expert can be granted in two ways: (1) a state legislature can determine that one group of professionals should be considered experts for a given purpose; or (2) in most cases, the court that is hearing a particular case decides if an individual should be deemed an expert on the issue in question (Gutheil & Appelbaum, 1982).

The Scope of Expert Testimony

Within the strict rules of evidence, the expert is allowed greater flexibility to express opinions than nonexpert witnesses. In general, witnesses are permitted to testify only to *facts* relevant to a given case; *opinions* are excluded. For example, if a nonexpert witness inserts an implicit opinion, by saying that a disabled client did not perform a task in a work sample test "because he was lazy," it would be stricken from the record as a violation of the "opinion rule." According to Gutheil and Appelbaum (1982), the rule is based on the belief that it is the job of the judge (or jury), not of the witness, to evaluate the factual information presented; to the extent that the witness has no greater ability to do so than does the judge or jury.

On the other hand, the expert is allowed to state an opinion in situations in which the average person would be unable to form a meaningful opinion of the facts of the case. Furthermore, expert testimony is permitted only when the judge determines, as a matter of law, that the facts in question cannot be properly analyzed by a layperson. Moreover, in some cases an expert might be allowed to offer an opinion on one aspect of an individual's behavior, but not on another because the judge might believe that the latter can be determined by an untrained person. In addition to the topic of opinion admissibility, it is important to mention briefly the "hearsay rule" and "hypothetical questioning."

The Hearsay Rule   Ordinarily, an individual's testimony is permitted to be based only on facts that have been observed directly (and selective opinions from qualified experts). Anything else is considered to be hearsay. In practice this means that if a disabled client has told another to that person's face that the disability is a sham with the intent to elicit rehabilitation benefits, the latter can testify to the reality of that statement. If that person has told the insurance carrier about the statement, however, the insurance carrier may not offer the statement as evidence, because it would be hearsay. The rationale for this rule is that it is improper to admit evidence that cannot be subjected to cross examination (Gutheil & Appelbaum, 1982).

The Hypothetical Question   It was mentioned before that among the questions posed to expert witnesses are those dealing with hypothetical situations based upon admissable evidence submitted in the case. The expert witness has the right to answer a hypothetical question, a function that ordinary witnesses (whose testimonies are limited to recounting observations) cannot fulfill. The hypothetical question is useful in obtaining the expert's opinion about a factual situation other than the one presumed to exist in the case at hand. Because a judge or jury is under no obligation to accept the expert's version of the facts, a hypothetical question or situation allows both sides of a case to place the expert's opinion on record with regard to any number of factual situations that might be determined to have been present. Although hypothetical questions sometimes stretch the bounds of an expert's imagination, they allow attorneys to probe more carefully into the basis for an expert's opinion. Furthermore, the expert witness cannot refuse to answer hypothetical questions. Yet, the well-prepared expert will have anticipated them and thought through potential responses in advance.

The Adversary System and the Expert Witness

It has long been the presumption in Anglo-American jurisprudence that truth can be ascertained only by witnessing the combat of minds, each attempting to prove the falsehood of the other's position. So important is this belief that a large part of procedural law is devoted to enhancing the ability of the contesting parties to attack each other as vigorously as possible. Rules in civil cases such as pretrial discovery, and in criminal cases as the Constitutional rights of notice of the charges, speedy and public trial, confrontation of witnesses, power of subpoena, and representation of counsel, were all devised to equalize and maximize the ability of each side to prove its point.

There are, of course, other approaches to truth. The "collaborative model," in which all the involved parties pool their information and share their collective insights, is the more familiar schema in scientific and clinical work, as well as in insurance disability compensation systems. But the law generally rejects such methods as insufficiently protective of individual rights. In those instances when expert witnesses enter the truly adversarial model, attacks to one's professional expertise, competence, and integrity during cross examination can be emotionally unsettling, especially when before an audience of nonprofessionals. Although this degree of "combat" and its after-effects on the expert are matters for personal introspection and resolution, it is a situation that requires the expert's consideration and mental preparation.

Ethical Issues for Expert Witnesses

Most expert witnesses are hired not by the court, but by one side or the other in a given case. This frequently leads to confusion in the expert's mind as to the extent of his or her obligation to those who are paying the fee for testimony. For example, should the expert try to support the point of view the "employer" (fee payor) is espousing when the evidence for it is weak to the point of nonexistence? How much "prepping" before the trial or hearing is legitimate with the attorney for the side that hired the expert witness? When confronted in court with evidence that seems to negate the basis for the witness' opinion, how obstinately should the expert stand by the original conclusion? In short, is the expert a "hired gun" who is being paid to express only the opinion that will favor the "employer's" case, or does the expert owe allegiance to some higher principle? To these, and similar questions, the following guidelines should help resolve some of the issues:

1. An expert witness should never take sides during testimony.
2. Do not be afraid to express an opinion because of who is paying for the services.
3. Never get involved in cases in which the expert has a personal interest and/or bias.

4. An expert should never set the fee for services on a contingency basis, wherein the amount received is based on the amount of the settlement or other outcomes of the case.
5. Above all, an expert witness is paid for his or her time spent in the preparation and delivery of testimony, *not for the testimony given per se.*

Preparation for the Expert Witness Role

In addition to being knowledgeable about the laws, regulations, and rules governing the case for which testimony is being provided, vocational experts must be prepared to establish their qualifications as experts. Furthermore, it cannot be overstated that much time and attention must be given to preparing testimony that is easy to understand, concise, and able to withstand the rigors of cross examination. Because of the importance of these factors, individually and collectively, the following guidelines are designed to aid rehabilitation professionals prepare for testimony:

1. Develop two resumes. The first should be a detailed description of personal biographical data, educational and vocational experiences that qualify the rehabilitation professional to testify in a given area(s), professional activities that indicate further expertise, and references of individuals who can confirm the information contained in the resume. The second resume should be a one page summary of experience. This can be used for marketing services and submitted to attorneys as evidence of expertise.
2. Determine what is expected by the person requesting services and whether or not these expectations can be fulfilled professionally and ethically. If it is difficult to accept the expectations of the person requesting the service, the rehabilitation professional can refuse to serve.
3. Identify the questions that are vocationally relevant to the case. This may be the most important service provided because vocationally relevant information usually is absent or, at best, minimal in many cases. Quite often, once the questions have been identified and answers have been obtained, the case will be settled before going to a formal hearing or trial.
4. Meet with the attorney requesting the expert witness service prior to the court appearance to review the vocationally relevant questions and answers. At this point, the attorney may conclude that the testimony might be harmful to the case and decide not to call the expert as a witness.
5. Be prepared to present the rationale that led to the opinions being expressed. This is frequently presented as a summary of the critical information that led to the conclusions being stated and the recommendation being made.

6. Evaluate *all* medical, psychological, social, vocational, and educational data pertaining to the client. If differing opinions are presented in these records, the rehabilitation professional should be prepared to present opinions based on each. On the other hand, it is not the rehabilitation professional's responsibility to evaluate which differing opinion is right or wrong.

7. Briefly summarize the vocationally relevant information found in each exhibit or report and record the summary in a manner that may be used as a quick reference. Any notes taken to the hearing or trial may become part of the evidence to be reviewed by both plaintiff and defense. Therefore, notes should contain only factual information and opinions based on certain assumptions.

8. Be prepared to cite supporting literature or similar cases of other experts. This can include information from associations formed to serve persons with similar disabilities as the case in question, experiences of public and private agencies, and policies of employers.

9. Answer only those questions the rehabilitation professional is qualified by training or experience to answer. Frequently, an attorney will attempt to discredit a witness by asking for opinions that are not in the realm of the expert's field. Be alert to this possibility and avoid interpreting the meanings of experts in other fields.

10. Answer only the question that has been asked, and attempt to avoid offering more information than is requested.

11. Be prepared to change an opinion if new evidence reveals its weakness(es), and anticipate questions based on assumptions that were not previously considered.

12. Be deliberate and thoughtful when answering questions. Two questions that sound familiar may indeed be very different.

13. Ask for clarification from the hearing officer or judge if a question does not appear relevant to the case in order to determine if the question must be answered.

14. Dress appropriately and, if possible, conservatively.

15. Persevere in avoiding provocation into a counterattack directed toward an aggressive attorney. Strive to maintain composure throughout testimony, especially during cross examination.

16. Never answer questions until they are understood. Do not be afraid to ask for clarification from either the attorney or the judge.

17. Never base opinions on a concept of the "average person." There is no average individual, only those who have one or more qualities equal to the average population.

18. Never say that payment is being received *for* testimony. Payment received is for the time involved in studying, analyzing, synthesizing, and preparing information for the case, as well as the knowledge gained through experience. *Testimony cannot be purchased, but time can.*

19. Do not be lulled into complacency by an ingratiating, mild, good-humored, relaxed, and friendly cross examiner. Always evaluate the implications of the questions being asked, as well as the answers to be given, before answering.

20. Do not expect the attorney to know the types of questions that are vocationally relevant in the case, and do not hesitate to suggest questions (and how they should be asked) prior to testimony. Once in the courtroom, however, the attorney should have complete control.

Summary

In 1981, there were more than 600,000 lawyers in the United States serving 230 million people. In that same year, approximately 13 million civil suits came to trial in federal and state courts (Cannon, 1983). Although it is difficult to determine how many of these cases involved vocational expert witnesses, it is safe to say that the rise of rehabilitation professionals in the courtroom continues to increase each year. Indeed, current trends in the rehabilitation field designed to assure the rights of handicapped individuals suggest that many rehabilitation professionals will be involved in legal proceedings regardless of their wishes. Although some rehabilitation professionals are uncomfortable with the prospect of becoming involved in the legal arena, others accept it as a means to achieve professional recognition and growth. Perhaps those who are uncomfortable are those who are prepared poorly for such a role. Indeed, however, typical rehabilitation training has not attended to this area of service application as perhaps it should. On the other hand, traditional rehabilitation training programs have provided members of the field with the basic concepts of professional ethics and accountability, both of which are tested in the courtroom.

This chapter has provided an overview of the types of judicial systems that are present in the United States; ranging from the state and federal court structures, to less formal hearings and prehearing conferences. Within those various legal situations, methods of inquiry were identified and discussed in order to familiarize readers with methods such as subpoenas, depositions, direct examination, cross examination, redirect examination, and recross examination. Finally, the chapter concluded with information about preparation, qualifications, and issues surrounding vocational expert witnesses. With these issues in mind, along with information presented in previous chapters, the reader should be prepared to understand many of the accountability issues presented in Chapter 10 as they relate to the rehabilitation field in general and its application within an insurance context in particular.

10   Accountability: A Professional Obligation

E very action taken or avoided, as well as every decision made or not by
rehabilitation professionals is susceptible to challenge regardless of work
setting. This is true especially within an insurance rehabilitation context
whereby professional judgments not only affect long-range career decisions,
but also influence the amount and duration of compensation payments and
the magnitude of award settlements. As a result, rehabilitation services provided
and the information contained in reports must be thorough, well-substantiated,
and sufficiently detailed to convince the most cost-conscious insurance representative, the most skeptical of attorneys, the most cautious of physicians,
and the most ambivalent of clients. Furthermore, the actions and decisions
of rehabilitation professionals during the course of the rehabilitation process
must be able to pass the judicious review of rehabilitation supervisors, state
or federal regulatory bureaus, and administrative law judges. Indeed, the degree
of scrutiny present in an insurance rehabilitation framework reinforces the
need for sound service programming, appropriate training and experience
among service providers, and adherence to acceptable professional and business practices.

    The purpose of this final chapter is to provide information about account-
ability methods applicable to businesses and service providers operating within
an insurance rehabilitation context. To accomplish that goal, the chapter is
divided into three sections: (1) program evaluation; (2) practitioner preparation and behavior; and (3) credentialing issues. The intent of the chapter is
to provide the reader with an appreciation for methods designed to upgrade
and enhance both the quality of rehabilitation services, as well as the rehabilitation professional's ability to perform them.

Program Evaluation

According to Graham (1980), both the professional literature and the prevailing social climate are defining accountability and documentation of service effectiveness as critical issues in the rehabilitation field. In order to address these issues adequately, rehabilitation administrators, supervisors, and direct-service providers are being asked for evidence of service impact and progress of disabled clients receiving those services. Indeed, those rehabilitation agencies and professionals that can make the "best case for both the value of their programs' (services') results and the maximization of available resources, will be the ones who will flourish in a new era of accountability" (Commission on Accreditation of Rehabilitation Facilities, 1979, p. 1). One form of accountability that can be useful for measuring service effectiveness and efficiency is program evaluation.

Definition

Emanating from personnel assessments of performance (dating back to the use of "character books" and "character blocks" developed by Robert Owen around 1800 in Scotland), program evaluation is a systematic method used to determine, on a regular basis, what post- programmatic benefits have been achieved. According to Frank (1979), program evaluation is useful for measuring program benefits (i.e., effectiveness), the associated time and cost to derive those benefits (i.e., efficiency), and descriptive data about the persons served or the product produced. When establishing any evaluation method, however, practitioners usually are confronted with major pragmatic, conceptual, and tactical problems that must be overcome or at least considered in terms of their effects.

According to Davidson (1980), pragmatic problems refer to those promises offered or implied by a specific service area that are beyond that which can be empirically documented. In other words, a service program attempts to oversell its benefits. Conceptual problems are those that generally result from improperly or inadequately designed forms of evaluation. That is to say, most rehabilitation professionals are trained to design, implement, or assess program evaluations. Finally, tactical problems are those that occur from faulty methods used to collect information that will be analyzed.

In order to eliminate or reduce the likelihood of these problems occurring, Matkin (1982b) suggests several steps be included in any program evaluation procedure:

1. Identify every significant aspect that must be achieved to complete the project.
2. Determine the order that these events are to occur.
3. Diagram the flow of activities from the project's start to its conclusion.

Purpose

The major purpose of program evaluation is to influence program decisions by providing information about the methods used within a service area to attain its goals. Spaniol (1977) reports that program evaluation is a measurement function with a permanent structure and role within rehabilitation firms, rather than a periodic and unsystematically applied set of activities. This suggests that the nature of an evaluation system, if to be used for maximum benefit, should be an ongoing process. Furthermore, the initial motivation for developing and using such a process has been suggested by Frank (1979) as threefold: (1) searching for means to upgrade the business of rehabilitating disabled clients; (2) offering more effective and efficient programs as a method to increase vocational benefits derived by disabled clients; and (3) growing pressure from regulatory agencies, referral sources, and client consumers to become more accountable for outcomes and monies spent.

In addition to these purposes, Anderson and Ball (1978) specify two other important uses for program evaluation. The first concerns decisions to be made about a program's continuation and expansion. Program evaluations used for this purpose generally are *summative* in nature and frequently are referred to as "impact evaluations," that is, assessing how well a program works. Among the questions addressed by an impact evaluation are the continued need for a service area, global effectiveness of the service to meet specified needs of disabled clients and referral sources, identifying important positive outcomes and negative side-effects of services, assessing the costs associated with each or all services offered, and the demand for and support of programs offered by would-be consumers. A second related purpose of program evaluations then, is to influence decisions about and directions for program modification. For example, if an evaluation of a rehabilitation service area reveals that it is not achieving its expected goals, rehabilitation professionals may want to examine and possibly modify specific components of the service or assign other personnel to perform those activities.

Criteria for Using Program Evaluation

The literature suggests that several criteria must be met in order for any differentiating outcome assessment to be useful. First, an evaluation system must be compatible with the goals and objectives of the overall rehabilitation agency or service area. Second, the system chosen should be simple to understand by those using it, as well as by those who will receive the information. Third, the results should be objective and observable in quantifiable dimensions. Fourth, the time and effort expended during a program evaluation can be minimized when additional paperwork requirements are reduced. Fifth, the time and effort spent for implementation of the assessment system should be minimal, yet adequate for the scope of the project. Sixth, any system used for evaluation cannot interfere with the rights of disabled clients being served. Lastly, the evaluation system chosen should be flexible enough to be used for as many different types of service programs as possible, taking into consideration slight modifications when needed.

Before implementing any program evaluation system, however, several important considerations must be made. Matkin (1981a) suggests that rehabilitation professionals take the time to (a) decide who the "client" is for the purpose of the evaluation (e.g., the funding source, disabled client), (b) specify the goals and objectives of the program evaluation, (c) record all relevant data in terms of the stated goals and objectives, (d) compare the value of alternative methods of data collection in terms of both time and cost saving benefits, and (e) provide feedback to staff personnel who will be confronted with the responsibility for collecting the data. Each of these steps can enhance the accuracy of data to be collected by communicating their relevancy to subsequent administrative decisions affecting service areas.

Implementing and Applying Program Evaluations

Implementing a program evaluation project depends upon the intent of the assessment. For example, evaluation criteria may be used to estimate the need for a program, identify alternative forms of evaluation, ascertain how well a program works or is working, or monitor the state of a service component (Rossi & Wright, 1977). Furthermore, once a decision has been made to proceed with a program evaluation, taking into account the preceding recommendations, the rehabilitation professional must design an evaluation system. Walker (1975) suggests the following seven elements be incorporated for any future assessment needs:

1. Measures of effectiveness and efficiency must be applied to all clients or a statistically valid representation.
2. Client benefits must be determined *after* cessation of a program or service's treatment has been rendered.
3. Both the length and cost of a program should be determined.
4. Reports need to be generated on a regular basis in order to optimize standardization of procedure, as well as present a long-term perspective of the service or program situation.

5. Reports should indicate the degree to which effectiveness and efficiency data are consistent with the established program or service goals.
6. Feedback offered should be presented in such a manner that the reader knows and understands the information in a matter of minutes.
7. The system must be followed from initiation until termination of the program evaluation system.

These criteria become very useful when developing strategies for three of the most common applications of program assessment: (1) summative evaluation, (2) formative evaluation, and (3) benefit-cost analysis.

Summative Evaluations   Summative evaluations, which are also known as outcome, impact, or effectiveness evaluations, include measures of how well an entire program or service area works (Evaluation Research Society, 1980). Summative evaluations assume that the service treatment procedures have been implemented properly and, as such, are concerned with how effective the program is in attaining its objectives (Wortman, 1975). The challenges for rehabilitation professionals are to find or devise appropriate indicators of effectiveness and to be able to attribute both the type and amount of effectiveness to the program, rather than to other influencing conditions (e.g., the Hawthorne Effect). Therefore, some knowledge or estimate of conditions *before* application of the program, or knowledge or estimates of conditions in the absence of the program, is necessary. For those reasons, careful consideration must be given to outcome measures; many of which may already exist and are available to rehabilitation professionals in the form of case records and monthly or weekly reports of client activities. On the other hand, if the reliability of these records is in doubt, this may indicate a starting point for research efforts.

Assuming that a goal-oriented program evaluation model is used, the rehabilitation professional must first determine a way of organizing rehabilitation activities into "programs" that will be subjected to evaluation. Management decisions and postprogrammatic client benefits can be improved by a program structure that measures the degree to which each client achieves the goal(s) of the program. Several examples of program structure in an insurance rehabilitation context may be helpful. It is important to mention, however, that program structure may vary between rehabilitation companies, not to mention private practitioners, who have identical outcome goals.

Figure 10–1 portrays one method for identifying a program structure based on the specific service areas offered (i.e., vocational evaluation, labor market research, and job placement services). In this example, the rehabilitation professional would establish methods to assess whether the three programs are successful in achieving their respective goals. A second type of program structure is found in Figure 10–2 in which the three programs noted in Figure 10–1 are assessed in terms of the number of disabled client referrals from various sources such as insurance companies, claimant attorneys, and state industrial commissions. Assuming that each of the referral sources requests any of the three service programs, the rehabilitation professional would have a total of nine areas to evaluate; three service programs for each of the three referral sources. Finally, Figure 10–3 depicts an evaluation model based on the nature of referred clients' disabilities. Using the three-program model from Figure 10–1, the rehabilitation professional may wish to assess program outcome based on orthopedic versus psychiatric disabilities; resulting in six areas to evaluate, that is, three service programs for each of the two broad disability categories.

Once the program structure has been developed, it will be necessary to define the services offered that should lead to the accomplishment of the program goals (Commission on Accreditation of Rehabilitation Facilities, 1980). The set of services provided within a program are determined by the characteristics of the system in which the rehabilitation program is operating (e.g., insurance, public sector). Additionally, the set of services available must comprise all services required to achieve the outcome or benefits. Using an example of a goal-oriented structure, a summative evaluation of a competitive-employment job placement program might include primary objectives such as performing a job analysis to determine whether a disabled client could perform the work required of a specific job, placing a client in a modified job with the same employer, or the length of time it takes to accomplish job placement.

Figure 10–1. Service-Based Evaluation (3 program evaluations).

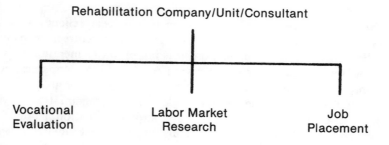

Rehabilitation Company/Unit/Consultant

Vocational Evaluation   Labor Market Research   Job Placement

Figure 10–2. Referral Source-Based Evaluation (9 program evaluations).

Figure 10–3. Type of Clients Served-Based Evaluation (6 program evaluations).

Once the primary objectives of a program have been identified, a determination must be made regarding the appropriate measures for each, to whom the measures are applied, when the measures are to be taken or recorded, what the sources of the data are, who are responsible for gathering the data, what the expected outcomes should be, and what the relative weight of each objective is to the others. Table 10–1 has been constructed to offer a clearer idea of how program objectives can be constructed in an assessable format. Of course, the reader should be aware that the criteria used to measure objectives are a personal choice or may be stipulated within insurance or other policies and procedures under which the rehabilitation professional is operating.

Before turning attention to formative evaluations, the reader should note categories labeled "expectancies" and "weights" in Table 10–1. *Expectancies* are the degree to which each objective is to be achieved and the criteria against which the actual performance of each objective is compared, while *weights* are the relative importance of the objectives expressed in either rank order or numerically with the total of them equaling 100 in the latter instance (Commission on Accreditation of Rehabilitation Facilities, 1980; Walker, 1975). Expectancy standards can be determined in terms of practitioner roles and functions. That is to say, these standards may be based on past performance, the duties identified as part of a person's job, the frequency with which the duties are performed, past or present flow of clients, and so forth. Weights may be determined, on the other hand, on the basis of social validation measures such as the relative importance of an objective as perceived by the referral source, other rehabilitation professionals, client advocates, or clients themselves. In the event that objectives are not meeting expected levels of achievement, further investigation of specific procedures may be warranted by using a formative evaluation process.

Formative Evaluations   Formative evaluations, which are also known as developmental or process evaluations, include testing or appraising the processes of an ongoing program in order to make immediate modifications and improvements (Evaluation Research Society, 1980). Activities may include analysis of management strategies and interactions among persons involved in the program, personnel appraisal, attitudes toward a program, or specific component services (Anderson & Ball, 1978). In some cases, formative evaluations may mean field testing a program or service on a small scale to assess the time, cost, and efficacy of procedures before implementing it on a larger scale. At this point, several examples of formative evaluations may be helpful.

The reader will recall from Chapter 6 that job analysis assists rehabilitation professionals to determine the suitability of specific work activities in relation to a client's disability. Without a bona fide medical opinion from the client's attending physician regarding the physical requirements of the work

Table 10-1. Program Evaluation Example for Job Placement

Primary Objectives	Measures	Applied To	Time of Measure	Data Source	Expectancies Min.	Goal	Opt.	Relative Weight
Same job, same employer	Percentage of clients	All terminees	60 days postplacement	Employer, Case Record	%	%	%	
Modified job, same employer	Percentage of clients	All terminees	60 days postplacement	Employer, Case Record	%	%	%	
Different job, same employer	Percentage of clients	All terminees	60 days postplacement	Employer, Case Record	%	%	%	
Same-modified job, different employer	Percentage of clients	All terminees	60 days postplacement	Employer, Case Record	%	%	%	
Different job, different employer	Percentage of clients	All terminees	60 days postplacement	Employer, Case Record	%	%	%	
Self-employment	Percentage of clients	All terminees	60 days postplacement	Employer, Case Record	%	%	%	
Obtain on-the-job training	Percentage of clients	All terminees	As event occurs	Employer, Case Record	%	%	%	

Table 10-1. (continued)

Primary Objectives	Measures	Applied To	Time of Measure	Data Source	Expectancies Min.	Goal	Opt.	Relative Weight
Apprenticeship	Percentage of clients	All terminees	As event occurs	Employer, Case Record	%	%	%	
Formal job train.	Percentage of clients	All terminees	As event occurs	Training Program	%	%	%	
Obtain full-time employment	Percentage of clients	All terminees	60 days post-hire	Employer	%	%	%	
Obtain part-time employment	Percentage of clients	All terminees	60 days post-hire	Employer	%	%	%	
Obtain competitive wage	Average wage rate	All terminees	60 days post-hire	Employer	%	%	%	
Minimize time from referral to employ.	Average # weeks	All terminees	At time of placement	Case Record	%	%	%	
Minimize cost for services	Average cost per client	All terminees	At termination	Accounting Records	%	%	%	

analyzed in relation to the nature of the disability, however, the rehabilitation professional can only speculate whether or not the job is suitable. On the other hand, when responses from an attending physician are delayed or simply not forthcoming, rehabilitation efforts may be unnecessarily prolonged. The use of a formative evaluation strategy could assist in investigating means to increase the likelihood of physicians responding in a timely manner. Assuming that the content and style of the written report are not problems in themselves, attention can be focused on other interventions as methods to increase physician response rates, such as the use of telephone prompts, video recording, hand-carrying reports and so forth.

Another area of concern among insurance rehabilitation professionals and referral sources that use their services are the findings and recommendations of vocational evaluations. Frequently the information contained in reports such as these is the foundation upon which subsequent vocational goals rest. Regardless of whether vocational evaluations are conducted by an outside agency or the rehabilitation professional, the use of a formative evaluation strategy may assist in identifying how often specific vocational goal recommendations match the occupation into which clients were placed. If significant differences are found to exist between the actual job obtained and those recommended by the evaluation, the rehabilitation professional may wish to adjust or recommend adjusting the assessment battery, change the manner of the evaluation process, or scrutinize the work of personnel performing the evaluation service.

Research methods used to perform formative and summative evaluations can take many forms, ranging from simple frequency counts to more complex statistical analyses. Furthermore, the use of single-subject, quasi-experimental, or true experimental research designs aids in the identification of whether program or service objectives are being achieved and the degree to which various intervention strategies assist or detract from desired outcomes. Although it is beyond the scope of this book to provide an adequate coverage of research design, methodological strategies, and statistical analyses, it is important to mention that rehabilitation professionals who use program evaluation need to at least be aware of the strengths and weaknesses associated with research techniques. Issues such as reliability and validity of the methods used, as well as their applicability in applied settings and practice, are discussed thoroughly by several authors, among whom Anne Anastasi perhaps is most noted.

Benefit-Cost Analysis　The reader will recall from Chapter 4 that economic benefits are associated with rehabilitation services. Within the public sector program, tax monies generated from earnings of those persons who have been rehabilitated successfully typically exceed the revenues allocated for rehabilitation service programs. On the other hand, rehabilitation services provided within an insurance context assist in holding down costs by returning disabled claimants to work as quickly as possible. The principle difference between the two sectors in terms of economic benefits demonstrated by rehabilitation services is that money paid for rehabilitation services in the public sector is returned directly to that system in the form of tax dollars resulting in a higher return than initial investment. Insurance dollars paid for rehabilitation services, on the other hand, are not recovered directly through taxes, but through premium payments by policyholders. In the latter method, premium costs may not increase substantially when costs are spread widely among all policyholders or when purchased services achieve cost-containment goals. Thus, a third application of program evaluation strategies is for determining the benefit-cost ratios for various rehabilitation services.

Although determining the benefit-cost ratio or cost-effectiveness of rehabilitation services is an involved and detailed process, Thompson (1980, pp. 47–48) provides useful guidelines to follow:

Step 1. *Identify the decisionmakers and their values:*   This usually consists of indicating which people are to be considered in the analysis and how heavily the effects on different persons and different types of effects are to be weighted relative to each other.

Step 2. *Identify alternatives:*   This requires understanding clearly what the decision choices are in terms of optimum and inadequate outcomes.

Step 3. *Identify costs:*   A cost is considered to be incurred for every person who feels *worse off* due to the program or services rendered. Cost may be program expenses, disincentives, or benefits lost as resources.

Step 4. *Identify benefits:*   Every person who is *better off* as the result of the program is a beneficiary. Direct costs and benefits usually are not hard to identify, whereas identifying *potential* gainers and losers is more difficult.

Step 5. *Valuing effects monetarily:*   All identified costs and benefits should be valued as compensating variations for each person affected by the program.

Step 6. *Discounting:*   All identified and valued effects occurring at different times should be discounted at the appropriate discount rate to make them commensurable. Thus, if all effects occur at about the same time, discounting is not necessary.

Step 7. *Taking distributional effects into account:*   An understanding of decisionmaker values may enable the rehabilitation professional to value distributional effects numerically. If this is not possible, however, then all judgments of valuation should be deferred to the decisionmaker(s).

Step 8. *Aggregating and interpreting the valued effects:*   The various valued effects of a program can be combined in a calculation of net benefits (cost-effectiveness) or in terms of a benefit-cost ratio.

Practitioner Preparation and Behavior

Although program evaluation strategies attempt to address accountability issues surrounding vocational rehabilitation services offered to disabled clients, they do not address directly the skills and knowledge required by practitioners responsible for service delivery. Aside from training received in a specific occupational discipline, rehabilitation professionals need to be aware of how best to apply their knowledge and skills in an insurance rehabilitation system. Additionally, practitioner training must identify acceptable standards of behavior and potential consequences for those who do not adhere to established codes of professional conduct. Thus, practitioner accountability issues include acquisition of the requisite training and experience to perform rehabilitation services, behaving in a manner acceptable to and in accordance with an occupation's ethical principles, and being cognizant of liability issues governing unacceptable practices and behaviors.

Rehabilitation Training and Experience

The demand for trained professionals within the insurance rehabilitation arena continues to grow in a manner commensurate with the expansion of that sector. An example of that growth was estimated by Lauterbach (1982, p. 53) as having "grown from nothing in 1970 to nearly 1,000 companies and total revenues approaching $250 million." Within those companies, individuals who offer vocational rehabilitation services to disabled clients perceive themselves to be competent professionals accountable for their practices. These beliefs held collectively as a group and individually among practitioners are founded, according to Matkin (1983a), on facts and opinions such as acquired education level, completion of specialty training, supervised work experiences, perceived quality of training received, quantity of successful client and work-related outcomes achieved, continued or increased instances of case referrals, earned annual income, and much more. On the other hand, review of the rehabilitation literature indicates that professionals believe that training programs need to be modified to better prepare practitioners for employment in the insurance rehabilitation system(s). In addition to the areas covered thus far in this book, authors note that practitioners require an awareness of the free enterprise system, an introduction to business administration and basic accounting, and an understanding of employee benefit programs (McMahon, 1979; Matkin, 1980d; Organist, 1979; Sales, 1979; Scher, 1979). Based upon these earlier recommendations, more recent studies of rehabilitation professionals' roles and functions have assisted in further defining training content areas (see Chapter 4). Finally, results of four current projects deserve brief mention concerning their findings and recommendations for adequate training content within an insurance rehabilitation context.

Lynch and Martin (1982) Study   These authors conducted a survey among members of the National Association of Rehabilitation Professionals in the Private Sector (NARPPS) to identify training needs among practitioners. Based on a 71.3% return rate to a 41-item skill and knowledge content survey questionnaire, Lynch and Martin grouped each item into one of six broad categorical headings: Medical, Business, Legislation, Counseling, Vocational, or Psychological. Furthermore, because the items were derived from the literature addressing areas of relevance to the private sector, the authors noted that all were considered at the least to be of minimum importance. Notwithstanding the initial "selectivity" of the work items in relation to the population surveyed, Lynch and Martin were careful to identify those items that were rated as most important versus those considered to be only marginally important. Their results concluded that skill areas related to assessment, job analysis and placement, communication, and organization were indeed of primary importance. On the other hand, those activities rated as least important included those areas typically associated with generic interpersonal counseling, such as group, family, cross-cultural, and employee assistance counseling.

Administration Studies   Several authors recently have speculated that rehabilitation professionals, particularly those trained as counselors, require basic training in supervisory and administrative techniques. The underlying assumption among these writers is that despite lack of training specifically in these management areas, rehabilitation administrators typically come to their positions from the counselor ranks (Feindel, 1980a, 1980b; Matkin, 1982a; Matkin et al., 1982; Sullivan, 1982). Based on these assumptions, Riggar and Matkin (1984) conducted a pilot investigation among a random sample of professionals who had graduated from four rehabilitation training programs specializing in either counseling or vocational evaluation and work adjustment between 1978 and 1982. Based on a 72.5% response rate to an 11-item survey questionnaire, these authors found that nearly three-fourths of the respondents were performing management duties in spite of having no prior formal training in that area, over half of these professionals were spending 20 or more hours per week engaged in administrative or supervisory duties, and the average time from graduation until these persons were placed in managerial roles was 14¼ months.

NARPPS and NCRE Investigations   During the summer of 1982, the Training and Research Committee of NARPPS and a special Task Force of the National Council on Rehabilitation Education (NCRE) conducted independent studies and prepared separate reports focused on training needs for rehabilitation counselors entering the private insurance sector. These two reports were sent separately to the Council on Rehabilitation Education (CORE), which serves as the national accrediting agency for all graduate rehabilitation counselor training programs, making recommendations for curriculum modifications. Although developed independently, both reports concluded that adequate preparation for rehabilitation counselors entering the insurance sector should include coursework in job placement and development, program planning and evaluation methodologies, legal and ethical issues, medical case management as related and contrasted to vocational management and medical/psychosocial aspects of disability, and identification and use of labor market issues (McMahon & Matkin, 1983).

Board for Rehabilitation Certification Studies   Although rehabilitation credentials is an area that will be discussed in more detail later in this chapter, it is important to mention a report prepared by a Task Force of the Commission on Rehabilitation Counselor Certification. In March, 1983, a study was initiated to identify the knowledge and content areas required of rehabilitation professionals who work within an insurance context. Based upon the literature available at that time, as well as input from persons representing many employment settings and professional disciplines in the rehabilitation field, six areas of knowledge were identified for subsequent development into an insurance rehabilitation certification examination. Although the content areas of the proposed Certified Insurance Rehabilitation Specialist examination (administered by the Board for Rehabilitation Certification) are undergoing validation procedures currently, they include: (1) Overview of Disability Compensation Systems; (2) Structures and Processes of Disability Compensation Systems; (3) Professional Terminology; (4) Insurance Rehabilitation Case Management; (5) Gathering, Synthesizing, and Disseminating Information; and (6) Forensic Rehabilitation (Matkin, 1984).

Professional Ethics

Rehabilitation professionals are confronted daily with issues requiring decisions that affect disabled clients either directly or indirectly. Frequently, the ability to make sound rehabilitation decisions rests on the knowledge and skills acquired through a combination of formal training and work experience in a particular occupation. In other instances, however, rehabilitation professionals seek guidance and support through standards of behavior established by the disciplines with which they identify (e.g., administration, counseling, medicine, nursing, or psychology). These standards, or ethical codes, consist of written and tacitly assumed models of conduct and moral judgment advocated by a particular philosophy or group (Stude & McKelvey, 1979). Ethical codes, on the other hand, do not provide guidance for every situation, but rather are statements of *principles* that must be interpreted and applied to a specific situation. Thus, they represent an underlying rationale for behavior that is *ideally* consistent with a specific philosophical or group orientation.

It is important that the reader become aware that ethical codes have both strengths and weaknesses because of their "interpretability" depending on the situation in which they are applied. In other words, there are frequently no "right" or "wrong" answers for situations requiring judgment calls, only "best" or "least-best" supportable alternatives. Thus, what may be the best decision in one situation under a given set of circumstances, may be interpreted as improper under alternative conditions. Keeping in mind that professional ethics represent an ingredient in the larger issue of accountability, strengths and limitations of ethical codes require identification and brief discussion.

Strengths   Ethical codes of conduct are among the characteristic elements of occupations that have acquired "professional" status according to Brubaker (1977). Not only do such standards provide general behavioral guidelines, but they also attempt to identify practitioners' responsibilities to maintain or increase their levels of occupational competence, as well as methods to reduce or remediate conflicts that may threaten the welfare of clients being served. Furthermore, ethical codes provide would-be consumers with general assurances upon which to build trust. For example, ethical codes found within human service occupations address issues such as privacy of communication between clients and practitioners, safeguarding controlled substances and materials (e.g., prescription medicines and tests), responsibility for individual and subordinates' actions, and the focus of primary allegiance by the professional in service performance. Thus, the substance contained within ethical codes promotes the development of client and practitioner expectations about the responsibilities of specific occupational groups in relation to the services covered or ascribed to their particular professional domain.

Limitations   Although ethical codes exist for virtually all human service disciplines under the rehabilitation "umbrella," they are binding only to members of the group or organization that adopts them. In other words, organizations have no ability to impose sanctions against nonmembers for conduct that may be considered to be in violation of a group's ethical codes. On the other hand, sanctions may be imposed on nonmembers by other agencies when the practices of a given occupation are regulated through credentialing mechanisms such as licensing, registration, or certification. Another limitation, especially within the rehabilitation field, is the absence of a single ethical code applicable to all the specialty disciplines within it (Cottone, Simmons, & Wilfley, 1983). Unlike the American Medical Association, the American Association for Counseling and Development, the American Psychological Association, and others that have one code of ethics for all their respective internal specialty divisions, the rehabilitation field contains separate ethical codes for most of its specialty areas (e.g., administration, counseling, vocational evaluation and work adjustment, and job development and placement).

Compounding this situation are the ethical codes contained in a variety of independent rehabilitation associations. This leads to another limitation concerning such codes of conduct, potential areas of internal and external conflict.

For those rehabilitation professionals who belong to several rehabilitation associations, each of which having its own code of ethics, areas of conflict may arise. For example, Cottone and his associates (1983) mention that under the NARPPS "Standards and Ethics" a rehabilitation professional has a responsibility to provide objective testimony when requested. However, if that same professional also is a member of the American Association for Counseling and Development, such behavior may be considered unethical unless direct client consent was obtained first. On the other hand, internal conflicts may be present within a single code of ethics. For example, a rehabilitation professional may be expected to be loyal to his or her employer and simultaneously be required to protect the welfare of the client being served. Although this stipulation appears to present no problems, assuming that the goals of the rehabilitation employer and the practitioner are one and the same, several authors disagree. The potential conflict in this situation rests in the lack of "client" definition. Thus, "allegiance" is required of the rehabilitation professional to more than one "master," i.e., the employer, the disabled client, and possibly the referral source "client" (Cottone, 1982; Matkin, 1980c; Matkin & May, 1981; Nadolsky, 1979). Issues such as these, not to mention failure to follow less ambiguous professional responsibilities contained in ethical codes, create a fertile climate for judicial inquiry into legal liabilities of rehabilitation professionals.

Legal Liabilities

Throughout this book, emphasis has been placed on the legal framework surrounding rehabilitation service delivery within insurance systems. Given the litigious nature of these systems, rehabilitation services and practitioner behaviors are under constant scrutiny by disabled clients, referral sources, plaintiff and defense attorneys, state and/or federal agencies, and possibly professional peers and colleagues. Thus, decisions made or not made, actions taken or not taken, by the rehabilitation professional in each case must be defensible whether called into question by others or not. As a result, it is important to mention several areas that deserve attention among both indirect and direct rehabilitation service providers, that if left unattended or performed inadequately, could result in legal liabilities against the rehabilitation professional and/or the rehabilitation company.

Malpractice / Negligence In order for negligence to exist, Schwitzgebel and Schwitzgebel (1980) identify four elements that must exist to establish a course of action: (1) a *duty* on the part of the professional must exist; (2)

a *breach* of that duty must occur; (3) an *actual loss or injury* must be sustained by the client; and (4) a *causal relationship* between the breach of duty and the resultant injury must be established. On the other hand, claims of negligence may be reduced by conformity to the established standards of professional conduct that are often considered implicit in an agreement ("contract") between a professional and a client. Under contract theory, a plaintiff will look for some implied or expressed promise that has been breached. In the absence of such a warranty, the rehabilitation practitioner will not be liable for an honest mistake of judgment, where the proper course of action is open to reasonable doubt. Similarly, a rehabilitation professional usually will avoid negligence liability when releasing information considered to be confidential by following consent issue guidelines, when the client initiates such a release of information, or in good faith efforts (Matkin, 1980a, 1980c). Generally, good faith efforts alone are insufficient to avoid malpractice liability, but the probability of a successful claim against the rehabilitation professional is small.

Confidential Communications   Rehabilitation professionals, although obligated by their various ethical codes to treat *all* communications between themselves and disabled clients in a confidential fashion, generally are not included as a legal class covered by the doctrine of privileged communication. Privileged communication applies only to attorneys and their clients, physicians and their patients, clergy and their parishioners, and any other occupational groups so designated by statute. Under this doctrine, professional disciplines so affected are bound under penalty of law not to divulge information about or between the practitioner and the clients served (Black, 1979). As a result, the rehabilitation professional, except where noted, is not legally immune from being compelled to testify in court concerning a disabled client or requested by subpoena to produce records and files about a specific case in question. Furthermore, failure to comply with a court's request to reveal sensitive material concerning communications with or about a disabled client will result in a contempt charge being issued against the rehabilitation professional and/or the employing agency or company. Therefore, to reduce the risks involved in releasing confidential materials, rehabilitation professionals should first inform disabled clients of the legal limits of the practitioner's confidentiality and seek separate consent for each disclosure.

Consent Issues   It should be apparent that consent is a fundamental concept applicable to human service delivery systems. The primary value of consent for rehabilitation service providers is that it permits disabled clients to exercise their rights of self-determination, by enabling them to assess a proposed service thoughtfully and with adequate information, thereby encouraging and permitting professionals to carefully safeguard the rights of clients (American Association of Mental Deficiency, 1977). Furthermore, consent reduces a professional's civil and criminal liability to charges of acting without prior consent, and should be obtained whenever a proposed activity or treatment procedure: (a) will require a client to incur significant *risks*; (b) will have a potentially *irreversible* impact on a client; or (c) will *intrude* physically, psychologically, or socially on a client.

According to the American Association of Mental Deficiency (1977), the legal concept of consent contains three elements; capacity, information, and voluntariness. *Capacity* is recognized in the law as being measured by both adaptive behavior and measured intelligence in combination (Black, 1979). For consent to be *informative*, the client must receive and understand a full, but not exhaustive, explanation of the material and relevant facts of the procedure(s) to be administered. Finally, consent is *voluntary* when there is an absence of overbearing coercion, duress, threats of inducements, and undue influence (Black, 1979). Moreover, the means used for obtaining consent and the criteria by which it is received must reflect the degree of risk, intrusiveness, and irreversibility of the proposed activity or procedure.

Finally, a consent system should be designed to avoid procedural complexities that will delay decision-making in situations where prompt action is essential. Three forms of consent provide clarification regarding who has the legal authority to furnish consent; direct, concurrent, and substitute. *Direct consent* always involves the agreement of the client who is directly affected. *Concurrent consent* consists of permission from both the directly affected client and another person, such as a spouse or relative. *Substitute consent*, or third-party consent, is provided by a client's advocate when the client lacks the capacity to give or withhold their own consent. For example, a client may in fact lack capacity (i.e., de facto), yet their consent must be obtained unless a court has adjudicated the client to be incompetent (i.e., de jure). Because of the legal nature of consent issues, three general guidelines are helpful to remember. First, the riskier, more intrusive, and more irreversible the activity, the more formal the consent process must be. Second, the less mentally capable the disabled client is, the more likely it will be that the consent of another will be required. Third, consent should be obtained for a specific, clearly defined purpose; thereby avoiding "blanket" consent to a number of activities of uncertain nature and duration (American Association of Mental Deficiency, 1977).

Individual and Supervisory Responsibilities   Related to the issue of practitioner training, are the responsibilities incumbent on both individual rehabilitation professionals and those who supervise them. Under the doctrine of respondeat superior, or as sometimes referred to as the doctrine of "vicarious liability," rehabilitation supervisors are responsible for the acts of their subordinates undertaken in the course and scope of the employment situation (Cohen, 1979). For example, supervisors have been held legally liable for actions taken by their subordinates who were inadequately or not trained to perform the job duties required in client treatment, and as a result, caused detrimental effects to their clients (Martin, 1975). Although each rehabilitation professional ultimately is responsible for his or her own conduct, the rehabilitation supervisor has a legal obligation to ensure that subordinates possess the proper training to carry out their assigned duties, as well as identify and take corrective actions if activities are not proceeding properly.

Malpractice Insurance   It should be stressed that although insurance alone will not cover all of the costs of a malpractice suit in the broad sense of the word (e.g., time, reputation, peace of mind), it will certainly help to defray much of the monetary expenses should a rehabilitation professional be named in a law suit. Therefore, it is important for rehabilitation professionals to read their insurance policies carefully with special attention to the types and kinds of suits the policy does and does not cover. For example, the professional liability insurance offered to members of the American Psychological Association does not protect psychologists from office or property liability. That is, any damages resulting from a client's slipping on the office floor or tripping on the carpet will not be reimbursed. Similarly, the insurance offered to members of the American Association of Counseling and Development, as well as the National Rehabilitation Association or NARPPS, does not insure supervisors against damages caused by the negligent acts of their subordinates.

Finally, Cohen (1979) recommends that rehabilitation professionals purchase their own liability insurance, regardless whether their employers provide "blanket" coverage for all employees or not. The rationale for this suggestion is that in any action taken against an individual professional, the employer is likely to be named also as a co-defendant. If this happens, the employer may only provide one attorney to argue for its interests as well as those of the employee. Needless to say, the rehabilitation professional probably will be better served if he or she has an attorney representing the professional's interests exclusively.

Credentialing Issues

Accountability operates on at least two levels; the programs of service to be delivered, and the qualifications of practitioners providing those services. A third area of accountability runs through both in a complementary fashion, although its very existence often is presupposed within program and practitioner issues. This third area consists of the credentials possessed by programs and practitioners that are designed to provide additional credibility to training and service programs, as well as individuals' qualifications. The four credentialing areas affecting practitioners and programs include accreditation, certification, registration, and licensure. Moreover, these areas represent relatively recent developments in the rehabilitation field, and as such, are in various stages of formation presently. Before proceeding, however, it is important to understand basic credentialing terminology in order to differentiate those terms applicable to individuals from those concerning programs and services.

Definition of Terms

Credentials   This term refers to evidence that attests to and provides assurance of the competency of a person or program to perform specific services. Within this definition, the term "competence" can be used to denote either skills or knowledge, or a combination of both, in a particular discipline when applied to an individual practitioner. When applicable to program credentials, on the other hand, competence is less at issue; opting instead for demonstration of program or service relevancy to the specific occupation with which it is associated. Examples of professional credentials include an academic diploma or degree, certificate of accreditation, certification, license, and registration. Generally, the hierarchy of professional credentials follows that first an individual acquires a degree or diploma from an accredited training program, followed by licensure within the confines of a specified jurisdiction to practice the degreed occupational discipline, followed by certification within a specialty area of the occupation.

Accreditation   This activity defines the requisite knowledge and skills to be *addressed* by training programs responsible for preparing individuals to enter a specific occupational discipline, or by a service delivery program responsible for providing a set of designated activities to consumers. Examples of the former include programs designed to prepare individuals as rehabilitation counselors, nurses, or physicians; whereas the latter refers to service delivery standards applied to programs such as those found in rehabilitation facilities, hospitals, or nursing homes. Most important, accreditation represents a credentialing mechanism applied to programs or services, *not* to practitioners of those services or teachers within training programs. On the other hand, one of the criteria of accreditation may stipulate that a credentialed practitioner must perform the specified service within a designated program.

Certification   This is a process by which a governmental or nongovernmental agency, such as an association or professional certifying board, grants formal recognition to an *individual* who has met certain predetermined professional standards established by that group. The purpose of certification is to enable the public in general and employers in particular to identify those practitioners who meet a standard that is usually set well above that required for licensure (Shimberg, 1981). Unlike licensure, however, certification does not prohibit uncertified individuals from practicing their chosen occupation, but rather is simply a form of "title control" applied to practitioners who perform a defined set of activities within a broad occupational field. Thus, when certification is instituted by either a governmental or nongovernmental agency, only those persons who at least meet the qualification standards established are permitted to use the designated occupational title; although nongovernmental agencies have a lesser degree of "title control." Examples of certification in the rehabilitation field include Certified Rehabilitation Counselor, Certified Vocational Evaluator, Certified Work Adjustment Specialist, or the newly initiated Certified Insurance Rehabilitation Specialist.

Licensure   This is a means by which agencies of the state or federal governments define, limit, and regulate the practice of a trade or profession. The purpose of such control is to protect the public health, safety, and welfare by restricting those persons from practicing a specified occupation in which they have neither recognized nor approved training and experience. By definition, licensing represents the most restrictive form of occupational regulation because the power to grant or withhold a license can be used to deny individuals the opportunity to earn a livelihood in their chosen occupations, or deny a business from being allowed to operate in a given location. According to Shimberg (1981), approximately 800 occupations in the United States are regulated by state licensing laws; ranging from the familiar, such as nurse and physician, to the more obscure, such as horseshoer and lightning rod installer. Within the field of rehabilitation, however, the prevalence of licensing requirements for the many disciplines within it vary according to occupation and location of practice. For example, although physicians must be licensed in each state where they practice, counselors are required to be licensed in only 10 states at present (i.e., Alabama, Arkansas, Florida, Georgia, Idaho, Ohio, South Carolina, Tennessee, Texas, and Virginia). Counselor licensing in South Carolina, on the other hand, more properly represents a form of professional "registration."

Registration   This is a process that is closely akin to certification and licensure, insofar that once these forms of credentials are issued, the professional becomes listed by name and other pertinent information among other similarly designated members of a particular discipline. Thus, a registry is a document that assists the public in identifying qualified practitioners or businesses to perform specific services. According to Gianforte (1976), registration can be defined at the national or state level, or both; whereby national registration assures reciprocity and the legal ability to practice in any jurisdiction, while state registration is territorially restrictive. Within the rehabilitation field, examples of registered disciplines include Registered Nurses, Registered Rehabilitation Therapists, and Registered Rehabilitation Specialists.

Credentialing in Rehabilitation

Although the purpose of rehabilitation credentialing groups, such as the Commission on Accreditation of Rehabilitation Facilities, Commission on Certification of Work Adjustment and Vocational Evaluation Specialists, Board for Rehabilitation Certification (which oversees the Certification of Insurance Rehabilitation Specialists Commission and the Commission on Rehabilitation Counselor Certification), and the Council on Rehabilitation Education is to identify, develop, and implement methods for assessing the knowledge of various practitioner disciplines, or service delivery programs, several emerging issues are noteworthy. In a series of articles, Matkin (1981b, 1981c, 1983a, 1983d, 1984) notes that rehabilitation certification credentials typically *precede* occupational licensing, rather than follow it. The reason for this seemingly "reverse" approach appears to be twofold.

First, certification generally is recognized nationally, rather than being confined to a particular jurisdiction, such as in the case of licensure. Specifically, this means that professionals who are certified as rehabilitation counselors, vocational evaluators, work adjustment specialists, or insurance rehabilitation specialists can use their designated title(s) in all states unless precluded by statutes that control these occupational titles further (i.e., licensure). The second reason that certification of rehabilitation professionals precedes licensure in most cases is the fact that few states have enacted laws that regulate who can be titled and practice as counselors, vocational evaluators, and so forth. In many ways, the relative absence of regulations applied to these occupational groups has contributed to the formation of nongovernmental rehabilitation specialty boards designed to provide assurances to would-be consumers of practitioner qualifications and service program efficacy.

Related to the formation of nongovernmental rehabilitation credentialing boards are several perplexing issues. One concern is the increasing abundance of independent, yet seemingly redundant and/or ambiguous, rehabilitation certification agencies. Another issue involves the potential confusion created for both would-be consumers and rehabilitation professionals when attempting to select "appropriate" credentials/credentialing agencies for needed services. These concerns have led to questions such as:

1. If counseling services are being offered by a rehabilitation practitioner, should that person be a Certified Rehabilitation Counselor, a National Certified Counselor, a Licensed Psychologist, a Licensed Employment Counselor, and so forth?

2. If a Rehabilitation Nurse provides patient care, should that person be certified by the Association of Rehabilitation Nurses, the Professional Rehabilitation Association, by both organizations, or by neither group?
3. If rehabilitation practitioners are certified by their respective occupational disciplines, should they also seek additional certification as Certified Insurance Rehabilitation Specialists in order to offer their services to disabled clients receiving disability compensation insurance?
4. Should a rehabilitation service program be accredited by the Commission on Accreditation of Rehabilitation Facilities, the International Institute of Rehabilitation, by both organizations, or by neither group?

Although answers to these and similar questions about rehabilitation credentials remain unresolved, it is important to note that these issues continue to be discussed in the rehabilitation literature and during meetings of practitioners. Because dialogue continues to be active in this area, it may be reasonable to assume that efforts to adequately resolve these issues will be forthcoming. Indeed, present events and future trends in rehabilitation accountability issues appear to suggest such a possibility.

Future Trends

The growing momentum for the development and implementation of professional standards among rehabilitation professionals and programs is illustrated by several events. First, the 1973 Rehabilitation Act (P.L. 93–112) and the 1978 Amendments (P.L. 95–602) place a premium on service accountability that indirectly affects practitioners' abilities to effectively identify and deliver appropriate vocational rehabilitation services to disabled clients. Second, the 1984 Amendments to the Rehabilitation Act (P.L. 98–221) require that "qualified personnel" be employed to deliver services to disabled clients. Third, federal legislation, as well as that found at the state level regarding workers' compensation, over the years has expanded client populations to include a wide variety of eligible disabilities, many of which require specialized knowledge and skills to treat effectively. Fourth, a national survey conducted among members of the American Rehabilitation Counseling Association revealed an overwhelming opinion (86%) favoring licensure for rehabilitation professionals in both public and private sectors (Hardy, Luck, & Chandler, 1982). Fifth, a review of state codes regulating activities of private employment agencies (see Appendix I) appears to reveal that rehabilitation professionals who perform job placement activities need to be licensed as employment counselors or their companies require licensure under existing statutes (Matkin, 1982c). Sixth, research conducted within public vocational rehabilitation agencies indicates that if such agencies desire greater professional attitudes, behaviors, and job satisfaction among their rehabilitation staff, they should hire only those persons who are certified or have an intent to become certified in a rehabilitation discipline (Tunick & Tseng, 1981). Finally, rehabilitation counselor career forecasting indicates that state licensure and designation as a Certified Rehabilitation Counselor significantly will govern the practices and hiring of rehabilitation practitioners by 1990 (Anderson & Parente, 1982).

In addition to these issues, the rehabilitation field must continue its efforts to reduce the fragmenting effects caused by the rise of special interest groups and credentialing boards that are frequently redundant in their purposes. In other words, the proliferation of seemingly diverse rehabilitation credentials within an occupational group has the same destructive potential for a profession as does the rise of a multitude of special interest groups purportedly representing a limited number of professional specialties (Brubaker, 1980; Matkin, 1983a). Among the proposed methods for resolving these problems are consolidation of seemingly redundant rehabilitation associations and credentialing boards (e.g., Matkin, 1981c, 1983a; Rasch, 1979).

In final analysis, after nearly 70 years of existence, the field of rehabilitation is beginning to realize the breadth of its applicability to the world of work for both disabled and able-bodied persons alike. Most important, however, in becoming aware of its potential the rehabilitation field is striving to remediate its own areas of deficiency by continuously refining its educational training programs and credentialing mechanisms to enhance the field's internal and external accountability.

Summary

Accountability issues in the field of vocational rehabilitation affect practitioners, service delivery systems, and training programs. Among the methods used to assess the effectiveness and efficiency of rehabilitation services are outcome evaluations, process evaluations, and benefit-cost analyses. These three uses of program evaluation assist rehabilitation personnel to better understand how well their services are attaining their identified goals. Moreover, program evaluation strategies provide information that can be useful for identifying service components that may require modification or elimination to enhance goal attainment. Complementing program evaluation, as a method of accountability, are activities associated with practitioner preparation and professional credentials. Appropriate educational and work experiences are prerequisites for the effective and efficient delivery of vocational rehabilitation services regardless of employment setting or system in which professionals are located. In addition to training received for entry into a rehabilitation occupational discipline, consumers and professionals alike frequently demand further evidence of knowledge and skills among service providers. These demands are often satisfied by rehabilitation professionals adhering to ethical codes of conduct and by possessing professional credentials in the form of certification, licensure, and/or registration. Service programs, on the other hand, satisfy demands for accountability through possession of and adherence to accreditation standards. Thus, in spite of its relative "youth" among health service occupations, the rehabilitation field is making significant strides toward professionalization.

GLOSSARY A
Insurance Terms*

Accident: An event causing loss, which takes place without being expected, in most cases specific to time and place.

Actuary: A person professionally trained to apply probability and statistics to the practical problems of insurance and related fields.

Adjuster: A person who handles claims. The term is becoming obsolete because its connotation is often negative and misunderstood (see Claims Service Representative).

Administrative Services Only Plan: An arrangement under which an insurance carrier or an independent organization will, for a fee, handle the administration of claims, benefits, and other administrative functions of a self-insured group.

Agent: An insurance company representative licensed by the state who solicits, negotiates, or effects contracts of insurance, and provides service to the policyholder for the insurer.

Aggregate Indemnity: The maximum dollar amount that may be collected for any disability, period of disability, or under the policy.

Amendment: A formal document changing the provisions of an insurance policy signed jointly by the insurance company officer and the policyholder or the authorized representative.

Approval: (1) word used in connection with the filing of policy and certificate forms and rates with the state insurance department; (2) a word used in connection with the underwriting process of an insurance company and consisting of the acceptance of the risk as set forth in the application as made or modified by the insurer; (3) acceptance of an offer from an applicant or policyholder in the form of a contract for new insurance, reinstatement of a terminated policy, request for a policy loan, etc., by an officer of the company.

Assurance/Insurance: The term "assurance" is used more commonly in Canada and Great Britain. The term "insurance" is the spreading of risk among many, among whom a few are likely to suffer loss. Today the terms are generally accepted as synonymous.

Audit: An examination of the books of account, vouchers, and other records of a person, corporation, firm, or other organization for the purpose of ascertaining the accuracy or inaccuracy of the records. An audit of the employer's payroll is used in calculating workers' compensation premiums.

Beneficiary: The person designated or provided for by the policy terms to receive the proceeds upon the death of the insured.

Benefits: The amount payable by the insurance company to a claimant, assignee, or beneficiary under each coverage.

Blanket Contract: A contract of health insurance affording benefits, such as accidental death and dismemberment, for all of a class of persons not individually identified.

---

*For definitions not included here, a convenient reference source is Health Insurance Association of America. 1982. Source Book of Health Insurance Data 1981-1982. 23rd Ed. Health Insurance Association of America, Washington, D.C.

Blanket Medical Expense: A provision which entitles the insured person to collect up to a maximum established in the policy for all hospital and medical expenses incurred, without any limitation on individual types of medical expenses.

Broker: An insurance solicitor, licensed by the state, who places business with a variety of insurance companies. A broker represents the buyer of insurance rather than the companies, but is paid commissions by the company.

Business Insurance: A policy that primarily provides coverage of benefits to a business as contrasted to an individual. It is issued to indemnify a business for the loss of services of a key employee or a partner who becomes disabled.

Captive: An insurance company formed by an employer to assume its workers' compensation and other risks and provide services.

Carrier: The insurance company or the one who agrees to pay the losses. The carrier may be organized as a company, either stock, mutual, or reciprocal, or as an Association of Underwriters.

Case Reserve: The dollar amount stated in a claim file which represents the estimate of the amount unpaid.

Casualty Insurance: A general class of insurance covering liability resulting from accidents; some types of property insurance and workers' compensation insurance.

Certificate of Insurance: A statement of coverage issued to an individual insured under a group insurance contract, outlining the insurance benefits and principal provisions applicable to the member.

Change in Loss Reserve: A recorded increase or decrease in the estimated cost of a claim.

Claim: A request for payment of reparation for a loss covered by an insurance contract.

Claimant: One who seeks a claim.

Claim Severity: Average loss per claim.

Claims Closed: Claims against an insurance carrier which have been settled by payment to the claimant or closed without payment.

Claims Pending: Claims in the process of disposition.

Claims Service Representative: A person who investigates losses and settles claims for an insurance carrier or the insured. A term preferred to adjuster.

Classification: The identification of policyholders in terms of their risk or potential loss category for rating purposes. There are three main categories of classification in workers' compensation: (1) manufacturing; (2) contracting; and (3) all other. Additionally, there are many classifications within each category.

Coinsurance: A policy provision frequently found in major medical insurance, by which both the insured person and the insurer share the covered losses under a policy in a specified ratio.

Commissioner of Insurance: Usual title of the head of the state insurance department and the official responsible for the enforcement of all insurance laws.

Comprehensive Major Medical Insurance: A policy designed to give the protection offered by both a basic and a major medical health insurance policy. It is characterized by a low deductible amount, a coinsurance feature, and high maximum benefits.

Consideration: One of the elements for a binding contract. Consideration is acceptance by the insurance company of the payment of the premium and the statement made by the prospective policyholder in the application.

Contributory: A group insurance plan issued to an employer under which both the employer and employee contribute to the cost of the plan; 75% of the eligible employees must be insured.

Conversion Privilege: A privilege granted in an insurance policy to convert to a different plan of insurance without providing evidence of insurability.

Covered Expenses: Hospital, medical, and miscellaneous health care expenses incurred by the insured that entitle him or her to a payment of benefits under a health insurance policy.

Deductible: The amount of covered charges incurred by the protected person which must be assumed or paid by the insured before benefits by the insurance carrier become payable.

Direct Writer: An insurer that sells through its own resources and does not employ independent agents.

Disability: The state of being disabled from earning full wages at the work at which the employee was last employed.

Disability Income Insurance: A form of health insurance that provides periodic payments to replace income when an insured person is unable to work as a result of illness, injury, or disease.

Dismemberment: Loss of a body member(s), or use thereof, or loss of sight due to injury.

Domestic Carrier: An insurance company organized and headquartered in a given state is referred to in that state as a domestic carrier.

Double Indemnity: A policy provision usually associated with death, which doubles payment of a designated benefit when certain kinds of accidents occur.

Dread Disease Insurance: Insurance providing an unallocated benefit, subject to a maximum amount, for expenses incurred in connection with the treatment of specified diseases, such as cancer, poliomyelitis, encephalitis, and spinal meningitis.

Duplication of Benefits: Overlapping or identical coverage of the same insured under two or more health plans, usually the result of contracts of different insurance companies, service organizations, or prepayment plans; also known as multiple coverage.

Eligibility Date: The date on which an individual member of a specified group becomes eligible to apply for insurance under the insurance plan.

Eligibility Period: A specified length of time, frequently 31 days, following the eligibility date during which an individual member of a particular group will remain eligible to apply for insurance under a group life or health insurance policy without evidence of insurability.

Eligible Employees: Those members of a group who have met the eligibility requirements under a group life or health insurance plan.

Elimination Period: A period of time between the period of disability and the start of disability income insurance benefits, during which no benefits are payable (see Waiting Period).

Evidence of Insurability: Any statement of proof of a person's physical condition and/or other factual information affecting his/her acceptance for insurance.

Exclusions: Specific conditions or circumstances listed in the policy for which the policy will not provide benefit payments.

Experience: A term used to describe the relationship, usually in a percentage or ratio, of premium to claims for a plan, coverage, or benefits for a stated period of time. Insurance companies in workers' compensation report three types of experience to rating bureaus: (1) policy year experience; (2) calendar year experience; and (3) accident year experience.

* *Policy Year Experience:* Represents the premiums and losses on all policies that go into effect within a given 12-month period.
* *Calendar Year Experience:* Represents losses incurred and premiums earned within a given 12-month period.
* *Accident Year Experience:* Represents accidents that occur within a given 12-month period and the premiums earned during that time.

Experience Rating: The process of determining the premium rate for a group risk, wholly or partially on the basis of that group's experience.

Experience Refund: A provision in most group policies for the return of premium to the policyholder because of lower than anticipated claims.

Fiscal Year: A certain 12-month period selected by an organization for its financial accounting period. For insurance companies, this always coincides with the calendar year.

Flat Schedule: A type of schedule in group insurance under which everyone is insured for the same benefits regardless of salary, position, or other circumstances.

Franchise Insurance: A form of insurance in which individual policies are issued to the employees of a common employer or the members of an association under an arrangement by which the employer or association agrees to collect the premiums and remit them to the insurer.

Fraternal Insurance: A cooperative type of insurance provided by social organizations for their members.

Group Contract: A contract of insurance made with an employer or other entity that covers a group of persons identified as individuals by reference to their relationship to the entity.

Guaranteed Renewable Contract: A contract that the insured person or entity has the right to continue in force by the timely payment of premiums for a substantial period of time, during which period the insurer has no right to make unilaterally any change in any provision of the contract, while the contract is in force, other than a change in the premium rate for classes of policyholders.

Health Insurance: Protection which provides payment of benefits for covered sickness or injury. Included under this heading are various types of insurance such as accident insurance, disability income insurance, medical expense insurance, and accidental death and dismemberment insurance.

Hospital Expense Insurance: Health insurance protection against the cost of hospital care resulting from the illness or injury of the insured person.

Hospital Indemnity: A form of health insurance which provides a stipulated daily, weekly, or monthly indemnity during hospital confinement.

Hospital Medical Insurance: A term used to indicate protection which provides benefits for the cost of any or all of the numerous health care services normally covered under various health care plans.

Impairment: The inability or lessened ability to function in the performance of work duties because of injury or illness from a work-related accident or disease.

Incontestable Clause: An optional clause which may be used in noncancellable or guaranteed renewable health insurance contracts providing that the insurer may not contest the validity of the contract after it has been in force for two or sometimes three years.

Indemnity: Security against possible loss or damages. Reimbursement for loss that is paid in a predetermined amount in the event of a covered loss.

Individual Insurance: Policies which provide protection to the policyholder and/or family. Sometimes referred to as Personal Insurance as distinct from group and blanket insurance.

Injury: Harm to a worker subject to treatment and/or compensable under workers' compensation.

Insurable Risk: The conditions that make a risk insurable are: (a) the peril insured against must produce a definite loss not under the control of the insured; (b) there must be a large number of homogeneous exposures subject to the same perils; (c) the loss must be calculable and the cost of insuring it must be economically feasible; (d) the peril must be unlikely to affect all insureds simultaneously; and (e) the loss produced by a risk must be definite and have a potential to be financially serious.

Insurance: Protection by written contract against the financial hazards, in whole or in part, of the happenings of specified fortuitous events.

Insured: The person, organization, or other entity who purchases insurance.

Insurer: The insurance company or any other organization which assumes the risk and provides the policy to the insured.

Insuring Clause: The clause that sets forth the type of loss being covered by the policy and the parties to the insurance contract.

Integration: A coordination of the disability income insurance benefit with other disability income benefits, such as Social Security, through a specific formula to insure reasonable income replacement.

Key-Men or Key-Person Health Insurance: An individual or group insurance policy designed to protect a firm against the loss of income resulting from disability to a key employee.

Lapse: Termination of a policy upon the policyholder's failure to pay the premium within the time required.

Legal Reserve: The minimum reserve which a company must keep to meet future claims and obligations as they are calculated under the state insurance code.

Liabilities: An insurance company's liabilities consist of its immediate or contingent policy obligations and unpaid claims.

Limited Policy: A contract which covers only certain specified diseases or accidents.

Long-Term Disability Income Insurance: Insurance issued to an employee, group, or individual to provide a reasonable replacement of a portion of an employee's earned income lost through a serious and prolonged illness during the normal work career (see Integration).

Loss Control: Efforts by the insurer and the insured to prevent accidents and reduce loss through the maintenance and updating of health and safety procedures.

Loss Expense Allocated: That part of expense paid by an insurance company in settling a particular claim, such as legal fees, but excluding the payments to the claimant.

Loss Expense Unallocated: Salaries and other expenses incurred in the general operation of the claim department of an insurance carrier which cannot be charged to individual claims.

Loss Ratio: The percent relationship which losses bear to premiums for a given period.

Loss Reserve: The dollar amount designated as the estimated cost of an accident at the time the first notice is received.

Major Medical Insurance: Health insurance to finance the expense of major illness and injury.

Manual Rate: The premium rate developed for a group insurance coverage from the company's standard rate tables normally referred to as its rate manual or underwriting manual.

Medicaid: State programs of public assistance to persons regardless of age whose income and resources are insufficient to pay for health care. Provided under Title XIX of the Federal Social Security Act of 1966.

Medicare: The hospital insurance system and the supplementary medical insurance for the aged created by the 1965 amendments to the Social Security Act.

Minimum Group: The least number of employees permitted under state law to effect a group for insurance purposes. The purpose is to maintain some sort of proper division between individual policy insurance and the group forms.

Morbidity: The incidence and severity of sicknesses and accidents in a well-defined class or classes of people.

Multiple Employer Group: A plan where the employees of two or more employers not financially related, are covered under one master policy.

Mutual Insurance Company: An insurance company which has no stockholders. It is managed by a board of directors, elected by its policyholders. Any earnings in excess of operating costs are returned to the policyholders in the form of dividends (see Stock Insurance).

National Association of Insurance Commissioners: The association of insurance commissioners of various states formed to promote national uniformity in the regulation of insurance.

National Council on Compensation Insurance: A rate-making and administrative organization for most companies which write workers' compensation insurance.

Noncontributory: A term applied to employee benefit plans under which the employer bears the full cost of the benefits for the employees. One hundred percent of the eligible employees must be insured.

Nondisabling Injury: An injury which may require medical care, but does not result in loss of working time or income.

Nonoccupational Policy: Contract which insures a person against off-the-job accident or sickness.

Nonparticipating Insurance: A plan of insurance under which the policyholder is not entitled to share in the dividend distribution of the company.

Nonprofit Insurers: Persons organized under special state laws to provide hospital, medical, or dental insurance on a nonprofit basis.

Occupational Disease: Any disease or specified diseases that are common to or a result of a particular occupation or specific work environment.

Occupational Hazard: Occupations that expose the insured to greater than normal physical dangers by the very nature of the work in which the insured is engaged, and the varying periods of absence from the occupation, due to the disability, that can be expected.

Occurrence: Any incident or happening involving possible loss to a policyholder.

Overhead Insurance: A type of short-term disability income contract that reimburses the insured person for specified, fixed, monthly expenses, normal and customary in the operation and conduct of the business or office.

Partial Disability: The result of an illness or injury which prevents an insured from performing one or more of the functions of his/her regular job.

Policy: The legal document issued by the company to the policyholder which outlines the conditions and terms of the insurance.

Policyholder: One who owns an insurance policy.

Pre-Existing Condition: A physical and/or mental condition of an insured which first manifested itself prior to the issuance of the individual policy or which existed prior to issuance and for which treatment was received.

Premium: The periodic payment required to keep a policy in force.

Principal Sum: The amount payable in one sum in the event of accidental death and in some cases accidental dismemberment.

Proration: The adjustment of benefits paid because of a mistake in the amount of the premiums paid or the existence of other insurance covering the same accident or disability.

Qualified Impairment Insurance: A form of substandard or special class insurance which restricts benefits for the injured person's particular condition.

Rate: The charge per unit of payroll which is used to determine workers' compensation or other insurance premiums. The rate varies according to the risk classification within which the policyholder may fall.

Rating: The application of the proper classification rate and possibly other factors to set the amount of premium for a policyholder. The three principal forms of rating are: (1) manual rating; (2) experience rating; and (3) retrospective rating.

Rehabilitation: Restoration of a totally disabled person to a meaningful occupation. A provision in some long-term disability policies that provides for continuation of benefits or other financial assistance while a totally disabled insured is retraining or attempting to resume productive employment.

Reinsurance: The insuring by one insurer of the liability of another insurance carrier. Two basic methods of reinsurance are the *pro rata* method (share of loss) and the *excess of loss* (loss above a specific amount) method.

Residual Disability Benefits: A provision in an insurance policy that provides benefits in proportion to a reduction of earnings as a result of disability, as opposed to the inability to work full-time.

Rider: A document which amends the policy or certificate. It may increase or decrease benefits, waive the conditions of coverage, or in any other way amend the original contract.

Risk: The uncertainty of loss with respect to person, liability, or the property of the insured.

Self-Administration: The procedure where an employer maintains all records regarding the employees covered under a group insurance plan.

Self-Insurer: An employer who can meet the state legal and financial requirements to assume by him or herself all of its risk and pay for the losses, although the employer may contract with an insurance carrier or others to provide certain essential services.

Short-Term Disability Income Insurance: The provision to pay benefits to a covered disabled person as long as he/she remains disabled up to a specified period not exceeding two years.

Social Security Freeze: A long-term disability policy provision that establishes that the offset from benefits paid by Social Security will not be changed regardless of subsequent changes in the Social Security law.

Special Risk Insurance: Coverage for risks or hazards of a special or unusual nature.

Standard Insurance: Insurance written on the basis of regular morbidity underwriting assumptions used by an insurance company and issued at normal rates.

Standard Provision: Those contract provisions generally required by state statutes until superseded by the uniform policy provision.

Standard Risk: A person who, according to a company's underwriting standards, is entitled to insurance protection without extra rating or special restrictions.

State Disability Plan: A plan for accident and sickness, or disability insurance required by state legislation of those employers doing business in that particular state.

State Insurance Department: A department of a state government whose duty is to regulate the business of insurance and give the public information on insurance.

Stock Insurance Company: An insurance company organized and owned by the stockholders who share in any profits, as distinguished from the mutual form of company which is owned by the policyholders.

Substandard Insurance: Insurance issued with an extra premium or special restriction to those persons who do not qualify for insurance at standard rates.

Substandard Risk: An individual, who, because of health history or physical limitations, does not meet the qualifications of a standard risk.

Third-Party Administration: Administration of a group insurance plan by some person or firm other than the insurer or the policyholder.

Tort Liability: The legal requirement that a person responsible, or at fault, shall pay for the damages and injuries caused.

Total Disability: An illness or injury that prevents an insured person from continuously performing every duty pertaining to his/her occupation or engaging in any other type of work.

Underwriter: The term generally is used for either: (a) a company that receives the premiums and accepts responsibility for the fulfillment of the insurance policy contract; (b) the company employee who decides whether or not the insurance company should assume a particular risk; or (c) the agent who sells the policy.

Underwriting: The process by which an insurer determines whether or not on what basis an application for insurance will be accepted.

Underwriting Profit or Loss: The profit or loss realized by an insurance company after deducting from earned premiums the incurred losses and expenses of doing business, but before provision for federal income tax and excluding investment income.

Unearned Premium: That portion of the paid premium applying to the unexpired portion of the policy term; or that portion of the paid premium for which protection has not been received.

Uninsurable Risk: One not acceptable for insurance due to excessive risk.

Valuation: The process of determining a company's liabilities under its policy obligations is termed "policy valuation." The process of determining the value of a company's investments is known as "asset valuation."

Waiting Period: The length of time an employee must wait from his/her date of employment or application for coverage, to the date the insurance policy is effective.

Waiver: An agreement attached to a policy that exempts from coverage certain disabilities or injuries which are normally covered by the policy.

Waiver of Premium: A provision included in some policies that exempts the policyholder from paying the premiums while an insured is totally disabled, during the life of the contract.

Workers' Compensation: The social insurance system for industrial and work injury regulated primarily among the separate states, but regulated in certain specified occupations by the federal government.

Workers' Compensation Commission: One of many terms identifying the state public body which administers the workers' compensation laws, holds hearings on contested cases, promotes industrial safety, rehabilitation, etc. It is often located within the state labor department. The national organization is the International Association of Industrial Accident Boards and Commissions.

GLOSSARY B
Legal Terms*

Access: The right of access to public records includes not only the legal right of access, but a reasonable opportunity to avail oneself of same.

Action: A proceeding brought to enforce any right.

Actionable Tort: A legal duty, imposed by statute or otherwise, owing by defendant to the one injured.

Adjudication: The giving or pronouncing a judgment or decree in a cause.

Administrative Law: That branch of public law that deals with the various organs of federal, state, and local governments which prescribes in detail the manner of their activities.

Adversary Proceeding: One having opposing parties, as distinguished from an ex parte proceeding.

Advisory Opinion: A formal opinion by judge or judges or a court or a law officer upon a question of law submitted by a legislative body or a governmental official, but not actually presented in a concrete case of law.

Affidavit: A written statement of fact signed and sworn before a person authorized to administer an oath.

Affirmative Action: The action that a governmental agency or unit is authorized to take to implement governmental policies in order to protect those people who are intended to benefit from such policies.

Aggrieved Party: One whose legal right is invaded by an act that constitutes a complaint, or whose primary interest is directly affected by a decree or judgment.

Amicus Curiae: A friend of the court or a person who has no right to appear in a suit but is allowed to introduce argument, authority, or evidence to protect his/her interests.

Answer: A formal written statement made by a defendant setting forth the ground of his/her defense.

Appeal: The process whereby a court of appeals reviews the record of written materials from a trial court proceeding to determine if errors were made that might lead to a reversal of the trial court's decision.

Appeal Bond: The bond given on taking an appeal, by which the appellant and his/her sureties are bound to pay damages and costs if he/she fails to prosecute the appeal with effect.

Appellant: The party who takes an appeal from one court or jurisdiction to another.

Appellee: The party in a cause against whom an appeal is taken; that is, the party who has an interest adverse to setting aside or reversing the judgment.

Assumption of Risk: A doctrine based upon voluntary exposure to a known risk. It is distinguished from contributory negligence, which is based on carelessness, in that it involves a comprehension that a peril is to be encountered and a willingness to encounter it.

---

*For definitions not included here, a convenient reference source is: Black, H.C. 1979. Black's Law Dictionary. 5th Ed. West Publishing Co., St. Paul, MN.

Bad Faith: Generally involving actual or constructive fraud, or a design to mislead or deceive another.

Beyond a Reasonable Doubt: The test applied in a criminal case that means facts proven must, by virtue of their probative force, establish guilt.

Bilateral Contract: A contract in which both contracting parties are bound to fulfill obligations reciprocally towards each other.

Bill: In general terms, it is a formal declaration, complaint, or statement of particular things in writing.

Bona Fide: Literally translated as "in good faith."

Bond: A certificate or evidence of a debt.

Breach of Duty: The neglect or failure to fulfill in a just and proper manner the duties of an office or fiduciary employment.

Brief: A written document prepared by an attorney addressed to the court summarizing facts and arguments in support of a litigant's position.

Burden of Proof: The duty of producing evidence as the case progresses, and/or the duty to establish the truth of the claim by a preponderance of the evidence. The former may pass from party to party, the latter rests throughout upon the party asserting the affirmative of the issue.

Case Law: The aggregate of reported cases forming a body of jurisprudence, or the law of a particular subject as evidenced or formed by the adjudged cases, in distinction to statutes and other sources of law.

Certiorari: The name of a writ of review or inquiry. Certiorari is an appellate proceeding for re-examination of action of inferior tribunal or as auxiliary process to enable appellate courts to obtain further information in pending cases.

Change of Venue: The removal of a suit begun in one jurisdiction to another jurisdiction.

Circuit Court of Appeals: The United States is divided into 11 judicial circuits in each of which there is established a court of appeals known as the United States Court of Appeals for the circuit.

Circumstantial Evidence: Indirect evidence that does not directly establish a fact, but from which a logical inference may be drawn that the fact exists.

Civil Case or Suit: A case brought by one or more individuals to seek redress of some legal injury (or aspect of an injury) for which there are civil (non-criminal) remedies.

Civil Rights: Rights pertaining to a person in virtue of his/her citizenship in a state or community.

Claim: A broad, comprehensive word that is the cause of a suit or a cause of action.

Claimant: One who asserts a right or a demand in a legal proceeding.

Class Action: An action brought on behalf of other persons similarly situated.

Class Legislation: Legislation limited in operation to certain persons or classes of persons, natural or artificially formed.

Clear and Convincing Proof: More than a preponderance of the evidence, but less than is required in a criminal case.

Clerk of Court: An officer of a court of justice who has charge of the clerical part of its business.

Code of Federal Regulations: The compendium of regulations issued by federal regulatory agencies in order to carry out the policies mandated by Congressional Acts.

Code of Civil Procedure: A collection of the rules of court systems, both state and federal.

Color of Law: Acting under the actual or assumed authority of the law.

Common Law: A system of legal principles that does not derive its authority from statutory law, but from general usage and custom as evidenced by decisions of courts.

Comparative Negligence: Where negligence by both parties is concurrent and contributes to injury, recovery is not barred under such doctrine, but plaintiff's damages are diminished proportionately, provided fault is less than the defendant's, and that, by exercise of ordinary care, the plaintiff could not have avoided consequences of the defendant's negligence after it was or should have been apparent.

Compensation: An act that a court orders done, or money that a court or other tribunal orders to be paid, by a person whose acts or omissions have caused loss or injury to another, in order that thereby the person damnified may receive equal value for the loss, or be made whole in respect to the injury.

Complaint: A legal document submitted to the court by potential plaintiffs in which they inform the court and the defendants that they are bringing suit and set out the underlying causes of action.

Confidential Relation: A fiduciary relation; the law, in order to prevent undue advantage from the unlimited confidence or sense of duty, which the relation naturally creates, requires the utmost degree of good faith in all transactions between the parties. The term "confidential relation" covers every form of relation between parties wherein confidence is reposed by one in another, and the former relies and acts upon representations of the other and is guilty of no derelictions on his/her own part.

Confidential Communications: Certain classes of communications, passing between persons who stand in a confidential or fiduciary relation to each other (or who, on account of their relative situation, are under a special duty of secrecy and fidelity), that the law will not permit to be divulged.

Conflict of Laws: Conflict in the mind of a judge as to which of two systems of law should govern a given case.

Consent Agreement: An out-of-court agreement reached by the parties to a suit, that will be formally approved by the court.

Consent, Express: Consent given directly, either orally or in writing. It represents positive, direct, unequivocal consent, requiring no inference or implication to supply the meaning.

Consent, Implied: Consent manifested by signs, actions, or facts, or by the inaction or silence, which raise a presumption that the consent has been given.

Consideration: The promise or performance by the other party that the promisor demands as the price of his/her promise.

Constitutional Right: A legal right that is based on the United States Constitution or on a state constitution.

Constructive Assent: An assent or consent imputed to a party from a constructive or an interpretation of his/her conduct; as distinguished from one which he/she actually expresses.

Contempt of Court: Any act that is calculated to embarrass, hinder, delay, or obstruct the court in the administration of justice, or that is calculated to lessen its authority or its dignity.

Contingent Claim: One that has not accrued and that is dependent on some future event that may never happen.

Contingent Liability: One that is not now fixed and absolute, but that will become so in the case of occurrence of some future event.

Contract: A binding agreement based on the genuine assent of the parties, made for a lawful object, between competent parties, in the form required by the law, and generally supported by consideration.

Counterclaim: The term is broader than set-off or recoupment, and includes both. It is an offensive, as well as defensive, plea that is not necessarily confined to the justice of the plaintiff's claim. It represents the right of the defendant to have the claims of the parties counterbalanced in whole or in part, with judgment to be entered for the excess, if any.

Court of Claims: Its jurisdiction extends to all claims against the United States arising out of any contract with the government or based on an act of Congress or regulation of the executive, and all claims referred to it by either house of Congress, as well as to claims for exoneration by a disbursing officer.

Court of Probate: A court having jurisdiction over the probate of wills, the grant of administration, and the supervision of management and settlement of estates or descendants.

Court Order: Every direction of a court or judge made or entered in writing, and not included in a judgment. An application for an order is called a motion.

Court Systems: There are two court structures in the United States; the federal courts and the state courts. The former consists of federal district courts where cases are tried, the U.S. Courts of Appeals, and the U.S. Supreme Court. State courts consist of trial-level courts designated by various titles, and one or two levels of appeal courts.

Covenant: An agreement, convention, or promise of by two or more parties, by deed in writing, signed and delivered, by which either of the parties pledges to the other that something is either done or shall be done, or stipulated for the truth of certain facts.

Cross Action: An action brought by one who is a defendant in a suit against the party who is the plaintiff in the suit upon a cause of action growing out of the same transaction in which there is controversy, whether it be a contract or a tort. An independent suit brought by the defendant against the plaintiff.

Cross-Claim: A "cross-claim" is one brought by a defendant against a co-defendant in the same suit.

Cross Examination: The questioning of a witness during a trial or deposition by the party opposing those who originally asked him/her to testify.

Culpable: Implies the act of conduct spoken of is reprehensible or wrong, but not that it involves malice or guilty purpose. The term connotes fault rather than guilt.

Damages: Money awarded by a court to someone who has been injured (plaintiff) and that must be paid by the party responsible for the injury (defendant). *Normal damages* are awarded when the injury is judged to be slight. *Compensatory damages* are awarded to repay or compensate the injured party for the injury incurred. *Punitive damages* are awarded when the injury is judged to have been committed maliciously or in wanton disregard of the injured plaintiff's interests.

Declaratory Relief: A remedy granted by a court where the court declares or finds that a plaintiff has certain rights. A request for declaratory relief is usually coupled with a request for injunctive relief where the court orders a defendant to take or refrain from taking certain actions.

Decree: A sentence of order of the court, pronounced on hearing and understanding all the points in issue, and determining the rights of all parties to the suit, according to equity and good conscience.

Defamation: The taking of one's reputation. The distinction between "criticism" and defamation is that the former deals only with such issues that invite public attention or call for public comment, and does not follow a person into his/her private life, or attacks an individual instead of his/her work. The fundamental difference between a right to "privacy" and a right to freedom from "defamation" is that the former directly concerns one's peace of mind, whereas the latter concerns primarily one's reputation.

Defendant: The person against whom an action is brought because of alleged responsibility for violating one or more of the plaintiff's legally protected interests.

Defense: A reason cited by a defendant why a complaint against him/her is without merit or why he/she is not responsible for the injury or violation of rights as alleged by the plaintiff.

Deposition: The testimony of a witness taken upon interrogatories not in open court, but in pursuance of a commission to take testimony issued by a court, or under a general law on the subject, and reduced to writing and duly authenticated, and intended to be used upon the trial of an action in court.

Direct Examination: The first interrogation or examination of a witness, on the merits, by the party on whose behalf he/she is called.

Disability: In a legal sense the term means the incapacity for the full enjoyment of ordinary legal rights. In a non-legal sense the term refers to physical, mental, or emotional impairment diagnosed as such by an appropriate professional practitioner.

Disclosure: The impartation of that which is secret.

Discovery: The process by which one party to a civil suit can find out about matters that are relevant to his/her case, including information about what evidence the other side has, what witnesses will be called upon, and so on. Discovery devices for obtaining information may include depositions and interrogatories to obtain testimony, requests for documents or other tangibles, or requests for physical or mental examinations.

Discrimination: A failure to treat all equally.

Dismissal with Prejudice: An adjudication on the merits, and final disposition, barring the right to bring or maintain an action on the same claim or cause.

Dismissal without Prejudice: To prevent the decree of dismissal from operating as a bar to a subsequent suit.

Diversity of Citizenship: A phrase used with reference to the jurisdiction of the federal courts, that extends to cases between citizens of different states, designating the condition existing when the party on one side of a suit is a citizen of one state and the party on the other side is a citizen of another state.

Domicile: That place where a person has his/her true, fixed, and permanent home and principal establishment, and to which whenever he/she is absent, has the intention of returning. "Domicile" is distinguished from "residence" in that the former is the home, the fixed place of habitation; whereas residence is a transient place of dwelling.

Doubt, Reasonable: That state of the case which, after the entire comparison and consideration of all the evidence, leaves the minds of the jurors in that condition where they cannot say they feel an abiding conviction to a moral certainty of the truth of the charge.

Due Care: The term implies that not only has a party not been negligent or careless, but that the party has been guilty of no violation of law in relation to the subject matter or transaction that constitutes the course of action.

Due Course of Law: Synonymous with "due process of law." The general definition thereof is law in its regular course of administration through courts of justice.

Due Process of Law: Means substantial justice and fundamental fairness. Procedurally, it has been interpreted to mean that reasonable notice be given to parties of a pending action in a court of law or government agency, and a reasonable opportunity to be heard before a competent and impartial tribunal.

Duress: The unlawful constraint exercised upon a person whereby he/she is forced to do some act that he/she otherwise would not have done.

Duty: An obligation or responsibility to perform or refrain from performing an act that may arise from the relationship between the particular parties.

Equal Protection of the Law: Equal protection and security shall be given to all under the circumstances in a person's life, liberty, and property, and in the pursuit of happiness, and in the exemption from any greater burdens and charges than are equally imposed upon all others under like circumstances.

Equity: A system of law and courts emphasizing "fairness" that developed separate from, and as a complement to, common law.

Estate: The whole of the property owned by a person, the realty as well as the personal goods.

Evidence: Any species of proof, or probative matter, legally presented at the trial of an issue, by the act of the parties and through the medium of witnesses, records, documents, concrete objects, and the like, for the purpose of inducing beliefs in the minds of the court or jury as to their contention.

Ex Parte: A judicial proceeding, order, injunction, and so on, taken or granted at the instance and for the benefit of one party only, and without notice to, or contestation by, any person adversely interested.

Ex Post Facto: After the fact; by an act or fact occurring after some previous act or fact.

Execution of Judgment: Putting into effect of the final judgment of the court.

Exemplary Damages: An award of money given over and above that required to compensate the victim for loss where the wrong committed was done with malice. It has the intent of acting as punishment and to provide an "example" for others. The term is synonymous with "punitive damages."

Expert Witness: A person called to testify because of recognized competence in an area.

Fair Hearing: One in which authority is executed fairly; that is consistently with the fundamental principles of justice embraced within the conception of due process of law.

Felony: An act declared to be a crime by statute or common law of a jurisdiction. Generally, it is a class of crime for which the possible penalty for conviction is more than one year in a penal institution.

Fiduciary: A person having a special duty of trust to act primarily for another's benefit.

Fiduciary Relation: Formal and informal relations that exist whenever one person trusts and relies on another. It exists where there is a special confidence reposed in one who, in equity and good conscience, is bound to act in good faith and with due regard to interests of one reposing the confidence.

Final Judgment: Synonymous with "final determination," wherein it is the final settling of the rights of the parties to the action beyond all appeal.

Finding of Fact: A conclusion by way of reasonable inference from the evidence.

Fraud: A false representation of a matter of fact, whether by words or by conduct, by false or misleading allegation, or by concealment of that which should have been disclosed, that deceives and is intended to deceive another so that he/she shall act upon it to his/her legal injury.

Fraudulent Conveyance: A conveyance or transfer of property, the object of which is to defraud a creditor, or hinder or delay, or put such property beyond the person's reach.

Frauds, Statute of: A common designation of an English Statute, passed in 1677, that has been adopted generally in nearly all of the United States. Its principal characteristic is the provision that no suit or action shall be maintained on certain classes of contracts or engagements unless there shall be a note or memorandum thereof in writing signed by the party to be charged or by the party's authorized agent.

Garnishment: A statutory proceding whereby a person's property, money, or credits in the possession or under control of, or owing by, another are applied to payment of the former's debts to a third person by proper statutory process against debtor and garnishee.

Guardian Ad Litem: One who is appointed by the court to protect the interests of a minor in a suit. He/she is empowered to act in the child's behalf until the case is concluded.

Hearsay: Evidence not proceeding from the personal knowledge of the witness, but from the mere repetition of what has been heard from others.

Impeach: In the law of evidence, it is to call in question the veracity of a witness, by means of evidence adduced for that purpose.

Incapacity: Implies that the person in view has the right vested in him/her, but is prevented by some impediment from exercising it.

Incompetency: Lack of ability, legal qualification, or fitness to discharge the required duty.

Incumbrance: A claim, lien, charge, or liability attached to and binding against real or personal property.

Indemnity: To secure against loss or damage; to give security for the reimbursement of a person in case of an anticipated loss falling upon him/her.

Indictment: A written accusation found and presented by a grand jury to a court that charges that a party committed some act, or was guilty of some omission, that, by law, is a public offense, punishable on indictment.

Injunction: A judicial process requiring the party to whom it is directed to for or refrain from doing a particular thing.

Injunctive Relief: A remedy granted by the court forbidding or requiring some action by the defendant.

Injury: Any wrong, or damages done to another, either done to his/her person, rights, reputation, or property.

In Loco Parentis: Literally, "in place of parents." A party acting legally in behalf of the parents.

In Re: In the matter of; concerning; with reference to.

Intent: A state of mind, inferred from a person's actions, showing purpose or determination to act in a certain manner.

Inter Alia: As a part of a text or in between other sections.

Interlocutory: Temporary; not final.

Interrogatories: A set or series of written questions composed for the purpose of being propounded to a party in equity, a garnishee, or a witness whose testimony is taken in a deposition.

Intestacy: The state or condition of dying without having made a valid will, or without having disposed by will of a part of a person's property.

Ipso Facto: Literally, "by the fact itself."

Issue: A single, certain, and material point, deduced by the pleadings of the parties, which is affirmed on the one side and denied on the other.

Jeopardy: The condition of a person when placed on trial, before a court of competent jurisdiction, upon an indictment or information that is sufficient in form and substance to sustain a conviction, and a jury has been charged with the party's deliverance.

Joinder: Joining or coupling together; uniting with another person in some legal step or proceeding.

Joint Liability: One wherein the joint obligator has the right to insist that the co-obligator be joined as a co-defendant with him/her, that is, that they are to be sued jointly.

Judgment: The official and authentic decision of a court upon the respective rights and claims of the parties to an action or suit therein litigated and submitted to its determination.

Jurisdiction: The authority, capacity, power, or right to act.

Jurisprudence: The philosophy of law, or the science that treats the principles of positive law and legal relations.

Levy: To collect or seize.

Liability: The subjection of a person to having his/her legal relation affected by the conduct of a person or the state having a legal power.

Libel: A printed or written article that has a tendency to expose one to public contempt, scorn, ridicule, shame or disgrace, or tends to induce an evil opinion of the person in the minds of others, or injure the person in his/her profession, occupation, or trade.

License: A permission, by a designated authority, to perform some act which without such authorization would be illegal, or would be a trespass or a tort.

Lien: A charge or security or incumbrance upon property.

Limitation, Statute of: A statute prescribing limitations to the right of action on certain described causes of action; that is, declaring that no suit shall be maintained on such causes of action unless brought within a specified period of time after the right accrued.

Litigation: A contest in a court for the purpose of enforcing a right.

Malfeasance: Unlawful conduct; acts that are expressly prohibited.

Malice: The intentional doing of a wrongful act without just cause or excuse, with an intent to inflict injury or under circumstances that the law will imply an evil intent.

Malpractice: Any professional misconduct, unreasonable lack of skill or fidelity in professional or fiduciary duties, evil practice, or illegal or immoral conduct.

Mandamus: Literally, "we command." A writ or order of a superior court to a lower court or to a governmental body commanding that a certain act be performed or not performed.

Misdemeanor: An unlawful act not as serious as a felony; generally punishable by a fine or short-term imprisonment.

Misfeasance: The improper performance of an act that the person has a right or duty to perform.

Motion: A request to the court to take some action or to request the opposing side to take some action relating to a case.

Negligence: The omission to do something that a reasonable man or reasonable professional, guided by those ordinary considerations that tyically regulate human affairs, would do, or the doing of something that a reasonable man or professional would not do.

Nolo Contendere: Literally, "I will not contest it." Like a demurrer, this plea admits, for the purposes of the case, all the facts that are well pleaded, but is not to be used as an admission elsewhere.

Notice: Information, and advice or written warning, in more or less formal shape, intended to appraise a person of some proceeding in which his/her interests are involved, or informing him/her of some fact that it is his/her right to know and the duty of the notifying party to communicate.

Obiter Dictum: Statements in judicial opinions wherein courts indulge in generalities that had no actual bearing on the issues involved.

Order: Every direction of a court or judge made or entered in writing, and not included in a judgment. An application for an order is a "motion."

Pardon: An act of grace, proceeding from the power intrusted with the execution of the laws, that exempt the individual on whom it is bestowed from the punishment the law inflicts for a crime the person committed.

Parens Patriae: In the United States, the state, as a sovereign; referring to the sovereign power of guardianship over persons under disability.

Performance, Specific: The doctrine of specific performance is that, where damages would be an inadequate compensation for the breach of an agreement, the contractor will be compelled to perform specifically what he/she has agreed to do.

Per Se: Literally, "in and of itself."

Petition: An application to a court ex parte praying for the exercise of the judicial powers of the court in relation to some matter that is not the subject for a suit or action, or for authority to do some action that requires the sanction of the court.

Plaintiff: A person who brings a suit to court in the belief that one or more of his/her legal rights have been violated or that he/she has suffered legal injury.

Plea: The answer that the defendant in an action at law makes to the plaintiff's declaration, and in which the former sets up matter of fact as defense, thus distinguishing from a demurrer, which imposes objections on grounds of law.

Pleading: The process in which alternate and opposing written statements are presented by the contesting parties for the purpose of focusing on a particular issue.

Precedent: A decision by a judge or court that serves as a rule or guide to support other judges in deciding future cases involving similar or analogous legal questions.

Presumption: An inference affirmation or disaffirmation of the truth or falsehood of any proposition or fact drawn by a process of probable reasoning in the absence of actual certainty of its truth or falsehood, or until such certainty can be ascertained.

Prima Facie Evidence: A fact presumed to be true as a matter of initial appearance and logic.

Privacy, Right of: The right of an individual to withhold his/her person and property from public scrutiny, if so desired, as long as it is consistent with the law or public policy.

Private Action: A case brought on behalf of one or more persons to vindicate violation of their legally protected interests. As distinguished from a class action, where the relief will apply to all persons similarly situated or within the class represented by the plaintiffs, any relief granted in a private action applies only to those plaintiffs actually before the court.

Privilege: An advantage or exemption, beyond those commonly held by citizens, to perform or not to perform an act.

Privy: A person who is in direct contractual relationship with another.

Probative: An adjective used to describe evidence that tends to establish or prove a fact in question.

Procedural Right: A right relating to the process of enforcing substantive rights or to obtaining relief, such as the right to a hearing, the right to present evidence in one's defense, or the right to counsel (procedural due process).

Process: The means of compelling the defendant in an action to appear in court.

Proof: The establishment of a fact by evidence.

Pro Se: A person who appears in court "pro se" appears as his/her own attorney.

Proximate Cause: An event that, in an unbroken and ordinary chain of events, produces an injury.

Quasi-Judicial: The action of public administrative officials who are required to investigate facts or ascertain the evidence of facts and to exercise discretion of a judicial nature.

Rebuttal Presumption: A species of legal presumption that holds good until disproved.

Rejoinder: The second pleading on the part of the defendant, being his/her answer to the plaintiff's replication.

Release: The relinquishment of a right, claim, or privilege, by a person in whom it exists or to whom it accrues, to the person against whom it might have been demanded or enforced.

Relief: A remedy for some legal wrong. Relief is requested by the plaintiff, to be granted by the court, against a defendant.

Remand: To send back; as in sending a case back to the same court out of which it came for purposes of having some action taken on it there.

Remedy: The means by which a right is enforced or the violation of a right is prevented, redressed, or compensated.

Respondeat Superior: Literally, "let the master respond." This maxim means that an employer is liable in certain cases for the wrongful acts of his/her employees, and the principal for those of his/her agency.

Respondent: The party who makes an answer to a charge or the party who contends against an appeal.

Right: A power or claim, legally enforced, inherent in one person that may make demands on another.

Settlement: A "meeting of minds" of parties to a transaction or controversy which resolves some or all of the issues involved in a case.

Slander: The speaking of base and defamatory words tending to prejudice another in one's reputation, office, trade, business, or means of livelihood.

Statute: An act of a legislature declaring, commanding, or prohibiting an action, in contrast to unwritten common law.

Statutory Right: A right based on a statute or law passed by a unit of federal, state, or local government.

Stipulation: An agreement between opposing parties that a particular fact or principle of law is true and applicable.

Strict Liability: Liability without fault; whereby neither care nor negligence, neither good nor bad faith, neither knowledge nor ignorance will save the defendant.

Sub Nom: Literally, "in the name of."

Subpoena: A process commanding a witness to appear and give testimony in court.

Subpoena Duces Tecum: A court order to produce documents or otherwise to explain to the court why such documents should not have to be produced.

Substantive Right: An essential right such as the right to free speech and religion or to be free from involuntary servitude, guaranteed in federal and state constitutions (substantive due process).

Summons: A writ, directed to a sheriff or other proper authority, requiring notification of individuals named, that an action has been commenced against them in a court that issued the writ, on a day named, and answer the complaint in such action.

Tort: A civil wrong for which a private individual may recover money damages, arising from a breach of duty created by law.

Tort-Feasor: A wrong-doer who is legally liable for damage caused.

Undue Influence: Wrongful persuasion of a person thereby causing him/her to do what would not normally be done.

Waiver: The intentional or voluntary relinquishment of a known right.

Warrant: A writ or precept from a competent authority in pursuance of law, directing the doing of an act, and addressed to an officer of a person competent to do the act, and affording said person protection from damage, in performing the act.

Writ: A mandatory precept issuing from a court, addressed to a public officer, or directly to the person whose action the court desires to command, either at the commencement of a suit or other proceeding or as incidental to its progress, and requiring the performance of a specified act, or giving authority and commission to have it done.

GLOSSARY C
Occupational Terminology*

Job Components

Element: The smallest step into which it is practicable to subdivide any work activity without analyzing separate motions, movements, and mental processes.

Task: One or more elements that is a distinct activity that constitutes the logical and necessary steps in the performance of work by workers. A *task* is created whenever human effort (physical or mental) is exerted to accomplish a specific purpose.

Position: A collection of tasks constituting the total work of a single worker. There are as many *positions* as there are workers in the country.

Job: A group of positions which are identical with respect to their major or significant tasks and sufficiently alike to justify their being covered by a single analysis. There may be one or many persons employed in the same job.

Lifting Activities

Sedentary Work: Lifting 10 pounds maximum and occasionally lifting or carrying articles, such as dockets, ledgers, and small tools. Jobs are *sedentary* when standing and walking are required only occasionally.

Light Work: Lifting 20 pounds maximum and/or frequently lifting or carrying objects weighing up to 10 pounds. Even though the weight lifted may be only a negligible amount, a job will be in this category when it requires: (a) walking or standing to a significant degree; or (b) sitting most of the time, but entails pushing and pulling of arm or leg controls.

Medium Work: Lifting 50 pounds maximum and/or frequently lifting or carrying objects weighing up to 25 pounds.

Heavy Work: Lifting 100 pounds maximum and/or frequently lifting or carrying objects weighing up to 50 pounds.

Very Heavy Work: Lifting objects in excess of 100 pounds and/or frequently carrying or lifting objects weighing 50 pounds or more.

Physical Activities

Balancing: Maintaining body equilibrium to prevent falling when walking, standing, crouching, or running on narrow, slippery, or erratically moving surfaces; or maintaining body equilibrium when performing gymnastic feats. *Described* in terms of *type* or *condition* of *surface* and *activities* in which balance must be maintained.

Carrying: Moving an object, usually by holding it in hands or arms, or on shoulders. *Described* in terms of *weights, distances,* and *duration.*

Climbing: Ascending or descending ladders, stairs, scaffolding, ramps, poles, and the like, using feet and legs, and/or hands and arms. Body agility is emphasized. *Described* in terms of *height, steepness, duration,* and *type of structure* climbed.

Crawling: Moving about on hands and knees or hands and feet. *Described* in terms of *distance* and *duration.*

---

*For definitions not included here, a convenient reference source is United States Department of Labor, Employment and Training Administration. 1981. Selected Characteristics of Occupations Defined in the Dictionary of Occupational Titles. U.S. Government Printing Office, Washington, D.C.

Crouching: Bending body forward and downward by bending legs and spine. *Described* in terms of *duration.*

Feeling: Perceiving attributes of objects, such as size, shape, temperature, or texture, by touching with skin, particularly fingertips.

Fingering: Picking, pinching, or otherwise working primarily with fingers rather than with the whole hand or arm as in handling. *Described* in terms of *objects* and *duration.*

Handling: Seizing, holding, grasping, turning, or otherwise working with hand or hands. Fingers are involved only to the extent that they are an extension of the hand, such as to turn a switch or shift automobile gears. *Described* in terms of *objects* and *duration.*

Hearing: Perceiving the nature of sounds.

Kneeling: Bending legs at knees to come to rest on knees or knee. *Described* in terms of *duration.*

Lifting: Raising or lowering an object from one level to another, using hands, arms, and/or shoulders. Includes upward pulling. *Described* in terms of *weights* and *vertical distances.*

Pulling: Exerting force upon an object so that the object moves toward the force. Includes jerking. *Described* in terms of *weights, estimated force, distances, duration,* and/or *type of surface.*

Pushing: Exerting force upon an object so that the object moves away from the force. Includes slapping, striking, kicking, and treadle actions. *Described* in terms of *weights, estimated force, distances, duration,* and/or *type of surface.*

Reaching: Extending hand(s) and arm(s) in any direction.

Reclining: Lying on one's side or in a prone or supine position. *Described* in terms of *position* and *duration.*

Sitting: Remaining in the normal seated position. *Described* in terms of *duration.*

Standing: Remaining on one's feet in an upright position at a work station without moving about. *Described* in terms of *duration.*

Stooping: Bending the body forward and downward by bending the spine at the waist. *Described* in terms of *duration.*

Talking: Expressing or exchanging ideas by means of the spoken word.

Tasting (Smelling): Distinguishing, with a degree of accuracy, differences or similarities in intensity or quality of flavors and/or odors, or recognizing particular flavors and/or odors, using tongue and/or nose.

Walking: Moving about on foot. Includes running. *Described* in terms of *duration* and *distance.*

Visual Acuity

Color Vision: Ability to identify and distinguish colors.

Far Vision: Clarity of vision at 20 feet or more.

Field of Vision: Observing an area that can be seen up and down or to right or left while eyes are fixed on a given point.

Midrange Vision: Clarity of vision at distances of more than 20 inches and less than 20 feet.

Near Vision: Clarity of vision at 20 inches or less.

Visual Accommodation: Adjustment of lens of eyes to bring an object into sharp focus.

Environmental Conditions

Atmospheric Conditions: Exposure to conditions that affect the respiratory system or the skin, such as fumes, noxious odors, dusts, mists, gases, and poor ventilation.

Exposure to Weather: Exposure to hot, cold, wet, humid, or windy conditions, caused by weather, which result in marked bodily discomfort.

Extreme Cold: Exposure to nonweather-related temperatures that are sufficiently low to cause marked bodily discomfort.

Extreme Heat: Exposure to nonweather-related temperatures that are sufficiently high to cause marked bodily discomfort.

Inherent Hazards: Proximity to moving mechanical parts, exposure to electrical shock, working in high exposed places, exposure to radiant energy, working with explosives, exposure to toxic or caustic chemicals, exposure to noises sufficient to cause possible hearing impairment or loss.

Noise: Exposure to constant or intermittent sounds of a pitch or level sufficient to cause a worker to have difficulty hearing the voice of person three or four feet away unless voice is raised above normal conversational level.

Vibration: Exposure to a shaking object or surface that causes strain on the body or extremities.

Wet and/or Humid: Contact with water or other liquids; or exposure to nonweather-related humid conditions where humidity is sufficiently high to cause marked bodily discomfort.

APPENDIX A

Coverage of Workers' Compensation Laws

| Jurisdiction | Employments Covered | | Exceptions* |
	Private	Public	
Alabama	Compulsory for 3 or more employees. Elective for owner of business.	Compulsory for all public employments except municipalities of less than 2,000 people and school districts.	Domestic servants and casual employees.
Alaska	Compulsory for all employments including elected or appointed corporate executive officers.	Compulsory: State and political subdivisions, members of state boards, and commissions. Elective: Executive officers of municipal corporations.	Part-time baby sitters, cleaning persons, seasonal workers, etc.
Arizona	Compulsory for all employments. Employee may reject.	Compulsory: State, counties, cities, towns, municipal corporations, and school districts.	Domestic servants and casual employees.
Arkansas	Compulsory for 3 or more employees. Elective for partners and sole proprietors.	Compulsory: State agencies, departments, institutions, and counties. Excludes: unincorporated cities and towns.	Farm labor, domestic servants, casual workers, vendors, and distributors of newspapers and other publications.

| | Employments Covered | | |
Jurisdiction	Private	Public	Exceptions*
California	Compulsory for all employments including working members of partnerships.	Compulsory for all public employments except those working without pay.	Charity and volunteer workers at camps, etc. that are operated by non-profit organizations. Domestic servants who work less than 52 hours in 90 days or earn less than $100. Students in sporting events.
Colorado	Compulsory for all employments.	Compulsory for all salaried public employments to include job trainees deemed employees of training commissions.	Employees of religious or charitable organizations, domestic servants and casual employees who earn less than $2,000 annually, and volunteer ski lift operators.
Connecticut	Compulsory for all employments. Corporate officers may reject. Elective for sole proprietors or partners.	Compulsory for all state, public corporations, and members of the General Assembly. Municipalities may elect coverage of others.	Casual employees, domestic servants employed less than 26 hours weekly, officers of fraternal organizations paid less than $100 yearly.
Delaware	Compulsory for all employments.	Elective for state, certain counties, cities, and towns.	Domestic servants, casual employees earning less than $300 in 3 months from one household, farm laborers.
District of Columbia	Compulsory for all employments.	Compulsory for all employments.	Farm labor, casual employees, master or crew of any vessel, interstate railroad employees.

| | Employments Covered | | |
Jurisdiction	Private	Public	Exceptions*
Florida	Compulsory for 3 or more employees. Elective for corporate officers, partners, and sole proprietors.	Compulsory for all employments except elected officials.	Domestic servants, casual employees, 12 or less casual or 5 or less farm labor, professional athletes, employees of common carriers, volunteers in nonprofit agencies or federal programs.
Georgia	Compulsory for all employments with 3 or more employees	Compulsory for all employments. Voluntary for planning commissions.	Farm labor, domestic servants, employees of common carriers by railroad, and casual labor.
Hawaii	Compulsory for all employments.	Compulsory for all employments and elected or appointed officials.	Employees of religious, charitable, or non-profit organizations. Domestics who earn less than $250 per quarter. Unpaid 25% stockholders of corporations without employees.
Idaho	Compulsory for all employments. Elective for corporate officers who are 10% stockholders, sole proprietors, and working members of partnerships.	Compulsory for all employments except officials at secondary school athletic events.	Agricultural labor, domestic servants, casual labor, unpaid volunteers, airmen, commission real estate salesmen and brokers.

Employments Covered

Jurisdiction	Private	Public	Exceptions*
Illinois	Compulsory for all employments in hazardous occupations. Elective for non-hazardous employments.	Compulsory for all employments except fire and police departments in cities over 200,000.	Certain farm labor, domestic servants, casual labor, real estate brokers and salesmen paid by commission only.
Indiana	Compulsory for all employments. Elective for sole proprietors and partnerships.	Compulsory for all employments including elected or appointed officials.	Farm labor, domestic servants, casual workers, and railroad workers.
Iowa	Compulsory for all employments, but corporate officers may reject.	Compulsory for all employments, except firemen and police.	Domestic and casual workers earning under $200 per quarter, farm labor if the employer's payroll is under $2,500 yearly, or any regular employee working less than 40 hours per week during 13 weeks.
Kansas	Compulsory for all employments. Elective for partners, individuals, and self-employments.	Compulsory for all employments. Members of firemen's relief funds may elect to accept or reject.	Farm labor or any employer whose annual gross payroll is not more than $10,000.

	Employments Covered		
Jurisdiction	Private	Public	Exceptions*
Kentucky	Compulsory for all employments. Elective for business owners or partners. Workers may reject coverage prior to injury.	Compulsory for all employments including elected and appointed officials.	Domestic servants if the employer employs fewer than 2 each regularly employed 40 hours per week, casual labor employed less than 20 consecutive days, agricultural labor, workers for religious or charitable organizations who receive aid and sustenance for their work.
Louisiana	Compulsory for all employments. Corporate officers who are 10% stockholders, partners, and sole proprietors may reject.	Compulsory for all employments except sheriffs' deputies and officials.	Crews of crop spraying aircraft while acting as contractors, real estate brokers and salesmen, laborers for employers engaged principally in agriculture.
Maine	Compulsory for all employments. Elective for partners and self-employed. Corporate officers who are 20% stockholders may reject.	Compulsory for all employments.	Casual or seasonal farm labor, domestic servants, maritime employees in foreign or interstate commerce, lobster sternmen, employers of fewer than 5 agricultural laborers.
Maryland	Compulsory for all employments including farm and dairy farmers with 3 or more employees. Elective for partners and sole proprietors.	Compulsory for all employments including prisoners working for county road boards and jurors for nonfederal courts.	Certain maintenance workers, casual, seasonal, or migratory farm laborers who do not operate machinery.

	Employments Covered		
Jurisdiction	Private	Public	Exceptions*
Massachusetts	Compulsory for all employments.	Compulsory for all state employments. Elective for counties, cities, and districts with taxation powers.	Seasonal and casual workers, domestic servants employed less than 16 hours per week, masters and seamen covered by federal law.
Michigan	Compulsory for 3 or more employees, or less than 3 if one is employed for 35 hours per week for 13 consecutive weeks by the same employer.	Compulsory for all employments including trainees in federally funded training programs who are considered employees.	Professional athletes whose average weekly wage is more than 200% of the statewide average, domestic servants working less than 35 hours per week for 13 weeks per year.
Minnesota	Compulsory for all employments. Elective for business owners or farms, or close corporations and their families.	Compulsory for all employments. Elective for elected or appointed officers of political subdivisions.	Certain casual labor, household workers who earn less than $500 per 3 months from one private household, family farms with annual payrolls of less than $8,000, railroad workers under federal law, commercial thresher or balers for family farms, nonprofit organizations with annual payrolls under $500.

	Employments Covered		
Jurisdiction	Private	Public	Exceptions*
Mississippi	Compulsory for all employments with 5 or more employees. Corporate officers may reject.	Voluntary for all employments. Specifically excludes handicapped persons in state sheltered workshop programs.	Domestic servants, farmers, farm laborers, officers in nonprofit charitable, fraternal, cultural, or religious organizations.
Missouri	Compulsory for all employments with 5 or more employees.	Compulsory for all employments.	Farm labor, domestic servants, and occasional labor for private households.
Montana	Compulsory for all employments. Elective for partners and sole proprietors. Corporate officers may reject.	Compulsory for all employments.	Domestic and casual employments, family members, employees covered by federal law, persons who work for aid and sustenance only.
Nebraska	Compulsory for all employments. Corporate officers who are 25% stockholders may reject.	Compulsory for all employments.	Farm labor and domestic servants.
Nevada	Compulsory for all employments. Elective for sole proprietors.	Compulsory for all employments including unpaid members and members of bands and orchestras.	Farm labor, domestic servants, casual labor, actors (except employees of motion picture producers), unpaid volunteers, and voluntary ski patrolmen.

Employments Covered

Jurisdiction	Private	Public	Exceptions*
New Hampshire	Compulsory for all employments. Elective for partners and sole proprietors.	Compulsory for all employments.	Railroad workers covered under FELA.
New Jersey	Elective for all employments.	Compulsory for all employments.	Casual workers, maritime workers, railroad workers engaged in interstate commerce.
New Mexico	Compulsory for 3 or more employees. Corporate officers who are 10% stockholders may reject.	Compulsory for all employments.	Farm or ranch labor, domestic servants, casual employees.
New York	Compulsory for all employments except corporate officer who is sole shareholder.	Compulsory for all state and subdivisions when worker is engaged in hazardous jobs. Voluntary for municipal corporations in nonhazardous employments.	Elective for farm labor if annual payroll is less than $1,200, volunteer workers, and domestic servants not employed by the same employer at least 40 hours per week.
North Carolina	Compulsory for 4 or more employees, and all employments with exposure to radiation. Corporate officers may reject.	Compulsory for all employments.	Farm labor, domestic servants, casual workers, railroad workers, voluntary ski patrol, individual sawmill or logging operators with less than 10 employees who work less than 60 days over 6 months.

| | Employments Covered | | |
Jurisdiction	Private	Public	Exceptions*
North Dakota	Compulsory for all hazardous employments. Excludes corporate officers unless performing duties performed by other employes.	Compulsory for all employments.	Farm labor, domestic servants, casual labor, illegal jobs or enterprises.
Ohio	Compulsory for all employments. Elective for partners and sole proprietors.	Compulsory for all employments.	Casual and domestic laborers who are paid less than $160 by one employer in any 3 month period.
Oklahoma	Compulsory for all employments. Elective for partners and sole proprietors.	Compulsory for all employments in hazardous jobs, except where equivalent coverages are in force.	Domestic and casual laborers of homeowners whose annual payroll is under $10,000, workers covered by federal law, real estate salesmen and brokers, agriculture/horticulture employers whose annual payroll is under $100,000.
Oregon	Compulsory for all employments. Elective for partners and sole proprietors, and corporate officers.	Compulsory for all employments including volunteer trainees in state schools for deaf and blind persons.	Domestic servants, casual labor, interstate transportation, and certain charitable or relief work.

Employments Covered

Jurisdiction	Private	Public	Exceptions*
Pennsylvania	Compulsory for all employments.	Compulsory for all employments except elected officials.	Domestic or casual labor, farmers with one employee who works less than 20 days a year or earns less than $150 annually.
Rhode Island	Compulsory for 4 or more employees, and all who work in hazardous jobs.	Compulsory for all state and city of Providence employments. Elective for cities and towns.	Agriculture and domestic servants.
South Carolina	Elective for 4 or more employees including active partners and sole proprietors whose employees are eligible for benefits.	Compulsory for all employments except elected and appointed officials.	Casual employees, farm labor, railroad workers, express companies, state and county fair associations, sellers of agricultural products, employers with annual payrolls under $3,000.
South Dakota	Compulsory for all employments. Elective for employers performing incidental labor to the job.	Compulsory for all employments except elected or appointed officials.	Farm labor, domestic servants if employed less than 24 hours in any week or less than 6 weeks in any 13 week period.
Tennessee	Compulsory for 5 or more employees. Elective for partners and sole proprietors. Corporate officers may reject.	Voluntary for all employments.	Farm labor, casual workers, domestic servants, employees of interstate common carriers, voluntary ski patrol.

	Employments Covered		
Jurisdiction	Private	Public	Exceptions*
Texas	Elective for all employments including corporate officers, partners, and sole proprietors.	Compulsory for Highway Department, and Texas and Texas A & M Universities. All others are elective.	Farm and ranch labor, domestic servants, railroads used as common carriers, casual employments.
Utah	Compulsory for all employments. Elective for partners and sole proprietors.	Compulsory for all employments.	Casual employments, farm employers whose annual payroll is less than $2,500 and who employ less than 4 persons for 40 hours per week for 13 weeks annually, domestic servants who work less than 40 hours per week for one employer.
Vermont	Compulsory for all employments. Corporate officers may reject.	Compulsory for all employments.	Casual or domestic workers, amateur athletes, farm labor where the employer's payroll is under $2,000 per year.
Virginia	Compulsory for 3 or more employees (4 or more farm employees or farmers whose annual payroll is $15,000 or more). Elective for corporate officers, partners, and sole proprietors.	Compulsory for all employments except administrative personnel who are elected or appointed for a definite term of office.	Casual employees, farm/horticulture laborers, domestic servants, employees of steam railroads.

| | Employments Covered | | |
Jurisdiction	Private	Public	Exceptions*
Washington	Compulsory for all employments. Elective for partners, sole proprietors, joint venturers, and corporate officers who are shareholder directors.	Compulsory for all employments.	Home repair and gardening workers, railroad workers, jockeys, farm labor earning less than $150 from one employer in an annual quarter, children under 18 years of age on a family farm.
West Virginia	Compulsory for all employments. Elective for partners and sole proprietors.	Compulsory for all employments.	Domestic workers, farm labor of 5 or fewer, casual workers, employees working temporarily out of state.
Wisconsin	Compulsory for all employments (except farm labor) if paid $500 or more in any annual quarter.	Compulsory for all employments.	Domestic servants and casual employees.
Wyoming	Compulsory for all employments in jobs classified as "extra-hazardous." Elective for corporate officers.	Compulsory for all employments engaged in extra-hazardous work.	Domestic servants, casual employees, office workers, sales clerks, farm and ranch labor.
FECA		All civil employees of the federal government including those persons performing work of civil employees without pay.	

Employments Covered

Jurisdiction	Private	Public	Exceptions*
Longshore Act	Compulsory for all maritime work nationwide.	Officers and employees of the U.S. or any state or foreign governments are not covered.	Master or crew of any vessel and persons unloading or repairing vessels of less than 18 tons.

*Applies to private employment only. Exceptions for public employments are specified under that heading.

(Adopted from United States Chamber of Commerce. 1984. Analysis of Workers' Compensation Laws 1984. United States Chamber of Commerce, Washington, D.C.)

APPENDIX B

Rehabilitation Coverage in Workers' Compensation

Jurisdiction	Maintenance Allowance	Special Provisions
Alabama	Board, lodging, travel if away from home.	Physical and vocational rehabilitation services at employer's expense. Employee's refusal results in loss of compensation.
Alaska	Board, lodging, travel, and temporary disability benefits.	Employer pays full costs. Services for 37–74 weeks. Compensation suspended for any unreasonable refusal or failure to participate in approved or agreed plan.
Arizona	Subject to Commission authorization.	Vocational rehabilitation trainees are considered employees at $200 monthly wage rate for compensation benefits.
Arkansas	Reasonable expenses for maintenance, travel, and other necessary costs up to 60 weeks.	Commission may authorize vocational rehabilitation if reasonable in relation to the disability. Worker may refuse.
California	All additional necessary living expenses during rehabilitation.	Compulsory program for employer or carrier. Rehabilitation trainee considered an employee of training employer for insurance purposes.
Colorado	Maintenance, tuition, and transportation during 26 weeks.	Employee cannot receive disability benefits and maintenance simultaneously.

Jurisdiction	Maintenance Allowance	Special Provisions
Connecticut	Weekly subsistence allowance during vocational rehabilitation services.	Employer pays full cost of medical rehabilitation. Vocational rehabilitation is furnished by the state Division of Workers' Rehabilitation.
Delaware	Reasonable board, lodging, and travel.	Physical and vocational rehabilitation paid by the employer.
District of Columbia	Does not exceed $50 per week.	Employer must provide vocational rehabilitation. Failure of the employee to cooperate results in forfeiture of benefits.
Florida	Reasonable board, lodging, and travel.	Services provided by or at the expense of the employer. Services last up to 26 weeks with extension for 26 more weeks. Employee refusal to accept rehabilitation deemed necessary results in 50[PCT] reduction in benefits for each week of refusal.
Georgia	Boarding, lodging, and travel if away from home.	Vocational rehabilitation for 52 weeks or longer if necessary. Employee's unreasonable refusal may result in suspension of benefits.
Hawaii	Discretion of the Department of Labor.	State Department of Labor makes recommendations for physical and/or vocational rehabilitation as needed by the employee.
Idaho	Reasonable expenses for maintenance and travel.	Disability benefits paid up to 104 weeks when retraining is required.
Illinois	Maintenance costs and incidental expenses.	Physical, mental, and vocational rehabilitation services provided if needed by the employee.

Jurisdiction	Maintenance Allowance	Special Provisions
Indiana	No specific statutory provisions other than compensation may be suspended if employee refuses suitable employment.	
Iowa	$20 weekly in addition to other compensation for 13 weeks.	Medical care may include physical rehabilitation services.
Kansas	Reasonable expenses for board, lodging, and travel up to $2,000 for 26 weeks if employer provides vocational rehabilitation services.	Vocational rehabilitation services provided by employer if unavailable through a public facility. Employee's unreasonable refusal of physical and/or vocational rehabilitation results in suspension of benefits. After 90 days' refusal, benefits are cancelled.
Kentucky	Board, lodging, and travel if away from home.	Unlimited medical rehabilitation services. Vocational rehabilitation may be extended beyond 52 weeks. Employee refusal results in 50[PCT] loss of compensation benefits.
Louisiana	No specific statutory provision.	
Maine	$35 per week for 52 weeks.	Vocational and/or educational rehabilitation services may be extended a maximum of 104 weeks.
Maryland	Up to $40 per week paid by the employer.	Entitled to 24 months of vocational rehabilitation services with the expenses of compensation and vocational rehabilitation paid by the employer. Unreasonable refusal by the employee results in loss of compensation.
Massachusetts	Room, board, and travel may be approved by the state rehabilitation commission.	Necessary cost of rehabilitation services subject to approval by the state rehabilitation commission.
Michigan	Travel and other necessary expenses during 52 weeks of training.	Medical and vocational rehabilitation services may be authorized by state workers' compensation board. May extend training up to a maximum of 104 weeks.

Jurisdiction	Maintenance Allowance	Special Provisions
Minnesota	Subject to approval of the rehabilitation plan.	Employer must provide vocational rehabilitation services from an approved list of consultants. Failure of the employee to cooperate can result in the employer seeking termination or suspension of benefits.
Mississippi	Up to $10 per week for 52 weeks.	No special provisions.
Missouri	$40 weekly for physical rehabilitation.	Employer may be ordered to pay or provide transportation.
Montana	During training periods, $50 per week additional for living expenses, plus costs of travel, tuition, books, and equipment.	Employee's refusal to participate and/or cooperate in rehabilitation services may result in loss of compensation benefits.
Nebraska	Board, lodging, and travel in addition to compensation.	Insurer must furnish medical, physical, and vocational rehabilitation services voluntarily. Costs may be divided between the employer and the vocational rehabilitation fund.
Nevada	Maintenance may be allowed as needed.	Carrier provides all necessary rehabilitation services. Employee's refusal results in loss of all benefits.
New Hampshire	Board, lodging, travel, books, and basic materials in addition to compensation.	Carrier must provide rehabilitation services voluntarily for at least one year.
New Jersey	No allowances stipulated.	Benefits may be stopped after 450 weeks unless the employee has submitted to physical or educational retraining.
New Mexico	Board, lodging, travel, and maintenance for family up to $3,000 in addition to other compensation.	Employer must provide vocational rehabilitation services.
New York	Up to $30 per week.	Cooperative arrangement between state departments of Labor and Education.

Jurisdiction	Maintenance Allowance	Special Provisions
North Carolina	No allowances required.	Insurer must furnish rehabilitation services needed to minimize the effects of the disability. Employee's refusal to cooperate may result in loss of compensation.
North Dakota	25[PCT] allowance in addition to other compensation.	Retraining provided by the state bureau of rehabilitation. Additional allowance up to $5,000 during lifetime for remodeling living or business facilities if required. Employee's refusal to cooperate results in forfeiture of compensation benefits.
Ohio	Minimum of 50[PCT] of statewide average weekly wage for 6 months.	State rehabilitation division within the workers' compensation commission may make all necessary expenditures.
Oklahoma	Board, lodging, travel, tuition, and books.	Necessary rehabilitation services may be ordered up to 52 weeks.
Oregon	Temporary total disability received during rehabilitation.	Rehabilitation Reserve pays cost of physical rehabilitation. Vocational services may be provided by the state, employer, or insurer. State reimburses employer for temporary disability benefits paid after the medical condition is stationary. Employee's failure to participate may result in benefits being suspended.
Pennsylvania	Cashpayments for living expenses may be furnished.	Vocational rehabilitation, training, and services provided by state.
Rhode Island	Board, lodging, and travel.	Compensation suspended for willful refusal of rehabilitation by the employee.
South Carolina	No specific statutory provisions.	

Jurisdiction	Maintenance Allowance	Special Provisions
South Dakota	Provided by the state as needed.	Compensation paid while employee is undergoing rehabilitation services.
Tennessee	No allowances stipulated.	Feasible cases referred to the state's Department of Education. Full or partial recovery of costs from employer or insurer.
Texas	No allowances stipulated.	Insurer provides necessary medical care and physical rehabilitation services. State provides vocational rehabilitation.
Utah	$1,000 maximum for permanent and total disability paid during rehabilitation.	If employee cannot be rehabilitated, then receives benefits for life at a minimum rate of $85 per week.
Vermont	Board, lodging, travel, books, and tools.	Vocational rehabilitation may be ordered. Employee refusal of such services may result in suspension of compensation benefits.
Virginia	No allowances stipulated.	Compensation, medical care, and vocational rehabilitation may be awarded. Employee's unreasonable refusal may result in suspension of benefits.
Washington	Compensation, board, lodging, travel, books, equipment, and child care up to 52 weeks with a $3,000 maximum.	Benefits may be extended an additional 52 weeks. State pays for employer's cost of job modification. Employee's refusal without good cause may result in 50% reduction of compensation benefits.
West Virginia	Up to $10,000 plus temporary total disability payments if totally disabled.	Necessary rehabilitation services provided by state-employed rehabilitation counselors.
Wisconsin	Board, lodging, and travel up to 40 weeks. Temporary total disability paid during training.	State-employed rehabilitation specialists evaluate and refer injured employees for medical, physical, and vocational services.

Jurisdiction	Maintenance Allowance	Special Provisions
Wyoming	Up to $10 per week for up to 72 weeks.	Maintenance allowances based on Board of Education recommendations.
FECA	Up to $200 per month.	If employee fails to undergo rehabilitation, benefits may be reduced if such services sould have increased the employee's earnings.
Longshore Act	Up to $25 per week.	50[PCT] of special fund (second-injury).

APPENDIX C
Disabled Workers' Second-Injury Provisions

Jurisdiction	Injuries Covered	Benefits Payable By Employer	Benefits Payable By Fund
Alabama	Second injury which combined with prior permanent partial disability results in permanent total disability.	Disability caused by second injury.	Difference between compensation payable for second injury and permanent total disability.
Alaska	Second injury which added to pre-existing permanent impairment results in substantially greater disability than from the second injury alone.	Disability caused by second injury up to 104 weeks.	Compensation in excess of 104 weeks.
Arizona	Second injury involving loss of a member or eye which added to pre-existing loss of use of member or eye results in permanent total disability.	Disability caused by second injury.	Difference between compensation payable for second injury and compensation for combined disability.

Jurisdiction	Injuries Covered	Benefits Payable By		
		Employer	Fund	
Arkansas	Second injury which added to previous permanent partial disability or impairment results in additional disability greater than the second injury alone.	Disability caused by second injury.	Difference between compensation payable for second injury and permanent disability	
California	Second permanent partial injury which added to the pre-existing permanent partial disability resulting in 70% or more permanent disability. The second injury must account for 35% of the loss.	Disability caused by second injury.	Difference between compensation payable for second injury and permanent disability.	
Colorado	Second injury which added to pre-existing permanent partial disability results in permanent total disability.	Disability caused by second injury.	Difference between compensation payable for second injury and permanent total disability.	
Connecticut	Second injury or disease which added to pre-existing injury or disease results in permanent disability greater than from second injury alone.	Benefits for first 104 weeks less compensation payable for prior disability.	Benefits beyond first 104 weeks less the compensation payable for prior disability.	
Delaware	Second injury or disease which added to pre-existing permanent injury from any cause results in permanent total disability.	Disability caused by second injury.	Difference between compensation payable for second injury and permanent disability.	

Jurisdiction	Injuries Covered	Benefits Payable By		
		Employer	Fund	
District of Columbia	Second injury or disease which added to pre-existing injury or disease results in permanent disability greater than from second injury alone.	Disability caused by second injury for first 104 weeks and first $1,000 medical expenses.	Difference between compensation payable for second injury and permanent disability.	
Florida	Second injury or disease which merges with previous permanent physical disability and results in substantially greater disability than from the second injury alone.		Reimburses employer for 60% of impairment benefits, 60% of wage-loss benefits up to 5 years, and 75% thereafter.	
Georgia	Second injury or disease which merges with prior permanent disability and results in greater disability than the second injury alone.	Disability caused by second injury for first 104 weeks.	Employer reimbursed for 50% of medical expenses in excess of $5,000 up to $10,000, 100% in excess of $10,000, income benefits beyond 104 weeks.	
Hawaii	Second injury which added to pre-existing disabilities results in greater permanent disability, permanent total disability, or death.	Disability benefits for first 104 weeks.	Benefits beyond the first 104 weeks.	
Idaho	Second injury which combined with prior permanent disability results in permanent total disability.	Disability caused by second injury.	Difference between compensation payable for second injury and permanent disability.	

Jurisdiction	Injuries Covered	Benefits Payable By	
		Employer	Fund
Illinois	Second injury involving loss of use of major members or eye which added to pre-existing loss of member results in permanent total disability.	Disability caused by second injury.	Difference between compensation payable for second injury and permanent disability.
Indiana	Second injury involving loss of use of extremities or eyes which added to pre-existing loss of member results in permanent total disability.	Disability caused by second injury.	Difference between compensation payable for second injury and permanent total disability.
Iowa	Second injury involving loss of use of member or eye which added to pre-existing loss of use of member results in permanent total disability.	Disability caused by second injury.	Difference between compensation payable for second injury and permanent disability less the value of the previous loss.
Kansas	Second injury related to 17 types of handicaps listed in statutes: any physical or mental disability.	Difference between fund payment and maximum award.	Compensation to the extent pre-existing handicap contributed to second injury.
Kentucky	Second injury or disease which added to prior disability results in permanent disability greater than from second injury alone.	Disability caused by second injury or dormant condition.	Difference between compensation payable for second injury and greater disability less amount paid for prior injury.
Louisiana	Second injury which combined with prior permanent partial disability results in disability greater than from second injury alone, or in death.	Disability benefits for first 104 weeks or in death cases, first 175 weeks.	Employer reimbursed for disability payments after first 104 weeks, or after 175 weeks in death cases.

Jurisdiction	Injuries Covered	Benefits Payable By	
		Employer	Fund
Maine	Second injury caused by injury or disease which added to pre-existing disability results in permanent total disability.	Disability caused by second injury.	Employer reimbursed for difference between compensation payable for second injury and permanent total disability.
Maryland	Second injury which combined with pre-existing permanent disability results in a greater combined disability which is a hindrance to employment.	Disability caused by second injury.	If permanent disability exceeds 50% of the whole body, employee is entitled to additional compensation.
Massachusetts	Second injury which added to pre-existing disability results in substantial greater combined disability or death. Pre-existing condition must support 25% earnings loss or 90 weeks of benefits.	Benefits for first 104 weeks.	Employer reimbursed for half of benefits paid after first 104 weeks.
Michigan	Second injury involving loss of member or eye which added to pre-existing loss of member results in permanent total disability.	Disability caused by second injury.	Difference between compensation payable for second injury and permanent total disability.

Jurisdiction	Injuries Covered	Benefits Payable By		
		Employer	Fund	
Minnesota	Second injury that results in substantially greater disability than from the second injury alone.	Disability caused by second injury.	Employer reimbursed for disability after 52 weeks, medical after $2,000. If second injury results in permanent total disability, fund pays difference between compensation payable for second injury and greater disability.	
Mississippi	Second injury involving loss of member or eye which added to pre-existing loss of member or eye results in permanent total disability.	Disability caused by second injury.	Difference between compensation payable for second injury and permanent disability.	
Missouri	Second injury resulting in permanent partial disability which compounds either a greater permanent partial or a permanent total disability.	Disability caused by second injury.	Difference between compensation payable for second injury and compounded disability.	
Montana	Second injury which combined with prior permanent disability results in death or disability.	Benefits for first 104 weeks.	Employer reimbursed after first 104 weeks.	
Nebraska	Second injury which combined with pre-existing disability causes substantially greater disability. Pre-existing disability must support 25% earnings loss or 90 weeks of benefits.	Disability caused by second injury.	Difference between compensation payable for second injury and previous disability.	

Jurisdiction	Injuries Covered	Benefits Payable By		
		Employer	Fund	
Nevada	Second injury which combined with any previous permanent disability causes substantially greater disability.		Compensation payable by Subsequent Injury Fund in state treasury.
New Hampshire	Second injury which combined with any pre-existing disability results in substantially greater disability.	Benefits for first 104 weeks.	Employer reimbursed after first 104 weeks.
New Jersey	Second injury resulting in permanent partial disability which added to pre-existing partial disability, compensable or not, results in permanent total disability.	Disability caused by compensable injury.	Difference between compensation payable for second injury and permanent total disability.
New Mexico	Second injury which added to pre-existing disability results in permanent disability greater than from second injury alone, or second injury resulting in death.	Liability apportioned by judicial determination.	Liability apportioned by judicial determination.
New York	Second injury involving loss of member or eye which added to pre-existing injury results in permanent total disability.	Benefits for first 104 weeks.	Employer reimbursed after first 104 weeks.

Jurisdiction	Injuries Covered	Benefits Payable By Employer	Fund
North Carolina	Second injury involving loss of member or eye which added to pre-existing injury results in permanent total disability provided the original and increased disability were each 20% of the entire member.	Disability caused by second injury.	Difference between compensation payable for second injury and permanent total disability.
North Dakota	Second injury or aggravation of any previous injury or condition which results in further disability.	Disability caused by second injury.	Percent attributable to aggravation or second injury.
Ohio	Second injury which aggravated pre-existing disease or condition resulting in death, temporary, or permanent total disability, and disability compensable under a special schedule.	Disability attributable to injury or occupational disease sustained in employment.	Amount of disability or proportion of cost of death award determined to be attributed to pre-existing disability.
Oklahoma	Second injury to "physically impaired person" which results in added permanent disability greater than from second injury alone.	Disability caused by second injury.	Difference between compensation payable for second injury and compensation for combined injuries.
Oregon	Compensable injury which results in permanent disability that may be an obstacle to employment.	Claims cost charged against the employer for experience rating purposes only.	Provides job placement aid, work station modification, and wage subsidy and increased protection.

Jurisdiction	Injuries Covered	Benefits Payable By	
		Employer	Fund
Pennsylvania	Second injury involving loss which added to pre-existing loss results in permanent total disability.	Scheduled benefits as a result of second injury.	Remaining compensation due for total disability.
Rhode Island	Second injury which merges with pre-existing work-related disability resulting in greater disability or death.	Benefits for first 104 weeks.	Employer reimbursed after first 104 weeks.
South Carolina	Second injury which added to any previous permanent disability results in substantially greater disability or death.	Disability caused by second injury for first 78 weeks' compensation and medical care.	Employer reimbursed for all benefits after 78 weeks, plus 50% of medical payments over $3,000 during first 78 weeks.
South Dakota	Second injury which added to any pre-existing disability results in additional permanent partial or total disability or death.	Disability caused by second injury.	Difference between compensation payable for second injury and compensation for combined injuries.
Tennessee	Second injury involving loss of member or eye which added to pre-existing loss results in permanent total disability.	Disability caused by second injury.	Difference between compensation payable for second injury and permanent total disability.
Texas	Second injury which added to pre-existing injury results in permanent total disability.	Disability caused by second injury.	Difference between compensation payable for second injury and permanent total disability.

Jurisdiction	Injuries Covered	Benefits Payable By		
		Employer	Fund	
Utah	Second injury which combined with a previous permanent disability results in a substantially greater disability.	Disability caused by second injury.	Difference between compensation payable for second injury and compensation for combined injuries.	
Vermont	Second injury involving loss of member or eye which added to previous disability results in permanent total disability.	Disability caused by second injury.	Difference between compensation payable for second injury and permanent total disability.	
Virginia	Second injury involving 20% loss of member or eye which added to pre-existing disability of 20% or more results in total or partial disability.	Disability caused by second injury.	Employer reimbursed for compensation after all other compensation has expired, plus up to $7,500 each for medical and vocational rehabilitation expenses.	
Washington	Second injury or disease which added to pre-existing injury or disease results in permanent total disability or death.	Disability caused by second injury.	Difference between charge assessed against employer at time of second injury and total pension reserve.	
West Virginia	Second injury which combined with pre-existing disability results in permanent total disability.	Disability caused by second injury.		

| | Employments Covered | | |
Jurisdiction	Private	Public	Exceptions[a]
Wisconsin	Second injury with permanent disability of 200 weeks or more with a pre-existing disability of an equal degree or greater.	Disability caused by second injury.	Disability caused by lesser of 2 injuries, if the combined disabilities result in permanent total disability, fund pays difference between compensation payable for second injury and permanent total disability.
Wyoming	Second injury in extra-hazardous employment which added to pre-existing loss of member or eye results in permanent total disability.	Disability caused by second injury.	Difference between compensation payable for second injury and permanent disability.
Longshore Act	Second injury resulting in permanent partial disability which added to pre-existing injury results in permanent total disability.	Disability caused by second injury for first 104 weeks.	Difference between compensation payable for second injury and permanent total disability.

(Adopted from United States Chamber of Commerce. 1984. Analysis of Workers' Compensation Laws 1984. United States Chamber of Commerce, Washington, D.C.)

APPENDIX D
Directory of Workers' Compensation Administrative Offices

Jurisdiction	Offices
Alabama	Workmen's Compensation Division Department of Industrial Relations Industrial Relations Building Montgomery, AL 36130 (205) 832-5040
Alaska	Workmen's Compensation Division Department of Labor P.O. Box 1149 Juneau, AK 99801 (907) 465-2790 Workmen's Compensation Board (same address as above)
Arizona	Industrial Commission 1601 West Jefferson P.O. Box 19070 Phoenix, AZ 85005 (602) 255-4661 State Compensation Fund 1616 West Adams Phoenix, AZ 85007
Arkansas	Workers' Compensation Commission Justice Building State Capitol Grounds Little Rock, AR 72201 (501) 372-3930
California	Division of Industrial Accidents Department of Labor P.O. Box 603, First Floor San Francisco, CA 94101 (415) 557-3542 Workers' Compensation Appeals Board 455 Golden Gate Avenue San Francisco, CA 94102 State Compensation Insurance Fund 1275 Market Street San Francisco, CA 94103

Jurisdiction	Offices
Colorado	Division of Labor 1313 Sherman Street, Room 314 Denver, CO 80203 Industrial Commission States Services Building, 5th Floor 1525 Sherman Street Denver, CO 80203 (303) 866-2446 State Compensation Insurance Fund 950 Broadway Denver, CO 80203
Connecticut	Workers' Compensation Commission 295 Treadwell Street Hamden, CT 06514 (203) 789-7783
Delaware	Industrial Accident Board State Office Building, 6th Floor 820 North French Street Wilmington, DE 19801 (302) 571-2885
District of Columbia	Department of Employment Services Office of Workers' Compensation P.O. Box 56098 Washington, D.C. 20011 (202) 576-7088
Florida	Division of Workers' Compensation Department of Labor and Employment Security 1321 Executive Center Drive-East Tallahassee, FL 32301 (904) 488-2548
Georgia	Board of Workers' Compensation 1000 Omni International, 10th Floor Atlanta, GA 30335 (404) 656-3875

Jurisdiction	Offices
Hawaii	Disability Compensation Division Department of Labor and Industrial Relations 830 Punchbowl Street Honolulu, HI 96813 (808) 548-4131 Labor and Industrial Relations Appeals Board 888 Mililani Street, Room 400 Honolulu, HI 96813
Idaho	Industrial Commission 317 Main Street Boise, ID 83720 (208) 334-2193 State Insurance Fund P.O. Box 1038 Boise, ID 83704
Illinois	Industrial Commission 160 North LaSalle Street Chicago, IL 60601 (312) 793-6611
Indiana	Industrial Board 601 State Office Building 100 North Senate Avenue Indianapolis, IN 46204 (317) 232-3808
Iowa	Industrial Commissioner's Office 507 10th Street Des Moines, IA 50319 (515) 281-5935
Kansas	Division of Workers' Compensation Department of Human Resources, 6th Floor 535 Kansas Avenue Topeka, KS 66603 (913) 296-3441
Kentucky	Workers' Compensation Board 127 Building U.S. 127 South Frankfort, KY 40601 (502) 564-5550

Jurisdiction	Offices
Louisiana	Department of Labor 5260 Florida Boulevard Baton Rouge, LA 70806 (504) 925-4227
Maine	Workers' Compensation Commission State Office Building State House Station 27 Augusta, ME 04333 (207) 289-3751
Maryland	Workmen's Compensation Commission 108 East Lexington Street Baltimore, MD 21202 (301) 659-4700 State Accident Fund 8722 Loch Raven Boulevard Towson, MD 21204
Massachusetts	Industrial Accidents Board Leverett Saltonstall Office Building 100 Cambridge Street Boston, MA 02202 (617) 727-3400
Michigan	Bureau of Workers' Disability Compensation Department of Labor 309 North Washington Square Lansing, MI 48909 (517) 373-3480 Workers' Compensation Appeal Board 309 North Washington Square Leonard Plaza Building Lansing, MI 48909 State Accident Fund 232 South Capitol Street Lansing, MI 48914
Minnesota	Workers' Compensation Division Department of Labor and Industry 444 Lafayette Road St. Paul, MN 55101 (612) 296-2432

Jurisdiction	Offices
	Worker's Compensation Court of Appeals MEA Building, 2nd Floor 55 Sherburne Avenue St. Paul, MN 55103
Mississippi	Workmen's Compensation Commission 1428 Lakeland Drive P.O. Box 5300 Jackson, MS 39216 (601) 987-4200
Missouri	Division of Workers' Compensation Department of Labor and Industrial Relations P.O. Box 58 Jefferson City, MO 65102 (314) 751-4231 Labor and Industrial Relations Commission 1904 Missouri Boulevard P.O. Box 599 Jefferson City, MO 65102
Montana	Division of Workers' Compensation 815 Front Street Helena, MT 59604 (406) 449-2047 Workers' Compensation Court 1422 Cedar-Airport Way P.O. Box 4127 Helena, MT 59601 State Compensation Insurance Fund (same address as Division)
Nebraska	Workmen's Compensation Court State House, 12th Floor Lincoln, NE 68509 (402) 471-2568
Nevada	State Industrial Insurance System 515 East Musser Street Carson City, NV 89714 (702) 885-5284 Department of Industrial Relations 1390 South Curry Street Carson City, NV 89710 (702) 885-3032

Jurisdiction	Offices
New Hampshire	Department of Labor 19 Pillsbury Street Concord, NH 03301 (603) 271-3171
New Jersey	Division of Workers' Compensation Department of Labor and Industry P.O. Box CN 381 John Fitch Plaza Trenton, NJ 08625 (609) 292-2414
New Mexico	Labor and Industrial Commission 509 Camino De Los Marquez, Suite 2 Santa Fe, NM 87501 (505) 827-9884 Workmen's Compensation Division (same address as above) (505) 827-9876
New York	Workers' Compensation Board Two World Trade Center New York, NY 10047 (212) 488-3033 State Insurance Fund 199 Church Street New York, NY 10007
North Carolina	Industrial Commission Dobbs Building 430 North Salisbury Street Raleigh, NC 27611 (919) 733-4820
North Dakota	Workmen's Compensation Bureau Russell Building Highway 83 North Bismarck, ND 58505 (701) 224-2700 Workmen's Compensation Fund (same address as above)
Ohio	Bureau of Workers' Compensation 246 North High Street Columbus, OH 43215 (614) 466-2950

Jurisdiction	Offices
	Industrial Commission (same address as Bureau) State Insurance Fund (same address as Bureau)
Okahoma	Oklahoma Workers' Compensation Court Jim Thorpe Building 2101 North Lincoln Boulevard Oklahoma City, OK 73105 (405) 521-8025 State Insurance Fund 5th and Walnut Oklahoma City, OK 73105
Oregon	Workers' Compensation Department Labor and Industries Building Salem, OR 97310 (503) 378-3304 Workers' Compensation Board 480 Church Street Salem, OR 97310
Pennsylvania	Bureau of Workers' Compensation Department of Labor and Industry 3607 Derry Street Harrisburg, PA 17111 (717) 783-5421 Workers' Compensation Appeal Board 2601 Herr Street, 3rd Floor Harrisburg, PA 17103 State Workmen's Insurance Fund 100 Lackawanna Avenue Scranton, PA 18503
Rhode Island	Workers' Compensation Commission 1 Dorrance Plaza Providence, RI 02903 (401) 277-3097
South Carolina	Industrial Commission Middleburg Office Park 1800 St. Julian Place Columbia, SC 29204 (803) 758-2556

Jurisdiction	Offices
South Dakota	Division of Labor and Management Department of Labor Kneip Building, 2nd Floor 700 North Illinois Street Pierre, SD 57501-2277 (605) 773-3681
Tennessee	Workers' Compensation Division Department of Labor 501 Union Building, 2nd Floor Nashville, TN 37219
Texas	Industrial Accident Board 200 East Riverside Drive, 1st Floor Austin, TX 78704 (512) 475-2251
Utah	Industrial Commission 160 East 300 South Salt Lake City, UT 84110-5800 (801) 530-6800 State Insurance Fund (same address as above)
Vermont	Department of Labor and Industry Montpelier, VT 05502 (802) 828-2286
Virginia	Industrial Commission Blanton Building P.O. Box 1794 Richmond, VA 23214 (804) 786-3644
Washington	Department of Labor and Industries General Administration Building AX-31 Olympia, WA 98504 (206) 753-6308 Board of Industrial Insurance Appeals 410 West 5th Street Capitol Center Building Olympia, WA 98504 Industrial Insurance Division (State Fund) (same address as Department)

Jurisdiction	Offices
West Virginia	Workmen's Compensation Commissioner's Office 601 Morris Street Charleston, WV 25301 (304) 384-2580 Workmen's Compensation Appeal Board 112 California Avenue, Room 116 Charleston, WV 25305 Workmen's Compensation Fund (same address as Commissioner's Office)
Wisconsin	Workers' Compensation Division Department of Industry, Labor, and Human Relations P.O. Box 7901 201 East Washington Avenue, Room 152 Madison, WI 53707 (608) 266-1340 Labor and Industry Review Commission P.O. Box 8126 Madison, WI 53708
Wyoming	Workers' Compensation Division State Treasurer's Office 2305 Carey Avenue Cheyenne, WY 82002 (307) 777-7441 Industrial Accident Fund (same address as above)
United States	Department of Labor Employment Standards Administration Washington, D.C. 20210 (202) 523-6191 Office of Workers' Compensation Programs (202) 523-6579 Division of Coal Mine Workers' Compensation (202) 523-6692 Division of Federal Employees' Compensation (202) 523-8463 Division of Longshore and Harbor Workers' Compensation (202) 523-8721

Jurisdiction	Offices
	Division of State Workers' Compensation Program (202) 523-7391
	Benefits Review Board 1111 20th Street, N.W., Suite 757 Vanguard Building Washington, D.C. 20036
	Employees' Compensation Appeals Board 300 Reporters Building 7th and D Streets, S.W., Room 300 Washington, D.C. 20210

(Adapted from: Wright, N.D., and Allen, G.P. 1982. The National Directory of State Agencies 1982–1983. Information Resources Press, Arlington, VA.)

APPENDIX E
Employment Agency Licensing Requirements

Jurisdiction	Examination	License Fee	Penalties	Exemptions[a]
Alabama	No	$50.00	No provisions	No provisions
Alaska	No	No provisions	Up to $1,000 fine and 6 months imprisonment	1, 2a-e, 3
Arizona	Yes	$100-$300.00	$50-$100 fine and up to 6 months imprisonment	3
Arkansas	Yes	$250.00	$50-$250 fine and up to 3 months imprisonment	1, 2b, 2f-i, 10, 13
California	Yes	$200.00	$50-$500 fine and up to 60 days imprisonment	1, 2b, 2i, 13c
Colorado	No	$150.00	$300 fine and up to 30 days imprisonment	1, 2a-e, 3, 10, 12
Connecticut	No	$75.00	$100.00 fine	1, 2a, 10
Delaware	No	$150.00	No provisions	No provisions
District of Columbia	No	$100.00	No provisions	No provisions
Florida	No	$100.00	$500-$1,000 fine and up to 2 years imprisonment	1, 13

Jurisdiction	Examination	License Fee	Penalties	Exemptions[a]
Georgia	Yes	$100-$200.00	No provisions	No provisions
Hawaii	Yes	No provisions specified in statutes		
Idaho		Prohibits private, for-profit employment agencies		
Illinois	Yes	$150-$400.00	Up to $1,000 fine and up to 1 year imprisonment	1, 2, 13a
Indiana	No	$50.00	$50-$100 fine and up to 6 months imprisonment	1, 2c, 2e, 9
Iowa	No	$50.00	No provisions	No provisions
Kansas	No	$10-$25.00	$50-$100 fine and up to 6 months imprisonment	1, 2c
Kentucky	No	$125.00	$25-$1,000 fine and up to 30 days imprisonment	1, 2a-e
Louisiana	Yes	$100-$300.00	Up to $500 fine and 6 months imprisonment	1, 2
Maine	No	$100.00	Up to $500 fine and 11 months imprisonment	1, 2c, 8, 10, 11
Maryland	No	$200.00	$25-$500 fine	No provisions
Massachusetts	No	$60-$100.00	Up to $500 fine and 1 year imprisonment	1, 12

Jurisdiction	Examination	License Fee	Penalties	Exemptions[a]
Michigan	No	$50-$200.00	$300-$1,000 fine and up to 4 years imprisonment	1, 2a-e
Minnesota	No	$75-$150.00	$25-$100 fine and up to 3 months imprisonment	No provisions
Mississippi	No	$500.00	No provisions	No provisions
Missouri	No	$100.00	Up to $1,000 fine and 1 year imprisonment	1, 2a-d, 12
Montana	No	$100.00	Up to $2,000 fine	No provisions
Nebraska	No	$300.00	$50-$100 fine and up to 3 months imprisonment	No provisions
Nevada	No	$50.00	No provisions	No provisions
New Hampshire	No	$2.00	$10.00 per day	No provisions
New Jersey	Yes	$90-$360.00	$25-$250 fine and up to 1 year imprisonment	1, 2a, 2c, 3, 7, 10
New Mexico	No	$50.00	Up to $100 fine and 6 months imprisonment	1, 6, 7
New York	No	$200-$400.00	$100-$1,000 fine and 30 days to 1 year imprisonment	1, 2a-f, 4, 5, 10, 13c

Jurisdiction	Examination	License Fee	Penalties	Exemptions[a]
North Carolina	No	No provisions	$500-$1,000 fine and up to 6 months imprisonment	1
North Dakota	No	$200.00	Up to $1,000 fine and 1 year imprisonment	12
Ohio	No	$100.00	$500-$1,000 fine and 2–6 months imprisonment	1, 2a-e, 3, 12, 13b
Oklahoma	No	$100.00	$50-$100 fine and up to 6 months imprisonment	1, 2c, 12
Oregon	Yes	$250.00	$100-$2,000 fine	1, 2a-i, 3, 13d
Pennsylvania	Yes	$150.00	$100-$500 fine and up to 30 days imprisonment	1, 2f-g, 10, 11
Rhode Island	No	No provisions	$10.00 per day	1
South Carolina	No	$100.00	$25-$500 fine and up to 30 days imprisonment	11
South Dakota	No	$10.00	Up to $100 fine and 30 days imprisonment	1, 2a-g, 4, 10, 12
Tennessee	Yes	$75-$175.00	$100-$500 fine and up to 3 months imprisonment	1–3, 11, 12
Texas	Yes	$150.00	$100-$500 fine and up to 6 months imprisonment	1, 3, 11

Jurisdiction	Examination	License Fee	Penalties	Exemptions[a]
Utah	No	No provisions	$100-$500 fine and up to 3 months imprisonment	1, 2b-c, 11
Vermont			No provisions provided in statutes	
Virginia	No	$50.00	Up to $5,000 fine and 10 years imprisonment	1, 12
Washington			No provisions provided in statutes	
West Virginia	No	$15.00	$100-$500 fine and from 1-6 months imprisonment	1, 2b-c
Wisconsin	No	$50-$300.00	No provisions	12
Wyoming	No	$10-$25.00	$50-$100 fine and up to 6 months imprisonment	1

[a]1 = State, federal, municipal agencies
2 = Nonprofit organizations where *no fee* is charged:
   a = Educational Institutions
   b = Religious Organizations
   c = Charitable Organizations
   d = Fraternal Organizations
   e = Benevolent Organizations
   f = Medical Institutions
   g = Nursing School
   h = Business Schools
   i = Vocational Schools
3 = Bona fide labor organizations
4 = Incorporated societies of professional engineers, land surveyors, architects

5 = Incorporated bar associations
6 = Veterans' organizations
7 = Farmers or stock raisers
8 = Employment of seamen
9 = Baby sitting
10 = Nurses' registries
11 = Agencies for public school teachers and administrators
12 = Part-time or temporary help where the employer pays wages, Social Security, unemployment insurance taxes, workers' compensatio
13 = Management consulting firms where the annual salary of hired job seekers:
   a = over $15,000
   b = over $20,000
   c = over $25,000
   d = over $30,000

(Adopted from Matkin, R.E. 1982c. Rehabilitation placement services: Unlicensed employment agencies or something else? Journal of Applied Rehabilitation Counseling, *13*(1):24–33.)

APPENDIX F

Directory of Employment Agency Licensing Boards and Commissions

Jurisdiction	Offices
Alabama	Department of Revenue 202 Administration Building 64 North Union Street Montgomery, AL 36130 (205) 832-5780
Alaska	Division of Occupational Licensing Department of Commerce & Economic Development State Office Building, 9th Floor Pouch D Juneau, AK 99811 (907) 465-2534
Arizona	Industrial Commission Labor Department 104 Commerce Building 1601 West Jefferson Street P.O. Box 19070 Phoenix, AZ 85005 (602) 255-4515 State Boards Administrative Office Department of Administration 1645 West Jefferson Street Phoenix, AZ 85007 (602) 255-3095
Arkansas	Department of Labor 1022 High Street Little Rock, AR 72202 (501) 375-8442 ext. 403
California	Department of Consumer Affairs 1020 N Street Sacramento, CA 95814 (916) 445-4465

Jurisdiction	Offices
Colorado	Division of Labor Department of Labor & Employment 314 State Centennial Building 1313 Sherman Street Denver, CO 80203 (303) 866-2782 Department of Regulatory Agencies 110 State Services Building 1525 Sherman Street Denver, CO 80203 (303) 866-3304
Connecticut	Department of Labor 200 Folly Brook Boulevard Wethersfield, CT 06109 (203) 566-4384
Delaware	Department of Labor Elbert N. Carvel State Office Building, 6th Floor 820 North French Street Wilmington, DE 19801 (302) 571-2710 Division of Business & Occupational Regulation Department of Administration Services Margaret M. O'Neill Building Court & Federal Streets P.O. Box 1401 Dover, DE 19901 (302) 736-4522
District of Columbia	Office of Licenses Department of Licenses, Investigation, & Inspections 931 North Potomac Building 614 H Street, N.W. Washington, D.C. 20001 (202) 727-6040
Florida	Department of Professional Regulation Old Courthouse Square Building 130 North Monroe Street Tallahassee, FL 32301 (904) 487-2252

Jurisdiction	Offices
Georgia	Department of Labor 288 State Labor Building 254 Washington Street, S.W. Atlanta, GA 30334 (404) 656-3011 Examining Boards Division Office of Secretary of State 166 Pryor Street, S.W. Atlanta, GA 30303 (404) 656-3900
Hawaii	Department of Labor & Industrial Relations Keelikoloni Building 825 Mililani Street Honolulu, HI 96813 (808) 548-3150 Professional & Vocational Licensing Division Department of Commerce & Consumer Affairs 1010 Richards Street P.O. Box 3469 Honolulu, HI 96801 (808) 548-6520
Idaho	Bureau of Occupational Licenses Department of Self-Governing Agencies 2404 Bank Drive, Room 312 Boise, ID 83705 (208) 334-3233
Illinois	Department of Labor 910 South Michigan Avenue, Room 1863 Chicago, IL 60605 (312) 793-2810 Division of Licensing & Testing Department of Registration & Education Bicentennial Building 320 West Washington Street Springfield, IL 62786 (217) 785-0891

Jurisdiction	Offices
Indiana	Regulated Occupations & Professional Service Bureau 1021 State Office Building 100 North Senate Avenue Indianapolis, IN 46204 (317) 232-2980 Department of Revenue 202 State Office Building 100 North Senate Avenue Indianapolis, IN 46204 (317) 232-2101
Iowa	Bureau of Labor 307 East 7th Street Des Moines, IA 50319 (515) 281-3606 Consumer Protection Division Office of the Attorney General Hoover State Office Building 1300 East Walnut Street Des Moines, IA 50319 (515) 281-5926
Kansas	Division of Labor-Management Relations & Employment 　　Standards Department of Human Resources 512 West 6th Street Topeka, KS 66603-3178 (913) 296-7475
Kentucky	Division of Occupations & Professions Department of Administration Finance & Administration Cabinet 354 New Capitol Annex Frankfort, KY 40601 (502) 564-3296 Department of Health Services Cabinet for Human Resources Human Resources Building 275 East Main Street Frankfort, KY 40621 (502) 564-2970

Jurisdiction	Offices
Louisiana	Department of Labor Employment Security Building 1001 North 23rd Street P.O. Box 44094 Baton Rouge, LA 70804 (504) 342-3011 Office of Licensing & Regulation Department of Health & Human Resources 755 Riverside North Baton Rouge, LA 70821 (504) 342-6714
Maine	Central Licensing Division Department of Business Regulation State House, Station 35 Augusta, ME 04333 (207) 289-2217
Maryland	Division of Labor & Industry Department of Licensing & Regulation 203 East Baltimore Street Baltimore, MD 21202 (301) 659-4179 Department of Licensing & Regulation Stanbalt Building 501 St. Paul Street Baltimore, MD 21202 (301) 659-6200
Massachusetts	Department of Labor & Industries Leverett Saltonstall State Office Building 100 Cambridge Street Boston, MA 02202 (617) 727-3454 Division of Registration Executive Office of Consumer Affairs 1520 Leverett Saltonstall State Office Building 100 Cambridge Street Boston, MA 02202 (617) 727-3076

Jurisdiction	Offices
Michigan	Department of Licensing & Regulation Department of Labor 320 North Washington Avenue P.O. Box 30018 Lansing, MI 48909 (517) 373-1870
Minnesota	Department of Labor & Industry Space Center Building 444 Lafayette Road St. Paul, MN 55101 (612) 296-2342 Commerce Commission Department of Commerce Metro Square Building 7th & Roberts Streets St. Paul, MN 55101 (612) 296-2283
Mississippi	Consumer Protection Division Department of Agriculture & Commerce 1601 Walter Sillers Building 550 High Street P.O. Box 1609 Jackson, MS 39205 (601) 354-6258
Missouri	Division of Professional Registration Department of Consumer Affairs, Regulation, & Licensing 3523 North Ten Mile Drive P.O. Box 1335 Jefferson City, MO 65102 (314) 751-2334

Jurisdiction	Offices
Montana	Department of Labor & Industry Employment Security Building Lockey & Roberts Streets P.O. Box 1728 Helena, MT 59620 (406) 449-2723 Professional & Occupational Licensing Bureau Business & Professional Licensing Department of Commerce 1424 9th Avenue Helena, MT 59620-0407 (406) 449-3163
Nebraska	Department of Labor 550 South 16th Street P.O. Box 94600, State House Station Lincoln, NE 68509 (402) 475-8451
Nevada	Labor Commission 602 Kinkaid Building 505 East King Street Capitol Complex Carson City, NV 89710 (702) 885-4850
New Hampshire	Department of Employment Security 32 South Main Street Concord, NH 03301 (603) 224-3311
New Jersey	Department of Labor Labor & Industry Building John Fitch Plaza C.N. 110 Trenton, NJ 08625 (609) 292-2323 Division of Consumer Affairs Department of Law & Public Safety 219 East Hanover Street Trenton, NJ 08608 (609) 292-4676

Jurisdiction	Offices
New Mexico	Commerce & Industry Commission Bataan Memorial Building Santa Fe, NM 87503 (505) 827-5571
	Consumer & Economic Crimes Division Office of the Attorney General Bataan Memorial Building P.O. Box Drawer 1508 Santa Fe, NM 87504-1508 (505) 982-6060
New York	Division of Professional Licensing Services State Education Department Cultural Education Center Empire State Plaza Albany, NY 12230 (518) 474-3830
	Consumer Protection Board Executive Department 1020 Twin Towers 99 Washington Avenue Albany, NY 12210 (518) 474-3514
North Carolina	Department of Labor Labor Building 4 West Edenton Street Raleigh, NC 27601 (919) 733-7166
North Dakota	Department of Labor State Capitol Bismarck, ND 58505 (701) 224-2661
Ohio	Department of Commerce Two Nationwide Plaza Chestnut & High Streets Columbus, OH 43215 (614) 466-3636
Oklahoma	Department of Labor 118 State Capitol Lincoln Boulevard Oklahoma City, OK 73105 (405) 521-2461

Jurisdiction	Offices
Oregon	Bureau of Labor & Industries State Office Building 1400 S.W. 5th Avenue Portland, OR 97201 (503) 229-5735 Department of Commerce 428 Labor & Industries Building Capitol Mall Salem, OR 97310 (503) 378-4100
Pennsylvania	Department of Labor & Industry 1700 Labor & Industry Building 7th & Forster Streets Harrisburg, PA 17120 (717) 787-3756 Bureau of Professional & Occupational Affairs Department of State Transportation & Safety Building, 6th Floor Commonwealth Avenue & Forster Street P.O. Box 2646 Harrisburg, PA 17120 (717) 787-8503
Rhode Island	Department of Business Regulation 100 North Main Street Providence, RI 02903 (401) 277-2246
South Carolina	Labor Department Landmark Center 3600 Forest Drive P.O. Box 11329 Columbia, SC 29211 (803) 758-2852

Jurisdiction	Offices
West Virginia	Department of Labor B451 State Office Building 6 1900 Washington Street, East Charleston, WV 25305 (304) 348-7890
Wisconsin	Department of Industry, Labor & Human Relations 401 General Executive Facility I 201 East Washington Avenue P.O. Box 7946 Madison, WI 53707 (608) 266-7552 Department of Regulation & Licensing Washington Square Building 1400 East Washington Avenue Madison, WI 53702 (608) 266-8609
Wyoming	Department of Labor & Statistics Hathaway Building 2300 Capitol Avenue Cheyenne, WY 82002 (307) 777-7261

(Adapted from: Markin, R.E. 1982c. Rehabilitation placement servies: Unlicensed employment agencies or something else? Journal of Applied Rehabilitation Counseling. 13(1): 24–33; and Wright, N.D., and Allen, G.P. 1982. The National Directory of State Agencies 1982–1983. Information Resources Press, Arlington, VA.)

APPENDIX G
Directory of State Vocational Rehabilitation Central Offices

Jurisdiction	Offices
Alabama	Division of Rehabilitation & Crippled Children The Alabama Department of Education 2129 East South Boulevard P.O. Box 11586 Montgomery, AL 36111 (205) 281-8780
Alaska	Office of Vocational Rehabilitation The Alaska Department of Education State Office Building Pouch F, Mail Stop 0581 Juneau, AK 99811 (907) 586-6500 or 586-3270
Arizona	Rehabilitation Services Bureau The Arizona Department of Economic Security 1400 West Washington Phoenix, AZ 85007 (602) 271-3332
Arkansas	Rehabilitation Services The Arkansas Department of Social and Rehabilitation Services P.O. Box 3781 Little Rock, AR 72203 (501) 371-2571
California	Department of Rehabilitation The Human Relations Agency of the State of California 830 K Street Mall Sacramento, CA 95814 (916) 445-3971
Colorado	Division of Rehabilitation The Colorado Department of Social Services 1575 Sherman Street Denver, CO 80203 (303) 892-2285 or 892-2652
Connecticut	The Connecticut State Department of Education Division of Vocational Rehabilitation 600 Asylum Avenue Hartford, CT 06105 (203) 566-3316 or 566-7329

Jurisdiction	Offices
Delaware	Vocational Rehabilitation Service The Delaware Department of Labor 1500 Shallcross Avenue P.O. Box 1190 Wilmington, DE 19899 (302) 655-4444
District of Columbia	Bureau of Rehabilitation Services and Social Rehabilitation Administration Department of Human Resources 122 C Street, N.W., Room 816 Washington, D.C. 20001 (202) 629-5896
Florida	Office of Vocational Rehabilitation The Florida Department of Health and Rehabilitation Services 1309 Winwood Boulevard Tallahassee, FL 32301 (904) 488-6210
Georgia	The Georgia Department of Human Resources Division of Vocational Rehabilitation 610 State Office Building 47 Trinity Avenue, S.W. Atlanta, GA 30334 (404) 656-2621
Hawaii	Division of Vocational Rehabilitation The Hawaii Department of Social Services and Housing Room 216, Queen Liliuokalami Building P.O. Box 339 Honolulu, HI 96809 (808) 548-6367
Illinois	Division of Vocational Rehabilitation The Illinois State Board of Vocational Education and Rehabilitation 623 East Adams Street P.O. Box 1587 Springfield, IL 62706 (217) 782-2093 (312) 793-2920 - Chicago

Jurisdiction	Offices
Indiana	Rehabilitation Services Board 1028 Illinois Building 17 West Market Street Indianapolis, IN 46204 (317) 633-5687
Iowa	Division of Rehabilitation Education and Services The Iowa Department of Public Instruction 507 10th Street, 5th Floor Des Moines, IA 50309 (515) 281-4156 or 281-4311
Kansas	Division of Vocational Rehabilitation Kansas Department of Social and Rehabilitation Services State Office Building, 5th Floor Topeka, KS 66612 (913) 296-3911
Kentucky	Bureau of Rehabilitation Services The Kentucky Department of Education Capitol Plaza Office Tower Frankfort, KY 40601 (502) 564-4440
Louisiana	Division of Vocational Rehabilitation Louisiana Department of Health and Human Resources Administration Office of Rehabilitation Services 1755 Florida Boulevard P.O. Box 44371 Baton Rouge, LA 70804 (504) 389-2831
Maine	Bureau of Rehabilitation Services Maine Department of Health and Welfare 32 Winthrop Street Augusta, ME 04330 (207) 289-2266
Maryland	Division of Vocational Rehabilitation The Maryland State Department of Education P.O. Box 8717 Baltimore-Washington International Airport Baltimore, MD 21240 (301) 796-8300

Jurisdiction	Offices
Massachusetts	Massachusetts Rehabilitation Commission 296 Boylston Street Boston, MA 02108 (617) 727-5550
Michigan	Vocational Rehabilitation Service Michigan Department of Education P.O. Box 30010 Lansing, MI 48909 (517) 373-3390
Minnesota	Division of Vocational Rehabilitation The Minnesota Department of Economic Security 390 North Robert Street, 5th Floor St. Paul, MN 55101 (612) 296-5619
Mississippi	Division of Vocational Rehabilitation Mississippi Department of Education 1304 Walter Sillers State Office Building P.O. Box 1698 Jackson, MS 38205 (601) 354-6825
Missouri	Division of Vocational Rehabilitation The Missouri Department of Elementary and Secondary Education 3523 North Ten Mile Drive Jefferson City, MO 65101 (314) 751-3251
Montana	Rehabilitation Services Division The Montana Department of Social and Rehabilitation Services P.O. Box 4210 Helena, MT 59601 (406) 449-2590
Nebraska	Division of Rehabilitation Services The Nebraska State Department of Education 301 Centennial Mall, South (6th Floor) Lincoln, NE 68509 (402) 471-2961

Jurisdiction	Offices
Nevada	Rehabilitation Division The Nevada Department of Human Resources Kinkaid Building, 5th Floor 505 East King Street State Capitol Complex Carson City, NV 89710 (702) 885-4440
New Hampshire	Vocational Rehabilitation Division State Board of Education of New Hampshire 105 Loudon Road, Building #3 Concord, NH 03301 (603) 271-3121
New Jersey	New Jersey Division of Vocational Rehabilitation Department of Labor and Industry Labor and Industry Building, Room 1005 John Fitch Plaza P.O. Box 1098 Trenton, NJ 08625 (609) 292-7880 or 292-5987
New Mexico	Superintendent for Vocational Rehabilitation The New Mexico Department of Education 231 Washington Avenue P.O. Box 1830 Santa Fe, NM 87501 (505) 827-2266
New York	Office of Vocational Rehabilitation The New York State Education Department 99 Washington Avenue Albany, NY 12230 (518) 474-2712
North Carolina	Division of Vocational Rehabilitation Services The North Carolina Department of Human Resources 620 North West Street P.O. Box 26053 Raleigh, NC 27611 (919) 733-3364

Jurisdiction	Offices
North Dakota	Department of Vocational Rehabilitation The North Dakota State Board of Social Services 1025 North Third Street P.O. Box 1037 Bismarck, ND 58501 (701) 224-2907
Ohio	Ohio Rehabilitation Services Commission 4656 Heaton Road Columbus, OH 43229 (614) 466-5157
Oklahoma	Rehabilitative and Visual Services Department of Institutions, Social and Rehabilitative Services Sequoyah Memorial Office Building P.O. Box 25352 Oklahoma City, OK 73125 (405) 521-3374
Oregon	Vocational Rehabilitation Division The Oregon Department of Human Resources 2045 Silverton Road, N.E. Salem, OR 97310 (503) 378-3850
Pennsylvania	Bureau of Vocational Rehabilitation The Pennsylvania Department of Labor and Industry Labor and Industry Building, Room 1317 7th and Forster Streets Harrisburg, PA 17120 (717) 787-5244
Rhode Island	Division of Vocational Rehabilitation Rhode Island Social and Rehabilitative Services 40 Fountain Street Providence, RI 02903 (401) 421-7005
South Carolina	The South Carolina Vocational Rehabilitation Department 301 Landmark Center 3600 Forest Drive P.O. Box 4945 Columbia, SC 29240 (803) 758-3154 or 758-3237

Jurisdiction	Offices
South Dakota	Division of Rehabilitation Services The South Dakota Department of Social Services State Office Building Illinois Street Pierre, SD 57501 (605) 244-3195
Tennessee	Division of Vocational Rehabilitation The Tennessee Department of Education 1808 West End Building, Room 1400 Nashville, TN 37203 (615) 741-2521
Texas	The Texas Rehabilitation Commission 118 East Riverside Drive Austin, TX 78704 (512) 447-0106 or 447-0100
Utah	Division of Rehabilitation Services The Utah State Board of Education 250 East 5th Street Salt Lake City, UT 84111 (801) 533-5991
Vermont	Vocational Rehabilitation Division The Vermont Department of Social and Rehabilitation Services Agency of Human Services State Office Building Montpelier, VT 05602 (802) 244-5181
Virginia	Department of Vocational Rehabilitation The Virginia State Board of Vocational Rehabilitation 4901 Fitzhugh Avenue P.O. Box 11045 Richmond, VA 23230 (804) 786-2091
Washington	Division of Vocational Rehabilitation The Washington State Department of Social and Health Services State Office Building #2 P.O. Box 1788 (MS 311) Olympia, WA 98504 (206) 753-2544

Jurisdiction	Offices
West Virginia	Division of Vocational Rehabilitation The West Virginia State Board of Vocational Education P & G Building 2019 Washington Street, East Charleston, WV 25305 (304) 348-2375
Wisconsin	Division of Vocational Rehabilitation The Wisconsin Department of Health and Social Services State Office Building 131 West Wilson Street Madison, WI 53702 (608) 266-5466 or 266-1683
Wyoming	Division of Vocational Rehabilitation The Wyoming Department of Health and Social Services Hathaway State Office Building, West Cheyenne, WY 82002 (307) 777-7389 or 777-7387

APPENDIX H
Directory of Rehabilitation Medical and Engineering Centers and Resources of Suppliers and Manufacturers of Assistive Devices

Medical Rehabilitation Research & Training Centers

George Washington University
Research & Training Center
Job Development Laboratory
2300 Eye Street, N.W.
Washington, D.C. 20037

CORE AREA: Job Development and Bio-Engineering for Severely Disabled Persons.

Medical Rehabilitation Research
& Training Center
New York University
400 East 34th Street
New York, NY 10016

CORE AREA: Evaluation of Functional Performance of Devices for Severely Disabled

Medical Rehabilitation Research
& Training Center
Tufts University
171 Harrison Avenue
Boston, MA 02111

CORE AREA: Communication Systems for Individuals with Non-Vocal Disabilities

Rehabilitation Engineering Centers

California

Rehabilitation Engineering Center
Children's Hospital at Stanford
520 Willow Road
Palo Alto, CA 94034

CORE AREA: Communication Disorder for the Deaf and Non-Vocal.

Rehabilitation Engineering Center
Rancho Los Amigos Hospital
7601 East Imperial Highway
Downey, CA 90242

CORE AREA: Functional Electrical Stimulation of Paralyzed Nerves and Muscles.

Rehabilitation Engineering Center
Smith-Kettlewell Institute of
Visual Sciences
2232 Western Street
San Francisco, CA 94115

CORE AREA: Sensory Aids for the Blind and Deaf.

Illinois

Rehabilitation Engineering Center
  Northwestern University
  345 East Superior Street, Room 1441
  Chicago, IL 60611

CORE AREA: Internal Total Joint
Replacement.

Iowa

Rehabilitation Engineering Center
  University of Iowa
  Orthopedics Department
  Dill Children's Hospital
  Iowa City, IA 52242

CORE AREA: Low Back Pain.

Kansas

Rehabilitation Engineering Center
  Cerebral Palsy Research Foundation
  4320 East Kellogg Street
  Wichita, KS 67218

CORE AREA: Vocational Aspects
of Rehabilitation.

Massachusetts

Rehabilitation Engineering Center
  Children's Hospital Medical Center
  300 Longwood Avenue
  Boston, MA 02115

CORE AREA: Neuromuscular
Control using Sensory Feedback
Systems.

Michigan

Rehabilitation Engineering Center
  University of Michigan
  225 West Engineering
  Ann Arbor, MI 48109

CORE AREA: Automotive
Transportation for the
Handicapped.

Ohio

Rehabilitation Engineering Center
  Case Western Reserve University
  2219 Adelbert Road
  Cleveland, OH 44106

CORE AREA: Upper Extremity
Functional Electrical Stimulation.

Pennsylvania

Rehabilitation Engineering Center
  Krusen Research Center
  Moss Rehabilitation Hospital
  12th Street & Tabor Road
  Philadelphia, PA 19141

CORE AREA: Locomotion and
Mobility.

Tennessee

Rehabilitation Engineering Center
　University of Tennessee
　1248 La Paloma Street
　Memphis, TN 38114

CORE AREA: Mobility Systems
for Severely Disabled.

Texas

Rehabilitation Engineering Center
　Texas Institute for Rehabilitation
　Research
　1333 Moursund Avenue
　Houston, TX 77025

CORE AREA: Effects of Pressure
on Tissue.

Southwest Research Institute
　8500 Culebra Road
　P.O. Drawer 28501
　San Antonio, TX 78284

CORE AREA: Employability
Restoration Engineering Program
for Severely Handicapped.

Virginia

Rehabilitation Engineering Center
　University of Virginia
　P.O. Box 3368, University Station
　Charlottesville, VA 22903

CORE AREA: Spinal Cord Injury.

Resources of Suppliers and Manufacturers of Assistive Devices

Accent on Information, Inc.
　Box 700
　Bloomington, IL 61701

PUBLICATION: Accent on Living:
Buyer's Guide.

The Independence Factory
　P.O. Box 597
　Middletown, OH 45042

PUBLICATION: How To Make It Cheap
Manual.

The Texas Rehabilitation
　Commission IMPART Demonstration
　Center
　2203 Babcock Road
　San Antonio, TX 78229

PUBLICATION: Assistive Devices:
Purchasing & Supply Catalogue.

Wisconsin Vocational Studies Center
　University of Wisconsin-Madison
　964 Educational Science Building
　1025 West Johnson Street
　Madison, WI 53706

PUBLICATION: Tools, Equipment &
Machinery Adapted for the Vocational,
Educational & Employment of the
Handicapped.

APPENDIX I
Directory of Assessment Instrument Publishers

Alfano, Anthony M.
6263 Twilight Avenue
Kalamazoo, MI 49004

American Association on Mental
   Deficiency
5101 Wisconsin Avenue, Suite 405
Washington, D.C. 20016

American College Testing Program
Educational Services Division
P.O. Box 168
Iowa City, IA 52243

American Guidance Service
Publishers' Building
Circle Pines, MN 55014

Associates for Research in Behavior, Inc.
The Science Center
34th & Market Streets
Philadelphia, PA 19104

Brodhead-Garrett Company
4560 East 71st Street
Cleveland, OH 44105

Bruce, Martin M., Publishers
340 Oxford Road
New Rochelle, NY 10804

Bureau of Educational Research &
   Service
University of Iowa
Iowa City, IA 52240

California Test Bureau/McGraw-Hill
Del Monte Research Park
Monterey, CA 93940

Career Education Readiness
Measurement & Research
Southern Illinois University
Box 123
Edwardsville, IL 62025

Career Planning & Placement Service
100 Noyes Hall
University of Missouri
Columbia, MO 65211

Center for Occupational Education
North Carolina State University
P.O. Box 5096
Raleigh, NC 27607

CFKR Career Materials, Inc.
110 Glenn Way
P.O. Box 5096
Belmont, CA 94002

Chronicle Guidance Publications, Inc.
Moravia, NY 13118

The College Board
888 Seventh Avenue
New York, NY 10019

Consulting Psychologists Press, Inc.
577 College Avenue
Palo Alto, CA 94306

Designed Learning
14677 N.W. Forrestal Loop
Beaverton, OR 97005

Educational Achievement Corporation
P.O. Box 7310
Waco, TX 76710

Educational & Industrial Testing Service
Ed ITS
San Diego, CA 92107

Educational Guidance, Inc.
P.O. Box 511
Main Post Office
Dearborn, MI 48121

Edupac, Inc.
231 Norfolk Street
Walpole, MA 02081

Educational Testing Service
Princeton, NJ 08540

Evaluation Systems, Inc.
640 North LaSalle Street, Suite 698
Chicago, IL 60610

Harcourt Brace Jovanovich, Inc.
757 Third Avenue
New York, NY 10017

Human Systems Consultants, Inc.
110 North Tenth Street, Suite 7
Columbia, MO 65201

Industrial Relations Center
University of Chicago
1225 East 60th Street
Chicago, IL 60637

Institute for Crippled and Disabled
400 First Avenue
New York, NY 10009

Institute of Personality & Ability Testing
1602 Coronado Drive
Champaign, IL 61820

Instructional Materials Laboratory
Ohio State University
1885 Neil Avenue
Columbus, OH 43210

Interstate Printers & Publishers, Inc.
19–27 North Jackson Street
Danville, IL 61832

Jastak Associates, Inc.
1526 Gilpin Avenue
Wilmington, DE 19806

Learning Concepts
2501 North Lamar
Austin, TX 78705

Marathon Consulting & Press
575 Anfield Road
Columbus, OH 43209

McCarron-Dial Systems
P.O. Box 45628
Dallas, TX 75248

Minicomp Corporation
1780 South Bellaire, Suite 510
Denver, CO 80222

Monitor
P.O. Box 2337
Hollywood, CA 90028

NCS Interpretive Scoring Systems
P.O. Box 1416
Minneapolis, MN 55440

NSVCS
Route 4, Box 217
Gainesville, FL 32601

OSU Nisonger Center
1580 Cannon Drive
Columbus, OH 43206

Personnel Press
191 Spring Street
Lexington, MA 02173

Prep, Inc.
1007 Whitehead Road
Trenton, NJ 08628

PRO-ED, Inc.
5341 Industrial Oaks Boulevard
Austin, TX 78735

The Psychological Corporation
757 Third Avenue
New York, NY 10017

Psychological Test Specialists
Box 1441
Missoula, MT 59801

Psychometric Affiliates
Box 3167
Munster, IN 46321

Publishers Test Service
2500 Garden Road
Monterey, CA 93940

Research Psychologists Press, Inc.
P.O. Box 984
Port Huron, MI 48060

The Riverside Publishing Company
(A Houghton Mifflin Subsidiary)
3 O'Hare Towers
8420 Bryn Mawr Avenue
Chicago, IL 60631

Sahel, Shoukry D.
Department of Management Sciences
University of Waterloo
Waterloo, Ontario N2LG Canada

Scholastic Testing Service, Inc.
480 Meyer Road
Bensenville, IL 60106

Science Research Associates, Inc.
155 North Wacker Drive
Chicago, IL 60606

Sheridan Psychological Services
P.O. Box 6101
Orange, CA 92667

Singer Company
80 Commerce Drive
Rochester, NY 14623

Stanford University Press
Stanford, CA 94305

Stoelting
1350 South Kostner Avenue
Chicago, IL 60623

Talent Assessment, Inc.
P.O. Box 5087
Jacksonville, FL 32207

U.S. Government Printing Office
Washington, D.C. 20402

U.S. Military Enlistment Processing
 Command
Ft. Sheridan, IL 60037

Valpar Corporation
3801 East 34th Street
Tucson, AZ 85713

Vocational Diagnosis & Assessment of
 Residual Employability Service Bureau
P.O. Box 55
Roswell, GA 30077

Vocational Psychology Research
N620 Elliott Hall
75 East River Road

University of Minnesota
Minneapolis, MN 55455

Vocational Research Institutes Jewish
 Employment & Vocational Service
1700 Sansom Street
Philadelphia, PA 19103

Western Psychological Services
12031 Wilshire Boulevard
Los Angeles, CA 90025

World of Work, Inc.
2923 North 67th Place
Scottsdale, AZ 85251

(Compiled from: Anastasi, A. 1982. Psychological Testing. 5th Ed. Macmillan Company, New York; and Kapes, J.T., and Mastie, M.M. (eds.). 1982. A Counselor's Guide to Vocational Guidance Instruments. American Personnel and Guidance Association, National Vocational Guidance Association, Falls Church, VA.)

APPENDIX J
Directory of Associations

Accent on Information, Inc.
P.O. Box 700
Bloomington, IL 61701
(309) 378-2961

Advocates for the Handicapped
Merchandise Mart
Chicago, IL 60654
(312) 822-0435

AFL-CIO Department of Community
Services
815 16th Street, N.W.
Washington, D.C. 20006
(202) 637-5000

Alexander Graham Bell Association for
the Deaf
3417 Volta Place, N.W.
Washington, D.C. 20007
(202) 337-5220

Alcoholics Anonymous
P.O. Box 459, Grand Central Station
New York, NY 10017
(212) 686-1100

Alliance of American Insurers
1501 Woodfield Rd., Suite 400 West
Schaumburg, IL 60195-4980
(312) 490-8500

American Association for Counseling and
Development
5999 Stevenson Avenue
Alexandria, VA 22304
(703) 823-9800

American Association for Marriage and
Family Therapy
924 West 9th Street
Upland, CA 91786
(714) 981-0888

American Association on Mental
Deficiency
5101 Wisconsin Avenue, N.W.
Washington, D.C. 20016
(202) 686-5400

American Association on Occupational
Health Nurses, Inc.
575 Lexington Avenue
New York, NY 10022
(212) 355-7733

American Association for Rehabilitation
Therapy, Inc.
P.O. Box 93
North Little Rock, AR 72116
(501) 725-9100 ext 469

American Association of Workers for the
Blind, Inc.
1511 K Street, N.W.
Washington, D.C. 20005
(202) 347-1559

American Bar Association
1155 East 60th Street
Chicago, IL 60637
(312) 947-4000

American Civil Liberties Union, Inc.
132 West 43rd Street
New York, NY 10036
(212) 944-9800

American Coalition of Citizens with
Disabilities, Inc.
1200 15th Street, N.W., Suite 201
Washington, D.C. 20005
(202) 785-4265

American Congress of Rehabilitation
Medicine
30 North Michigan Avenue
Chicago, IL 60602
(312) 236-9512

American Council on Education
1 Dupont Circle
Washington, D.C. 20036
(202) 833-4700

American Deafness and Rehabilitation
Association, Inc.
814 Thayer Avenue
Silver Spring, MD 20910
(301) 589-0880

American Federation of State, County,
and Municipal Employees
1625 L Street, N.W.
Washington, D.C. 20036
(202) 452-4800

American Foundation for the Blind, Inc.
15 West 16th Street
New York, NY 10011
(212) 620-2000

American Heart Association, Inc.
7320 Greenville Avenue
Dallas, TX 75231
(214) 750-5300

American Hospital Association, Inc.
840 North Lake Shore Drive
Chicago, IL 60611
(312) 280-6000

American Industrial Hygiene
Association
66 South Miller Road
Akron, OH 44313
(216) 836-9537

American Law Institute
4025 Chestnut Street
Philadelphia, PA 19104
(215) 243-1611

American Lung Association
1740 Broadway
New York, NY 10019
(212) 245-8000

American Medical Association
535 North Dearborn Street
Chicago, IL 60610
(312) 751-6000

American Nurses Association, Inc.
2420 Pershing Road
Kansas City, MO 64108
(816) 474-5720

American Occupational Therapy
Association, Inc.
6000 Executive Boulevard, Suite 200
Rockville, MD 20852
(301) 770-2200

American Organization for Rehabilitation
through Training Federation, Inc.
817 Broadway
New York, NY 10003
(212) 677-4400

American Orthotic and Prosthetic
Association
1444 N Street, N.W.
Washington, D.C. 20005
(202) 234-8400

American Osteopathic Association
12 East Ohio Street
Chicago, IL 60611
(312) 944-2713

American Personnel and Guidance
Association (see—American Association for Counseling and Development)

American Physical Therapy Association
1156 15th Street N.W.
Washington, D.C. 20005
(202) 466-2070

American Printing House of the
Blind, Inc.
1839 Frankfort Avenue
Louisville, KY 40206
(502) 895-2405

American Psychiatric Association
1700 18th Street, N.W.
Washington, D.C. 20009
(202) 797-4900

American Psychological Association
1200 17th Street, N.W.
Washington, D.C. 20036
(202) 833-7600

American Public Health Association
1015 15th Street, N.W.
Washington, D.C. 20005
(202) 789-5600

American Red Cross
17th and D Streets, N.W.
Washington, D.C. 20006
(202) 737-8300

American Rehabilitation Counseling
Association (see American Association
for Counseling and Development)

American Speech-Language-Hearing
Association
10801 Rockville Pike
Rockville, MD 20852
(301) 897-5700

Arthritis Foundation
3400 Peachtree Road, N.E.
Atlanta, GA 30326
(404) 266-0795

Association of American Railroads
1920 L Street, N.W.
Washington, D.C. 20036
(202) 835-9126

Association of Medical Rehabilitation
Directors and Coordinators
87 Elm Street
Framingham, MA 01710
(617) 877-0517

Association for Retarded Citizens
2709 Avenue E East
Arlington, TX 76011
(817) 261-4961

Blue Cross Association
840 North Lake Shore Drive
Chicago, IL 60611
(312) 440-6000

Board for Rehabilitation
Certification
1156 Shure Drive, Suite 350
Arlington Heights, IL 60004
(312) 394-2104

Brookings Institute
1775 Massachusetts Avenue, N.W.
Washington, D.C. 20036
(202) 797-6000

Cancer Care, Inc., and the National
Cancer Foundation, Inc.
1 Park Avenue
New York, NY 10016
(212) 679-5700

Certification of Insurance Rehabilitation
Specialists Commission (see—Board for
Rehabilitation Certification)

Commission on Accreditation of
Rehabilitation Facilities
2500 North Pantano Road
Tucson, AZ 85715
(602) 886-8575

Commission on Certification of Work
Adjustment and Vocational Evaluation
Specialists (see Board for Rehabilitation
Certification)

Commission on Rehabilitation
Counselor Certification (see Board for
Rehabilitation Certification)

Council on Rehabilitation Education,
Inc.
185 North Wabash, Room 1617
Chicago, IL 60602
(312) 346-6027

Council of State Administrators of
Vocational Rehabilitation
1055 Thomas Jefferson Street, N.W.,
Suite 401
Washington, D.C. 20007
(202) 638-4634

Council on Social Work Education, Inc.
111 8th Avenue
New York, NY 10011
(212) 242-3800

Council of State Governments
P.O. Box 11910, Iron Works Pike
Lexington, KY 40578
(606) 252-2291

Cystic Fibrosis Foundation
6000 Executive Boulevard, Suite 309
Rockville, MD 20852
(301) 881-9130

Goodwill Industries of America, Inc.
9200 Wisconsin Avenue, N.W.
Washington, D.C. 20014
(301) 530-6500

Group Health Association of America,
Inc.
1717 Massachusetts Avenue, N.W.
Washington, D.C. 20036
(202) 483-4012

Health Insurance Association
of America
1850 K Street, N.W.
Washington, D.C. 20006
(202) 331-1336

Helen Keller International, Inc.
22 West 17th Street
New York, NY 10011
(212) 620-2100

Institute of Insurers of America
Providence and Sugartown Roads
Malvern, PA 19355
(215) 644-2100

International Association of Industrial
Accident Boards and Commissions
P.O. Box 2917
Olympia, WA 98507
(206) 754-3793

International Commission for the
Prevention of Alcoholism
6830 Laurel Street, N.W.
Washington, D.C. 20012
(202) 723-0800

International Hospital Federation
444 North Capitol Street, N.W.
Washington, D.C. 20001
(202) 638-1100

Job Placement Division (see National
Rehabilitation Association)

Joint Commission on Accreditation
of Hospitals
875 North Michigan Avenue
Chicago, IL 60611
(312) 642-6061

Leukemia Society of America, Inc.
800 2nd Avenue
New York, NY 10017
(212) 573-8484

Materials Development Center
Stout Vocational Rehabilitation Institute
University of Wisconsin-Stout
Menomonie, WI 54751
(715) 232-1380

March of Dimes Birth Defects
Foundations
275 Mamoroneck Avenue
White Plains, NY 10605
(914) 428-7100

Mental Health Materials Center, Inc.
30 East 29th Street
New York, NY 10016
(212) 889-5760

Mental Retardation Association of
America, Inc.
211 East 300 South, Suite 212
Salt Lake City, UT 84111
(801) 328-1575

Muscular Dystrophy Association, Inc.
810 7th Avenue
New York, NY 10019
(212) 586-0808

National Accreditation Council for
Agencies Serving the Blind and
Visually Handicapped
79 Madison Avenue
New York, NY 10016
(212) 683-8581

National Association for Hearing and
Speech Action
6110 Executive Boulevard, Suite 1000
Rockville, MD 20852
(301) 897-8682

National Association of the Deaf
814 Thayer Avenue
Silver Spring, MD 20910
(301) 587-1788

National Association of Jewish
Vocational Services
225 Park Avenue, South
New York, NY 10003
(212) 457-2400

National Association of Rehabilitation
Facilities
5530 Wisconsin Avenue, N.W.
Washington, D.C. 20015
(301) 654-5882

National Association of Rehabilitation
Professionals in the Private Sector
P.O. Box 708
Twin Peaks, CA 92391
(714) 337-0745

National Association of Social
Workers, Inc.:
1425 H Street, N.W.
Washington, D.C. 20005
(202) 628-6800

National Board for Certified
Counselors, Inc., (see American
Association for Counseling
and Development)

National Bureau of Economic
Research, Inc.
1050 Massachusetts Avenue
Cambridge, MA 02138
(617) 868-3900

National Association for Statewide
Health and Welfare
c/o National Conference on Social
Welfare
1730 M Street, N.W., Suite 911
Washington, D.C. 20036
(202) 785-0817

National Center for a Barrier Free
Environment
1140 Connecticut Avenue, N.W.,
Room 1006
Washington, D.C. 20036
(202) 466-6896

National Child Labor Committee
1501 Broadway, Room 1111
New York, NY 10036
(212) 840-1801

National Civil Service League
4340 East West Highway, Suite 900
Bethesda, MD 20014
(301) 654-8664

National Clearing House of
   Rehabilitation Materials
Oklahoma State University
115 Old USDA Building
Stillwater, OK 74078
(405) 624-7650

National Commission for Health
   Certifying Agencies
1101 30th Street, N.W.
Washington, D.C. 20007
(202) 333-9300

National Council on Alcoholism, Inc.
733 3rd Avenue, Suite 1405
New York, NY 10017
(212) 986-4433

National Council on Family Relations
1219 University Avenue, S.E.
Minneapolis, MN 55414
(612) 331-2774

National Council of Health Care
   Services
2600 Virginia Avenue, N.W., Suite 915
Washington, D.C. 20037
(202) 785-4754

National Council on Rehabilitation
   Education
2921 Ermine Way
Farmers Branch, TX 75234
(214) 241-4747

National Easter Seal Society for
   Crippled Children and Adults
2023 West Ogden Avenue
Chicago, IL 60612
(312) 243-8400

National Education Association
1201 16th Street, N.W.
Washington, D.C. 20036
(202) 883-4000

National Employment Counselor
   Association (see American Association
   for Counseling and Development)

National Environmental Health
   Association
1200 Lincoln Street, Suite 704
Denver, CO 80203
(303) 861-9090

National Federation of the Blind
1800 Johnson Street
Baltimore, MD 21230
(301) 655-7418

National Health Council, Inc.
1740 Broadway
New York, NY 10019
(212) 582-6040

National Health and Welfare Mutual Life
   Insurance Association, Inc.
666 5th Avenue
New York, NY 10019
(212) 399-1600

National Head Injury Foundation
280 Singletary Lane
Framingham, MA 01701
(617) 879-7473

National Industries for the Blind
1455 Broad Street
Bloomfield, NJ 07003
(201) 338-3804

National Kidney Foundation
2 Park Avenue
New York, NY 10016
(212) 889-2210

National League for Nursing, Inc.
10 Columbus Circle
New York, NY 10019
(212) 582-1022

National Medical Association
2109 E Street, N.W.
Washington, D.C. 20037
(202) 338-8266

National Mental Health Association
1800 North Kent Street
Arlington, VA 22209
(703) 528-6405

National Multiple Sclerosis Society
205 East 42nd Street
New York, NY 10017
(212) 986-3240

National Recreation and Park
Association
1601 North Kent Street
Arlington, VA 22209
(202) 525-0606

National Rehabilitation Association
633 South Washington Street
Alexandria, VA 22314
(703) 836-0850

National Rehabilitation Administration
Association (see National
Rehabilitation Association)

National Rehabilitation Counseling
Association (see National
Rehabilitation Association)
(703) 836-7677

National Rehabilitation Information
Center
The Catholic University of America
4407 8th Street, N.E.
Washington, D.C. 20017-2299
(202) 635-5826

National Rehabilitation Hospital
1636 Connecticut Avenue, N.W.
Washington, D.C. 20009

National Safety Council
444 North Michigan Avenue
Chicago, IL 60611
(312) 527-4800

National Society to Prevent
Blindness, Inc.
9 Madison Avenue
New York, NY 10016
(212) 684-3505

National Spinal Cord Injury
Foundation
369 Elliot Street
Newton Upper Falls, MA 02164
(617) 964-0521

National Tuberous Sclerosis
Association, Inc.
P.O. Box 159
Laguna Beach, CA 92652
(714) 494-8900

National Veterans Affairs and
Rehabilitation Commission
1608 K Street, N.W.
Washington, D.C. 20006
(202) 861-2700

Professional Rehabilitation Association
P.O. Box 772
Lindenhurst, NY 11757-0772

Railroad Retirement Board
844 North Rush Street
Chicago, IL 60611
(312) 751-4500

Rehabilitation International
423 Park Avenue, South
New York, NY 10016
(212) 679-6520

Rehabilitation Nurse's Society
P.O. Box 8480, Universal City Station
North Hollywood, CA 91608
(213) 760-2644

Seeing Eye, Inc.
P.O. Box 375
Morristown, NJ 07960
(201) 539-4425

Social Legislation Information
Service, Inc.
1346 Connecticut Avenue, N.W.
Washington, D.C. 20036
(202) 223-2396

The President's Committee on
Employment of the Handicapped
1111 20th Street, N.W.
Washington, D.C. 20036
(202) 653-5044

United Cancer Council, Inc.
1803 North Meridian Street
Indianapolis, IN 46202
(317) 923-6490

United Cerebral Palsy Associations, Inc.
66 East 34th Street
New York, NY 10016
(212) 481-6300

United States Chamber of Commerce
1615 H Street, N.W.
Washington, D.C. 20062
(301) 468-5128

United States Department of Education
  Rehabilitation Services Administration
400 Maryland Avenue, S.W.
Washington, D.C. 20202
(202) 245-8492

United States Department of Health and
  Human Services
200 Independence Avenue, S.W.
Washington, D.C. 20201
(202) 245-6296

United Mine Workers of America Health
  and Retirement Funds
2021 K Street, N.W.
Washington, D.C. 20006
(202) 452-5000

United Seamen's Service
1 World Trade Center
New York, NY 10048
(212) 755-1033

United Way of America
801 North Fairfax Street
Alexandria, VA 22314
(703) 386-7100

Vocational Evaluation and Work
  Adjustment Association (see National
  Rehabilitation Association)

W.E. Upjohn Institute for Employment
  Research
300 South Westnedge Avenue
Kalamazoo, MI 49007
(616) 343-5541

References

Alexander, C.P. (1983, May 30). The new economy. *Time*, pp. 62–70.

Alexander, F.G., & Selesnick, S.T. (1966). *The history of psychiatry.* New York: Harper & Row.

Allan, W.S. (1958). *Rehabilitation: A community challenge.* New York: John Wiley & Sons.

Allen, F.L. (1952). *The big change.* New York: Harper & Brothers.

American Association of Mental Deficiency. (1977). *Consent handbook.* Washington, DC: Author.

American Psychological Association. (1982). *Ethical standards of psychologists.* Washington, DC: Author.

Anastasi, A. (1982). *Psychological testing* (5th ed.). New York: Macmillan Publishing.

Andersen, R.H. (1979). Vocational expert testimony: The new frontier for the rehabilitation professional. *Journal of Rehabilitation, 45*(3), 39–40, 74.

Anderson, J.K., & Parente, F.R. (1982). Rehabilitation counselors forecast their future. *Journal of Rehabilitation, 48*(1), 36–42.

Anderson, S.B., & Ball, S. (1978). *The profession and practice of program evaluation.* San Francisco: Jossey-Bass.

Andrisani, P.J. (1978). The establishment of stable and successful careers: The role of work attitudes and labor market knowledge. In U.S. Department of Labor, *Conference report on youth unemployment, its measurements and meaning.* Washington, DC: Author.

Angell, D.L., DeSau, G.T., & Havrilla, A.A. (1969). Rehabilitation counselor versus coordinator . . . one of rehabilitation's great straw men. *NRCA Professional Bulletin, 9*(1), 7–8.

Baker, R.A. (1980). The purpose of reinsurance. In R.W. Strain (Ed.), *Reinsurance* (pp. 33–50). New York: The College of Insurance.

Baker, R.J. (1982). Vocational evaluation. In R.T. Roessler & S.E. Rubin, *Case management and rehabilitation counseling* (pp. 85–102). Baltimore: University Park Press.

Beals, R., & Hickman, N. (1972). Industrial injuries to the back and extremities. *Journal of Bone and Joint Surgery, 54,* 1593–1611.

Bell, M. (1979). *Marketing concepts and strategies* (3rd ed.). Boston: Houghton Mifflin.

Benjamin, A. (1974). *The helping interview* (2nd ed.). Boston: Houghton Mifflin.

Berkowitz, M. (1960). *Workmen's compensation.* New Brunswick, NJ: Rutgers University Press.

Berkowitz, M. (1980). *Work disincentives.* Falls Church, VA: Institute for Information Studies.

Berkowitz, M. (1981). Disincentives and the rehabilitation of disabled persons. In E.L. Pan, T.E. Backer, & C.L. Vash (Eds.), *Annual review of rehabilitation* (pp. 40–57). New York: Springer Publishing.

Bickelhaupt, D.L., & Magee, J. (1970). *General insurance.* Homewood, IL: Richard D. Irwin, Inc.

Biestek, F.P. (1957). *The casework relationship.* Chicago: Loyola University Press.

Bitter, J.A. (1979). *Introduction to rehabilitation.* St. Louis: C.V. Mosby.

Black, B.J. (1968). *Principles of industrial therapy for the mentally ill.* New York: Grune & Stratton.

Black, H.C. (1979). *Black's law dictionary* (5th ed.). St. Paul, MN: West Publishing Co.

Bloom, P.N., & Novelli, W.D. (1980). Problems and challenges in social marketing. *Journal of Marketing, 44*(2), 79–88.

Boehne, K.P. (1982). *Railroad retirement board operations: Field office structure and disability retirement* (Report No. 12–386–0). Washington, DC: Committee on Government Operations Subcommittee Hearings.

Botterbusch, K.F. (1980). *A comparison of commercial vocational evaluation systems.* Menomonie, WI: Materials Development Center, Stout Vocational Rehabilitation Institute.

Brandon, T.L. (1983). Vocational rehabilitation specialists in the courtroom. *Vocational Evaluation and Work Adjustment Bulletin, 16,* 103–108.

Brisolara, A. (1979). *The alcoholic employee: A handbook of useful guidelines.* New York: Human Sciences Press.

Brodsky, S. (1981). Ten commandments for an expert witness. *Social Action and the Law, 7*(1), 7.

Brolin, J., & Webster, D.B. (1978). Job modification in vocational evaluation. *Vocational Evaluation and Work Adjustment Bulletin, 11*(4), 7–12.

Brubaker, D.R. (1977). Professionalization and rehabilitation counseling. *Journal of Applied Rehabilitation Counseling, 8,* 208–217.

Brubaker, D.R. (1980). Diversity or destruction: The rise of special interest groups in rehabilitation counseling. *NRCA Professional Report, 21*(2), 1, 4.

California Association of Rehabilitation Professionals. (1982). *Guidelines for standards of professional behavior.* Santa Rosa, CA: Author.

California Department of Industrial Relations, Rehabilitation Bureau. (1979). *Sample of 1978 case closures.* San Francisco: Author.

Cannon, M.W. (1983). Contentious and burdensome litigation: A need for alternatives. *National Forum, 63*(4), 10–13.

Capshaw, T., Grenfell, J., & Savino, W.F. (1982). *Practical aspects of handling social security disability claims.* Madison, WI: Professional Educational Systems.

Cheit, E.F. (1961). *Injury and recovery in the course of employment.* New York: John Wiley & Sons.

Cheit, E.F., & Gordon, M.S. (Eds.). (1963). *Occupational disability and public policy.* New York: John Wiley & Sons.

Cohen, R.J. (1979). *Malpractice.* New York: The Free Press.

Commission on Accreditation of Rehabilitation Facilities. (1979). *Program evaluation in work activity facilities.* Tucson: Author.

Commission on Accreditation of Rehabilitation Facilities. (1980). *Standards manual for rehabilitation facilities.* Tucson: Author.

Conley, R.W. (1965). *The economics of vocational rehabilitation.* Baltimore: Johns Hopkins Press.

Conley, R.W. (1969). A benefit-cost analysis of the vocational rehabilitation program. *Journal of Human Resources, 4,* 226–252.

Cottone, R.R. (1982). Ethical issues in private-for-profit rehabilitation. *Journal of Applied Rehabilitation Counseling, 13*(3), 14–17, 24.

Cottone, R.R., Simmons, B., & Wilfley, D. (1983). Ethical issues in vocational rehabilitation: A review of the literature from 1970 to 1981. *Journal of Rehabilitation, 49*(2), 19–24.

Cross, D.L. (1979). A defense attorney looks at private rehabilitation. *Journal of Rehabilitation*, 45(3), 37–38, 74.

Davidson, P.O. (1980). Evaluating lifestyle change programs. In P.O. Davidson & S.M. Davidson (Eds.), *Behavioral medicines: Changing health lifestyles* (pp. 391—409). New York: Brunner / Mazel.

Deneen, L.J., & Hessellund, T.A. (1981). *Vocational rehabilitation of the injured worker.* San Francisco: Rehab Publications.

Diamond, C.R., & Petkas, E.J. (1979). A state agency's view of private-for-profit rehabilitation. *Journal of Rehabilitation*, 45(3), 30–31.

Dickman, F., & Emener, W.G. (in press). Employee assistance programs: Basic concepts, critical attributes, and an evaluation. *Personnel Administration.*

Dodd, W.F. (1936). *Administration of workmen's compensation.* New York: The Commonwealth Fund.

Dollard, J., & Miller, N.E. (1950). *Personality and psychotherapy.* New York: McGraw-Hill.

Donaldson, J.H. (1976). *Casualty claim practice.* Homewood, IL: Richard D. Irwin, Inc.

Dorken, H. (1980). Perspectives on national health insurance and rehabilitation. In E.L. Pan, T.E. Backer, & C.L. Vash (Eds.), *Annual review of rehabilitation* (pp. 13–54). New York: Springer Publishing Co.

Downey, E.H. (1924). *Workmen's compensation.* New York: Macmillan Co.

Dunn, D.J. (1973). Recording observations. *Consumer Brief*, 1(1), 1–3.

Dunn, D.J. (1974). *Placement services in the vocational rehabilitation program.* Menomonie, WI: Materials Development Center, Stout Vocational Rehabilitation Institute.

Eastman, C. (1969). *Work accidents and the law: American labor, from conspiracy to collective bargaining.* New York: Arno and the New York Times.

Eaton, M.W. (1979). Obstacles to the vocational rehabilitation of individuals receiving workers' compensation. *Journal of Rehabilitation*, 45(2), 59–63.

Elliott, C.M., & Vaughn, E.J. (1972). *Fundamentals of risk and insurance.* New York: John Wiley & Sons.

Emener, W.G., & Rubin, S.E. (1980). Rehabilitation counselor roles and functions and sources of role strain. *Journal of Applied Rehabilitation Counseling, 11,* 57–69.

Evaluation Research Society. (1980). *Standards for program evaluation.* Potomac, MD: Author.

Feinberg, L.B., & McFarlane, F.R. (1979). Setting-based factors in rehabilitation counselor role variability. *Journal of Applied Rehabilitation Counseling, 10,* 95–101.

Feindel, M. (1980a). A comparison of occupational values and opportunities of rehabilitation counselors and administrators. *Journal of Rehabilitation Administration, 4,* 14–18.

Feindel, M. (1980b). Confessions of an elevated counselor: Why don't they love me anymore? *Journal of Rehabilitation*, 46(2), 70–71, 80.

Ferguson, R.E. (1980). The bases of reinsurance. In R.W. Strain (Ed.), *Reinsurance* (pp. 51–78). New York: The College of Insurance.

Field, T.F. (1981). The consolidation of the rehabilitation professional associations: Pros and cons. *Journal of Applied Rehabilitation Counseling, 12,* 65–68.

Field, T.F., McCrosky, B., Sink, J.M., & Wattenbarger, W. (1978). The role and functions of the vocational expert in judicial hearings. *Psychology Rehabilitation, 2*(2), 17–27.

Field, T.F., & Sink, J.M. (1981). *The vocational expert.* Athens, GA: VDARE Service Bureau.

Fine, S.A. (1973). *Functional job analysis: An approach to a technology for manpower planning.* Kalamazoo, MI: W.E. Upjohn Institute for Employment Research.

Fine, S.A., Holt, A.M., & Hutchinson, M.F. (1974). *Functional job analysis: How to standardize task statements.* Kalamazoo, MI: W.E. Upjohn Institute for Employment Research.

Fine, S.A., & Wiley, W.W. (1971). *An introduction to functional job analysis: A scaling of selected tasks for the social welfare field.* Kalamazoo, MI: W.E. Upjohn Institute for Employment Research.

Fourth Institute on Rehabilitation Issues. (1977). *Rehabilitation of the severely handicapped homebound.* Hot Springs, AR: Arkansas Research and Training Center.

Francis, R.A. (1983). The development of federal accessibility law. *Journal of Rehabilitation, 49*(1), 29–32.

Frank, K. (1979). *Program evaluation systems for vocational rehabilitation programs.* Stryker, OH: Quadco Rehabilitation Center.

Gellman, W. (1968). The principles of vocational evaluation. *Rehabilitation Literature, 29,* 98–102.

Gianforte, G. (1976). Certification: A challenge and a choice. *Journal of Rehabilitation, 42*(5), 15–17, 39.

Goldberg, R., Bigwood, A., MacCarthy, S., Donaldson, W., & Conrad, S. (1972). Vocational profile of patients awaiting and following renal transplantation. *Archive of Physical Medicine and Rehabilitation, 53,* 28–33.

Goldberg, R., & Freed, M. (1973). Vocational adjustment, interest, work values, and career plans of persons with spinal cord injuries. *Scandanavian Journal of Rehabilitation Medicine, 5,* 3–11.

Gordon, M.S. (1963). Industrial injuries insurance in Europe and the British commonwealth before World War II. In E.F. Cheit & M.S. Gordon (Eds.), *Occupational disability and public policy* (pp. 191–220). New York: John Wiley & Sons.

Graham, C.S. (1980). An effectiveness measure for work adjustment: Providing evidence of impact. *Vocational Evaluation and Work Adjustment Bulletin, 13,* 98–102.

Grenfell, J.G. (1980). The attorney use of a vocational expert. In *How to profitably handle social security cases-1980.* Indianapolis: Indiana Continuing Legal Education Forum.

Gulledge, Z.L. (1963). Vocational rehabilitation of industrially injured workers. In E.F. Cheit & M.S. Gordon (Eds.), *Occupational disability and public policy* (pp. 395–420). New York: John Wiley & Sons.

Gutheil, T.G., & Appelbaum, P.S. (1982). *Clinical handbook of psychiatry and the law.* New York: McGraw-Hill.

Gutowski, M. (1979). *Rehabilitation in the private sector: Changing the structure of the rehabilitation industry.* Washington, DC: The Urban Institute.

Gutowski, M., Harder, P., & Koshel, J. (1980). *Forecasting manpower needs in the rehabilitation industry.* Washington, DC: The Urban Institute.

Hardy, R.E., Luck, R.S., & Chandler, A.L. (1982). Licensure of rehabilitation counselors and related issues: Results of a national survey. *Rehabilitation Counseling Bulletin, 25,* 157–161.

Hasbrook, R.F. (1981). (Editorial). If you have it—flaunt it. *Journal of Applied Rehabilitation Counseling, 12,* 143.

Health Insurance Association of America. (1982). *Source book of health insurance data 1981–1982* (23rd ed.). Washington, DC: Author.

Hinsie, L.E., & Campbell, R.J. (1973). *Psychiatric dictionary* (4th ed.). New York: Oxford University Press.

Insurance Institute of America. (1982). *Principles of insurance and liability claims adjusting: Course guide-adjuster 32.* Malvern, PA: Author.

Interdepartmental Committee to Study Workmen's Compensation for Seamen. (1941). *System of workmen's compensation for seamen* (Senate Doc. No. 113). Washington, DC: 77th Congress, 1st session.

Interdepartmental Workers' Compensation Task Force. (1977). *Workers' compensation: Is there a better way?* Washington, DC: U.S. Government Printing Office.

International Association of Industrial Accident Boards and Commissions. (1977). *Model medical care and rehabilitation program.* Atlanta: Author.

Isaacson, L.E. (1971). *Career information in counseling and teaching* (2nd ed.). Boston: Allyn & Bacon.

Isaacson, L.E. (1977). *Career information in counseling and teaching* (3rd ed.). Boston: Allyn & Bacon.

Jaffe, A.J. (Ed.). (1961). *Research conference on workmen's compensation and vocational rehabilitation.* New York: Bureau of Applied Social Research, Columbia University.

Jagim, R.D., Wittman, W.D., & Noll, J.0. (1978). Mental health professionals' attitudes toward confidentiality, privilege, and third-party disclosure. *Professional Psychologist, 9,* 458–466.

Jaques, M.E. (1970). *Rehabilitation counseling: Scope and services.* Boston: Houghton Mifflin Co.

Johnson, R., & Heal, L.W. (1976). Private employment agency responses to the physically handicapped applicant in a wheelchair. *Journal of Applied Rehabilitation Counseling, 7,* 12–21.

Jones, J.J., & DeCloths, T.A. (1969). Job analysis: National survey findings. *Personnel Journal, 49,* 805–809.

Kapes, J.T., & Mastie, M.M. (Eds.). (1982). *A counselor's guide to vocational guidance instruments.* Alexandria, VA: American Association for Counseling and Development.

Kornblum, G. (1974). The expert as a witness and consultant. *Practice and Law.*

Kramer, H.T. (1980). The nature of reinsurance. In R.W. Strain (Ed.), *Reinsurance* (pp. 1–32). New York: The College of Insurance.

Krusen, E.M., & Ford, D.E. (1958). Compensation factor in low-back injuries. *Journal of the American Medical Association, 166,* 1128–1133.

Kulp, C.A., & Hall, J.W. (1968). *Casualty insurance.* New York: The Ronald Press.

Kunce, J.T. (1969). Vocational interest, disability, and rehabilitation. *Rehabilitation Counseling Bulletin, 12,* 204–210.

Land, T. (1981). Global strategy: Confronting alcoholism at the workplace. *Alcoholism*, *1*, 41–42.

Larson, A. (1974). *Workmen's compensation for occupational injuries and death.* New York: Matthew Bender.

Lauterback, J.R. (1982, April 5). Coaching the disabled back to work. *Industry Week*, pp. 52–55.

Lewin, S.S., Ramseur, J.H., & Sink, J.M. (1979). The role of private rehabilitation: Founder, catalyst, competitor. *Journal of Rehabilitation*, *45*(3), 16–19.

Long, J.D. (1971). *Ethics, morality, and insurance: A long-range outlook.* Bloomington, IN: Bureau of Business Research, Graduate School of Business, Indiana University.

Lorenz, J.R. (1977). Our roots. In J.R. Lorenz, I.B. Hawley, & A.A. McDonald (Eds.), Rehabilitation administration: Fact or fiction? A symposium. *Journal of Rehabilitation Administration*, *1*(4), 24–37.

Lorenz, J.R., Graham, C.S., Hashey, P.L., & Baker, R.J. (1981). *Selected aspects of financial management in rehabilitation facilities: A resource manual.* Washington, DC: National Association of Rehabilitation Facilities.

Lucas, C.J. (1972). *Our western educational heritage.* New York: The Macmillan Co.

Lynch, R.K. (1978). Vocational rehabilitation of workers' compensation clients. *Journal of Applied Rehabilitation Counseling*, *9*, 164–167.

Lynch, R.K. (1983). The vocational expert. *Rehabilitation Counseling Bulletin*, *27*, 18–25.

Lynch, R.K., & Martin, T. (1982). Rehabilitation counseling in the private sector: A training needs survey. *Journal of Rehabilitation*, *48*(3), 51–52, 73.

Lytel, R.B., & Botterbusch, K.F. (1981). *Physical demands job analysis: A new approach.* Menomonie, WI: Materials Development Center, Stout Vocational Rehabilitation Institute.

McCahan, D. (1929). *State insurance in the United States.* Philadelphia: University of Pennsylvania Press.

McCormick, E.J. (1979). *Job analysis: Methods and applications.* New York: AMACOM.

McMahon, B.T. (1979). Private sector rehabilitation: Benefits, dangers, and implications for education. *Journal of Rehabilitation*, *45*(3), 56–58.

McMahon, B.T., & Matkin, R.E. (1983). Preservice graduate training needs for private sector rehabilitation counselors. *Rehabilitation Counseling Bulletin*, *27*, 54–60.

McMahon, B., Matkin, R., Growick, B., Mahaffey, D., & Gianforte, G. (1983). Recent trends in private sector rehabilitation. *Rehabilitation Counseling Bulletin*, *27*, 32–47.

Magarick, P. (1962). *Successful handling of casualty claims.* Englewood Cliffs, NJ: Prentice-Hall.

Mallik, K. (1979). Job accommodation through job restructuring and environmental modification. In D. Vandergoot & J.D. Worrall (Eds.), *Placement in rehabilitation: A career development perspective* (pp. 145–165). Baltimore: University Park Press.

Mallik, K., & Moretti, V. (1982). Unions as a resource in job placement. *Journal of Rehabilitation*, *48*(2), 20–24.

Malone, W.S., & Plant, M.L. (1963). *Cases and materials on workmen's compensation.* St. Paul, MN: West Publishing Co.

Martin, M.E. (1976). *Legal concerns of the rehabilitation counselor.* Menomonie, WI: Research and Training Center.

Martin, R. (1975). *Legal challenges to behavior modification: Trends in schools, corrections, and mental health.* Champaign, IL: Research Press.

Matkin, R.E. (1980a). Legal and ethical issues in vocational evaluation. *Vocational Evaluation and Work Adjustment Bulletin, 13*(2), 57–61.

Matkin, R.E. (1980b). Public/private rehabilitation during recession. A cooperative partnership. *Journal of Rehabilitation, 46*(4), 58–61.

Matkin, R.E. (1980c). Supervisory responsibilities relating to legal and ethical issues in rehabilitation settings. *Journal of Rehabilitation Administration, 4,* 133–143.

Matkin, R.E. (1980d). The rehabilitation counselor in private practice: Perspectives for education and preparation. *Journal of Rehabilitation, 46* (2), 60–62.

Matkin, R.E. (1980e). Vocational rehabilitation during economic recession. *Journal of Applied Rehabilitation Counseling, 11,* 124–127.

Matkin, R.E. (1981a). Program evaluation: Searching for accountability in private rehabilitation. *Journal of Rehabilitation, 47*(1), 65–68.

Matkin, R.E. (1981b). The certification dilemma in private rehabilitation. *Journal of Applied Rehabilitation Counseling, 12,* 9–14.

Matkin, R.E. (1981c). Will consolidation alone yield a profession? *Journal of Applied Rehabilitation Counseling, 12,* 82–84.

Matkin, R.E. (1982a). Preparing rehabilitation counselors to perform supervisory and administrative responsibilities. *Journal of Applied Rehabilitation Counseling, 13*(3), 21–24.

Matkin, R.E. (1982b). Program evaluation strategies for private for-profit rehabilitation. *Rehabilitation Counseling Bulletin, 25,* 268–277.

Matkin, R.E. (1982c). Rehabilitation placement services: Unlicensed employment agencies or something else? *Journal of Applied Rehabilitation Counseling, 13*(1), 24–33.

Matkin, R.E. (1982d). Rehabilitation services offered in the private sector: A pilot investigation. *Journal of Rehabilitation, 48*(4), 31–33.

Matkin, R.E. (1982e). The roles and functions of rehabilitation specialists in the private sector (Doctoral dissertation, Southern Illinois University, 1982). *Dissertation Abstracts International, 43,* 05A.

Matkin, R.E. (1983a). Credentialing the rehabilitation profession. *Journal of Rehabilitation, 49*(2), 25–28, 67.

Matkin, R.E. (1983b). Educating employers to hire disabled workers. *Journal of Rehabilitation, 49*(3), 60–64.

Matkin, R.E. (1983c). Insurance rehabilitation: Counseling the industrially injured worker. *Journal of Applied Rehabilitation Counseling, 14*(3), 47–50.

Matkin, R.E. (1983d). Legal and ethical challenges in the private rehabilitation sector. *Rehabilitation Literature, 44,* 206–209, 256.

Matkin, R.E. (1984). Certified insurance rehabilitation specialists: Issues and answers. *Rehabilitation Forum, 11*(1), 12–17.

Matkin, R.E., & May, V.R. (1981). Potential conflicts of interest in private rehabilitation: Identification and resolution. *Journal of Applied Rehabilitation Counseling, 12,* 15–18.

Matkin, R.E., & Rice, J.M. (1979). Integrating diagnostic and behavior assessment techniques. *Vocational Evaluation and Work Adjustment Bulletin, 12*(4), 18–24.

Matkin, R.E., & Riggar, T.F. (1985). *The rise of private sector rehabilitation and its effects on training programs.* Manuscript submitted for publication.

Matkin, R.E., Sawyer, H.W., Lorenz, J.R., & Rubin, S.E. (1982). Rehabilitation administrators and supervisors: Their work assignments, training needs, and suggestions for preparation. *Journal of Rehabilitation Administration, 6,* 170–183.

May, V.R. (1983). The vocational expert witness: Expanding the market place. *Vocational Evaluation and Work Adjustment Bulletin, 16,* 100–102.

Mehr, R.I., & Cammack, E. (1976). *Principles of insurance.* Homewood, IL: Richard D. Irwin, Inc.

Mehr, R.I., & Hedges, B.A. (1963). *Risk management in the business enterprise.* Homewood, IL: Richard D. Irwin, Inc.

Menniger, W.C. (1964). The meaning of work in western society. In H. Borow (Ed.), *Man in a world of work* (pp. xiii–xvii). Boston: Houghton Mifflin Co.

Meyer, W.F. (1971). *Life and health insurance law.* Rochester, NY: The Lawyers Cooperative Publishing Co.

Miner, M.G., & Miner, J.B. (1979). *Employee selection within the law.* Washington, DC: The Bureau of National Affairs, Inc.

Mink, J.A. (1975). MTM and the disabled. *Journal of Method-Time-Measurement, 2*(2).

Minton, E.B. (1977). Job placement: Strategies and techniques. *Rehabilitation Counseling Bulletin, 21,* 141–149.

Morrissey, A.B. (1951). *Rehabilitation nursing.* New York: G.P. Putnam's Sons.

Munts, R., & Garfinkel, I. (1974). *The work disincentive effect of unemployment insurance.* Kalamazoo, MI: W.E. Upjohn Institute for Employment Research.

Muthard, J.E., & Salomone, P.R. (1969). Role and functions of the rehabilitation counselor. *Rehabilitation Counseling Bulletin, 13,* 81–168.

Nadolsky, J.M. (1972). *Development of a model for vocational evaluation of the disadvantaged.* Auburn, AL: Duplicating Service, Auburn University.

Nadolsky, J.M. (1979). Profit and certification in vocational rehabilitation programs. *Journal of Rehabilitation, 45*(3), 65–69.

National Commission on Workmen's Compensation Laws. (1972). *The report of the national commission on state workmen's compensation laws* (Vols. 1–4). Washington, DC: U.S. Government Printing Office.

National Council on Rehabilitation. (1944). *Symposium on the processes of rehabilitation.* Cleveland: Author.

Neff, W.S. (1968). *Work and human behavior.* New York: Athertin Press.

Ninth Institute on Rehabilitation Issues. (1982). *Marketing: An approach to placement.* Menomonie, WI: Stout Vocational Rehabilitation Institute.

Obermann, C.E. (1965). *A history of vocational rehabilitation in America.* Minneapolis: T.S. Denison & Co.

Olshansky, S. (1957). An evaluation of rehabilitation counselor training. *Vocational Guidance Quarterly, 5,* 164–167.

Olshansky, S., & Hart, W.R. (1967). A study of curricula, psychologists in vocational rehabilitation or vocational rehabilitation counseling. *Journal of Rehabilitation, 33*(2), 28–30.

Organist, J. (1979). Private sector rehabilitation practitioners—organize within NRA. *Journal of Rehabilitation, 45*(3), 52–55.

Palluzzi, J.G. (1981). Marketing: The key ingredient. *Women in Management Quarterly,* 2, 3.

Pati, G.C., & Adkins, J.I. (1981). *Managing and employing the handicapped: The untapped potential.* Lake Forest, IL: Brace-Park, The Human Resource Press.

Patterson, C.H. (1957). Counselor or coordinator. *Journal of Rehabilitation, 23*(3), 13–15.

Patterson, C.H. (1966). The rehabilitation counselor: A projection. *Journal of Rehabilitation, 32*(2), 31, 49.

Patterson, C.H. (1967). Specialization in rehabilitation counseling. *Rehabilitation Counseling Bulletin, 10,* 147–154.

Patterson, C.H. (1968). Rehabilitation counseling: A profession or a trade? *Personnel Guidance Journal, 46,* 567–571.

Patterson, C.H. (1970). Power, prestige and the rehabilitation counselor. *Rehabilitation Research and Practice Review, 1,* 1–7.

Petersen, W. (1961). *Population.* New York: The Macmillan Co.

Pfeffer, I. (1966). The early history of insurance. *Annals of Social Charting Property and Casualty Underwriters, 19,* 11, 19, 23.

President's Commission on the Health Needs of the Nation. (1952). *Building America's health* (Vol. 2). Washington, DC: U.S. Government Printing Office.

Pruitt, W.A. (1977). *Vocational (work) evaluation.* Menomonie, WI: Walt Pruitt Associates.

Quey, R.L. (1968). Toward a definition of work. *Personnel Guidance Journal, 47,* 223–227.

Rados, D.L. (1981). *Marketing for non-profit organizations.* Boston: Auburn House Publishing Co.

Rasch, J.D. (1979). The case for an independent association of rehabilitation counselors. *Journal of Applied Rehabilitation Counseling, 10,* 171–176.

Rayback, J.G. (1966). *A history of American labor.* New York: The Free Press.

Reagles, K.W., & Wright, G.N. (1971). *A benefit-cost analysis of the Wood county project: An illustrated lecture.* Madison, WI: Regional Rehabilitation Research Institute, University of Wisconsin.

Reagles, S.A. (1981). Economic incentives and employment of the handicapped. *Rehabilitation Counseling Bulletin, 25,* 13–19.

Reich, N. (1980). Disability and accessibility: A look at shopping facilities. *Journal of Rehabilitation, 46*(3), 24–27.

Rhodes, J.E. (1917). *Workmen's compensation.* New York: The Macmillan Co.

Riegel, R., Miller, J.S., & Williams, C.A. (1976). *Insurance principles and practices: Property and liability* (6th ed.). Englewood Cliffs, NJ: Prentice-Hall.

Riesenfeld, S.A., & Maxwell, R.C. (1950). *Modern social legislation.* Brooklyn: The Foundation Press.

Riggar, T.F., & Matkin, R.E. (1984). Rehabilitation counselors working as administrators: A pilot investigation. *Journal of Applied Rehabilitation Counseling, 15*(1), 9–13.

Roche, G.S. (1973). *Entitlements to unemployment insurance benefits.* Kalamazoo, MI: W.E. Upjohn Institute for Employment Research.

Roessler, R.T., & Rubin, S.E. (1982). *Case management and rehabilitation counseling.* Baltimore: University Park Press.

Roman, P.M. (1981). From employee alcoholism to employee assistance. *Journal for the Study of Alcoholism, 42,* 244–272.

Rosove, B. (1982). Employability assessment: Its importance and one method of doing it. *Journal of Employment Counseling, 19,* 113–123.

Rossi, P.H., & Wright, S.R. (1977). Evaluation research: An assessment of theory, practice and politics. *Evaluation Quarterly, 1*(1), 5–48.

Rubin, S.E., Matkin, R.E., Ashley, J.M., Beardsley, M.M., May, V.R., Onstott, K.L., & Puckett, F.D. (1984). Roles and functions of certified rehabilitation counselors. *Rehabilitation Counseling Bulletin, 27,* 199–224, 238–245.

Rubin, S.E., & Roessler, R.T. (1983). *Foundations of the vocational rehabilitation process* (2nd ed.). Baltimore: University Park Press.

Rule, W.R., & Wright, K.C. (1981). Rehabilitation's unheralded partner: Economics. *Journal of Applied Rehabilitation Counseling, 12,* 208–211.

Sabini, S.E. (1983). *Rehabilitation management of group health insurance claims.* Newark, NJ: Mutual Benefit Life.

Sales, A. (1979). Rehabilitation counseling in the private sector: Implications for graduate education. *Journal of Rehabilitation, 45*(3), 59–61, 72.

Sandor, A.A. (1957). The history of professional liability suits in the United States. *Journal of the American Medical Association, 163,* 459–466.

Sartain, A.Q., & Baker, A.W. (1978). *The supervisor and the job* (3rd ed.). New York: McGraw-Hill.

Sauvain, H.C. (1967). *Investment management* (3rd ed.). Englewood Cliffs, NJ: Prentice-Hall.

Sawyer, H.W., & Schumacher, B. (1980). Stress and the rehabilitation administrator. *Journal of Rehabilitation Administration, 4,* 49–56.

Scher, P.L. (1979). NARPPS—key to the survival of rehabilitation in the nineteen-eighties. *Journal of Rehabilitation, 45*(3), 50–51, 74.

Schumacher, B. (1977). Rehabilitation counseling. In P.J. Valletutti & F. Christoplos (Eds.), *Interdisciplinary approaches to human services* (pp. 357–372). Baltimore: University Park Press.

Schwitzgebel, R.L., & Schwitzgebel, R.K. (1980). *Law and psychological practice.* New York: John Wiley & Sons.

Shaffer, G.W., & Lazarus, R.S. (1952). *Fundamental concepts in clinical psychology.* New York: McGraw-Hill.

Shimberg, B. (1981). Testing for licensure and certification. *American Psychologist, 36,* 1138–1146.

Shinnick, M.D., Black, J.B., & Decker, R. (1983). Industrial engineering procedures and vocational evaluation. *Vocational Evaluation and Work Adjustment Bulletin, 16,* 24–29.

Shrey, D.E. (1979). The rehabilitation counselor in industry: A new frontier. *Journal of Applied Rehabilitation Counseling, 9,* 168–172.

Silberman, L.J., Rothaus, B., & Sharpnick, S. (1980). *Rehabilitation: The California system.* Santa Ana, CA: Alliance of Vocational Educators.

Sinick, D. (1969). Training, job placement, and follow-up. In D. Malikin & H. Rusalem (Eds.), *Vocational rehabilitation of the disabled: An overview* (pp. 129–153). New York: New York University Press.

Sixth Institute on Rehabilitation Issues. (1979). *Rehabilitation engineering: A counselor's guide.* Menomonie, WI: Stout Vocational Rehabilitation Institute.

Social Security Administration. (1982). *Social security handbook.* Washington, DC: U.S. Government Printing Office.

Somers, H.M., & Somers, A.R. (1954). *Workmen's compensation.* New York: John Wiley & Sons.

Spaniol, L. (1977). A program evaluation model for rehabilitation agencies and facilities. *Journal of Rehabilitation Administration, 1*(3), 4–13.

Stude, E.W., & McKelvey, J. (1979). Ethics and the law: Friend or foe? *Personnel Guidance Journal, 57,* 453–456.

Sullivan, M. (1982). A follow-up study of rehabilitation counseling graduates. *Journal of Applied Rehabilitation Counseling, 13*(1), 6–10.

Suojanen, W.W. (1977). Responsibility and professional management in vocational rehabilitation agencies: A reaction to Crawford's research. *Journal of Rehabilitation Administration, 1*(1), 21–26.

Super, D.E. (1969). The development of vocational potential. In D. Malikin & H. Rusalem (Eds.), *Vocational rehabilitation of the disabled: An overview* (pp. 75–90). New York: New York University Press.

Tenth Institute on Rehabilitation Issues. (1983). *Private-public rehabilitation: A better understanding.* Menomonie, WI: Stout Vocational Rehabilitation Institute.

Tenth Institute on Rehabilitation Issues. (1983). *Projects with industry.* Hot Springs, AR: Arkansas Rehabilitation Research and Training Center.

Thomas, S.W. (1981). Rehabilitation engineering in vocational evaluation and work adjustment. *Vocational Evaluation and Work Adjustment Bulletin, 14,* 120–124.

Thompson, M.S. (1980). *Benefit-cost analysis for program evaluation.* Beverly Hills, CA: Sage Publications.

Treon, R.T. (1979). Private rehabilitation of injured persons: A plaintiff lawyer's perspective. *Journal of Rehabilitation, 45*(3), 34–36.

Tunick, R.H., & Tseng, M.S. (1981). Professional identity, job satisfaction, and rehabilitation counselor certification. *Rehabilitation Counseling Bulletin, 25,* 74–79.

Tyler, A.F. (1944). *Freedom's ferment: Phases of American social history from the colonial period to the outbreak of the civil war.* New York: Harper & Brothers.

Ugland, R.P. (1977). Job seeker's aids: A systematic approach for organizing employer contacts. *Rehabilitation Counseling Bulletin, 21,* 107–115.

United States Chamber of Commerce. (1984). *Analysis of workers' compensation laws.* Washington, DC: Author.

United States Department of Education, Office of Special Education and Rehabilitative Services. (1980). *Resource guide: Rehabilitation engineering and product information.* Washington, DC: U.S. Government Printing Office.

United States Department of Health, Education and Welfare, Rehabilitation Services Administration. (1978). *State vocational rehabilitation agency program data: Fiscal year 1978.* Washington, DC: U.S. Government Printing Office.

United States Department of Health, Education and Welfare, Rehabilitation Services Administration. (1979). *State vocational rehabilitation agency program data: Fiscal year 1979.* Washington, DC: U.S. Government Printing Office.

United States Department of Health, Education and Welfare, Rehabilitation Services Administration. (1980). *State vocational rehabilitation agency program data: Fiscal year 1980.* Washington, DC: U.S. Government Printing Office.

United States Department of Health and Human Services, Health Care Financing Administration. (1981). *Health care financing review.* Washington, DC: U.S. Government Printing Office.

United States Department of Health and Human Services, Social Security Administration. (1982). *Social security rulings 1982* (SSA Pub. No. 65–002). Washington, DC: Office of Operational Policy and Procedure.

United States Department of Labor, Bureau of Apprenticeship. (1964). *The national apprenticeship program.* Washington, DC: U.S. Government Printing Office.

United States Department of Labor, Employment Standards Administration. (1980). *Guidelines for rehabilitation services from private rehabilitation agencies.* Washington, DC: U.S. Government Printing Office.

United States Department of Labor, Employment Standards Administration. (1980). *The fair labor standards act of 1938, as amended.* Washington, DC: U.S. Government Printing Office.

United States Department of Labor, Employment and Training Administration. (1977). *Dictionary of occupational titles* (4th ed.). Washington, DC: U.S. Government Printing Office.

United States Department of Labor, Employment and Training Administration. (1981). *Selected characteristics of occupations defined in the dictionary of occupational titles.* Washington, DC: U.S. Government Printing Office.

United States Department of Labor, Employment and Training Administration. (1982). *A guide to job analysis: A "how-to" publication for occupational analysts.* Menomonie, WI: Materials Development Center, Stout Vocational Rehabilitation Institute.

United States Department of Labor, Manpower Administration. (1970). *Handbook for job restructuring.* Washington, DC: U.S. Government Printing Office.

United States Department of Labor, Manpower Administration. (1972). *Handbook for analyzing jobs.* Menomonie, WI: Materials Development Center, Stout Vocational Rehabilitation Institute.

Vactor, H., & Hubach, J. (1979). The industrial engineering approach to work evaluation. *Vocational Evaluation and Work Adjustment Bulletin, 12*(2), 14–17.

Vandergoot, D. (1982). Work readiness assessment. *Rehabilitation Counseling Bulletin, 26,* 84–87.

Vandergoot, D., Swirsky, J., & Rice, K. (1982). Using occupational information in rehabilitation counseling. *Rehabilitation Counseling Bulletin, 26,* 94–100.

Vocational Evaluation and Work Adjustment Association. (1975). The tools of vocational evaluation. *Vocational Evaluation and Work Adjustment Bulletin, 8,* 49–64.

Walker, R.A. (1975). *Planning for program evaluation.* Minneapolis: Office of Rehabilitation Services.

Walls, R.T., Masson, C., & Werner, T.J. (1977). Negative incentives to vocational rehabilitation. *Rehabilitation Literature, 38,* 143–150.

Warren, D. (1979). Rehabilitation engineering . . . take another look. *Continuing Education News, 5*(4), 1–3.

Weber, M. (1930). *The Protestant work ethic and the spirit of capitalism.* New York: Charles Scribner's Sons.

Weiss, R.J., & Bergen, B.J. (1968). Social supports and the reduction of psychiatric disability. *Psychiatry, 31,* 107–115.

Welch, G.T. (1979). The relationship of rehabilitation with industry. *Journal of Rehabilitation, 45*(3), 24–25.

White, A.W. (1969). Low-back pain in men receiving workmen's compensation: A follow-up study. *Canadian Medical Association Journal, 95,* 50–56.

Whitehouse, F.A. (1953). Habilitation—concept and process. *Journal of Rehabilitation, 19*(2), 3–7.

Willett, A.H. (1951). *The economic theory of risk and insurance.* Philadelphia: The University of Pennsylvania.

Williams, R. (1984, February). The machine breakers. *Review,* pp. 132, 134, 137.

Witte, E.E. (1930, December). The theory of workmen's compensation. *American Labor Legislation Review,* p. 411.

Wortman, P.M. (1975). Evaluation research: A psychological perspective. *American Psychologist, 30,* 562–575.

Wright, G.N., & Fraser, R.T. (1975). Task analysis for the education, preparation, classification, and utilization of rehabilitation counselor-track personnel. *Wisconsin studies in vocational rehabilitation monographs, 3*(22). Madison, WI: University of Wisconsin.

Wright, N.D., & Allen, G.P. (1982). *The national directory of state agencies 1982-1983.* Arlington, VA: Information Resource Press.

Young, W.M. (1977). Rehabilitation administration from the perspective of a rehabilitation counselor turned administrator. In J.R. Lorenz, I.B. Hawley, & A.A. McDonald (Eds.), Rehabilitation administration: Fact or fiction? A symposium. *Journal of Rehabilitation Administration, 1*(4), 24–37.

Zadny, J.J., & James, L.F. (1978). A survey of job-search patterns among state vocational rehabilitation clients. *Rehabilitation Counseling Bulletin, 22,* 60–65.

Zadny, J.J., & James, L.F. (1979). Job placement in state vocational rehabilitation agencies: A survey of technique. *Rehabilitation Counseling Bulletin, 22,* 361–378.

Zisman, J. (1946). *Workmen's compensation and the protection of seamen* (Bulletin 869). Washington, DC: U.S. Department of Labor, Bureau of Labor Statistics.

Author Index

Adkins, J.I., 159, 173, 174, 345.
Alexander, C.P., 155, 174, 337.
Alexander, F.G., 130, 337.
Allan, W.S., 64, 82, 83, 337.
Allen, F.L., 19, 337.
Allen, G.P., 290, 306, 349.
American Association of Mental Deficiency, 218, 219, 337.
American Psychological Association, 139, 337.
Anastasi, A., 135, 213, 322, 337.
Andersen, R.H., 189, 193, 194, 337.
Anderson, J.K., 227, 337.
Anderson, S.B., 203, 210, 337.
Andrisani, P.J., 155, 337.
Angell, D.L., 78, 337.
Appelbaum, P.S., 184, 189, 194, 195, 340.
Ashley, J.M., 346.
Baker, A.W., 28, 346.
Baker, R.A., 49, 50, 337.
Baker, R.J., 134, 337, 342.
Ball, S., 203, 210, 337.
Beals, R., 146, 147, 337.
Beardsley, M.M., 346.
Bell, M., 177, 337.
Benjamin, A., 142, 144, 337.
Bergen, B.J., 148, 349.
Berkowitz, M., 65, 148-150, 337.
Bickelhaupt, D.L., 39, 44, 45, 337.
Biestek, F.P., 143, 337.
Bigwood, A., 340.
Bitter, J.A., 24, 64, 66-68, 113, 133, 135, 142, 144, 158, 159, 163, 168, 170, 171, 337.
Black, B.J., 1, 337.
Black, H.C., 183, 218, 219, 337.
Black, J.B., 123, 124, 237, 346.
Bloom, P.N., 179, 338.
Boehne, K.P., 23, 338.
Botterbusch, K.F., 116, 117, 137, 338, 342.
Brandon, T.L., 189, 338.
Brisolara, A., 69, 338.

Brodsky, S., 191, 338.
Brolin, J., 123, 124, 338.
Brubaker, D.R., 216, 225, 338.
California Association of Rehabiliation Professionals, 105, 121, 138, 165, 338.
California Department of Industrial Relations, 146, 147, 172, 338.
Cammack, E., 34, 42, 45, 53, 58, 334.
Campbell, R.J., 148, 341.
Cannon, M.W., 198, 338.
Capshaw, T., 193, 338.
Chandler, A.L., 224, 340.
Cheit, E.F., 10, 11, 13, 15, 17-22, 65, 73, 96, 147, 171, 338.
Cohen, R.J., 182, 184, 186, 219, 220, 338.
Commission on Accreditation of Rehabilitation Facilities, 202, 206, 208, 338.
Conley, R.W., 68, 338.
Conrad, S., 340.
Cottone, R.R., 216, 217, 338.
Cross, D.L., 194, 339.
Davidson, P.O., 202, 339.
Decker, R., 123, 124, 346.
DeCloths, T.A., 114, 115, 341.
Deneen, L.J., 68, 105, 143, 144, 146, 153, 154, 339.
DeSau, G.T., 78, 337.
Diamond, C.R., 66, 74, 339.
Dickman, F., 69, 339.
Dodd, W.F., 11, 339.
Dollard, J., 148, 339.
Donaldson, J.H., 58, 339.
Donaldson, W., 340.
Dorken, H., 53, 339.
Downey, E.H., 12, 339.
Dunn, D.J., 136, 168, 169, 339.
Eastman, C., 5, 6, 339.
Eaton, M.W., 145, 146, 148, 339.
Elliott, C.M., 37-39, 44-51, 54, 339.
Emener, W.G., 69, 170, 339.

351

Subject Index